THE COMPLETE RESULTS AND LINE-UPS OF THE UEFA CHAMPIONS LEAGUE 2021-2024

Dirk Karsdorp

British Library Cataloguing in Publication Data
A catalogue record for this book is available from the British Library

ISBN: 978-1-86223-527-4

Website   www.soccer-books.co.uk
e-mail   info@soccer-books.co.uk

Printed in the UK by 4edge Ltd

FOREWORD

'Hail Wolves – Champions of the World', screamed the headlines one grey December morning in 1954. Wolverhampton Wanderers had recovered from a two-goal deficit to beat Honvéd of Budapest, a significant event maybe, but hardly justifying such a headline.

Much of the euphoria stemmed from the make-up of the Hungarian team. Puskas, Kocsis and four others had been in the national side, which had twice beaten England in the previous 13 months, scoring 13 goals in the process. But Wolves had been favoured by the conditions, had more incentive than their opponents (who were simply on a European jaunt), and had survived a number of goalmouth escapes earlier in the game. While English eyes viewed the result through rose-tinted spectacles, more objectivity was revealed elsewhere in Europe.

The most far-sighted reaction came from France. In the daily sports paper L'Equipe, the editor Gabriel Hannot decried the overreaction of the English. He wrote: 'We must wait for Wolves to visit Moscow or Budapest before we proclaim their invincibility. There are other clubs of international prowess, notably Milan and Real Madrid to name but two…'

Hannot's opinion was not baseless. The next day the paper devoted much space to outline plans for a European tournament, in which patriotic boasts could be put to the test. It was not an original idea; there had already been international competitions like the Mitropa Cup before the Second World War, which featured the leading club sides in Austria, Czechoslovakia, Hungary, Yugoslavia and later Switzerland, Italy and Romania. After the War, France, Italy, Spain and Portugal played one another for the Latin Cup. But L'Equipe's plan provided for the whole of Europe, and Gabriel Hannot also called for the support of the European football's governing body, UEFA.

This campaign from France originated an entirely new era in football. Not only did UEFA accept the proposal, except for the name (UEFA preferred European Champion Clubs' Cup to Hannot's European Cup, which they wanted to keep for a national team competition), but in their acceptance they took a step which certainly cracked and even broke down much of the traditional insularity of top class club football. Aided by the parallel development of floodlighting, which made practicable the extra fixtures which had to be played in midweek, the European Champion Club's Cup became a tremendous success – though officials might have been a little peeved that their lengthy nomenclature was immediately shortened into the European Cup by the media and most other commentators.

As the European dream became reality, the commercial prospects of international club competition were not lost on the continent's leading participants. Before the end of the decade, the European Cup Winners' Cup had been instituted as a spin-off tournament, while in 1958 the first official contest between national sides, the European Nations' Cup, began its life span. Oddly enough, the actual name 'European Cup' has never been utilised.

The first 'European Cup' tie was played on 4th September 1955, between Sporting Club de Portugal from Lisbon and Partizan of Belgrade; just four days later Real Madrid set out on an astounding run during which they would not lose an aggregate tie for five years!

This first competition comprised 16 entrants, 8 of whom were not actually the reigning champions of their countries at the time. Over the years the number of entrants increased until there were regularly 32 teams competing for the trophy. Between the years of 1955 and 1991 each tie was played on a knock-out basis over two legs and a sister title to our books covering the Champions League, The Complete Results and Line-ups of the European Champion Clubs' Cup 1955-1991 – The Knockout Years, is also available from Soccer Books Ltd. This contains full statistics for every game played in the competition during this period.

The 1991-92 season saw the beginning of a new era with the start of the so-called "Champions League", a money-spinning format which saw entrants grouped in Leagues of four teams in certain stages of the competition. Together with a gradual increase in entrants this led to a huge rise in the number of lucrative matches to be played meaning qualification for the Champions League is now vitally important for Europe's major teams.

Sister titles to this book containing full statistics for every game played in the European Champions League from 1991-2004, 2004-2009, 2009-2012, 2012-2015, 2015-2018 and 2018-2021 are also available from Soccer Books Ltd as are other books containing full statistics for a variety of European football competitions (including the UEFA Cup, Fairs Cup, UEFA Europa League, UEFA Europa Conference League and Mitropa Cup), and other World competitions. Further details of these titles can be found on the back cover.

We have endeavoured to make the contents of this book as accurate as possible but often, checking two different sources leads to different information for the same match. In cases such as this we have used the most trustworthy information we could find.

Throughout this book, rather than use English spellings, we have used the correct spelling of Club names and places as used in the country of origin. For example, Rome is Roma, Copenhagen is København etc.

UEFA CHAMPIONS LEAGUE
2021-2022

PRELIMINARY ROUND

Semi-Final Round

22.06.21   Elbasan Arena, Elbasan (ALB): SS Folgore/Falciano – Prishtina KF 0-2 (0-0)
SS Folgore/Falciano: Alessandro Semprini (90+2' Emanuele Semprini), Cristian Brolli,
Nicholas Arrigoni, Daniel Piscaglia (76' Federico Di Addario), Assane Fall (68' Riccardo
Aluigi), Mirco Spighi (90+2' Matteo Giardi), Andrea Nucci, Fabio Sottile, Marco Bernardi,
Lorenzo Dormi, Eric Fedeli (67' William Garcia). Coach: Omar Lepri.
Prishtina KF: Ardit Nika, Gledi Mici, Besnik Krasniqi, Lumbardh Dellova (90+3' Gentian
Muça), Tun Bardhoku, Sabien Lilaj, Laurit Boshnjaku (64' Qendrim Zyba), Endrit Krasniqi
(90+2' Albin Prapashtica), Gauthier Mankenda (64' Xhevdet Shabani), Oto John (64'
Mendurim Hoti), Leutrim Kryeziu. Coach: Zekirija Ramadani.
Goals: 51' Endrit Krasniqi 0-1, 90+1' Mendurim Hoti 0-2.
Referee: Joni Hyytiä (FIN)

22.06.21   Stadiumi Niko Dovana, Durrës (ALB):
            HB Tórshavn – Inter Club d'Escaldes 0-1 (0-0)
HB Tórshavn: Teitur Gestsson, Hørdur Askham, Bartal Wardum (88' Hanus Sørensen), Daniel
Johansen, René Joensen, Hedin Hansen, Michal Przybylski (85' Áki Samuelsen), Mads
Mikkelsen (88' Stefan Radosavljevic), Hilmar Leon Jakobsen, Adrian Justinussen (66' Pæter
Petersen), Mikkel Dahl. Coach: Jonas Dal Andersen.
Inter Club d'Escaldes: Josep Gómes, Federico Bessone, Emili García, Adrià Gallego, Pau
Bosch, Iván De Nova, Sergi Moreno (85' Joel Paredes Leones), Jordi Roca (62' François
Gomis), Jordi Betriu (75' Ludovic Clemente), Genís Soldevila (85' Ildefons Lima), Gerard
Artigas. Coach: Lopo.
Goal: 61' Jordi Betriu 0-1.
Referee: Joonas Jaanovits (EST)

Final Round

25.06.21   Elbasan Arena, Elbasan: Prishtina KF – Inter Club d'Escaldes 2-0 (1-0)
Prishtina KF: Ardit Nika, Gledi Mici, Besnik Krasniqi, Leotrim Bekteshi, Lumbardh Dellova,
Sabien Lilaj (88' Oto John), Xhevdet Shabani (71' Gauthier Mankenda), Laurit Boshnjaku,
Endrit Krasniqi (89' Tun Bardhoku), Mendurim Hoti (78' Qendrim Zyba), Leutrim Kryeziu.
Coach: Zekirija Ramadani.
Inter Club d'Escaldes: Josep Gómes, Federico Bessone (56' Ildefons Lima), Emili García,
Adrià Gallego, Pau Bosch (70' Toni Lao), Iván De Nova, Sergi Moreno (56' Ludovic
Clemente), François Gomis (46' Jordi Roca), Jordi Betriu (56' Joel Paredes Leones), Genís
Soldevila, Gerard Artigas. Coach: Lopo.
Goals: 44', 58' Endrit Krasniqi 1-0, 2-0.
Referee: Adam Ladebäck (SWE)

FIRST QUALIFYING ROUND

06.07.21   Bolt Arena, Helsinki: HJK Helsinki – FK Buducnost Podgorica 3-1 (3-1)
HJK Helsinki: Jakob Tånnander, Valtteri Moren, Janne Saksela, Daniel O'Shaughnessy, Miro
Tenho, Filip Valencic, Lucas Lingman, Jair, Atomu Tanaka, Roope Riski, David Browne.
Coach: Toni Koskela.
FK Buducnost Podgorica: Milos Dragojevic, Vladan Adzic, Luka Mirkovic (72' Bogdan
Milic), Anto Babic, Petar Grbic, Milos Raickovic (73' Jovan Baosic), Miomir Djurickovic,
Vasilije Terzic, Andrija Raznatovic, Lazar Mijovic, Viktor Djukanovic (46' Marko
Mrvaljevic). Coach: Mladen Milinkovic.
Goals: 5' Roope Riski 1-0, 7' Filip Valencic 2-0, 13' Janne Saksela 3-0,
36' Milos Raickovic 3-1 (p).
Referee: Nicolas Laforge (BEL)   Attendance: 2,365

06.07.21   Groupama Aréna, Budapest: Ferencvárosi TC – Prishtina KF 3-0 (0-0)
Ferencvárosi TC: Dénes Dibusz, Miha Blazic, Lasha Dvali, Eldar Civic, Henry Wingo, Róbert
Mak (79' Somália), Dávid Sigér, Igor Kharatin (89' Bálint Vécsei), Tokmac Nguen, Franck
Boli (68' Ryan Mmaee), Myrto Uzuni. Coaches: Serhiy Rebrov & Peter Stöger.
Prishtina KF: Ardit Nika, Gledi Mici, Besnik Krasniqi (80' Tun Bardhoku), Leotrim Bekteshi,
Sabien Lilaj, Laurit Boshnjaku (71' Gauthier Mankenda), Endrit Krasniqi, Qendrim Zyba,
Mendurim Hoti (80' Xhevdet Shabani), Oto John (80' Bleart Tolaj), Leutrim Kryeziu.
Coach: Zekirija Ramadani.
Goals: 71' Tokmac Nguen 1-0, 74' Ryan Mmaee 2-0, 78' Miha Blazic 3-0.
Referee: David Munro (SCO)   Attendance: 8,765

06.07.21   A. Le Coq Arena, Tallinn: FC Flora Tallinn – Hibernians FC 2-0 (0-0)
FC Flora Tallinn: Matvei Igonen, Märten Kuusk, Henrik Pürg, Marco Lukka, Michael
Lilander, Konstantin Vassiljev, Henrik Ojamaa, Martin Miller, Markus Soomets, Sergei
Zenjov, Rauno Sappinen. Coach: Jürgen Henn.
Hibernians FC: Ryan Vella, Leandro Almeida, Andrei Agius, Sergio Raphael, Ferdinando
Apap, Zachary Grech, Dunstan Vella, Jake Grech (88' Timothy Tabone Desira), Jurgen
Degabriele (76' Edafe Uzeh), Thaylor Lubanzadio (76' Wilfried Domoraud), Ayrton Attard.
Coach: Stefano Sanderra.
Goals: 75', 89' Rauno Sappinen 1-0, 2-0.
Referee: Lazar Lukic (SRB)   Attendance: 1,804
Sent off: 73' Sergio Raphael.

06.07.21   Stadionul Dr. Constantin Radulescu, Cluj-Napoca:
            CFR Cluj – Borac Banja Luka 3-1 (2-1)
CFR Cluj: Giedrius Arlauskis, Mateo Susic (79' Cristian Manea), Camora, Mike Cestor,
Ciprian Deac, Rúnar Sigurjónsson, Rachid Bouhenna, Adrian Paun (67' Claudiu Petrila),
Jonathan Rodríguez, Billel Omrani (67' Gabriel Debeljuh), Valentin Costache (61' Alexandru
Chipciu). Coach: Marius Sumudica.
Borac Banja Luka: Nikola Lakic, Dino Coric, Djordje Cosic, Aleksandar Vojinovic (61' Amar
Begic), Djordje Milojevic, Stojan Vranjes, Goran Zakaric, Dejan Meleg (74' Donald Molls
Ntchamda), Aleksandar Subic (68' Marko Jovanovic), Almedin Dino Ziljkic (74' Milan
Vusurovic), Panagiotis Moraitis (68' Ante Zivkovic). Coach: Marko Maksimovic.
Goals: 11' Billel Omrani 1-0, 28' Ciprian Deac 2-0, 45+1' Panagiotis Moraitis 2-1,
60' Rúnar Sigurjónsson 3-1.
Referee: Jochem Kamphuis (HOL)   Attendance: 4,500

06.07.21   Vilniaus LFF stadionas, Vilnius: FK Zalgiris – Linfield FC 3-1 (2-0)
FK Zalgiris: Edvinas Gertmonas, Saulius Mikoliūnas, Joël Bopesu, El Hadji Pape Diaw, Nemanja Ljubisavljevic, Milen Gamakov (83' Karolis Uzėla), Hugo Vidémont, Ovidijus Verbickas (59' Ogenyi Onazi), Francis Kyeremeh (84' Marko Karamarko), Jakub Sylvestr (83' Josip Tadic), Tomislav Kis. Coach: Vladimir Cheburin.
Linfield FC: Christopher Johns, Matthew Clarke, Niall Quinn (77' Jordan Stewart), Michael Newberry, Jamie Mulgrew, Chris Shields, Jimmy Callacher, Conor Pepper, Stephen Fallon, Cameron Palmer, Christy Manzinga (78' Navid Nasseri). Coach: David Healy.
Goals: 38' Hugo Vidémont 1-0, 45' Tomislav Kis 2-0 (p), 54' Christy Manzinga 2-1, 67' Christopher Johns 3-1 (og).
Referee: Alex Troleis (FRO)   Attendance: 1,500

06.07.21   Stade Émile Mayrisch, Esch-sur-Alzette:
           CS FOLA Esch – Lincoln Red Imps 2-2 (0-1)
CS FOLA Esch: Emmanuel Cabral, Grégory Grisez, Julien Klein, Jean Sylvio Ouassiero, Veldin Muharemovic (46' Denis Ahmetxhekaj), Rodrigue Dikaba (84' Gauthier Caron), Mirza Mustafic (46' Bruno Ramírez), Bruno Freire, Lucas Correia (80' Idir Boutrif), Stefano Bensi, Michael Omosanya (46' Rodrigo Parreira). Coaches: Sébastien Grandjean & Fábio Martins.
Lincoln Red Imps: Lolo Soler, Scott Wiseman, Bernardo Lopes, Jesús Toscano, Roy Chipolina, Fernando Carralero (46' Ethan Britto), Liam Walker (90' Kian Ronan), Mustapha Yahaya, Marco Rosa (72' Graeme Torrilla), Lee Casciaro (71' Braian Gómez), Thay De Barr (89' Nikita Kovalonoks). Coach: Michael McElwee.
Goals: 26' Fernando Carralero 0-1, 50' Ethan Britto 0-2, 65' Stefano Bensi 1-2, 66' Denis Ahmetxhekaj 2-2.
Referee: Michal Ocenás (SVK)   Attendance: 385

06.07.21   Tose Proeski Arena, Skopje: KF Shkëndija 79 – NS Mura 0-1 (0-1)
KF Shkëndija 79: Kostadin Zahov, Mevlan Murati, Antonio Pavic, Egzon Bejtulai, Ján Krivák, Armend Alimi, Kamer Qaka, Arbin Zejnullai (64' Rubin Hebaj), Besart Ibraimi, Valmir Nafiu (64' Igor), Ljupco Doriev (82' Dashmir Elezi). Coach: Ernest Gjoka.
NS Mura: Matko Obradovic, Ziga Kous (85' Amadej Marosa), Klemen Sturm, Ján Gorenc, Zan Karnicnik, Matic Marusko, Nino Kouter, Luka Bobicanec (85' Alen Kozar), Tomi Horvat, Mihael Klepac (74' Klemen Pucko), Kai Cipot (64' Stanisa Mandic). Coach: Ante Simundza.
Goal: 29' Luka Bobicanec 0-1 (p).
Referee: António Nobre (POR)   Attendance: 3,200

FK Shkëndija 79 played their home match at Tose Proeski Arena, Skopje, instead of their regular stadium Ecolog Arena, Tetovo, which did not meet UEFA requirements.

07.07.21   Aspmyra Stadion, Bodø: FK Bodø/Glimt – Legia Warszawa 2-3 (1-2)
FK Bodø/Glimt: Nikita Haikin, Brede Moe, Marius Lode (88' Marius Høibråten), Alfons Sampsted, Fredrik Bjørkan (41' Morten Konradsen), Ulrik Saltnes, Patrick Berg, Sondre Fet, Hugo Vetlesen (69' Sebastian Tounekti), Erik Botheim, Lasse Nordås (46' Pernambuco). Coach: Kjetil Knutsen.
Legia Warszawa: Artur Boruc, Artur Jedrzejczyk, Filip Mladenovic, Mateusz Wieteska, Mateusz Holownia, André Martins (83' Ernest Muçi), Bartosz Kapustka, Bartosz Slisz, Luquinhas, Kacper Skibicki (83' Mattias Johansson), Mahir Emreli (79' Rafael Lopes). Coach: Czeslaw Michniewicz.
Goals: 2' Luquinhas 0-1, 41' Mahir Emreli 0-2, 45+1' Erik Botheim 1-2, 61' Mahir Emreli 1-3, 78' Pernambuco 2-3.
Referee: Juxhin Xhaja (ALB)   Attendance: 2,283
Sent off: 82' Morten Konradsen.

7

07.07.21   Boris Paichadze Dinamo Arena, Tbilisi: Dinamo Tbilisi – Neftçi PFK 1-2 (1-1)
Dinamo Tbilisi: Roin Kvaskhvadze, Fabian Sporkslede (83' Barnes Osei), Simon Gbegnon,
Levan Kharabadze (73' Tornike Morchiladze), Saba Khvadagiani, Giorgi Papava, Milán
Rádin, Bakar Kardava, Giorgi Kutsia (68' Nodar Kavtaradze), Giorgi Gabedava (68' Tornike
Akhvlediani), Zoran Marusic. Coach: Kakhaber Tskhadadze.
Neftçi PFK: Aqil Mammadov, Vojislav Stankovic, Mamadou Mbodj, Mert Çelik, Emin
Makhmudov, Namiq Alasgarov, Sabir Bougrine (90+1' Mirabdulla Abbasov), Mamadou Kané,
Yusuf Lawal (86' Omar Buludov), César Meza Colli (88' Khayal Najafov), Harramiz.
Coach: Samir Abbasov.
Goals: 23' Namiq Alasgarov 0-1, 36' Zoran Marusic 1-1, 58' Emin Makhmudov 1-2 (p).
Referee: David Fuxman (ISR)   Attendance: 5,890

07.07.21   Tehelné pole, Bratislava: Slovan Bratislava – Shamrock Rovers 2-0 (1-0)
Slovan Bratislava: Adrián Chovan, Guram Kashia, Vasil Bozhikov, Vernon De Marco, Jurij
Medvedev, Jaba Kankava (73' Jaromír Zmrhal), Ibrahim Rabiu (90+2' Filip Lichý), Joeri de
Kamps, Aleksandar Cavric (74' Dávid Hrncár), Ezekiel Henty (63' Vladimír Weiss), Rafael
Ratão (90+2' Dávid Strelec). Coach: Vladimir Weiss.
Shamrock Rovers: Alan Mannus, Roberto Lopes, Sean Gannon (68' Daniel Mandriou), Sean
Hoare, Lee Grace, Liam Scales, Ronan Finn, Richie Towell (68' Graham Burke), Gary
O'Neill, Rory Gaffney, Aaron Greene (68' Dylan Watts). Coach: Stephen Bradley.
Goals: 28', 47' Rafael Ratão 1-0, 2-0.
Referee: Sebastian Gishamer (AUT)   Attendance: 500

Vladimír Weiss missed a penalty kick (90').

07.07.21   Malmö Stadion, Malmö: Malmö FF – Riga FC 1-0 (0-0)
Malmö FF: Johan Dahlin, Eric Larsson, Lasse Nielsen, Jonas Knudsen, Anel Ahmedhodzic,
Søren Rieks (46' Veljko Birmancevic), Jo Inge Berget (73' Amin Sarr), Oscar Lewicki (73'
Bonke Innocent), Erdal Rakip, Sebastian Nanasi (67' Adi Nalic), Antonio Colak.
Coach: Jon Dahl Tomasson.
Riga FC: Roberts Ozols, Armands Pētersons, Antonijs Cernomordijs, Milos Vranjanin, Ritvars
Rugins, Ivan Paurevic, Felipe Brisola (90+2' Wesley Natã), Nedeljko Piscevic, Vladislavs
Fjodorovs (60' Kule Mbombo, 90+2' Edgar Babayan), Mikael Soisalo, Yunusa Muritala.
Coach: Andris Riherts.
Goal: 50' Antonio Colak 1-0.
Referee: Kaarlo Oskari Hämäläinen (FIN)   Attendance: 4,012
Sent off: 41' Yunusa Muritala.

07.07.21   Stadiumi Niko Dovana, Durrës: KF Teuta Durrës – FC Sheriff Tiraspol 0-4 (0-2)
KF Teuta Durrës: Stivi Frashëri, Renato Arapi, Blagoja Todorovski, Jackson (78' Blerim
Kotobelli), Rustem Hoxha (68' Asion Daja), Emiljano Vila, Albano Aleksi, Sheriff Kallaku,
Dejvi Bregu, Taulant Seferi (85' Pepi Georgiev), Lorenco Vila. Coach: Eduard Martini.
FC Sheriff Tiraspol: Georgios Athanasiadis, Cristiano, Danilo Arboleda, Gustavo Dulanto,
Keston Julien, Sébastien Thill (90' John Charles Petro), Moussa Kyabou, Henrique Luvannor
(67' Lovro Bizjak), Adama Traoré (78' Hansel Zapata), Frank Castañeda (90+1' Alexandr
Belousov), Nadrey Dago (46' Momo Yansané). Coach: Yuriy Vernydub.
Goals: 15', 45+1' Henrique Luvannor 0-1, 0-2, 56' Adama Traoré 0-3,
89' Frank Castañeda 0-4.
Referee: Amine Kourgheli (BLS)   Attendance: 500

8

07.07.21   Sammy Ofer Stadium, Haifa: Maccabi Haifa – FK Kairat 1-1 (1-0)
Maccabi Haifa: Josh Cohen, Rami Gershon, Bogdan Planic, Sun Menachem, Tjaronn Chery (66' Dolev Haziza), Raz Meir, Ali Mohamed (66' Ori Dahan), Neta Lavi (14' José Rodríguez), Mohammad Abu Fani, Godsway Donyoh (66' Din David), Omer Atzili (82' Ben Sahar). Coach: Barak Bakhar.
FK Kairat: Stas Pokatilov, Denis Polyakov, Gafurzhan Suyombaev, Rade Dugalic, Nuraly Alip, Kamo Hovhannisyan (85' Dino Mikanovic), Nebojsa Kosovic, Aybol Abiken (70' Daniyar Uzenov), Vágner Love, José Kanté (85' Arsen Buranchiev), Artur Shushenachev (70' Gulzhygit Alykulov). Coach: Kirill Keker.
Goals: 45' Omer Atzili 1-0, 76' Nuraly Alip 1-1.
Referee: Milovan Milacic (MNE)   Attendance: 25,200

07.07.21   Huvepharma Arena, Razgrad:
PFC Ludogorets Razgrad – Shakhtyor Soligorsk 1-0 (0-0)
PFC Ludogorets Razgrad: Kristijan Kahlina, Igor Plastun, Jordan Ikoko, Anton Nedyalkov, Olivier Verdon, Stéphane Badji (72' Elvis Manu), Cauly Souza, Claude Gonçalves, Claudiu Keserü (60' Pieros Sotiriou), Kiril Despodov (79' Mavis Tchibota), Bernhard Tekpetey (60' Wanderson). Coach: Valdas Dambrauskas.
Shakhtyor Soligorsk: Alyaksandr Gutor, Egor Filipenko, Aleksandr Sachivko (82' Ruslan Khadarkevich), Nikola Antic, Gleb Shevchenko, Yuriy Kendysh, Nikita Korzun (33' Július Szöke), Valon Ahmedi, Dmitri Podstrelov (46' Igor Ivanovic, 83' Roman Begunov), Djordje Ivanovic (68' Igor Stasevich), Dembo Darboe. Coach: Roman Grygorchuk
Goal: 90+2' Cauly Souza 1-0.
Referee: Rohit Saggi (NOR)   Attendance: 4,762

07.07.21   Park Avenue, Aberystwyth: Connah's Quay Nomads – FC Alashkert 2-2 (1-2)
Connah's Quay Nomads: Oliver Byrne, George Horan, Danny Holmes (58' Tom Moore), John Disney, Danny Harrison (46' Kris Owens), Jay Owen (46' Aeron Edwards), Callum Morris, Declan Poole, Jamie Mullan (90+7' Aron Williams), Michael Wilde, Craig Curran. Coach: Andy Morrison.
FC Alashkert: Ognjen Cancarevic, Dejan Boljevic, Didier Kadio, Taron Voskanyan, Tiago Cametá, James, Artak Grigoryan, Rumyan Hovsepyan (67' Artak Edigaryan), David Khurtsidze, David Davidyan (90+14' Nikita Tankov), José Embaló (68' Aleksandar Glisic). Coach: Aleksandr Grigoryan.
Goals: 19' Craig Curran 1-0, 21', 44' David Khurtsidze 1-1, 1-2, 79' George Horan 2-2.
Referee: Vasilis Dimitriou (CYP)   Attendance: 145

Connah's Quay Nomads played their home match at Park Avenue, Aberystwyth, instead of Deeside Stadium, Connah's Quay, which did not meet UEFA requirements.

07.07.21   Stadion Maksimir, Zagreb: Dinamo Zagreb – Valur Reykjavík 3-2 (2-0)
Dinamo Zagreb: Danijel Zagorac, Kévin Théophile-Catherine, Petar Stojanovic, Rasmus Lauritsen, Daniel Stefulj, Arijan Ademi, Josip Misic (59' Lirim Kastrati), Kristijan Jakic (85' Martin Baturina), Lovro Majer (74' Marko Tolic), Duje Cop (74' Sandro Kulenovic), Luka Menalo (59' Mario Cuze). Coach: Damir Krznar.
Valur Reykjavík: Hannes Halldórsson, Birkir Sævarsson, Rasmus Christiansen, Orri Ómarsson (76' Johannes Vall), Sebastian Hedlund, Haukur Sigurdsson (66' Christian Køhler), Krinstinn Sigurdsson, Gudmundur Tryggvason, Birkir Heimisson (76' Almarr Ormarsson), Sigurdur Lárusson (66' Andri Adolphsson), Patrick Pedersen (66' Sverrir Páll Hjaltested). Coach: Heimir Gudjónsson.
Goals: 8' Arijan Ademi 1-0, 41' Lovro Majer 2-0 (p), 72' Arijan Ademi 3-0, 88' Krinstinn Sigurdsson 3-1 (p), 89' Andri Adolphsson 3-2.
Referee: Genc Nuza (RKS)   Attendance: 987

Arijan Ademi missed a penalty kick (82').

Kristinn Sigurdsson missed a penalty Kick (88').

13.07.21   Victoria Stadium, Gibraltar: Lincoln Red Imps – CS FOLA Esch 5-0 (2-0)
Lincoln Red Imps: Kyle Goldwin, Scott Wiseman, Bernardo Lopes, Jesús Toscano, Roy Chipolina (80' John Sergeant), Ethan Britto (68' Kike Gómez), Liam Walker (80' Lee Casciaro), Mustapha Yahaya, Marco Rosa (72' Graeme Torrilla), Kian Ronan, Thay De Barr (80' Braian Gómez). Coach: Michael McElwee.
CS FOLA Esch: Thomas Hym, Grégory Grisez, Julien Klein, Jean Sylvio Ouassiero, Bruno Freire, Lucas Correia (66' Emmanuel Cabral *goalkeeper*), Diogo Pimentel, Denis Ahmetxhekaj (46' Mirza Mustafic), Stefano Bensi (75' Cristiano Pascoal), Gilson Delgado, Idir Boutrif (62' Jules Diallo). Coaches: Sébastien Grandjean & Fábio Martins.
Goals: 18' Thay De Barr 1-0, 39' Liam Walker 2-0 (p), 58' Kian Ronan 3-0, 67' Liam Walker 4-0 (p), 73' Thay De Barr 5-0.
Referee: Ian McNabb (NIR)   Attendance: 621
Sent off: 64' Thomas Hym.

13.07.21   Stadions Skonto, Riga: Riga FC – Malmö FF 1-1 (0-1)
Riga FC: Roberts Ozols, Armands Pētersons, Antonijs Cernomordijs, Milos Vranjanin (46' Jean-Baptiste Léo), Ritvars Rugins (87' Olegs Laizāns), Ivan Paurevic, Felipe Brisola (72' Marko Djurisic), Nedeljko Piscevic, Vladislavs Fjodorovs (72' Edgar Babayan), Mikael Soisalo, Wesley Natã (80' Kule Mbombo). Coach: Andris Riherts.
Malmö FF: Johan Dahlin, Eric Larsson, Lasse Nielsen, Jonas Knudsen, Anel Ahmedhodzic, Felix Beijmo, Søren Rieks (59' Bonke Innocent), Anders Christiansen (84' Franz Brorsson), Oscar Lewicki, Erdal Rakip (59' Sebastian Nanasi), Antonio Colak. Coach: Jon Dahl Tomasson.
Goals: 33' Antonio Colak 0-1, 57' Ivan Paurevic 1-1.
Referee: Gergö Bogár (HUN)   Attendance: 637

13.07.21   MFA Centenary Stadium, Ta'Qali: Hibernians FC – FC Flora Tallinn 0-3 (0-2)
Hibernians FC: Ryan Vella, Leandro Almeida (53' Timothy Tabone Desira), Andrei Agius, Ferdinando Apap, Zachary Grech (46' Myles Beerman), Bjorn Kristensen, Dunstan Vella, Jake Grech, Wilfried Domoraud (72' Francis Mensah), Jurgen Degabriele, Thaylor Lubanzadio (63' Ayrton Attard). Coach: Stefano Sanderra.
FC Flora Tallinn: Matvei Igonen, Märten Kuusk, Henrik Pürg, Marco Lukka, Michael Lilander, Konstantin Vassiljev, Henrik Ojamaa (88' Danil Kuraksin), Martin Miller (46' Markus Poom), Markus Soomets, Sergei Zenjov, Rauno Sappinen (68' Sten Reinkort). Coach: Jürgen Henn.
Goals: 25' Sergei Zenjov 0-1, 33' Rauno Sappinen 0-2, 87' Sten Reinkort 0-3.
Referee: Manfredas Lukjancukas (LTU)   Attendance: 155

13.07.21   Origovöllurinn, Reykjavík: Valur Reykjavík – Dinamo Zagreb 0-2 (0-1)
Valur Reykjavík: Hannes Halldórsson, Birkir Sævarsson, Rasmus Christiansen, Johannes Vall, Sebastian Hedlund, Krinstinn Sigurdsson, Gudmundur Tryggvason (83' Arnór Smárason), Christian Køhler (81' Haukur Sigurdsson), Birkir Heimisson (81' Almarr Ormarsson), Sverrir Páll Hjaltested (63' Patrick Pedersen), Sigurdur Lárusson (63' Andri Adolphsson). Coach: Heimir Gudjónsson.
Dinamo Zagreb: Danijel Zagorac, Kévin Théophile-Catherine, François Moubandje, Petar Stojanovic, Rasmus Lauritsen, Arijan Ademi, Kristijan Jakic (58' Bartol Franjic), Luka Ivanusec (58' Josip Misic), Lovro Majer (71' Lirim Kastrati), Mislav Orsic (89' Luka Menalo), Bruno Petkovic (71' Mario Gavranovic). Coach: Damir Krznar.
Goals: 31' Luka Ivanusec 0-1, 88' Mislav Orsic 0-2.
Referee: Zaven Hovhannisyan (ARM)   Attendance: 800

13.07.21   Bolshaya Sportivnaya Arena, Tiraspol:
             FC Sheriff Tiraspol – KF Teuta Durrës 1-0 (1-0)
FC Sheriff Tiraspol: Georgios Athanasiadis, Cristiano, Danilo Arboleda, Gustavo Dulanto (46' Stjepan Radeljic), Keston Julien, Sébastien Thill, Moussa Kyabou, Henrique Luvannor (46' Momo Yansané), Adama Traoré (82' Lovro Bizjak), Frank Castañeda (71' Hansel Zapata), Nadrey Dago (60' Peter Banda). Coach: Yuriy Vernydub.
KF Teuta Durrës: Stivi Frashëri, Renato Arapi, Blagoja Todorovski, Rustem Hoxha, Blerim Kotobelli (64' Jackson), Erindo Karabeci (64' Sheriff Kallaku), Emiljano Vila, Asion Daja (80' Ledio Beqja), Taulant Seferi, Lorenco Vila (39' Albano Aleksi), Ildi Gruda (46' Pepi Georgiev). Coach: Eduard Martini.
Goal: 6' Adama Traoré 1-0.
Referee: Vladimir Moskalev (RUS)   Attendance: 1,920

13.07.21   Gradski Stadion, Banja Luka: Borac Banja Luka – CRF Cluj 2-1 (0-0,2-0) (AET)
Borac Banja Luka: Nikola Cetkovic, Marko Jovanovic (88' Donald Molls Ntchamda), Dino Coric, Djordje Cosic, Aleksandar Vojinovic, Djordje Milojevic (74' Aleksandar Subic), Stojan Vranjes, Goran Zakaric, Sinisa Dujakovic (46' Milan Vusurovic), Amar Begic (104' Dejan Meleg), Panagiotis Moraitis (99' Ante Zivkovic). Coach: Marko Maksimovic.
CFR Cluj: Giedrius Arlauskis, Camora, Mike Cestor, Cristian Manea, Ciprian Deac, Rúnar Sigurjónsson, Rachid Bouhenna, Adrian Paun (80' Claudiu Petrila, 120' Ovidiu Hoban), Jonathan Rodríguez, Billel Omrani (79' Gabriel Debeljuh), Valentin Costache (66' Alexandru Chipciu, 120' Iasmin Latovlevici). Coach: Marius Sumudica.
Goals: 60 Stojan Vranjes 1-0, 64' Panagiotis Moraitis 2-0, 118' Alexandru Chipciu 2-1.
Referee: Urs Schnyder (SUI)   Attendance: 8,300

13.07.21   Mestni Stadion Fazanerija, Murska Sobota: NS Mura – KF Shkëndija 79 5-0 (2-0)
NS Mura: Matko Obradovic, Ziga Kous, Klemen Sturm (81' Klemen Pucko), Ján Gorenc, Zan Karnicnik (68' Marin Karamarko), Matic Marusko, Nino Kouter (68' Alen Kozar), Luka Bobicanec (76' Amadej Marosa), Tomi Horvat, Mihael Klepac, Kai Cipot (68' Stanisa Mandic). Coach: Ante Simundza.
KF Shkëndija 79: Kostadin Zahov, Mevlan Murati, Antonio Pavic, Egzon Bejtulai, Ján Krivák, Armend Alimi (85' Florent Ramadani), Kamer Qaka, Arbin Zejnullai (46' Medjit Neziri), Igor (46' Valmir Nafiu), Besart Ibraimi (58' Rubin Hebaj), Ljupco Doriev (69' Dashmir Elezi). Coach: Ernest Gjoka.
Goals: 25' Luka Bobicanec 1-0, 45+1' Nino Kouter 2-0, 54' Mihael Klepac 3-0, 64' Ziga Kous 4-0, 87' Mihael Klepac 5-0.
Referee: Marcel Bîrsan (ROM)   Attendance: 3,100
Sent off: 42' Ján Krivák.

13.07.21   Stadiumi Fadil Vokrri, Pristina: Prishtina KF – Ferencváros TC 1-3 (0-0)
Prishtina KF: Ardit Nika, Gledi Mici, Besnik Krasniqi, Leotrim Bekteshi, Sabien Lilaj (64' Tun Bardhoku), Laurit Boshnjaku, Endrit Krasniqi, Qendrim Zyba (52' Mendurim Hoti), Gauthier Mankenda, Oto John (60' Xhevdet Shabani), Leutrim Kryeziu.
Coach: Zekirija Ramadani.
Ferencvárosi TC: Dénes Dibusz, Miha Blazic, Eldar Civic, Henry Wingo, Samy Mmaee, Somália (69' Bálint Vécsei), Róbert Mak (61' Oleksandr Zubkov), Igor Kharatin, Tokmac Nguen (89' Roko Baturina), Myrto Uzuni (88' Damir Redzic), Ryan Mmaee (70' Dávid Sigér). Coach: Peter Stöger.
Goals: 49' Myrto Uzuni 0-1, 67' Mendurim Hoti 1-1, 80', 86' Myrto Uzuni 1-2, 1-3.
Referee: Laurent Kopriwa (LUX)   Attendance: 0

13.07.21   Stadion pod Goricom, Podgorica:
          FK Buducnost Podgorica – HJK Helsinki 0-4 (0-3)
FK Buducnost Podgorica: Milos Dragojevic, Vladan Adzic, Luka Mirkovic (58' Aleksa Cetkovic), Jovan Baosic, Bogdan Milic (46' Anto Babic), Petar Grbic, Milos Raickovic, Miomir Djurickovic, Andrija Raznatovic (79' Nemanja Sekulic), Igor Ivanovic (79' Viktor Djukanovic), Lazar Mijovic. Coach: Mladen Milinkovic.
HJK Helsinki: Jakob Tånnander, Valtteri Moren, Janne Saksela (67' David Browne), Daniel O'Shaughnessy, Luis Murillo (67' Riku Riski), Miro Tenho, Filip Valencic (74' Matti Peltola), Lucas Lingman, Jair (53' Sebastian Dahlström), Atomu Tanaka, Roope Riski (53' Luís Henrique). Coach: Toni Koskela.
Goals: 6' Roope Riski 0-1, 35' Filip Valencic 0-2, 39' Jair 0-3, 49' Roope Riski 0-4.
Referee: Dragomir Draganov (BUL)   Attendance: 1,450

13.07.21   Windsor Park, Belfast: Linfield FC – FK Zalgiris 1-2 (0-2)
Linfield FC: Christopher Johns, Matthew Clarke (46' Jordan Stewart), Niall Quinn (72' Navid Nasseri), Michael Newberry, Trai Hume, Jamie Mulgrew (72' Cameron Palmer), Chris Shields, Jimmy Callacher, Kirk Millar, Stephen Fallon, Christy Manzinga (86' Andrew Clarke). Coach: David Healy.
FK Zalgiris: Edvinas Gertmonas, Saulius Mikoliūnas, Ivan Tatomirovic, Joël Bopesu, El Hadji Pape Diaw, Nemanja Ljubisavljevic, Ogenyi Onazi (78' Ovidijus Verbickas), Milen Gamakov (86' Karolis Uzéla), Hugo Vidémont, Francis Kyeremeh (86' Marko Karamarko), Jakub Sylvestr (70' Josip Tadic). Coach: Vladimir Cheburin.
Goals: 17' Saulius Mikoliūnas 0-1, 44' Ogenyi Onazi 0-2, 66' Chris Shields 1-2 (p).
Referee: Matthew De Gabriele (MLT)   Attendance: 888
Sent off: 64' El Hadji Pape Diaw, 89' Karolis Uzéla.

13.07.21   Tallaght Stadium, Dublin: Shamrock Rovers – Slovan Bratislava 2-1 (1-0)
Shamrock Rovers: Alan Mannus, Joey O'Brien (81' Sean Hoare), Roberto Lopes, Lee Grace,
Liam Scales, Ronan Finn, Richie Towell (84' Aaron Greene), Gary O'Neill (71' Dylan Watts),
Daniel Mandriou, Rory Gaffney, Graham Burke. Coach: Stephen Bradley.
Slovan Bratislava: Adrián Chovan, Guram Kashia, Vasil Bozhikov, Vernon De Marco, Jurij
Medvedev, Jaba Kankava, Vladimír Weiss (90' Alen Mustafic), Joeri de Kamps (90' Myenty
Abena), Dávid Hrncár (59' Aleksandar Cavric), Ezekiel Henty (59' Ibrahim Rabiu), Rafael
Ratão (82' Jaromír Zmrhal). Coach: Vladimir Weiss.
Goals: 16' Graham Burke 1-0 (p), 64' Richie Towell 2-0, 72' Vladimír Weiss 2-1.
Referee: Mario Zebec (CRO)   Attendance: 1,500

*Loser Shamrock Rovers received a bye to the UEFA Europa Conference League Third
Qualifying Round.*

13.07.21   Stadion na Banovom brdu, Beograd (SRB):
              Shakhtyor Soligorsk – PFC Ludogorets Razgrad 0-1 (0-0)
Shakhtyor Soligorsk: Alyaksandr Gutor, Egor Filipenko, Aleksandr Sachivko, Nikola Antic,
Gleb Shevchenko, Igor Stasevich (84' Roman Begunov), Yuriy Kendysh (90+1' Nikita
Korzun), Valon Ahmedi (62' Roman Debelko), Július Szöke (85' Igor Ivanovic), Djordje
Ivanovic (84' Dmitri Podstrelov), Dembo Darboe. Coach: Roman Grygorchuk.
PFC Ludogorets Razgrad: Kristijan Kahlina, Igor Plastun, Jordan Ikoko, Anton Nedyalkov,
Olivier Verdon, Wanderson (61' Alex Santana), Stéphane Badji, Cauly Souza, Claude
Gonçalves, Pieros Sotiriou (87' Bernhard Tekpetey), Kiril Despodov (76' Mavis Tchibota).
Coach: Valdas Dambrauskas.
Goal: 71' Kiril Despodov 0-1.
Referee: Arda Kardesler (TUR)   Attendance: 0

*Shakhtyor Soligorsk played their home match at Stadion na Banovom brdu, Beograd (Serbia),
instead of their regular stadium Stroitel Stadium, Soligorsk, following UEFA's suspension of
all matches to be played in Belarus during 2021. The suspension followed European Union
sanctions in response to the Ryanair Flight 4978 incident, which banned all European airlines
from flying over Belarusian airspace.*

14.07.21   Ortaliq Stadion, Almaty: FK Kairat – Maccabi Haifa 2-0 (1-0)
FK Kairat: Stas Pokatilov, Denis Polyakov, Gafurzhan Suyombaev, Rade Dugalic, Nuraly
Alip, Kamo Hovhannisyan (86' Gulzhygit Alykulov), Nebojsa Kosovic, Aybol Abiken (86'
Arsen Buranchiev), Vágner Love, José Kanté (90+6' João Paulo), Artur Shushenachev (78'
Dino Mikanovic). Coach: Kirill Keker.
Maccabi Haifa: Josh Cohen, Rami Gershon, Bogdan Planic, Sean Goldberg (80' Sun
Menachem), Tjaronn Chery, José Rodríguez (46' Ali Mohamed), Raz Meir (69' Ben Sahar),
Mohammad Abu Fani (80' Maor Levi), Omer Atzili, Din David (64' Godsway Donyoh),
Dolev Haziza. Coach: Barak Bakhar.
Goals: 10' Vágner Love 1-0, 66' Aybol Abiken 2-0.
Referee: Viktor Kopiievskyi (UKR)   Attendance: 7,952
Sent off: 90+2' Sergey Keiler, 90+2' Ali Mohamed.

14.07.21   Vazgen Sargsyan anvan Hanrapetakan Marzadasht, Yerevan:
FC Alashkert – Connah's Quay Nomads 1-0 (0-0,0-0) (AET)
FC Alashkert: David Yurchenko, Artak Edigaryan, Didier Kadio, Taron Voskanyan, Tiago Cametá, James (62' Branko Mihajlovic), Artak Grigoryan (120' Wangu Gome), David Khurtsidze (111' Vincent Bezecourt), David Davidyan (90+3' Nikita Tankov), José Embaló (62' Grigor Aghekyan), Aleksandar Glisic (46' Rumyan Hovsepyan).
Coach: Aleksandr Grigoryan.
Connah's Quay Nomads: Oliver Byrne, John Disney, Kris Owens, Tom Moore, Aeron Edwards, Callum Morris, Declan Poole, Jamie Mullan (120' Harry Owen), Craig Curran, Jordan Davies, Jamie Insall (105' Aron Williams). Coach: Andy Morrison.
Goal: 112' Vincent Bezecourt 1-0.
Referee: Ondrej Pechanec (CZE)   Attendance: 4,000

FC Alashkert played their home match at Vazgen Sargsyan anvan Hanrapetakan Marzadasht, Yerevan, instead of their regular stadium Alashkert Stadium, Yerevan, which did not meet UEFA requirements.

14.07.21   Bakcell Arena, Baku: Neftçi PFK – Dinamo Tbilisi 2-1 (0-0)
Neftçi PFK: Aqil Mammadov, Vojislav Stankovic, Mamadou Mbodj, Omar Buludov, Mert Çelik, Emin Makhmudov, Namiq Alasgarov (90+3' Mirabdulla Abbasov), Sabir Bougrine (76' Khayal Najafov), Mamadou Kané, Yusuf Lawal, César Meza Colli (72' Harramiz).
Coach: Samir Abbasov.
Dinamo Tbilisi: Roin Kvaskhvadze, Fabian Sporkslede (70' Tornike Morchiladze), Simon Gbegnon, Levan Kharabadze (89' Nodar Kavtaradze), Saba Khvadagiani, Giorgi Papava, Milán Rádin (89' Nodar Iashvili), Bakar Kardava (74' Anzor Mekvabishvili), Giorgi Kutsia (70' Barnes Osei), Giorgi Gabedava, Zoran Marusic. Coach: Kakhaber Tskhadadze.
Goals: 51' Milán Rádin 0-1, 58' Emin Makhmudov 1-1 (p), 68' Namiq Alasgarov 2-1.
Referee: Dumitri Muntean (MOL)   Attendance: 3,218

14.07.21   Stadion Miejski Legii Warszawa im. Marszalka Józefa Pilsudskiego, Warszawa:
Legia Warszawa – FK Bodø/Glimt 2-0 (1-0)
Legia Warszawa: Artur Boruc, Artur Jedrzejczyk, Filip Mladenovic, Mateusz Wieteska, Mateusz Holownia, Josip Juranovic (80' Mattias Johansson), André Martins, Bartosz Kapustka (72' Rafael Lopes), Bartosz Slisz, Luquinhas, Mahir Emreli (83' Tomás Pekhart).
Coach: Czeslaw Michniewicz.
FK Bodø/Glimt: Nikita Haikin, Marius Høibråten, Brede Moe (60' Sigurd Kvile), Marius Lode, Alfons Sampsted, Ulrik Saltnes, Patrick Berg, Sondre Fet (90+1' Elias Hagen), Hugo Vetlesen (60' Sebastian Tounekti), Erik Botheim (60' Lasse Nordås), Pernambuco (75' Axel Lindahl). Coach: Kjetil Knutsen.
Goals: 40' Luquinhas 1-0, 90+4' Tomás Pekhart 2-0.
Referee: Aristotelis Diamantopoulos (GRE)   Attendance: 17,473

14

SECOND QUALIFYING ROUND

(Champions Path)

20.07.21   Vazgen Sargsyan anvan Hanrapetakan Marzadasht, Yerevan:
FC Alashkert – FC Sheriff Tiraspol 0-1 (0-0)
FC Alashkert: David Yurchenko, Dejan Boljevic, Didier Kadio, Taron Voskanyan, Tiago
Cametá, James (46' Aghvan Papikyan), Artak Grigoryan, Rumyan Hovsepyan (66' Wangu
Gome), David Khurtsidze (46' Vincent Bezecourt), David Davidyan (81' Nikita Tankov), José
Embaló (77' Aleksandar Glisic). Coach: Aleksandr Grigoryan.
FC Sheriff Tiraspol: Georgios Athanasiadis, Cristiano, Danilo Arboleda, Gustavo Dulanto,
Keston Julien, Sébastien Thill, Edmund Addo, Moussa Kyabou, Henrique Luvannor (90+3'
Lovro Bizjak), Adama Traoré (64' Momo Yansané), Frank Castañeda (88' Peter Banda).
Coach: Yuriy Vernydub.
Goal: 84' Henrique Luvannor 0-1.
Referee: Rade Obrenovic (SVN)   Attendance: 5,800

*FC Alashkert played their home match at Vazgen Sargsyan anvan Hanrapetakan Marzadasht,
Yerevan, instead of their regular stadium Alashkert Stadium, Yerevan, which did not meet
UEFA requirements.*

20.07.21   Victoria Stadium, Gibraltar: Lincoln Red Imps – CFR Cluj 1-2 (1-0)
Lincoln Red Imps: Kyle Goldwin, Scott Wiseman, Bernardo Lopes, Jesús Toscano, Roy
Chipolina, Ethan Britto (69' Emmanuel Ocran), Liam Walker (83' Graeme Torrilla), Mustapha
Yahaya, Marco Rosa, Kian Ronan (59' Lee Casciaro), Kike Gómez (69' Fernando Carralero).
Coach: Raúl Castillo Pérez.
CFR Cluj: Giedrius Arlauskis, Iasmin Latovlevici, Mateo Susic (74' Cristian Manea), Danijel
Graovac, Ciprian Deac (81' Anas Tahiri), Rúnar Sigurjónsson (90+2' Guessouma Fofana),
Rachid Bouhenna, Adrian Paun (81' Claudiu Petrila), Jonathan Rodríguez, Valentin Costache
(46' Alexandru Chipciu), Gabriel Debeljuh. Coach: Marius Sumudica.
Goals: 45' Marco Rosa 1-0, 52', 58' Gabriel Debeljuh 1-1, 1-2.
Referee: Willy Delajod (FRA)   Attendance: 1,039

20.07.21   Stadion Maksimir, Zagreb: Dinamo Zagreb – Omonia Nicosia 2-0 (0-0)
Dinamo Zagreb: Dominik Livakovic, Kévin Théophile-Catherine, François Moubandje, Stefan
Ristovski, Rasmus Lauritsen, Arijan Ademi (42' Josip Misic), Kristijan Jakic, Luka Ivanusec
(63' Lirim Kastrati), Lovro Majer, Mislav Orsic (79' Duje Cop), Bruno Petkovic (79' Mario
Gavranovic). Coach: Damir Krznar.
Omonia Nicosia: Fabiano, Jan Lecjaks, Tomás Hubocan, Ádám Lang, Ioannis Kousoulos,
Jordi Gómez, Éric Bauthéac, Mikkel Diskerud (62' Marinos Tzionis), Abdullahi Shehu, Michal
Duris (82' Andronikos Kakoullis), Marko Scepovic (82' Loizos Loizou).
Coach: Henning Berg.
Goals: 65' Lovro Majer 1-0, 81' Kristijan Jakic 2-0.
Referee: Pawel Gil (POL)   Attendance: 2,234

20.07.21   Groupama Aréna, Budapest: Ferencváros TC – FK Zalgiris 2-0 (2-0)
Ferencvárosi TC: Dénes Dibusz, Miha Blazic, Eldar Civic (90+2' Bálint Vécsei), Henry
Wingo, Samy Mmaee, Somália, Igor Kharatin, Oleksandr Zubkov (69' Róbert Mak), Tokmac
Nguen (69' Kristoffer Zachariassen), Myrto Uzuni, Ryan Mmaee (76' Franck Boli).
Coach: Peter Stöger.
FK Zalgiris: Edvinas Gertmonas, Saulius Mikoliūnas, Ivan Tatomirovic, Joël Bopesu, Nemanja
Ljubisavljevic, Ogenyi Onazi (84' Mantas Kuklys), Milen Gamakov (59' Tomislav Kis), Hugo
Vidémont, Ovidijus Verbickas, Francis Kyeremeh (59' Marko Karamarko), Josip Tadic (65'
Jakub Sylvestr). Coach: Vladimir Cheburin.
Goals: 25' Myrto Uzuni 1-0, 39' Tokmac Nguen 2-0.
Referee: Giorgi Kruashvili (GEO)   Attendance: 10,107

21.07.21   Ortaliq Stadion, Almaty: FK Kairat – Crvena Zvezda Beograd 2-1 (1-0)
FK Kairat: Stas Pokatilov, Denis Polyakov, Gafurzhan Suyombaev (46' Arsen Buranchiev, 75'
Gulzhygit Alykulov), Dino Mikanovic, Rade Dugalic, Nuraly Alip, Kamo Hovhannisyan,
Nebojsa Kosovic (12' Yan Vorogovskiy), Vágner Love, José Kanté, Artur Shushenachev (68'
Macky Bagnack). Coach: Kirill Keker.
Crvena Zvezda Beograd: Milan Borjan, Aleksandar Dragovic, Milan Rodic, Milan Gajic,
Radovan Pankov, Nenad Krsticic, Aleksandar Katai (83' Axel Bakayoko), Sékou Sanogo,
Mirko Ivanic (68' Guélor Kanga), El Fardou Ben Nabouhane (90' Filippo Falco), Milan
Pavkov (46' Loïs Diony). Coach: Dejan Stankovic.
Goals: 24' José Kanté 1-0, 56' Dino Mikanovic 1-1 (og), 79' Macky Bagnack 2-1.
Referee: Halil Umut Meler (TUR)   Attendance: 7,000

21.07.21   Eleda Stadion, Malmö: Malmö FF – HJK Helsinki 2-1 (1-0)
Malmö FF: Johan Dahlin, Eric Larsson (77' Niklas Moisander), Lasse Nielsen, Anel
Ahmedhodzic, Felix Beijmo (90+5' Franz Brorsson), Søren Rieks (69' Veljko Birmancevic),
Anders Christiansen, Oscar Lewicki (77' Erdal Rakip), Bonke Innocent, Antonio Colak, Adi
Nalic (69' Jo Inge Berget). Coach: Jon Dahl Tomasson.
HJK Helsinki: Jakob Tånnander, Valtteri Moren, Janne Saksela, Daniel O'Shaughnessy, Luis
Murillo, Miro Tenho, Filip Valencic (90+4' Luís Henrique), Lucas Lingman, Jair (59' David
Browne), Atomu Tanaka, Roope Riski (79' Riku Riski). Coach: Toni Koskela.
Goals: 45+1' Antonio Colak 1-0, 68' Roope Riski 1-1, 74' Anders Christiansen 2-1.
Referee: Mykola Balakin (UKR)   Attendance: 5,324

21.07.21   Mestni Stadion Fazanerija, Murska Sobota:
            NS Mura – PFC Ludogorets Razgrad 0-0
NS Mura: Matko Obradovic, Ziga Kous, Klemen Sturm, Ján Gorenc, Zan Karnicnik, Matic
Marusko, Nino Kouter, Luka Bobicanec (90+2' Stanisa Mandic), Tomi Horvat, Mihael Klepac
(90+2' Amadej Marosa), Kai Cipot (81' Klemen Pucko). Coach: Ante Simundza.
PFC Ludogorets Razgrad: Kristijan Kahlina, Igor Plastun, Jordan Ikoko, Anton Nedyalkov,
Olivier Verdon, Cauly Souza, Claude Gonçalves, Alex Santana (81' Mavis Tchibota), Dominik
Yankov (63' Wanderson), Pieros Sotiriou (70' Elvis Manu), Kiril Despodov.
Coach: Valdas Dambrauskas.
Referee: Harm Osmers (GER)   Attendance: 3,450

16

21.07.21   Stadion Tehelné pole, Bratislava: Slovan Bratislava – BSC Young Boys 0-0
Slovan Bratislava: Adrián Chovan, Guram Kashia, Vasil Bozhikov, Vernon De Marco, Jurij
Medvedev (30' Lukás Pauschek), Jaba Kankava, Vladimír Weiss, Joeri de Kamps (90+2' Filip
Lichý), Aleksandar Cavric (74' Dejan Dzazic), Jaromír Zmrhal (90+2' Dávid Strelec), Rafael
Ratão (74' Ezekiel Henty). Coach: Vladimir Weiss.
BSC Young Boys: David von Ballmoos, Ulisses Garcia (84' Jordan Lefort), Cédric Zesiger,
Silvan Hefti (80' Quentin Maceiras), Mohamed Ali Camara, Nicolas Moumi Ngamaleu (84'
Marvin Spielmann), Vincent Sierro, Michel Aebischer, Jordan Siebatcheu, Meschack Elia,
Felix Mambimbi (55' Christian Fassnacht). Coaches: David Wagner & Matteo Vanetta.
Referee: Chris Kavanagh (ENG)   Attendance: 1,000

21.07.21   Stadion Miejski Legii Warszawa im.Marszalka Józefa Pilsudskiego, Warszawa:
               Legia Warszawa – FC Flora Tallinn 2-1 (1-0)
Legia Warszawa: Artur Boruc, Artur Jedrzejczyk, Filip Mladenovic, Mateusz Wieteska,
Mateusz Holownia (60' Rafael Lopes), Josip Juranovic, André Martins, Bartosz Kapustka (7'
Bartosz Slisz), Luquinhas, Tomás Pekhart, Mahir Emreli (56' Josué).
Coach: Czeslaw Michniewicz.
FC Flora Tallinn: Matvei Igonen, Märten Kuusk, Henrik Pürg, Marco Lukka (74' Ken
Kallaste), Michael Lilander, Konstantin Vassiljev, Henrik Ojamaa, Martin Miller, Markus
Soomets (80' Markus Poom), Sergei Zenjov, Rauno Sappinen (80' Sten Reinkort).
Coach: Jürgen Henn.
Goals: 3' Bartosz Kapustka 1-0, 53' Rauno Sappinen 1-1, 90+1' Rafael Lopes 2-1.
Referee: Vitali Meshkov (RUS)   Attendance: 16,721

21.07.21   Stadio Georgios Karaiskáki, Piraeus: Olympiakos Piraeus – Neftçi PFK 1-0 (1-0)
Olympiakos Piraeus: Konstantinos Tzolakis, Rúben Semedo, Oleg Reabciuk, Svetozar
Markovic (78' Marios Vrousai), Andreas Bouchalakis (18' Mathieu Valbuena), Pierre Malong
(69' Vasilios Sourlis), Giorgos Masouras, Athanasios Androutsos, Lazar Randjelovic (46' Pape
Cissé), Mohamed Mady Camara, Ahmed Hassan "Koka" (79' Aguibou Camara).
Coach: Pedro Martins.
Neftçi PFK: Aqil Mammadov, Vojislav Stankovic, Mamadou Mbodj, Mert Çelik, Emin
Makhmudov (89' Romain Basque), Namiq Alasgarov (45+1' Mirabdulla Abbasov), Sabir
Bougrine (87' Omar Buludov), Mamadou Kané, Yusuf Lawal, César Meza Colli (86' Khayal
Najafov), Harramiz. Coach: Samir Abbasov.
Goal: 29' Mohamed Mady Camara 1-0.
Referee: João Pinheiro (POR)   Attendance: 7,305
Sent off: 43' Mohamed Camara, 63' Mert Çelik.

27.07.21   Neo GSP Stadium, Nicosia: Omonia Nicosia – Dinamo Zagreb 0-1 (0-0)
Omonia Nicosia: Fabiano, Jan Lecjaks, Tomás Hubocan, Ádám Lang, Jordi Gómez, Éric
Bauthéac (76' Andronikos Kakoullis), Mikkel Diskerud (87' Paris Psaltis), Abdullahi Shehu,
Marinos Tzionis (76' Michal Duris), Marko Scepovic, Loizos Loizou (76' Fotis Papoulis).
Coach: Henning Berg.
Dinamo Zagreb: Dominik Livakovic, Kévin Théophile-Catherine (87' Dino Peric), François
Moubandje, Stefan Ristovski, Rasmus Lauritsen, Josip Misic (82' Bartol Franjic), Kristijan
Jakic, Luka Ivanusec (87' Jakov Vasilj), Lovro Majer (82' Amer Gojak), Mislav Orsic (65'
Luka Menalo), Bruno Petkovic. Coach: Damir Krznar.
Goal: 79' Luka Menalo 0-1.
Referee: Glenn Nyberg (SWE)   Attendance: 7,256

17

27.07.21   A. Le Coq Arena, Tallinn: FC Flora Tallinn – Legia Warszawa 0-1 (0-0)
FC Flora Tallinn: Matvei Igonen, Märten Kuusk, Henrik Pürg, Marco Lukka (74' Ken Kallaste), Michael Lilander, Konstantin Vassiljev, Henrik Ojamaa (74' Sten Reinkort), Martin Miller, Markus Poom, Sergei Zenjov (80' Markus Soomets), Rauno Sappinen. Coach: Jürgen Henn.
Legia Warszawa: Artur Boruc, Artur Jedrzejczyk, Filip Mladenovic, Mateusz Wieteska, Mateusz Holownia, Josip Juranovic, Josué, André Martins, Luquinhas, Rafael Lopes (83' Bartosz Slisz), Mahir Emreli (70' Tomás Pekhart). Coach: Czeslaw Michniewicz.
Goal: 67' Rafael Lopes 0-1.
Referee: Anastasios Papapetrou (GRE)   Attendance: 3,691

27.07.21   Bolt Arena, Helsinki: HJK Helsinki – Malmö FF 2-2 (1-1)
HJK Helsinki: Jakob Tånnander, Valtteri Moren, Daniel O'Shaughnessy, Luis Murillo (77' Riku Riski), Miro Tenho, Filip Valencic, Lucas Lingman, Jair, Atomu Tanaka (85' Anthony Olusanya), Roope Riski, David Browne. Coach: Toni Koskela.
Malmö FF: Johan Dahlin, Niklas Moisander, Franz Brorsson, Anel Ahmedhodzic, Søren Rieks (72' Veljko Birmancevic), Anders Christiansen, Jo Inge Berget (72' Adi Nalic), Oscar Lewicki, Erdal Rakip (61' Eric Larsson), Bonke Innocent (61' Felix Beijmo), Antonio Colak. Coach: Jon Dahl Tomasson.
Goals: 1' Miro Tenho 1-0, 11' Anders Christiansen 1-1, 76' Veljko Birmancevic 1-2, 78' Riku Riski 2-2.
Referee: Stuart Attwell (ENG)   Attendance: 6,465

27.07.21   Vilniaus LFF stadionas, Vilnius: FK Zalgiris – Ferencvárosi TC 1-3 (0-1)
FK Zalgiris: Edvinas Gertmonas, Saulius Mikoliūnas, Joël Bopesu, Elhadji Pape Diaw, Nemanja Ljubisavljevic, Ogenyi Onazi (61' Tomislav Kis), Hugo Vidémont, Ovidijus Verbickas, Francis Kyeremeh (87' Gustas Jarusevicius), Karolis Uzéla, Jakub Sylvestr (61' Josip Tadic). Coach: Vladimir Cheburin.
Ferencvárosi TC: Dénes Dibusz, Miha Blazic (76' Bálint Vécsei), Henry Wingo, Samy Mmaee, Dominik Csontos, Somália (57' Dávid Sigér), Igor Kharatin, Kristoffer Zachariassen, Tokmac Nguen (70' Oleksandr Zubkov), Myrto Uzuni (76' Róbert Mak), Ryan Mmaee. Coach: Peter Stöger.
Goals: 44', 72' Ryan Mmaee 0-1, 0-2, 90+3' Elhadji Pape Diaw 1-2, 90+4' Róbert Mak 1-3.
Referee: Erik Lambrechts (BEL)   Attendance: 2,032

28.07.21   Malaya Sportivnaya Arena, Tiraspol: FC Sheriff Tiraspol – FC Alashkert 3-1 (2-1)
FC Sheriff Tiraspol: Georgios Athanasiadis, Cristiano, Danilo Arboleda, Gustavo Dulanto, Keston Julien, Sébastien Thill (90' Stjepan Radeljic), Edmund Addo, Peter Banda (60' Hansel Zapata), Henrique Luvannor (90' Lovro Bizjak), Adama Traoré, Frank Castañeda (81' Nadrey Dago). Coach: Yuriy Vernydub.
FC Alashkert: Ognjen Cancarevic, Artak Yedigaryan (77' Nikita Tankov), Didier Kadio, Taron Voskanyan, Tiago Cametá, Artak Grigoryan, Rumyan Hovsepyan (46' Vincent Bezecourt), Branko Mihajlovic (46' James), David Khurtsidze, David Davidyan (68' Aghvan Papikyan), Aleksandar Glisic (58' José Embaló). Coach: Aleksandr Grigoryan.
Goals: 11' Aleksandar Glisic 0-1, 15' Gustavo Dulanto 1-1, 23' Henrique Luvannor 2-1, 87' Sébastien Thill 3-1 (p).
Referee: Bojan Pandzic (SWE)   Attendance: 2,046

18

28.07.21   Bakcell Arena, Baku: Neftçi Baku – Olympiakos 0-1 (0-1)
Neftçi PFK: Aqil Mammadov, Vojislav Stankovic, Mamadou Mbodj, Omar Buludov (31'
Mirabdulla Abbasov, 82' Fahmin Muradbayli), Emin Makhmudov, Romain Basque, Sabir
Bougrine (82' Khayal Najafov), Mamadou Kané, Yusuf Lawal (82' Asim Alizade), César
Meza Colli (65' Ismayil Zülfüqarli), Harramiz. Coach: Samir Abbasov.
Olympiakos Piraeus: Konstantinos Tzolakis, Kenny Lala, Rúben Semedo, Pape Cissé, Svetozar
Markovic, Ousseynou Ba, Mathieu Valbuena (76' Lazar Randjelovic), Pierre Malong, Giorgos
Masouras, Ahmed Hassan "Koka" (86' Youssef El-Arabi), Vasilios Sourlis (82' Marios
Vrousai). Coach: Pedro Martins.
Goal: 15' Giorgos Masouras 0-1.
Referee: Ricardo de Burgos (ESP)   Attendance: 5,500

28.07.21   Stadionul Dr. Constantin Radulescu, Cluj-Napoca:
           CFR Cluj – Lincoln Red Imps 2-0 (1-0)
CFR Cluj: Giedrius Arlauskis, Mateo Susic, Camora, Mike Cestor, Danijel Graovac, Ciprian
Deac (46' Anas Tahiri), Rúnar Sigurjónsson (74' Guessouma Fofana), Alexandru Chipciu (62'
Valentin Costache), Ovidiu Hoban (46' Jonathan Rodríguez), Adrian Paun, Gabriel Debeljuh
(62' Billel Omrani). Coach: Marius Sumudica.
Lincoln Red Imps: Lolo Soler, Scott Wiseman, Bernardo Lopes, Jesús Toscano, Roy Chipolina
(90+3' John Sergeant), Ethan Britto (46' Graeme Torrilla), Fernando Carralero (68' Emmanuel
Ocran), Liam Walker, Mustapha Yahaya, Marco Rosa (68' Braian Gómez (ARG)), Kike
Gómez (79' Lee Casciaro). Coach: Michael McElwee.
Goals: 18' Mike Cestor 1-0, 58' Rúnar Sigurjónsson 2-0.
Referee: Yigal Frid (ISR)   Attendance: 5,230

28.07.21   Huvepharma Arena, Razgrad: PFC Ludogorets Razgrad – NS Mura 3-1 (1-0)
PFC Ludogorets Razgrad: Kristijan Kahlina, Igor Plastun, Jordan Ikoko, Anton Nedyalkov,
Olivier Verdon, Cauly Souza (90+2' Dominik Yankov), Claude Gonçalves, Alex Santana (64'
Stéphane Badji), Pieros Sotiriou (76' Elvis Manu), Kiril Despodov (90+2' Mavis Tchibota),
Bernard Tekpetey (46' Wanderson). Coach: Valdas Dambrauskas.
NS Mura: Matko Obradovic, Ziga Kous (83' Tio Cipot), Klemen Sturm (85' Klemen Pucko),
Ján Gorenc, Zan Karnicnik, Matic Marusko, Nino Kouter, Luka Bobicanec, Tomi Horvat,
Mihael Klepac (85' Amadej Marosa), Kai Cipot (58' Stanisa Mandic). Coach: Ante Simundza.
Goals: 4' Pieros Sotiriou 1-0, 64' Tomi Horvat 1-1, 82' Elvis Manu 2-1, 90' Cauly Souza 3-1.
Referee: Marco Di Bello (ITA)   Attendance: 5,008

28.07.21   Stadion Wankdorf, Bern: BSC Young Boys – Slovan Bratislava 3-2 (2-0)
BSC Young Boys: David von Ballmoos, Ulisses Garcia, Cédric Zesiger, Silvan Hefti,
Mohamed Ali Camara, Nicolas Moumi Ngamaleu (58' Marvin Spielmann), Christian
Fassnacht, Vincent Sierro (70' Christopher Martins Pereira), Michel Aebischer, Jordan
Siebatcheu (58' Wilfried Kanga), Meschack Elia (89' Sandro Lauper).
Coaches: David Wagner & Matteo Vanetta.
Slovan Bratislava: Adrián Chovan, Guram Kashia, Vasil Bozhikov, Lukás Pauschek, Vernon
De Marco (87' Myenty Abena), Jurij Medvedev (46' Jaromír Zmrhal), Jaba Kankava, Vladimír
Weiss, Joeri de Kamps (81' Ibrahim Rabiu), Ezekiel Henty (81' Dávid Strelec), Rafael Ratão
(73' Aleksandar Cavric). Coach: Vladimir Weiss.
Goals: 10' Jordan Siebatcheu 1-0 (p), 24' Ulisses Garcia 2-0, 48' Michel Aebischer 3-0,
58' Wilfried Kanga 3-1 (og), 62' Ezekiel Henty 3-2.
Referee: Irfan Peljto (BIH)   Attendance: 19,564

Rafael Ratão missed a penalty kick (21').

19

28.07.21   Stadion Rajko Mitic, Beograd: Crvena Zvezda Beograd – Kairat 5-0 (3-0)
Crvena Zvezda Beograd: Milan Borjan, Aleksandar Dragovic, Milan Rodic, Marko Gobeljic
(59' Milan Gajic), Radovan Pankov, Aleksandar Katai (79' Marko Lazetic), Filippo Falco (68'
El Fardou Ben Nabouhane), Sékou Sanogo, Guélor Kanga (79' Nenad Krsticic), Mirko Ivanic,
Loïs Diony (68' Nikola Krstovic). Coach: Dejan Stankovic.
FK Kairat: Danil Ustimenko, Denis Polyakov, Dino Mikanovic (34' Gulzhygit Alykulov), Yan
Vorogovskiy, Rade Dugalic (77' Alexandr Shirobokov), Nuraly Alip, Kamo Hovhannisyan,
Aybol Abiken, Arsen Buranchiev (63' Andrey Ulshin), Vágner Love, Artur Shushenachev (63'
Ricardo Alves). Coach: Kirill Keker.
Goals: 9' Aleksandar Katai 1-0, 21' Loïs Diony 2-0, 42' Aleksandar Katai 3-0,
49' Mirko Ivanic 4-0, 56' Filippo Falco 5-0.
Referee: Andris Treimanis (LAT)   Attendance: played behind closed doors.

(League Path)

20.07.21   Allianz Stadion, Vienna: Rapid Wien – Sparta Prague 2-1 (0-1)
Rapid Wien: Richard Strebinger, Kevin Wimmer, Filip Stojkovic, Maximilian Hofmann,
Maximilian Ullmann, Christoph Knasmüllner (87' Thorsten Schick), Dejan Petrovic (73'
Srdjan Grahovac), Robert Ljubicic, Ercan Kara, Marco Grüll, Kelvin Arase (64' Taxiarchis
Fountas). Coach: Dietmar Kühbauer.
Sparta Prague: Florin Nita, Lukás Stetina, Andreas Vindheim, Casper Højer Nielsen, Dávid
Hancko, Tomás Wiesner (83' David Moberg-Karlsson), Borek Dockal (83' Adam Karabec),
David Pavelka, Ladislav Krejcí (I) (69' Jakub Pesek), Ladislav Krejcí (II), Adam Hlozek.
Coach: Pavel Vrba.
Goals: 3' Ladislav Krejci (II) 0-1, 63', 70' Christoph Knasmüllner 1-1, 2-1.
Referee: Serdar Gözübüyük (HOL)   Attendance: 19,500

20.07.21   Celtic Park, Glasgow: Celtic FC – FC Midtjylland 1-1 (1-0)
Celtic FC: Vasilis Barkas, Anthony Ralston, Greg Taylor, Stephen Welsh, Nir Bitton, Callum
McGregor, Ryan Christie, David Turnbull (78' Tom Rogic), Ismaila Soro, Odsonne Édouard
(77' Albian Ajeti), Liel Abada (45' Dane Murray). Coach: Ange Postecoglou.
FC Midtjylland: Jonas Lössl, Daniel Høegh, Erik Sviatchenko, Henrik Dalsgaard, Paulinho
(88' Joel Andersson), Pione Sisto, Anders Dreyer, Evander, Mikael Anderson (72' Awer
Mabil), Raphael Onyedika (82' Nicolas Madsen), Júnior Brumado (87' Mads Hansen).
Coach: Bo Henriksen.
Goals: 39' Liel Abada 1-0, 66' Evander 1-1.
Referee: Sandro Schärer (SUI)   Attendance: 9,000
Sent off: 44' Nir Bitton, 56' Anders Dreyer.

21.07.21   Philips Stadion, Eindhoven: PSV Eindhoven – Galatasaray 5-1 (2-1)
PSV Eindhoven: Joël Drommel, Philipp Mwene, André Ramalho, Philipp Max, Olivier
Boscagli, Mario Götze, Marco van Ginkel (62' Davy Pröpper), Ibrahim Sangaré, Eran Zahavi
(90' Pablo Rosario), Noni Madueke (76' Ryan Thomas), Yorbe Vertessen (62' Cody Gakpo).
Coach: Roger Schmidt.
Galatasaray: Fernando Muslera, Ömer Bayram, Alpaslan Öztürk (61' Yunus Akgün), Marcão
Teixeira, Christian Luyindama, Arda Turan (61' Sofiane Féghouli), Aytaç Kara, Emre Kilinç
(89' Emre Tasdemir), Kerem Aktürkoglu (89' Radamel Falcao), Ryan Babel (61' Mostafa
Mohamed), Jesse Sekidika. Coach: Fatih Terim.
Goals: 2', 35' Eran Zahavi 1-0, 2-0, 42' Emre Kilinç 2-1, 51' Mario Götze 3-1,
84' Eran Zahavi 4-1, 88' Mario Götze 5-1.
Referee: Alejandro Hernández (ESP)   Attendance: 23,500

28.07.21   MCH Arena, Herning: FC Midtjylland – Celtic FC 2-1 (0-0,1-1) (AET)
FC Midtjylland: Jonas Lössl, Erik Sviatchenko, Henrik Dalsgaard, Joel Andersson (105' Dion Cools), Paulinho (89' Nikolas Dyhr), Juninho (113' Rasmus Nicolaisen), Pione Sisto, Awer Mabil (89' Victor Lind), Evander, Charles (59' Raphael Onyedika), Júnior Brumado (77' Mads Hansen). Coach: Bo Henriksen.
Celtic FC: Scott Bain, Anthony Ralston, Greg Taylor (105' Adam Montgomery), Stephen Welsh, Dane Murray, Callum McGregor, Ryan Christie, David Turnbull (105' Albian Ajeti), Ismaila Soro (98' Tom Rogic), Odsonne Édouard, Liel Abada (59' James Forrest). Coach: Ange Postecoglou.
Goals: 48' Callum McGregor 0-1, 61' Awer Mabil 1-1, 94' Raphael Onyedika 2-1.
Referee: Bartosz Frankowski (POL)   Attendance: 4,890

FC Midtjylland won after extra time.

28.07.21   Basaksehir Fatih Terim Stadyumu, Istanbul:
            Galatasaray – PSV Eindhoven 1-2 (0-1)
Galatasaray: Fernando Muslera, Ömer Bayram (76' Atalay Babacan), DeAndre Yedlin, Marcão Teixeira, Christian Luyindama, Aytaç Kara, Emre Kilinç (67' Emre Tasdemir), Kerem Aktürkoglu (67' Arda Turan), Jesse Sekidika, Mostafa Mohamed (46' Mbaye Diagne), Baris Yilmaz (46' Ryan Babel). Coach: Fatih Terim.
PSV Eindhoven: Joël Drommel, Philipp Mwene, André Ramalho, Philipp Max, Olivier Boscagli, Mario Götze (90+2' Jordan Teze), Marco van Ginkel (69' Davy Pröpper), Ibrahim Sangaré, Eran Zahavi (75' Nick Viergever), Cody Gakpo (90+2' Bruma), Noni Madueke (69' Mauro Júnior). Coach: Roger Schmidt.
Goals: 37' Noni Madueke 0-1, 59' Marco van Ginkel 0-2, 84' Mbaye Diagne 1-2.
Referee: Massimiliano Irrati (ITA)   Attendance: 5,775
Sent off: 74' Olivier Boscagli.

28.07.21   Generali Ceská pojistovna Arena, Prague: Sparta Prague – Rapid Wien 2-0 (1-0)
Sparta Prague: Florin Nita, Lukás Stetina, Casper Højer Nielsen (62' Matej Polidar), Dávid Hancko, Tomás Wiesner, Borek Dockal, David Pavelka (35' Michal Sácek), David Moberg-Karlsson (77' Ladislav Krejcí (I)), Jakub Pesek, Ladislav Krejcí (II), Adam Hlozek. Coach: Pavel Vrba.
Rapid Wien: Richard Strebinger, Kevin Wimmer, Filip Stojkovic, Maximilian Ullmann, Leo Greiml (59' Christopher Dibon), Dejan Petrovic (86' Jonas Auer), Lion Schuster, Taxiarchis Fountas, Ercan Kara (78' Christoph Knasmüllner), Marco Grüll, Kelvin Arase (78' Thorsten Schick). Coach: Dietmar Kühbauer.
Goals: 16' David Moberg-Karlsson 1-0 (p), 81' Jakub Pesek 2-0.
Referee: Bobby Madden (SCO)   Attendance: 9,105

THIRD QUALIFYING ROUND

(Champions Path)

03.08.21 Eleda Stadion, Malmö: Malmö FF – Glasgow Rangers FC 2-1 (0-0)
Malmö FF: Johan Dahlin, Niklas Moisander, Lasse Nielsen, Anel Ahmedhodzic, Søren Rieks (88' Felix Beijmo), Anders Christiansen (89' Erdal Rakip), Jo Inge Berget, Oscar Lewicki, Bonke Innocent, Veljko Birmancevic (74' Adi Nalic), Antonio Colak (88' Malik Abubakari). Coach: Jon Dahl Tomasson.
Glasgow Rangers FC: Allan McGregor, James Tavernier, Connor Goldson, Filip Helander, Borna Barisic, Steven Davis, Scott Arfield, John Lundstram, Scott Wright, Cedric Itten (63' Fashion Sakala), Ryan Kent. Coach: Steven Gerrard.
Goals: 47' Søren Rieks 1-0, 49' Veljko Birmancevic 2-0, 90+5' Steven Davis 2-1.
Referee: Szymon Marciniak (POL)   Attendance: 5,820

03.08.21 Stadionul Dr. Constantin Radulescu, Cluj-Napoca:
                  CFR Cluj – BSC Young Boys 1-1 (1-0)
CFR Cluj: Giedrius Arlauskis, Mateo Susic, Camora, Mike Cestor, Cristian Manea, Ciprian Deac, Rúnar Sigurjónsson (85' Valentin Costache), Rachid Bouhenna, Jonathan Rodríguez, Denis Alibec (22' Adrian Paun), Billel Omrani (62' Gabriel Debeljuh). Coach: Marius Sumudica.
BSC Young Boys: David von Ballmoos, Ulisses Garcia (71' Jordan Lefort), Cédric Zesiger, Silvan Hefti, Mohamed Ali Camara (56' Fabian Rieder), Christopher Martins Pereira (84' Vincent Sierro), Nicolas Moumi Ngamaleu (71' Marvin Spielmann), Christian Fassnacht (56' Sandro Lauper), Michel Aebischer, Jordan Siebatcheu, Meschack Elia. Coaches: David Wagner & Matteo Vanetta.
Goals: 4' Cristian Manea 1-0, 90+3' Vincent Sierro 1-1.
Referee: Danny Makkelie (HOL)   Attendance: 9,500

03.08.21 Stadio Georgios Karaiskáki, Piraeus:
                  Olympiakos Piraeus – PFC Ludogorets Razgrad 1-1 (0-0)
Olympiakos Piraeus: Konstantinos Tzolakis, Kenny Lala (61' Athanasios Androutsos), Rúben Semedo, Pape Cissé (53' Youssef El-Arabi), Oleg Reabciuk, Ousseynou Ba, Mathieu Valbuena (72' Aguibou Camara), Pierre Malong (46' Yann M'Vila), Giorgos Masouras, Mohamed Mady Camara, Ahmed Hassan "Koka". Coach: Pedro Martins.
PFC Ludogorets Razgrad: Kristijan Kahlina, Igor Plastun, Jordan Ikoko, Anton Nedyalkov, Olivier Verdon, Stéphane Badji, Cauly Souza (73' Alex Santana), Claude Gonçalves, Pieros Sotiriou (89' Wanderson), Kiril Despodov, Bernard Tekpetey (82' Cicinho). Coach: Valdas Dambrauskas.
Goals: 50' Kiril Despodov 0-1, 87' Aguibou Camara 1-1.
Referee: Bobby Madden (SCO)   Attendance: 9,212

03.08.21   Stadion Rajko Mitic, Beograd:
Crvena Zvezda Beograd – FC Sheriff Tiraspol 1-1 (1-1)
Crvena Zvezda Beograd: Milan Borjan, Aleksandar Dragovic, Milan Rodic, Marko Gobeljic, Radovan Pankov, Aleksandar Katai, Filippo Falco (77' El Fardou Ben Nabouhane), Sékou Sanogo (68' Nenad Krsticic), Guélor Kanga, Mirko Ivanic, Loïs Diony (56' Nikola Krstovic). Coach: Dejan Stankovic.
FC Sheriff Tiraspol: Georgios Athanasiadis, Cristiano, Danilo Arboleda, Gustavo Dulanto, Keston Julien (75' Fernando Costanza), Sébastien Thill, Dimitris Kolovos, Edmund Addo, Adama Traoré, Frank Castañeda (76' Lovro Bizjak), Momo Yansané. Coach: Yuriy Vernydub.
Goals: 33' Frank Castañeda 0-1, 45+1' Loïs Diony 1-1.
Referee: Ovidiu Hategan (ROM)   Attendance: 24,433
Sent off: 57' Guélor Kanga.

04.08.21   Stadion Maksimir, Zagreb: Dinamo Zagreb – Legia Warszawa 1-1 (0-0)
Dinamo Zagreb: Dominik Livakovic, Kévin Théophile-Catherine, Stefan Ristovski, Rasmus Lauritsen, Josip Misic (85' Marko Bulat), Kristijan Jakic, Luka Ivanusec, Lovro Majer (65' Lirim Kastrati), Bartol Franjic, Mislav Orsic (85' Luka Menalo), Bruno Petkovic. Coach: Damir Krznar.
Legia Warszawa: Artur Boruc, Artur Jedrzejczyk, Filip Mladenovic, Mateusz Wieteska, Josip Juranovic, Maik Nawrocki, André Martins, Bartosz Slisz, Luquinhas, Rafael Lopes (75' Ernest Muçi), Mahir Emreli (75' Tomás Pekhart). Coach: Czeslaw Michniewicz.
Goals: 60' Bruno Petkovic 1-0, 82' Ernest Muçi 1-1.
Referee: Antonio Mateu Lahoz (ESP)   Attendance: 4,597

04.08.21   Groupama Aréna, Budapest: Ferencvárosi TC – Slavia Praha 2-0 (1-0)
Ferencvárosi TC: Dénes Dibusz, Miha Blazic, Eldar Civic (86' Endre Botka), Henry Wingo, Samy Mmaee, Igor Kharatin, Kristoffer Zachariassen (86' Oleksandr Zubkov), Aïssa Laïdouni, Tokmac Nguen (90+2' Adnan Kovacevic), Myrto Uzuni, Ryan Mmaee (75' Stjepan Loncar). Coach: Peter Stöger.
Slavia Praha: Ondrej Kolár, Taras Kacharaba, Alexander Bah, David Zima, Nicolae Stanciu, Tomás Holes (72' Ondrej Lingr), Lukás Masopust (53' Ivan Schranz), Petr Sevcík (25' Ibrahim Traoré), Srdjan Plavsic (46' Peter Olayinka), Oscar Dorley, Jan Kuchta (53' Petar Musa). Coaches: Jindrich Trpisovský & Zdenek Houstecky.
Goals: 44' Taras Kacharaba 1-0 (og), 50' Igor Kharatin 2-0 (p).
Referee: Jesús Gil Manzano (ESP)   Attendance: 17,127

10.08.21   Bolshaya Sportivnaya Arena, Tiraspol:
FC Sheriff Tiraspol – Crvena Zvezda Beograd 1-0 (1-0)
FC Sheriff Tiraspol: Georgios Athanasiadis, Cristiano, Danilo Arboleda, Gustavo Dulanto, Keston Julien, Sébastien Thill, Dimitris Kolovos (67' Momo Yansané), Edmund Addo, Henrique Luvannor, Adama Traoré (85' Lovro Bizjak), Frank Castañeda. Coach: Yuriy Vernydub.
Crvena Zvezda Beograd: Milan Borjan, Aleksandar Dragovic, Milan Rodic, Milos Degenek, Milan Gajic, Aleksandar Katai (64' Nenad Krsticic), Slavoljub Srnic (60' Veljko Nikolic), Filippo Falco (46' El Fardou Ben Nabouhane), Sékou Sanogo (77' Zeljko Gavric), Mirko Ivanic, Loïs Diony (46' Nikola Krstovic). Coach: Dejan Stankovic.
Goal: 45+2' Danilo Arboleda 1-0.
Referee: Felix Zwayer (GER)   Attendance: 4,950

23

10.08.21   Sinobo Stadium, Prague: Slavia Praha – Ferencvárosi TC 1-0 (1-0)
Slavia Praha: Ondrej Kolár, Taras Kacharaba, Alexander Bah, Nicolae Stanciu, Tomás Holes,
Lukás Masopust (75' Petar Musa), Jakub Hromada (65' Ibrahim Traoré), Oscar Dorley,
Stanislav Tecl (65' Jan Kuchta), Ivan Schranz (65' Srdjan Plavsic), Peter Olayinka (16'
Abdallah Sima). Coach: Jindrich Trpisovský
Ferencvárosi TC: Dénes Dibusz, Endre Botka (78' Oleksandr Zubkov), Miha Blazic, Eldar
Civic, Henry Wingo, Samy Mmaee (46' Adnan Kovacevic), Igor Kharatin, Kristoffer
Zachariassen (71' Somália), Aïssa Laïdouni, Tokmac Nguen (67' Ryan Mmaee), Myrto Uzuni.
Coach: Peter Stöger.
Goal: 36' Lukás Masopust 1-0.
Referee: Tobias Stieler (GER)   Attendance: 15,238
Sent off: 84' Eldar Civic.

10.08.21   Huvepharma Arena, Razgrad:
         PFC Ludogorets Razgrad – Olympiakos Piraeus 2-2 (0-1,2-2) (AET)
PFC Ludogorets Razgrad: Kristijan Kahlina, Igor Plastun, Josué Sá (94' Dorin Rotariu), Jordan
Ikoko (106' Cicinho), Anton Nedyalkov, Olivier Verdon, Stéphane Badji (88' Alex Santana),
Cauly Souza (106' Dominik Yankov), Claude Gonçalves, Pieros Sotiriou, Kiril Despodov.
Coach: Valdas Dambrauskas.
Olympiakos Piraeus: Konstantinos Tzolakis, Rúben Semedo, Oleg Reabciuk, Ousseynou Ba,
Yann M'Vila (91' Pierre Malong), Andreas Bouchalakis (54' Sokratis Papastathopoulos),
Giorgos Masouras (88' Pape Cissé), Athanasios Androutsos (119' Kenny Lala), Mohamed
Mady Camara, Youssef El-Arabi (106' Ahmed Hassan "Koka"), Marios Vrousai (65' Mathieu
Valbuena). Coach: Pedro Martins.
Goals: 31' Yann M'Vila 0-1, 49' Rúben Semedo 1-1 (og), 57' Pieros Sotiriou 2-1 (p),
68' Youssef El-Arabi 2-2 (p).
Referee: Orel Grinfeld (ISR)   Attendance: 5,118
Sent off: 86' Ousseynou Ba.

PFC Ludogorets Razgrad won on penalties (4:1).

Penalties: Sotiriou 1-0, Valbuena missed, Alex Santana 2-0, Ahmed Hassan "Koka" missed,
*   Verdon 3-0, Lala 3-1, Cicinho 4-1.*

10.08.21   Stadion Wankdorf, Bern: BSC Young Boys – CFR Cluj 3-1 (3-1)
BSC Young Boys: Guillaume Faivre, Ulisses Garcia, Cédric Zesiger, Silvan Hefti (82' Quentin
Maceiras), Mohamed Ali Camara, Christopher Martins Pereira (87' Vincent Sierro), Nicolas
Moumi Ngamaleu, Christian Fassnacht, Michel Aebischer (67' Fabian Rieder), Jordan
Siebatcheu (88' Wilfried Kanga), Meschack Elia (82' Felix Mambimbi).
Coaches: David Wagner & Matteo Vanetta.
CFR Cluj: Giedrius Arlauskis, Mateo Susic, Camora, Mike Cestor, Cristian Manea, Ciprian
Deac, Rúnar Sigurjónsson (46' Denis Alibec), Gussouma Fofana (46' Jonathan Rodríguez),
Rachid Bouhenna, Adrian Paun, Billel Omrani (77' Valentin Costache).
Coach: Marius Sumudica.
Goals: 4' Billel Omrani 0-1, 23' Jordan Siebatcheu 1-1, 25' Nicolas Moumi Ngamaleu 2-1,
42' Jordan Siebatcheu 3-1.
Referee: Cüneyt Çakir (TUR)   Attendance: 21,145
Sent off: 63' Adrian Paun.

10.08.21   Stadion Miejski Legii Warszawa im. Marszalka Józefa Pilsudskiego, Warszawa:
Legia Warszawa – Dinamo Zagreb 0-1 (0-1)
Legia Warszawa: Artur Boruc, Artur Jedrzejczyk, Filip Mladenovic, Mateusz Wieteska, Josip
Juranovic, Maik Nawrocki, André Martins (46' Josué), Bartosz Slisz, Luquinhas, Rafael Lopes
(71' Ernest Muçi), Mahir Emreli (56' Tomás Pekhart). Coach: Czeslaw Michniewicz.
Dinamo Zagreb: Dominik Livakovic, Kévin Théophile-Catherine, Stefan Ristovski, Rasmus
Lauritsen (25' Dino Peric), Josip Misic, Kristijan Jakic (46' François Moubandje), Luka
Ivanusec (64' Luka Menalo), Lovro Majer (77' Amer Gojak), Bartol Franjic, Mislav Orsic,
Bruno Petkovic. Coach: Damir Krznar.
Goal: 20' Bartol Franjic 0-1.
Referee: Benoît Bastien (FRA)   Attendance: 26,769

10.08.21   Ibrox Stadium, Glasgow: Glasgow Rangers FC – Malmö FF 1-2 (1-0)
Glasgow Rangers FC: Allan McGregor, Leon Balogun, James Tavernier, Connor Goldson,
Borna Barisic, Steven Davis, Scott Arfield (70' Ianis Hagi), Scott Wright (62' Fashion Sakala),
Joe Ayodele-Aribo, Alfredo Morelos, Ryan Kent. Coach: Steven Gerrard.
Malmö FF: Johan Dahlin, Niklas Moisander, Lasse Nielsen, Anel Ahmedhodzic, Søren Rieks,
Anders Christiansen, Jo Inge Berget (83' Felix Beijmo), Oscar Lewicki, Bonke Innocent,
Veljko Birmancevic (74' Erdal Rakip), Antonio Colak (90+1' Malik Abubakari).
Coach: Jon Dahl Tomasson.
Goals: 18' Alfredo Morelos 1-0, 53', 57' Antonio Colak 1-1, 1-2.
Referee: Slavko Vincic (SVN)   Attendance: 47,021
Sent off: 45+1' Bonke Innocent.

(League Path)

03.08.21   Generali Ceska pojistovna Arena, Prague: Sparta Prague – AS Monaco 0-2 (0-1)
Sparta Prague: Florin Nita, Filip Panák, Dávid Hancko, Tomás Wiesner, Borek Dockal (60'
Adam Karabec), David Pavelka, David Moberg-Karlsson (46' Lukas Julis), Jakub Pesek, Matej
Polidar (77' Andreas Vindheim), Michal Sácek, Adam Hlozek. Coach: Pavel Vrba.
AS Monaco: Alexander Nübel, Ruben Aguilar, Axel Disasi, Caio Henrique, Benoît Badiashile,
Gelson Martins (88' Anthony Musaba), Aleksandr Golovin (76' Ismail Jakobs), Aurélien
Tchouaméni, Youssouf Fofana, Kevin Volland (76' Cesc Fàbregas), Wissam Ben Yedder (57'
Sofiane Diop). Coach: Niko Kovac.
Goals: 37' Aurélien Tchouaméni 0-1, 59' Kevin Volland 0-2.
Referee: Michael Oliver (ENG)   Attendance: 10,533

03.08.21   Philips Stadion, Eindhoven: PSV Eindhoven – FC Midtjylland 3-0 (3-0)
PSV Eindhoven: Joël Drommel, Philipp Mwene (70' Jordan Teze), André Ramalho, Philipp
Max, Armando Obispo, Mario Götze, Marco van Ginkel (70' Davy Pröpper), Ibrahim Sangaré,
Eran Zahavi, Cody Gakpo (87' Yorbe Vertessen), Noni Madueke (90+2' Bruma).
Coach: Roger Schmidt.
FC Midtjylland: Jonas Lössl, Erik Sviatchenko, Joel Andersson, Paulinho (82' Nikolas Dyhr),
Rasmus Nicolaisen, Awer Mabil (57' Gustav Isaksen), Anders Dreyer (69' Victor Lind),
Evander, Charles (46' Dion Cools), Raphael Onyedika, Júnior Brumado (68' Mads Hansen).
Coach: Bo Henriksen.
Goals: 19' Noni Madueke 1-0, 29' Mario Götze 2-0, 32' Cody Gakpo 3-0.
Referee: Sergei Karasev (RUS)   Attendance: 22,700

25

03.08.21 Luminus Arena, Genk: KRC Genk – Shakhtar Donetsk 1-2 (1-0)
KRC Genk: Maarten Vandevoordt, Jhon Lucumí, Gerardo Arteaga, Daniel Muñoz, Mujaid Sadick, Patrik Hrosovský (83' Carel Eiting), Bryan Heynen, Mike Trésor (67' Kristian Thorstvedt), Paul Onuachu (82' Cyriel Dessers), Théo Bongonda, Junya Ito.
Coach: John van den Brom.
Shakhtar Donetsk: Anatoliy Trubin, Marlon, Mykola Matvienko (64' Marlos), Dodô, Vitão, Manor Solomon (46' Alan Patrick), Maycon, Marcos Antônio (73' Taras Stepanenko), Pedrinho, Tetê (64' Ismaily), Lassina Traoré (86' Dentinho). Coach: Roberto De Zerbi.
Goals: 39' Paul Onuachu 1-0, 63' Tetê 1-1 (p), 81' Alan Patrick 1-2.
Referee: Anastasios Sidiropoulos (GRE)   Attendance: 5,096

04.08.21 Otkrytiye Arena, Moscow: Spartak Moscow – SL Benfica 0-2 (0-0)
Spartak Moscow: Aleksandr Maksimenko, Georgi Dzhikiya, Samuel Gigot, Ayrton, Nikolai Rasskazov, Roman Zobnin (59' Mikhail Ignatov), Jorrit Hendrix (78' Ezequiel Ponce), Zelimkhan Bakaev (68' Viktor Moses), Nail Umyarov, Jordan Larsson (77' Alex Král), Alexander Sobolev. Coach: Rui Vitória.
SL Benfica: Odisseas Vlachodimos, Jan Vertonghen, Nicolás Otamendi, Álex Grimaldo (84' Gil Dias), Lucas Veríssimo, Pizzi (65' Éverton), João Mário, Rafa Silva (84' Adel Taarabt), Julian Weigl, Diogo Gonçalves (65' Gilberto), Haris Seferovic (37' Gonçalo Ramos).
Coach: Jorge Jesus.
Goals: 50' Rafa Silva 0-1, 73' Gilberto 0-2.
Referee: Srdjan Jovanovic (SRB)   Attendance: 2,933

10.08.21 NSC Olimpiyskiy, Kyiv: Shakhtar Donetsk – KRC Genk 2-1 (1-0)
Shakhtar Donetsk: Anatoliy Trubin, Marlon, Mykola Matvienko, Dodô, Vitão, Alan Patrick (67' Marlos), Maycon (84' Taras Stepanenko), Marcos Antônio, Pedrinho (37' Georgiy Sudakov, 67' Yevgen Konoplyanka), Tetê, Lassina Traoré (85' Danylo Sikan).
Coach: Roberto De Zerbi.
KRC Genk: Maarten Vandevoordt, Jhon Lucumí (68' Cyriel Dessers), Carlos Cuesta, Gerardo Arteaga, Daniel Muñoz, Patrik Hrosovský (62' Carel Eiting), Bryan Heynen, Kristian Thorstvedt (62' Mike Trésor), Paul Onuachu (82' Joseph Paintsil), Théo Bongonda, Junya Ito (82' Mujaid Sadick). Coach: John van den Brom.
Goals: 27' Lassina Traoré 1-0, 76' Marcos Antônio 2-0, 90' Cyriel Dessers 2-1.
Referee: István Kovács (ROM)   Attendance: 20,594

10.08.21 MCH Arena, Herning: FC Midtjylland – PSV Eindhoven 0-1 (0-0)
FC Midtjylland: Jonas Lössl, Joel Andersson, Paulinho, Dion Cools, Rasmus Nicolaisen, Nikolas Dyhr (46' Gustav Isaksen), Awer Mabil (72' Victor Lind), Anders Dreyer, Evander (83' Charles), Raphael Onyedika (80' Oscar Fraulo), Júnior Brumado (80' Mads Hansen).
Coach: Bo Henriksen.
PSV Eindhoven: Joël Drommel, André Ramalho, Philipp Max, Olivier Boscagli, Jordan Teze, Mario Götze (76' Marco van Ginkel), Davy Pröpper (89' Mauro Júnior), Ibrahim Sangaré, Eran Zahavi (88' Fodé Fofana), Cody Gakpo (64' Yorbe Vertessen), Noni Madueke (64' Bruma). Coach: Roger Schmidt.
Goal: 90+3' Bruma 0-1.
Referee: Clément Turpin (FRA)   Attendance: 6,288

26

10.08.21   Stade Louis II, Monaco: AS Monaco – Sparta Prague 3-1 (0-0)
AS Monaco: Alexander Nübel, Djibril Sidibé, Axel Disasi, Caio Henrique (59' Ismail Jakobs),
Benoît Badiashile, Gelson Martins (59' Krépin Diatta), Aleksandr Golovin (60' Sofiane Diop),
Aurélien Tchouaméni (60' Eliot Matazo), Youssouf Fofana, Kevin Volland (67' Cesc
Fàbregas), Wissam Ben Yedder. Coach: Niko Kovac.
Sparta Prague: Florin Nita, Filip Panák, Dávid Hancko, Tomás Wiesner (84' Adam Gabriel),
David Pavelka, Jakub Pesek (67' David Moberg-Karlsson), Matej Polidar, Michal Sácek (59'
Matej Pulkrab), Filip Soucek, Adam Karabec (83' Vojtech Patrák), Adam Hlozek (66' Martin
Minchev). Coach: Pavel Vrba.
Goals: 50' Gelson Martins 1-0, 56' Aleksandr Golovin 2-0, 78' David Moberg-Karlsson 2-1,
81' Sofiane Diop 3-1.
Referee: Daniele Orsato (ITA)   Attendance: 5,476

10.08.21   Estádio do Sport Lisboa e Benfica, Lisboa: SL Benfica – Spartak Moscow 2-0 (0-0)
SL Benfica: Odisseas Vlachodimos, Jan Vertonghen (46' Morato), Nicolás Otamendi, Álex
Grimaldo, Lucas Veríssimo, Pizzi (65' Éverton), João Mário, Rafa Silva (86' Adel Taarabt),
Julian Weigl, Diogo Gonçalves (78' Gilberto), Gonçalo Ramos (65' Roman Yaremchuk).
Coach: Jorge Jesus.
Spartak Moscow: Aleksandr Maksimenko, Georgi Dzhikiya, Samuel Gigot, Ayrton, Nikolai
Rasskazov, Roman Zobnin, Zelimkhan Bakaev (65' Reziuan Mirzov), Aleksandr Lomovitskiy,
Nail Umyarov (65' Alex Král), Ezequiel Ponce (81' Alexander Sobolev), Jordan Larsson (81'
Mikhail Ignatov). Coach: Rui Vitória.
Goals: 57' João Mário 1-0, 90+2' Samuel Gigot 2-0 (og).
Referee: Anthony Taylor (ENG)   Attendance: 16,312

PLAY-OFF ROUND

(Champions Path)

17.08.21   Red Bull Arena, Wals-Siezenheim: Red Bull Salzburg – Brøndby IF 2-1 (0-1)
Red Bull Salzburg: Philipp Köhn, Andreas Ulmer, Maximilian Wöber, Rasmus Kristensen,
Oumar Solet, Nicolas Seiwald, Mohamed Camara, Luka Sucic, Nicolás Capaldo (46' Brenden
Aaronson), Karim Adeyemi (82' Noah Okafor), Benjamin Sesko (77' Chikwubuike Adamu).
Coach: Matthias Jaissle.
Brøndby IF: Mads Hermansen, Kevin Mensah, Andreas Maxsø, Jens Martin Gammelby (86'
Mathias Kvistgaarden), Andreas Bruus, Kevin Tshiembe, Anton Skipper, Morten Frendrup,
Anis Ben Slimane, Simon Hedlund (72' Andrija Pavlovic), Mikael Uhre (65' Andreas Pyndt).
Coach: Niels Frederiksen.
Goals: 4' Mikael Uhre 0-1, 56' Karim Adeyemi 1-1, 90' Brenden Aaronson 2-1.
Referee: Szymon Marciniak (POL)   Attendance: 17,538

17.08.21   Bolshaya Sportivnaya Arena, Tiraspol:
           FC Sheriff Tiraspol – Dinamo Zagreb 3-0 (1-0)
FC Sheriff Tiraspol: Georgios Athanasiadis, Cristiano, Danilo Arboleda, Gustavo Dulanto,
Keston Julien (53' Fernando Costanza), Sébastien Thill, Dimitris Kolovos (87' Lovro Bizjak),
Edmund Addo (87' John Charles Petro), Henrique Luvannor (90+2' Stjepan Radeljic), Adama
Traoré, Momo Yansané. Coach: Yuriy Vernydub.
Dinamo Zagreb: Dominik Livakovic, Kévin Théophile-Catherine, Stefan Ristovski, Dino Peric
(21' François Moubandje), Josip Misic (65' Luka Menalo), Kristijan Jakic, Luka Ivanusec,
Lovro Majer (65' Amer Gojak), Bartol Franjic, Mislav Orsic (80' Duje Cop), Bruno Petkovic.
Coach: Damir Krznar.
Goals: 45' Adama Traoré 1-0, 54' Dimitris Kolovos 2-0, 80' Adama Traoré 3-0.
Referee: Cüneyt Çakir (TUR)   Attendance: 5,281

18.08.21   Stadion Wankdorf, Bern: BSC Young Boys – Ferencvárosi TC 3-2 (2-1)
BSC Young Boys: Guillaume Faivre, Ulisses Garcia, Cédric Zesiger, Silvan Hefti, Mohamed
Ali Camara, Christopher Martins Pereira, Nicolas Moumi Ngamaleu, Christian Fassnacht (86'
Quentin Maceiras), Vincent Sierro (76' Fabian Rieder), Jordan Siebatcheu (58' Wilfried
Kanga), Meschack Elia (86' Felix Mambimbi). Coaches: David Wagner & Matteo Vanetta.
Ferencvárosi TC: Dénes Dibusz, Endre Botka (69' Ryan Mmaee), Miha Blazic, Adnan
Kovacevic, Henry Wingo, Somália, Igor Kharatin, Oleksandr Zubkov (79' Róbert Mak), Aïssa
Laïdouni, Franck Boli, Myrto Uzuni (86' Regő Szánthó). Coach: Peter Stöger.
Goals: 14' Franck Boli 0-1, 16' Meschack Elia 1-1, 40' Vincent Sierro 2-1,
65' Ulisses Garcia 3-1, 82' Franck Boli 3-2.
Referee: Willie Collum (SCO)   Attendance: 15,652
Sent off: 25' Silvan Hefti.

Myrto Uzuni missed a penalty kick (27').

18.08.21   Eleda Stadion, Malmö: Malmö FF – PFC Ludogorets Razgrad 2-0 (1-0)
Malmö FF: Johan Dahlin, Niklas Moisander (34' Eric Larsson), Lasse Nielsen, Franz
Brorsson, Søren Rieks, Anders Christiansen, Jo Inge Berget (81' Felix Beijmo), Oscar
Lewicki, Erdal Rakip (81' Malik Abubakari), Veljko Birmancevic (88' Adi Nalic), Antonio
Colak. Coach: Jon Dahl Tomasson.
PFC Ludogorets Razgrad: Kristijan Kahlina, Igor Plastun, Jordan Ikoko, Anton Nedyalkov,
Olivier Verdon, Stéphane Badji, Cauly Souza, Claude Gonçalves, Alex Santana (73' Mavis
Tchibota), Pieros Sotiriou, Bernard Tekpetey (61' Wanderson). Coach: Valdas Dambrauskas.
Goals: 26' Veljko Birmancevic 1-0, 61' Jo Inge Berget 2-0.
Referee: Antonio Mateu Lahoz (ESP)   Attendance: 5,463

24.08.21   Groupama Aréna, Budapest: Ferencvárosi TC – BSC Young Boys 2-3 (2-1)
Ferencvárosi TC: Dénes Dibusz, Miha Blazic, Adnan Kovacevic, Eldar Civic, Henry Wingo, Somália (86' Róbert Mak), Kristoffer Zachariassen (76' Stjepan Loncar), Aïssa Laïdouni, Franck Boli (71' Oleksandr Zubkov), Myrto Uzuni, Ryan Mmaee. Coach: Peter Stöger.
BSC Young Boys: David von Ballmoos, Ulisses Garcia, Cédric Zesiger, Mohamed Ali Camara, Quentin Maceiras, Christopher Martins Pereira, Nicolas Moumi Ngamaleu, Christian Fassnacht, Vincent Sierro (62' Michel Aebischer), Jordan Siebatcheu (85' Felix Mambimbi), Meschack Elia (85' Sandro Lauper). Coaches: David Wagner & Matteo Vanetta.
Goals: 4' Cédric Zesiger 0-1, 18' Henry Wingo 1-1, 27' Ryan Mmaee 2-1,
56' Christian Fassnacht 2-2, 90+3' Felix Mambimbi 2-3.
Referee: Sergei Karasev (RUS)   Attendance: 20,667
Sent off: 64' Aïssa Laïdouni.

Jordan Siebatcheu missed a penalty kick (72').

24.08.21   Huvepharma Arena, Razgrad: PFC Ludogorets Razgrad – Malmö FF 2-1 (1-1)
PFC Ludogorets Razgrad: Kristijan Kahlina, Igor Plastun, Jordan Ikoko (46' Cicinho), Anton Nedyalkov, Olivier Verdon (63' Josué Sá), Wanderson (74' Mavis Tchibota), Stéphane Badji (46' Alex Santana), Cauly Souza (31' Dominik Yankov), Claude Gonçalves, Pieros Sotiriou, Kiril Despodov. Coach: Valdas Dambrauskas.
Malmö FF: Johan Dahlin (40' Ismael Diawara), Lasse Nielsen, Franz Brorsson, Anel Ahmedhodzic, Søren Rieks, Anders Christiansen, Jo Inge Berget, Oscar Lewicki (90+2' Erdal Rakip), Bonke Innocent, Veljko Birmancevic, Antonio Colak (90+2' Malik Abubakari). Coach: Jon Dahl Tomasson.
Goals: 10' Anton Nedyalkov 1-0, 42' Veljko Birmancevic 1-1, 60' Pieros Sotiriou 2-1 (p).
Referee: Clément Turpin (FRA)   Attendance: 5,130

25.08.21   Brøndby Stadium, Brøndbyvester: Brøndby IF – Red Bull Salzburg 1-2 (0-2)
Brøndby IF: Mads Hermansen, Kevin Mensah (59' Jens Martin Gammelby), Andreas Maxsø, Andreas Bruus, Kevin Tshiembe, Josip Radosevic, Mathias Greve (59' Anis Ben Slimane), Tobias Borchgrevink Børkeeiet (59' Anton Skipper), Morten Frendrup (84' Sigurd Rosted), Simon Hedlund (78' Andrija Pavlovic), Mikael Uhre. Coach: Niels Frederiksen.
Red Bull Salzburg: Philipp Köhn, Andreas Ulmer, Maximilian Wöber, Rasmus Kristensen, Oumar Solet, Brenden Aaronson (85' Bernardo), Nicolas Seiwald, Mohamed Camara (66' Zlatko Junuzovic), Luka Sucic, Karim Adeyemi (71' Mërgim Berisha), Benjamin Sesko (71' Noah Okafor). Coach: Matthias Jaissle.
Goals: 4' Benjamin Sesko 0-1, 10' Brenden Aaronson 0-2, 62' Andreas Maxsø 1-2.
Referee: Carlos del Cerro Grande (ESP)   Attendance: 22,397

25.08.21   Stadion Maksimir, Zagreb: Dinamo Zagreb – FC Sheriff Tiraspol 0-0)
Dinamo Zagreb: Dominik Livakovic, Kévin Théophile-Catherine, Stefan Ristovski, Sadegh
Moharrami (62' Lirim Kastrati), Josip Misic (84' Amer Gojak), Luka Ivanusec, Lovro Majer,
Bartol Franjic, Duje Cop (69' Deni Juric), Mislav Orsic (85' Luka Menalo), Bruno Petkovic.
Coach: Damir Krznar.
FC Sheriff Tiraspol: Georgios Athanasiadis, Cristiano, Danilo Arboleda, Gustavo Dulanto,
Fernando Costanza, Sébastien Thill, Dimitris Kolovos (74' John Charles Petro), Edmund
Addo, Henrique Luvannor (88' Stjepan Radeljic), Adama Traoré, Frank Castañeda (58' Momo
Yansané). Coach: Yuriy Vernydub.
Referee: Daniele Orsato (ITA)   Attendance: 8,015

(League Path)

17.08.21   Stade Louis II, Monaco: AS Monaco – Shakhtar Donetsk 0-1 (0-1)
AS Monaco: Radoslaw Majecki, Djibril Sidibé, Guillermo Maripán, Caio Henrique, Benoît
Badiashile, Gelson Martins (67' Krépin Diatta), Aleksandr Golovin (60' Sofiane Diop),
Aurélien Tchouaméni, Youssouf Fofana (46' Jean Lucas), Kevin Volland, Wissam Ben Yedder
(67' Myron Boadu). Coach: Niko Kovac.
Shakhtar Donetsk: Anatoliy Trubin, Marlon, Mykola Matvienko, Dodô, Vitão, Manor Solomon
(66' Yevgen Konoplyanka), Maycon (74' Taras Stepanenko), Marcos Antônio, Pedrinho (46'
Alan Patrick), Tetê (89' Marlos), Lassina Traoré (90' Danylo Sikan).
Coach: Roberto De Zerbi.
Goal: 19' Pedrinho 0-1.
Referee: Danny Makkelie (HOL)   Attendance: 5,700

18.08.21   Estádio do Sport Lisboa e Benfica, Lisboa: SL Benfica – PSV Eindhoven 2-1 (2-0)
SL Benfica: Odisseas Vlachodimos, Nicolás Otamendi, Álex Grimaldo, Lucas Veríssimo,
Morato, Pizzi (72' André Almeida), João Mário (86' Adel Taarabt), Rafa Silva, Julian Weigl
(71' Éverton), Diogo Gonçalves (73' Soualiho Meïté), Roman Yaremchuk (71' Gonçalo
Ramos). Coach: Jorge Jesus.
PSV Eindhoven: Joël Drommel, Philipp Mwene, André Ramalho, Philipp Max (89' Jordan
Teze), Olivier Boscagli (64' Armando Obispo), Mario Götze, Marco van Ginkel (65' Davy
Pröpper), Ibrahim Sangaré, Eran Zahavi (89' Yorbe Vertessen), Cody Gakpo, Noni Madueke
(74' Bruma). Coach: Roger Schmidt.
Goals: 10' Rafa Silva 1-0, 42' Julian Weigl 2-0, 51' Cody Gakpo 2-1.
Referee: Dr. Felix Brych (GER)   Attendance: 18,199

24.08.21   Philips Stadion, Eindhoven: PSV Eindhoven – SL Benfica 0-0
PSV Eindhoven: Joël Drommel, Philipp Mwene (90' Ryan Thomas), André Ramalho, Philipp
Max (89' Jordan Teze), Olivier Boscagli (70' Armando Obispo), Mario Götze, Marco van
Ginkel (70' Bruma), Ibrahim Sangaré, Eran Zahavi, Cody Gakpo, Noni Madueke (70' Yorbe
Vertessen). Coach: Roger Schmidt.
SL Benfica: Odisseas Vlachodimos, Nicolás Otamendi, Gilberto (61' André Almeida), Álex
Grimaldo, Lucas Veríssimo, Morato, Adel Taarabt (54' Jan Vertonghen), João Mário (74'
Éverton), Rafa Silva (74' Soualiho Meïté), Julian Weigl, Roman Yaremchuk (61' Gonçalo
Ramos). Coach: Jorge Jesus.
Referee: Slavko Vincic (SVN)   Attendance: 21,855
Sent off: 32' Lucas Veríssimo.

25.08.21   Oblasny SportKomplex Metalist, Kharkiv:
         Shakhtar Donetsk – AS Monaco 2-2 (0-2,1-2) (AET)
Shakhtar Donetsk: Andry Pyatov, Marlon, Mykola Matvienko (46' Ismaily), Dodô, Vitão (101'
Sergiy Kryvtsov), Alan Patrick, Manor Solomon (82' Mykhailo Mudryk), Maycon, Marcos
Antônio (86' Taras Stepanenko), Tetê (66' Marlos), Lassina Traoré (101' Fernando).
Coach: Roberto De Zerbi.
AS Monaco: Alexander Nübel, Djibril Sidibé (98' Ruben Aguilar), Guillermo Maripán, Caio
Henrique (117' Ismail Jakobs), Benoît Badiashile, Gelson Martins (71' Jean Lucas), Aleksandr
Golovin (76' Wilson Isidor), Aurélien Tchouaméni (117' Axel Disasi), Youssouf Fofana,
Kevin Volland, Wissam Ben Yedder (76' Sofiane Diop). Coach: Niko Kovac.
Goals: 18', 39' Wissam Ben Yedder 0-1, 0-2, 74' Marlos 1-2, 114' Ruben Aguilar 2-2 (og).
Referee: Anthony Taylor (ENG)   Attendance: 26,697

*Shakhtar Donetsk played their home match at Oblasny SportKomplex Metalist, Kharkiv,
instead of their regular stadium Donbass Arena, Donetsk, due to the war in Eastern Ukraine.*

GROUP STAGE

GROUP A

Manchester City	6	4	0	2	18	-	10	12
Paris Saint-Germain	6	3	2	1	13	-	8	11
RB Leipzig	6	2	1	3	15	-	14	7
Club Brugge KV	6	1	1	4	6	-	20	4

GROUP B

Liverpool FC	6	6	0	0	17	-	6	18
Atlético Madrid	6	2	1	3	7	-	8	7
FC Porto	6	1	2	3	4	-	11	5
AC Milan	6	1	1	4	6	-	9	4

GROUP C

AFC Ajax	6	6	0	0	20	-	5	18
Sporting CP	6	3	0	3	14	-	12	9
Borussia Dortmund	6	3	0	3	10	-	11	9
Besiktas JK	6	0	0	6	3	-	19	0

GROUP D

Real Madrid CF	6	5	0	1	14	-	3	15
Internazionale Milano	6	3	1	2	8	-	5	10
FC Sheriff Tiraspol	6	2	1	3	7	-	11	7
Shakhtar Donetsk	6	0	2	4	2	-	12	2

GROUP E

Bayern München	6	6	0	0	22	-	3	18
SL Benfica	6	2	2	2	7	-	9	8
FC Barcelona	6	2	1	3	2	-	9	7
Dynamo Kyiv	6	0	1	5	1	-	11	1

GROUP F

Manchester United	6	3	2	1	11	-	8	11
Villarreal CF	6	3	1	2	12	-	9	10
Atalanta Bergamo	6	1	3	2	12	-	13	6
BSC Young Boys	6	1	2	3	7	-	12	5

GROUP G

Lille OSC	6	3	2	1	7 - 4	11
Red Bull Salzburg	6	3	1	2	8 - 6	10
Sevilla FC	6	1	3	2	5 - 5	6
VfL Wolfsburg	6	1	2	3	5 - 10	5

GROUP H

Juventus FC	6	5	0	1	10 - 6	15
Chelsea FC	6	4	1	1	13 - 4	13
Zenit Saint Petersburg	6	1	2	3	10 - 10	5
Malmö FF	6	0	1	5	1 - 14	1

GROUP A

15.09.21   Etihad Stadium, Manchester: Manchester City – RB Leipzig 6-3 (3-1)
Manchester City: Ederson Moraes, João Cancelo, Nathan Aké, Rúben Dias, Kevin de Bruyne
(71' Phil Foden), Jack Grealish (81' Gabriel Jesus), Oleksandr Zinchenko, Bernardo Silva (59'
Ilkay Gündogan), Rodri (59' Fernandinho), Riyad Mahrez, Ferrán Torres (72' Raheem
Sterling). Coach: Pep Guardiola.
RB Leipzig: Péter Gulácsi, Willi Orban, Lukas Klostermann, José Angeliño, Nordi Mukiele,
Emil Forsberg (61' Dominik Szoboszlai), Konrad Laimer (60' Amadou Haïdara), Christopher
Nkunku (81' Josko Gvardiol), Dani Olmo (72' Brian Brobbey), Tyler Adams, André Silva (60'
Yussuf Poulsen). Coach: Jesse Marsch.
Goals: 16' Nathan Aké 1-0, 28' Nordi Mukiele 2-0 (og), 42' Christopher Nkunku 2-1,
45+2' Riyad Mahrez 3-1 (p), 51' Christopher Nkunku 3-2, 56' Jack Grealish 4-2,
73' Christopher Nkunku 4-3, 75' João Cancelo 5-3, 85' Gabriel Jesus 6-3.
Referee: Serdar Gözübüyük (HOL)   Attendance: 38,062
Sent-off: 79' José Angeliño.

15.09.21   Jan Breydelstadion, Brugge: Club Brugge KV – Paris Saint-Germain 1-1 (1-1)
Club Brugge KV: Simon Mignolet, Eduard Sobol, Clinton Mata, Jack Hendry, Stanley N'Soki,
Mats Rits, Hans Vanaken, Éder Balanta, Kamal Sowah (90+2' Faitout Maouassa), Charles De
Ketelaere, Noa Lang. Coach: Philippe Clement.
Paris Saint-Germain: Keylor Navas, Marquinhos, Presnel Kimpembe, Abdou Diallo (75' Nuno
Mendes), Achraf Hakimi, Georginio Wijnaldum (46' Julian Draxler), Ander Herrera, Leandro
Paredes (46' Danilo Pereira), Lionel Messi, Neymar, Kylian Mbappé (51' Mauro Icardi).
Coach: Mauricio Pochettino.
Goals: 15' Ander Herrera 0-1, 27' Hans Vanaken (27').
Referee: Sandro Schärer (SUI)   Attendance: 27,546

28.09.21   Red Bull Arena, Leipzig: RB Leipzig – Club Brugge KV 1-2 (1-2)
RB Leipzig: Péter Gulácsi, Willi Orban, Lukas Klostermann, Nordi Mukiele (46' Josko
Gvardiol), Mohamed Simakan (78' Tyler Adams), Emil Forsberg, Kevin Kampl, Konrad
Laimer (46' Amadou Haïdara), Christopher Nkunku, Dominik Szoboszlai (58' André Silva),
Yussuf Poulsen (78' Brian Brobbey). Coach: Jesse Marsch.
Club Brugge KV: Simon Mignolet, Eduard Sobol (79' Federico Ricca), Clinton Mata, Jack
Hendry, Stanley N'Soki, Mats Rits (79' Ruud Vormer), Hans Vanaken, Éder Balanta, Kamal
Sowah (68' Ignace Van Der Brempt), Charles De Ketelaere (72' Wesley), Noa Lang.
Coach: Philippe Clement.
Goals: 5' Christopher Nkunku 1-0, 22' Hans Vanaken 1-1, 40' Mats Rits (1-2).
Referee: Slavko Vincic (SVN)   Attendance: 23,500

28.09.21   Parc des Princes, Paris: Paris Saint-Germain – Manchester City 2-0 (1-0)
Paris Saint-Germain: Gianluigi Donnarumma, Marquinhos, Presnel Kimpembe, Achraf
Hakimi, Nuno Mendes, Ander Herrera, Marco Verratti (78' Georginio Wijnaldum), Idrissa
Gueye (90' Danilo Pereira), Lionel Messi, Neymar, Kylian Mbappé.
Coach: Mauricio Pochettino.
Manchester City: Ederson Moraes, Kyle Walker, João Cancelo, Aymeric Laporte, Rúben Dias,
Kevin de Bruyne, Jack Grealish (68' Phil Foden), Bernardo Silva, Rodri, Riyad Mahrez,
Raheem Sterling (78' Gabriel Jesus). Coach: Pep Guardiola.
Goals: 8' Idrissa Gueye 1-0, 2-0 Lionel Messi (74').
Referee: Carlos del Cerro Grande (ESP)   Attendance: 37,350

19.10.21   Jan Breydelstadion, Brugge: Club Brugge KV – Manchester City 1-5 (0-2)
Club Brugge KV: Simon Mignolet, Eduard Sobol, Clinton Mata, Jack Hendry, Stanley N'Soki
(79' Brandon Mechele), Mats Rits (56' Ruud Vormer), Hans Vanaken, Éder Balanta (68' Noah
Mbamba-Muanda), Kamal Sowah (56' Ignace Van Der Brempt), Charles De Ketelaere (79'
Bas Dost), Noa Lang. Coach: Philippe Clement.
Manchester City: Ederson Moraes, Kyle Walker, João Cancelo, Aymeric Laporte (57' Nathan
Aké), Rúben Dias, Kevin de Bruyne (64' Cole Palmer), Jack Grealish, Bernardo Silva (57'
Ilkay Gündogan), Rodri (71' Fernandinho), Phil Foden (64' Raheem Sterling), Riyad Mahrez.
Coach: Pep Guardiola.
Goals: 30' João Cancelo 0-1, 43' Riyad Mahrez 0-2 (p), 53' Kyle Walker 0-3,
67' Cole Palmer 0-4, 81' Hans Vanaken 1-4, 84' Riyad Mahrez 1-5.
Referee: István Kovács (ROM)   Attendance: 24,915

19.10.21   Parc des Princes, Paris: Paris Saint-Germain – RB Leipzig 3-2 (1-1)
Paris Saint-Germain: Keylor Navas, Marquinhos, Presnel Kimpembe, Achraf Hakimi, Nuno
Mendes, Ander Herrera (61' Georginio Wijnaldum), Marco Verratti, Idrissa Gueye (61' Danilo
Pereira), Julian Draxler (90' Thilo Kehrer), Lionel Messi, Kylian Mbappé.
Coach: Mauricio Pochettino.
RB Leipzig: Péter Gulácsi, Willi Orban, Lukas Klostermann (70' Josko Gvardiol), José
Angeliño (83' Benjamin Henrichs), Nordi Mukiele, Mohamed Simakan (83' Yussuf Poulsen),
Konrad Laimer, Christopher Nkunku, Tyler Adams, Amadou Haïdara (62' Ilaix Moriba),
André Silva (83' Emil Forsberg). Coach: Jesse Marsch.
Goals: 9' Kylian Mbappé 1-0, 28' André Silva 1-1, 57' Nordi Mukiele 1-2,
67', 74' Lionel Messi 2-2, 3-2 (p).
Referee: Marco Guida (ITA)   Attendancce: 47,359

Kylian Mbappé missed a penalty kick (90+4').

34

03.11.21   Red Bul Arena, Leipzig: RB Leipzig – Paris Saint-Germain 2-2 (1-2)
RB Leipzig: Péter Gulácsi, Willi Orban (46' Amadou Haïdara), José Angeliño, Nordi Mukiele, Mohamed Simakan, Josko Gvardiol, Emil Forsberg (59' Dominik Szoboszlai), Konrad Laimer (85' Benjamin Henrichs), Christopher Nkunku, Tyler Adams (74' Dani Olmo), André Silva (59' Yussuf Poulsen). Coach: Jesse Marsch.
Paris Saint-Germain: Gianluigi Donnarumma, Marquinhos, Presnel Kimpembe, Achraf Hakimi, Nuno Mendes, Georginio Wijnaldum (85' Ander Herrera), Ángel Di María (85' Julian Draxler), Idrissa Gueye, Danilo Pereira, Neymar, Kylian Mbappé (90+3' Mauro Icardi). Coach: Mauricio Pochettino.
Goals: 8' Christopher Nkunku 1-0, 21', 39' Georginio Wijnaldum 1-1, 1-2, 90+2' Dominik Szoboszlai 2-2 (p).
Referee: Andreas Ekberg (SWE)   Attendance: 39,794

André Silva missed a penalty kick (12').

03.11.21   Etihad Stadium, Manchester: Manchester City – Club Brugge KV 4-1 (1-1)
Manchester City: Ederson Moraes, Kyle Walker (80' Oleksandr Zinchenko), João Cancelo, Aymeric Laporte, John Stones, Ilkay Gündogan, Jack Grealish (68' Gabriel Jesus), Bernardo Silva (75' Kevin de Bruyne), Rodri, Phil Foden (80' Cole Palmer), Riyad Mahrez (69' Raheem Sterling). Coach: Pep Guardiola.
Club Brugge KV: Simon Mignolet, Eduard Sobol (73' Federico Ricca), Clinton Mata (78' Ignace Van Der Brempt), Brandon Mechele, Jack Hendry, Stanley N'Soki, Ruud Vormer, Mats Rits (78' Noah Mbamba-Muanda), Hans Vanaken, Charles De Ketelaere (87' Kamal Sowah), Noa Lang (78' Bas Dost). Coach: Philippe Clement.
Goals: 15' Phil Foden 1-0, 17' John Stones 1-1 (og), 54' Riyad Mahrez 2-1, 72' Raheem Sterling 3-1, 90+2' Gabriel Jesus 4-1.
Referee: Antonio Miguel Mateu Lahoz (ESP)   Attendance: 50,228

24.11.21   Etihad Stadium, Manchester: Manchester City – Paris Saint-Germain 2-1 (0-0)
Manchester City: Ederson Moraes, Kyle Walker, João Cancelo, John Stones, Rúben Dias, Ilkay Gündogan, Oleksandr Zinchenko (54' Gabriel Jesus), Bernardo Silva, Rodri, Riyad Mahrez, Raheem Sterling. Coach: Pep Guardiola.
Paris Saint-Germain: Keylor Navas, Marquinhos, Presnel Kimpembe, Achraf Hakimi, Nuno Mendes (67' Thilo Kehrer), Ander Herrera (61' Danilo Pereira), Idrissa Gueye (67' Ángel Di María), Leandro Paredes, Lionel Messi, Neymar, Kylian Mbappé. Coach: Mauricio Pochettino.
Goals: 50' Kylian Mbappé 0-1, 63' Raheem Sterling 1-1, 76' Gabriel Jesus (76').
Referee: Daniele Orsato (ITA)   Attendance: 52,030

24.11.21   Jan Breydelstadion, Brugge: Club Brugge KV – RB Leipzig 0-5 (0-4)
Club Brugge KV: Simon Mignolet, Clinton Mata, Jack Hendry, Stanley N'Soki (46' Federico Ricca), Ignace Van Der Brempt (60' Brandon Mechele), Hans Vanaken, Éder Balanta, Kamal Sowah (82' José Izquierdo), Charles De Ketelaere (82' Wesley), Bas Dost (46' Mats Rits), Noa Lang. Coach: Philippe Clement.
RB Leipzig: Josep Martínez, Lukas Klostermann (62' Benjamin Henrichs), José Angeliño, Nordi Mukiele, Josko Gvardiol (80' Solomon Bonnah), Emil Forsberg, Kevin Kampl, Konrad Laimer (62' Ilaix Moriba), Christopher Nkunku, André Silva, Brian Brobbey (66' Hugo Novoa). Coach: Jesse Marsch.
Goals: 12' Christopher Nkunku 0-1, 17' Emil Forsberg 0-2 (p), 26' André Silva 0-3, 45+1' Emil Forsberg 0-4, 90+3' Christopher Nkunku 0-5.
Referee: Davide Massa (ITA)   Attendance: 24,072

07.12.21   Red Bull Arena, Leipzig: RB Leipzig – Manchester City 2-1 (1-0)
RB Leipzig: Péter Gulácsi, Lukas Klostermann (46' Mohamed Simakan), José Angeliño, Nordi Mukiele (79' Benjamin Henrichs), Josko Gvardiol, Emil Forsberg (80' Brian Brobbey), Kevin Kampl, Konrad Laimer (63' Tyler Adams), Christopher Nkunku, Dominik Szoboszlai, André Silva (86' Ilaix Moriba). Coach: Achim Beierlorzer.
Manchester City: Zack Steffen, Kyle Walker, Nathan Aké (87' Rúben Dias), John Stones, Fernandinho, Ilkay Gündogan, Kevin De Bruyne (87' Cole Palmer), Jack Grealish, Oleksandr Zinchenko, Phil Foden (46' Raheem Sterling), Riyad Mahrez. Coach: Pep Guardiola.
Goals: 24' Dominik Szoboszlai 1-0, 71' André Silva 2-0, 76' Riyad Mahrez 2-1.
Referee: Sandro Schärer (SUI)   Attendance: 0
Sent-off: 82' Kyle Walker.

07.12.21   Parc des Princes, Paris: Paris Saint-Germain – Club Brugge KV 4-1 (3-0)
Paris Saint-Germain: Gianluigi Donnarumma, Marquinhos, Abdou Diallo, Achraf Hakimi, Nuno Mendes (50' Thilo Kehrer), Georginio Wijnaldum, Ángel Di María (71' Ander Herrera), Marco Verratti (83' Éric Dina-Ebimbe), Idrissa Gueye (71' Leandro Paredes), Lionel Messi, Kylian Mbappé (83' Mauro Icardi). Coach: Mauricio Pochettino.
Club Brugge KV: Simon Mignolet, Clinton Mata, Federico Ricca, Jack Hendry, Stanley N'Soki, Mats Rits (69' Ruud Vormer), Hans Vanaken, Éder Balanta (69' Noah Mbamba-Muanda), Charles De Ketelaere, Cisse Sandra (57' Ignace Van Der Brempt), Noa Lang. Coach: Philippe Clement.
Goals: 2', 7' Kylian Mbappé 1-0, 2-0, 38' Lionel Messi 3-0, 68' Mats Rits 3-1, 76' Lionel Messi 4-1 (p).
Referee: Jesús Gil Manzano (ESP)   Attendance: 47,492

GROUP B

15.09.21   Anfield, Liverpool: Liverpool FC – AC Milan 3-2 (1-2)
Liverpool FC: Alisson, Joel Matip, Andrew Robertson, Joe Gomez, Trent Alexander-Arnold, Jordan Henderson (84' James Milner), Fabinho, Naby Keïta (71' Thiago Alcântara), Mohamed Salah (84' Alex Oxlade-Chamberlain), Divock Origi (63' Sadio Mané), Diogo Jota (71' Curtis Jones). Coach: Jürgen Klopp.
AC Milan: Mike Maignan, Simon Kjær, Davide Calabria, Fikayo Tomori, Theo Hernández, Franck Kessié, Ismaël Bennacer (71' Sandro Tonali), Alexis Saelemaekers (62' Alessandro Florenzi), Ante Rebic (83' Daniel Maldini), Rafael Leão (62' Olivier Giroud), Brahim Díaz. Coach: Stefano Pioli.
Goals: 9' FikayoTomori 1-0 (og), 42' Ante Rebic 1-1, 44' Brahim Díaz 1-2, 49' Mohamed Salah 2-2, 69' Jordan Henderson 3-2.
Referee: Szymon Marciniak (POL)   Attendance: 51,445

Mohamed Salah missed a penalty kick (14').

15.09.21   Estadio Wanda Metropolitano, Madrid: Atlético Madrid – FC Porto 0-0
Atlético Madrid: Jan Oblak, Felipe Monteiro (75' Héctor Herrera), José Giménez, Mario Hermoso (56' Renan Lodi), Geoffrey Kondogbia, Koke (56' Ángel Correa), Yannick Carrasco, Thomas Lemar (36' Rodrigo de Paul), Marcos Llorente, Luis Suárez, João Félix (56' Antoine Griezmann). Coach: Diego Simeone.
FC Porto: Diogo Costa, Pepe (54' Iván Marcano), Chancel Mbemba, Zaidu Sanusi (46' Wendell), Mateus Uribe (66' Vitinha), Otávio, Marko Grujic, Jesús Corona, Mehdi Taremi, Toni Martínez (66' Sérgio Oliveira), Luis Díaz (84' Pepê Aquino). Coach: Sérgio Conceição.
Referee: Ovidiu Alin Hategan (ROM)   Attendance: 40,098
Sent-off: 90+5' Chancel Mbemba.

28.09.21   Stadio Giuseppe Meazza, Milano: AC Milan – Atlético Madrid 1-2 (1-0)
AC Milan: Mike Maignan, Alessio Romagnoli, Davide Calabria, Fikayo Tomori, Theo
Hernández, Franck Kessié, Ismaël Bennacer (81' Alessandro Florenzi), Alexis Saelemaekers
(82' Pierre Kalulu), Ante Rebic (34' Sandro Tonali), Rafael Leão (57' Olivier Giroud), Brahim
Díaz (57' Fodé Ballo-Touré). Coach: Stefano Pioli.
Atlético Madrid: Jan Oblak, Kieran Trippier (40' João Félix), Felipe Monteiro, José Giménez,
Mario Hermoso (46' Renan Lodi), Geoffrey Kondogbia (64' Thomas Lemar), Koke (61'
Antoine Griezmann), Yannick Carrasco (46' Rodrigo de Paul), Marcos Llorente, Luis Suárez,
Ángel Correa. Coach: Diego Simeone.
Goals: 20' Rafael Leão 1-0, 84' Antoine Griezmann 1-1, 90+7' Luis Suárez 1-2 (p).
Referee: Cüneyt Çakir (TUR)   Attendance: 35,374
Sent-off: 29' Franck Kessié.

28.09.21   Estádio do Dragão, Porto: FC Porto – Liverpool FC 1-5 (0-2)
FC Porto: Diogo Costa, Iván Marcano, Fábio Cardoso, Zaidu Sanusi (56' Wendell), Sérgio
Oliveira (67' Pepê Aquino), Mateus Uribe (56' Vitinha), Otávio (14' Fábio Vieira), Jesús
Corona, Mehdi Taremi, Toni Martínez (46' Marko Grujic), Luis Díaz.
Coach: Sérgio Conceição.
Liverpool FC: Alisson, Joel Matip, Virgil van Dijk, Andrew Robertson, James Milner (66' Joe
Gomez), Jordan Henderson (73' Alex Oxlade-Chamberlain), Fabinho, Curtis Jones, Mohamed
Salah (67' Roberto Firmino), Sadio Mané (67' Takumi Minamino), Diogo Jota (88' Divock
Origi). Coach: Jürgen Klopp.
Goals: 18' Mohamed Salah 0-1, 45' Sadio Mané 0-2, 60' Mohamed Salah 0-3,
75' Mehdi Taremi 1-3, 77', 81' Roberto Firmino 1-4, 1-5.
Referee: Sergey Karasev (RUS)   Attendance: 23,520

19.10.21   Estadio Wanda Metropolitano, Madrid: Atlético Madrid – Liverpool FC 2-3 (2-2)
Atlético Madrid: Jan Oblak, Kieran Trippier, Felipe Monteiro, Mario Hermoso (80' Marcos
Llorente), Geoffrey Kondogbia (46' José Giménez), Koke, Yannick Carrasco, Thomas Lemar
(80' Luis Suárez), Rodrigo de Paul (80' Renan Lodi), Antoine Griezmann, João Félix (80'
Ángel Correa). Coach: Diego Simeone.
Liverpool FC: Alisson, Joel Matip, Virgil van Dijk, Andrew Robertson, Trent Alexander-
Arnold (85' Joe Gomez), James Milner (63' Alex Oxlade-Chamberlain), Jordan Henderson,
Naby Keïta (46' Fabinho), Roberto Firmino, Mohamed Salah (90+2' Neco Williams), Sadio
Mané (62' Diogo Jota). Coach: Jürgen Klopp.
Goals: 8' Mohamed Salah 0-1, 13' Naby Keïta 0-2, 20', 34' Antoine Griezmann 1-2, 2-2,
78' Mohamed Salah 2-3 (p).
Referee: Daniel Siebert (GER)   Attendance: 60,725
Sent-off: 52' Antoine Griezmann.

19.10.21   Estádio do Dragão, Porto: FC Porto – AC Milan 1-0 (0-0)
FC Porto: Diogo Costa, Pepe, Wendell (46' Zaidu Sanusi), Chancel Mbemba, Sérgio Oliveira
(67' Vitinha), Mateus Uribe, Otávio (90+1' Marko Grujic), Mehdi Taremi (84' Toni Martínez),
Luis Díaz, João Mário, Evanilson (67' Jesús Corona). Coach: Sérgio Conceição.
AC Milan: Ciprian Tatarusanu, Simon Kjær, Davide Calabria, Fodé Ballo-Touré (58' Pierre
Kalulu), Fikayo Tomori (59' Alessio Romagnoli), Rade Krunic (82' Daniel Maldini), Ismaël
Bennacer, Alexis Saelemaekers, Sandro Tonali (66' Tiemoué Bakayoko), Olivier Giroud (58'
Zlatan Ibrahimovic), Rafael Leão. Coach: Stefano Pioli.
Goal: 65' Luis Díaz 1-0.
Referee: Dr. Felix Brych (GER)   Attendance: 32,130

03.11.21   Stadio Giuseppe Meazza, Milano: AC Milan – FC Porto 1-1 (0-1)
AC Milan: Ciprian Tatarusanu, Alessio Romagnoli, Davide Calabria (46' Pierre Kalulu),
Fikayo Tomori, Theo Hernández, Ismaël Bennacer, Alexis Saelemaekers, Sandro Tonali (68'
Franck Kessié), Olivier Giroud (76' Zlatan Ibrahimovic), Rafael Leão (85' Daniel Maldini),
Brahim Díaz (68' Rade Krunic). Coach: Stefano Pioli.
FC Porto: Diogo Costa, Pepe, Chancel Mbemba, Zaidu Sanusi, Sérgio Oliveira (70' Vitinha),
Otávio (85' Toni Martínez), Marko Grujic, Mehdi Taremi (86' Pepê Aquino), Luis Díaz (79'
Bruno Costa), João Mário, Evanilson (79' Francisco Conceição). Coach: Sérgio Conceição.
Goals: 6' Luis Díaz 0-1, 61' Chancel Mbemba 1-1 (og).
Referee: Clément Turpin (FRA)   Attendance: 39,675

03.11.21   Anfield, Liverpool: Liverpool FC – Atlético Madrid 2-0 (2-0)
Liverpool FC: Alisson, Joel Matip, Virgil van Dijk, Kostas Tsimikas, Trent Alexander-Arnold
(90+4' Nathaniel Phillips), Jordan Henderson, Alex Oxlade-Chamberlain (78' Takumi
Minamino), Fabinho (59' Thiago Alcântara), Mohamed Salah, Sadio Mané (46' Roberto
Firmino, 78' Divock Origi), Diogo Jota. Coach: Jürgen Klopp.
Atlético Madrid: Jan Oblak, Kieran Trippier, Felipe Monteiro, José Giménez, Mario Hermoso,
Koke (69' Matheus Cunha), Yannick Carrasco (69' Sime Vrsaljko), Rodrigo de Paul, Luis
Suárez (59' Héctor Herrera), Ángel Correa (75' Javier Serrano), João Félix (59' Renan Lodi).
Coach: Diego Simeone.
Goals: 13' Diogo Jota 1-0, 21' Sadio Mané 2-0.
Referee: Danny Makkelie (HOL)   Attendance: 51,347
Sent-off: 36' Felipe Monteiro.

24.11.21   Anfield, Liverpool: Liverpool FC – FC Porto 2-0 (0-0)
Liverpool FC: Alisson, Joel Matip, Kostas Tsimikas (63' Andrew Robertson), Ibrahima
Konaté, Neco Williams, Thiago Alcântara (63' Jordan Henderson), Alex Oxlade-Chamberlain
(82' James Milner), Tyler Morton, Mohamed Salah (71' Fabinho), Takumi Minamino, Sadio
Mané (72' Divock Origi). Coach: Jürgen Klopp.
FC Porto: Diogo Costa, Pepe (25' Fábio Cardoso), Chancel Mbemba, Zaidu Sanusi, Sérgio
Oliveira (64' Vitinha), Mateus Uribe (77' Marko Grujic), Otávio, Mehdi Taremi (64' Francisco
Conceição), Luis Díaz, João Mário, Evanilson (77' Toni Martínez). Coach: Sérgio Conceição.
Goals: 52' Thiago Alcântara 1-0, 70' Mohamed Salah 2-0.
Referee: Felix Zwayer (GER)   Attendance: 52,209

24.11.21   Estadio Wanda Metropolitano, Madrid: Atlético Madrid – AC Milan 0-1 (0-0)
Atlético Madrid: Jan Oblak, Stefan Savic, José Giménez, Mario Hermoso (64' Renan Lodi),
Koke, Yannick Carrasco, Thomas Lemar (64' Ángel Correa), Rodrigo de Paul (77' Sime
Vrsaljko), Marcos Llorente, Luis Suárez (77' Matheus Cunha), Antoine Griezmann (81'
Geoffrey Kondogbia). Coach: Diego Simeone.
AC Milan: Ciprian Tatarusanu, Simon Kjær, Alessio Romagnoli, Theo Hernández, Pierre
Kalulu (65' Alessandro Florenzi), Rade Krunic (65' Junior Messias), Franck Kessié, Alexis
Saelemaekers, Sandro Tonali (65' Tiemoué Bakayoko), Olivier Giroud (66' Zlatan
Ibrahimovic), Brahim Díaz (78' Ismaël Bennacer). Coach: Stefano Pioli.
Goal: 87' Junior Messias 0-1.
Referee: Slavko Vincic (SVN)   Attendance: 61,019

07.12.21 Estádio do Dragão, Porto: FC Porto – Atlético Madrid 1-3 (0-0)
FC Porto: Diogo Costa, Pepe, Chancel Mbemba, Zaidu Sanusi (63' Wendell), Otávio (82'
Fábio Vieira), Marko Grujic (81' Jesús Corona), Vitinha, Mehdi Taremi (82' Toni Martínez),
Luis Díaz, João Mário (81' Sérgio Oliveira), Evanilson. Coach: Sérgio Conceição.
Atlético Madrid: Jan Oblak, Sime Vrsaljko, Mario Hermoso, Geoffrey Kondogbia, Koke,
Yannick Carrasco, Thomas Lemar (66' Ángel Correa), Rodrigo de Paul, Marcos Llorente, Luis
Suárez (13' Matheus Cunha, 83' Renan Lodi), Antoine Griezmann. Coach: Diego Simeone.
Goals: 56' Antoine Griezmann 0-1, 90' Ángel Correa 0-2, 90+2' Rodrigo de Paul 0-3,
90+6' Sérgio Oliveira 1-3 (p).
Referee: Clément Turpin (FRA) Attendance: 38,830
Sent-off: 67' Yannick Carrasco, 72' Wendell, 75' Agustín Marchesin (not used sub).

07.12.21 Stadio Giuseppe Meazza, Milano: AC Milan – Liverpool FC 1-2 (1-1)
AC Milan: Mike Maignan, Alessio Romagnoli, Fikayo Tomori, Theo Hernández, Pierre Kalulu
(64' Alessandro Florenzi), Rade Krunic (83' Tiemoué Bakayoko), Franck Kessié, Sandro
Tonali (59' Alexis Saelemaekers), Zlatan Ibrahimovic, Brahim Díaz (59' Ismaël Bennacer),
Junior Messias. Coach: Stefano Pioli.
Liverpool FC: Alisson, Kostas Tsimikas, Ibrahima Konaté, Nathaniel Phillips, Neco Williams
(90+3' Conor Bradley), Alex Oxlade-Chamberlain, Tyler Morton, Mohamed Salah (64' Naby
Keïta), Takumi Minamino (90+3' Max Woltman), Sadio Mané (64' Joe Gomez), Divock Origi
(80' Fabinho). Coach: Jürgen Klopp.
Goals: 29' Fikayo Tomori 1-0, 36' Mohamed Salah 1-1, 55' Divock Origi 1-2.
Referee: Danny Makkelie (HOL) Attendance: 56,237

GROUP C

15.09.21 Vodafone Park, Istanbul: Besiktas JK – Borussia Dortmund 1-2 (0-2)
Besiktas JK: Ersin Destanoglu, Fabrice N'Sakala, Welinton Souza, Valentin Rosier, Javi
Montero, Atiba Hutchinson (78' Salih Uçan), Miralem Pjanic, Josef de Souza, Rachid Ghezzal
(89' Gökhan Töre), Michy Batshuayi, Cyle Larin (61' Kenan Karaman). Coach: Sergen Yalçin.
Borussia Dortmund: Gregor Kobel, Mats Hummels (70' Marin Pongracic), Thomas Meunier,
Raphaël Guerreiro, Manuel Akanji, Julian Brandt (46' Axel Witsel), Mahmoud Dahoud, Jude
Bellingham (69' Marius Wolf), Marco Reus, Donyell Malen (70' Youssoufa Moukoko), Erling
Haaland (86' Ansgar Knauff). Coach: Marco Rose.
Goals: 20' Jude Bellingham 0-1, 45+3' Erling Haaland 0-2, 90+4' Javi Montero 1-2.
Referee: Antonio Miguel Mateu Lahoz (ESP) Attendance: 22,445

15.09.21 Estádio José Alvalade, Lisboa: Sporting CP – AFC Ajax 1-5 (1-3)
Sporting CP: Antonio Adán, Luís Carlos Neto, Zouhair Feddal, Rúben Vinagre (46' Matheus
Reis), Pedro Porro, Gonçalo Inácio (21' Ricardo Esgaio), João Palhinha, Nuno Santos (60'
Tiago Tomás), Matheus Nunes, Paulinho (78' Daniel Bragança), Jovane Cabral (46' Pablo
Sarabia). Coach: Rúben Amorim.
AFC Ajax: Remko Pasveer, Daley Blind (81' Perr Schuurs), Noussair Mazraoui (70' Devyne
Rensch), Lisandro Martínez, Jurriën Timber, Edson Álvarez, Ryan Gravenberch, Dusan Tadic,
Steven Berghuis (77' Kenneth Taylor), Sébastien Haller, Antony (70 David Neres).
Coach: Erik ten Hag.
Goals: 2', 9' Sébastien Haller 0-1, 0-2, 33' Paulinho 1-2, 39' Steven Berghuis 1-3,
51', 63' Sébastien Haller 1-4, 1-5.
Referee: José María Sánchez Martínez (ESP) Attendance: 20,382

28.09.21   Johan Cruijff Arena, Amsterdam: AFC Ajax – Besiktas JK 2-0 (2-0)
AFC Ajax: Remko Pasveer, Daley Blind, Noussair Mazraoui, Lisandro Martínez, Jurriën
Timber, Edson Álvarez, Ryan Gravenberch, Dusan Tadic, Steven Berghuis (72' Davy
Klaassen), Sébastien Haller, Antony (71' David Neres). Coach: Erik ten Hag.
Besiktas JK: Ersin Destanoglu, Fabrice N'Sakala, Umut Meras (73' Berkay Vardar), Valentin
Rosier, Ridvan Yilmaz (46' Gökhan Töre), Serdar Saatçi, Josef de Souza, Salih Uçan (46'
Oguzhan Özyakup), Can Bozdogan, Michy Batshuayi, Kenan Karaman. Coach: Sergen Yalçin.
Goals: 17' Steven Berghuis 1-0, 43' Sébastien Haller 2-0.
Referee: Benoît Bastien (FRA)   Attendance: 52,628

28.09.21   Signal-Iduna-Park, Dortmund: Borussia Dortmund – Sporting CP 1-0 (1-0)
Borussia Dortmund: Gregor Kobel, Mats Hummels, Thomas Meunier, Raphaël Guerreiro (75'
Nico Schulz), Manuel Akanji, Axel Witsel, Thorgan Hazard (71' Marius Wolf), Mahmoud
Dahoud (8' Julian Brandt), Jude Bellingham, Marco Reus, Donyell Malen (75' Reinier).
Coach: Marco Rose.
Sporting CP: Antonio Adán, Luís Carlos Neto, Sebastián Coates, Zouhair Feddal, Matheus
Reis (84' Ricardo Esgaio), Pedro Porro (84' Bruno Tabata), Pablo Sarabia (74' Jovane Cabral),
João Palhinha (84' Daniel Bragança), Matheus Nunes, Paulinho, Tiago Tomás (58' Nuno
Santos). Coach: Rúben Amorim.
Goal: 37' Donyell Malen 1-0.
Referee: Srdjan Jovanovic (SRB)   Attendance: 25,000

19.10.21   Vodafone Park, Istanbul: Besiktas JK – Sporting CP 1-4 (1-3)
Besiktas JK: Ersin Destanoglu, Domagoj Vida, Fabrice N'Sakala, Welinton Souza, Valentin
Rosier, Miralem Pjanic, Alex Teixeira (80' Kenan Karaman), Josef de Souza, Rachid Ghezzal,
Michy Batshuayi, Cyle Larin (73' Gökhan Töre). Coach: Sergen Yalçin.
Sporting CP: Antonio Adán, Sebastián Coates, Zouhair Feddal (90+1' Luís Carlos Neto),
Matheus Reis (73' Ricardo Esgaio), Pedro Porro, Gonçalo Inácio, Pablo Sarabia (84' Tiago
Tomás), João Palhinha, Pedro Gonçalves "Pote" (90+2' Nuno Santos), Matheus Nunes (90+2'
Daniel Bragança), Paulinho. Coach: Rúben Amorim.
Goals: 15' Sebastián Coates 0-1, 24' Cyle Larin 1-1, 27 Sebastián Coates 1-2,
44' Pablo Sarabia 1-3 (p), 89' Paulinho 1-4.
Referee: Slavko Vincic (SVN)   Attendance: 22,936

19.10.21   Johan Cruijff Arena, Amsterdam: AFC Ajax – Borussia Dortmund 4-0 (2-0)
AFC Ajax: Remko Pasveer, Daley Blind, Noussair Mazraoui (83' Devyne Rensch), Lisandro
Martínez, Jurriën Timber, Edson Álvarez, Ryan Gravenberch, Dusan Tadic, Steven Berghuis
(69' Davy Klaassen), Sébastien Haller (83' Mohamed Daramy), Antony (76' David Neres).
Coach: Erik ten Hag.
Borussia Dortmund: Gregor Kobel, Mats Hummels (79' Marin Pongracic), Thomas Meunier
(79' Marius Wolf), Nico Schulz (46' Emre Can), Manuel Akanji, Axel Witsel, Julian Brandt
(88' Ansgar Knauff), Jude Bellingham, Marco Reus, Donyell Malen (53' Thorgan Hazard),
Erling Haaland. Coach: Marco Rose.
Goals: 11' Marco Reus 1-0 (og), 25' Daley Blind 2-0, 57' Antony 3-0,
72' Sébastien Haller 4-0.
Referee: Jesús Gil Manzano (ESP)   Attendance: 54,029

03.11.21   Signal-Iduna-Park, Dortmund: Borussia Dortmund – AFC Ajax 1-3 (1-0)
Borussia Dortmund: Gregor Kobel, Mats Hummels, Thomas Meunier, Manuel Akanji, Axel
Witsel, Thorgan Hazard (34' Marin Pongracic), Julian Brandt, Marius Wolf (58' Felix
Passlack), Jude Bellingham, Marco Reus (76' Ansgar Knauff), Steffen Tigges (76' Donyell
Malen). Coach: Marco Rose.
AFC Ajax: Remko Pasveer, Daley Blind, Noussair Mazraoui, Lisandro Martínez, Jurriën
Timber, Edson Álvarez (46' Davy Klaassen), Ryan Gravenberch, Dusan Tadic, Steven
Berghuis (67' Mohammed Kudus), Sébastien Haller, Antony. Coach: Erik ten Hag.
Goals: 37' Marco Reus 1-0 (p), 72' Dusan Tadic 1-1, 83' Sébastien Haller 1-2,
90+3' Davy Klaassen 1-3.
Referee: Michael Oliver (ENG)   Attendance: 54,820
Sent-off: 29' Mats Hummels.

03.11.21   Estádio José Alvalade, Lisboa: Sporting CP – Besiktas JK 4-0 (3-0)
Sporting CP: Antonio Adán, Sebastián Coates, Zouhair Feddal, Matheus Reis (72' Rúben
Vinagre), Pedro Porro (17' Ricardo Esgaio), Gonçalo Inácio, Pablo Sarabia, João Palhinha,
Pedro Gonçalves "Pote" (72' Jovane Cabral), Matheus Nunes (60' Daniel Bragança), Paulinho
(60' Nuno Santos). Coach: Rúben Amorim.
Besiktas JK: Ersin Destanoglu, Welinton Souza, Javi Montero (46' Alex Teixeira), Ridvan
Yilmaz, Mehmet Topal, Atiba Hutchinson (61' Salih Uçan), Josef de Souza, Necip Uysal,
Rachid Ghezzal (78' Gökhan Töre), Kenan Karaman, Cyle Larin (61' Can Bozdogan, 83'
Oguzhan Özyakup). Coach: Sergen Yalçin.
Goals: 31', 38' Pedro Gonçalves "Pote" 1-0 (p), 2-0, 41' Paulinho 3-0, 56' Pablo Sarabia 4-0.
Referee: Sergey Karasev (RUS)   Attendance: 40,835
Sent-off: 90' Josef de Souza.

24.11.21   Vodafone Park, Istanbul: Besiktas JK – AFC Ajax 1-2 (1-0)
Besiktas JK: Mert Günok, Domagoj Vida, Umut Meras, Valentin Rosier, Javi Montero (81'
Necip Uysal), Mehmet Topal (81' Atiba Hutchinson), Miralem Pjanic (81' Salih Uçan), Alex
Teixeira (59' Can Bozdogan), Rachid Ghezzal (67' Michy Batshuayi), Georges-Kévin
N'Koudou, Cyle Larin. Coach: Sergen Yalçin.
AFC Ajax: André Onana, Nico Tagliafico (77' Daley Blind), Noussair Mazraoui (72' Jurriën
Timber), Perr Schuurs (77' Devyne Rensch), Lisandro Martínez, Davy Klaassen, Ryan
Gravenberch, Dusan Tadic, Steven Berghuis (83' Kenneth Taylor), David Neres, Mohamed
Daramy (46' Sébastien Haller). Coach: Erik ten Hag.
Goals: 22' Rachid Ghezzal 1-0 (p), 54', 69' Sébastien Haller 1-1, 1-2.
Referee: Irfan Peljto (BIH)   Attendance: 11,712

24.11.21   Estádio José Alvalade, Lisboa: Sporting CP – Borussia Dortmund 3-1 (2-0)
Sporting CP: Antonio Adán, Sebastián Coates, Zouhair Feddal, Matheus Reis (67' Ricardo Esgaio), Pedro Porro (88' Manuel Ugarte), Gonçalo Inácio, Pablo Sarabia (67' Nuno Santos), João Palhinha, Pedro Gonçalves "Pote" (88' Flávio Nazinho), Matheus Nunes, Paulinho (82' Tiago Tomás). Coach: Rúben Amorim.
Borussia Dortmund: Gregor Kobel, Thomas Meunier, Nico Schulz (46' Emre Can), Manuel Akanji, Marin Pongracic (67' Steffen Tigges), Axel Witsel (66' Mahmoud Dahoud), Julian Brandt, Reinier (66' Dan-Axel Zagadou), Jude Bellingham, Marco Reus, Donyell Malen. Coach: Marco Rose.
Goals: 30', 39' Pedro Gonçalves "Pote" 1-0, 2-0, 81' Pedro Porro 3-0,
90+3' Donyell Malen 3-1.
Referee: Carlos del Cerro Grande (ESP)   Attendance: 41,341
Sent-off: 74' Emre Can.

Pedro Gonçalves "Pote" missed a penalty kick (81').

07.12.21   Johan Cruijff Arena, Amsterdam: AFC Ajax – Sporting CP 4-2 (2-1)
AFC Ajax: Remko Pasveer, Daley Blind (46' Nico Tagliafico), Noussair Mazraoui (77' Jurriën Timber), Perr Schuurs (59' Devyne Rensch), Lisandro Martínez, Edson Álvarez (72' Kenneth Taylor), Ryan Gravenberch, Steven Berghuis, Sébastien Haller, David Neres (60' Davy Klaassen), Antony. Coach: Erik ten Hag.
Sporting CP: João Virgínia, Luís Carlos Neto, Ricardo Esgaio, Matheus Reis, Gonçalo Esteves (73' Flávio Nazinho), Gonçalo Inácio, Nuno Santos (60' Paulinho), Manuel Ugarte (73' Pablo Sarabia), Daniel Bragança (81' Dario Essugo), Bruno Tabata, Tiago Tomás (60' Pedro Gonçalves "Pote"). Coach: Rúben Amorim.
Goals: 8' Sébastien Haller 1-0 (p), 22' Nuno Santos 1-1, 42' Antony 2-1, 58' David Neres 3-1, 62' Steven Berghuis 4-1, 78' BrunoTabata 4-2.
Referee: Davide Massa (ITA)   Attendance: 0

07.12.21   Signal-Iduna-Park, Dortmund: Borussia Dortmund – Besiktas JK 5-0 (2-0)
Borussia Dortmund: Gregor Kobel, Mats Hummels, Thomas Meunier (46' Reinier), Nico Schulz, Dan-Axel Zagadou (73' Marin Pongracic), Axel Witsel, Marius Wolf (62' Felix Passlack), Mahmoud Dahoud, Jude Bellingham (73' Raphaël Guerreiro), Marco Reus (63' Erling Haaland), Donyell Malen. Coach: Marco Rose.
Besiktas JK: Ersin Destanoglu, Welinton Souza, Umut Meras, Javi Montero, Mehmet Topal, Josef de Souza (82' Atiba Hutchinson), Necip Uysal, Can Bozdogan (76' Salih Uçan), Michy Batshuayi, Kenan Karaman (46' Valentin Rosier), Cyle Larin (69' Rachid Ghezzal).
Coach: Sergen Yalçin.
Goals: 29' Donyell Malen 1-0, 45+2', 52' Marco Reus 2-0 (p), 3-0,
68', 71' Erling Haaland 4-0, 5-0.
Referee: François Letexier (FRA)   Attendance: 15,000
Sent-off: 43' Welinton Souza.

GROUP D

15.09.21   Bolshaya Sportivnaya Arena, Tiraspol:
          FC Sheriff Tiraspol – Shakhtar Donetsk 2-0 (1-0)
FC Sheriff Tiraspol: Georgios Athanasiadis, Cristiano, Danilo Arboleda, Gustavo Dulanto, Fernando Costanza, Sébastien Thill, Dimitris Kolovos (55' Momo Yansané), Jasurbek Yaxshiboyev (67' Bruno Souza), Edmund Addo (85' Stjepan Radeljic), Adama Traoré, Frank Castañeda (85' Boban Nikolov). Coach: Yuriy Vernydub.
Shakhtar Donetsk: Andry Pyatov, Ismaily, Marlon, Mykola Matvienko, Dodô, Maycon, Marcos Antônio (64' Alan Patrick), Pedrinho, Tetê (46' Marlos), Fernando (65' Mykhailo Mudryk), Lassina Traoré. Coach: Roberto De Zerbi.
Goals: 16' Adama Traoré 1-0, 62' Momo Yansané 2-0.
Referee: Deniz Aytekin (GER)   Attendance: 5,205

15.09.21   Stadio Giuseppe Meazza, Milano:
          Internazionale Milano – Real Madrid CF 0-1 (0-0)
Internazionale Milano: Samir Handanovic, Matteo Darmian (55' Denzel Dumfries), Stefan de Vrij, Milan Skriniar, Alessandro Bastoni, Ivan Perisic (55' Federico Dimarco), Marcelo Brozovic, Hakan Çalhanoglu (65' Arturo Vidal), Nicolò Barella (84' Matías Vecino), Edin Dzeko, Lautaro Martínez (65' Joaquín Correa). Coach: Simone Inzaghi.
Real Madrid CF: Thibaut Courtois, David Alaba, Nacho, Dani Carvajal, Éder Militão, Luka Modric (80' Eduardo Camavinga), Casemiro, Lucas Vázquez (66' Rodrygo), Federico Valverde, Karim Benzema, Vinícius Júnior (90+1' Marco Asensio). Coach: Carlo Ancelotti.
Goal: 89' Rodrygo 0-1.
Referee: Daniel Siebert (GER)   Attendance: 37,082

28.09.21   NSC Olimpiyskiy, Kyiv: Shakhtar Donetsk – Internazionale Milano 0-0
Shakhtar Donetsk: Andry Pyatov, Ismaily (78' Sergiy Kryvtsov), Marlon, Mykola Matvienko, Dodô, Taras Stepanenko, Alan Patrick (85' Marlos), Manor Solomon (78' Mykhailo Mudryk), Maycon, Pedrinho, Lassina Traoré (11' Tetê). Coach: Roberto De Zerbi.
Internazionale Milano: Samir Handanovic, Stefan de Vrij, Milan Skriniar, Federico Dimarco (81' Ivan Perisic), Denzel Dumfries, Alessandro Bastoni, Matías Vecino (81' Roberto Gagliardini), Marcelo Brozovic (55' Hakan Çalhanoglu), Nicolò Barella, Edin Dzeko (55' Joaquín Correa), Lautaro Martínez (72' Alexis Sánchez). Coach: Simone Inzaghi.
Referee: István Kovács (ROM)   Attendance: 26,170

Shakhtar Donetsk played their home matches at NSC Olimpiyskiy, Kyiv, instead of their regular stadium Donbass Arena, Donetsk, due to the war in Eastern Ukraine.

28.09.21   Estadio Santiago Bernabéu, Madrid:
          Real Madrid CF – FC Sheriff Tiraspol 1-2 (0-1)
Real Madrid CF: Thibaut Courtois, David Alaba, Nacho (66' Rodrygo), Éder Militão, Miguel Gutiérrez (66' Toni Kroos), Casemiro (66' Luka Modric), Federico Valverde, Eduardo Camavinga, Karim Benzema, Eden Hazard (66' Luka Jovic), Vinícius Júnior.
Coach: Carlo Ancelotti.
FC Sheriff Tiraspol: Georgios Athanasiadis, Cristiano, Danilo Arboleda, Gustavo Dulanto, Fernando Costanza, Sébastien Thill, Dimitris Kolovos (90+2' Boban Nikolov), Jasurbek Yaxshiboyev (57' Bruno Souza), Edmund Addo, Adama Traoré, Frank Castañeda (78' Keston Julien). Coach: Yuriy Vernydub.
Goals: 25' Jasurbek Yaxshiboyev 0-1, 65' Karim Benzema 1-1 (p), 89' Sébastien Thill 1-2.
Referee: Lawrence Visser (BEL)   Attendance: 24,522

19.10.21   NSC Olimpiyskiy, Kyiv: Shakhtar Donetsk – Real Madrid CF 0-5 (0-1)
Shakhtar Donetsk: Anatoliy Trubin, Sergiy Kryvtsov, Ismaily (75' Viktor Kornienko), Marlon, Dodô, Alan Patrick (79' Taras Stepanenko), Manor Solomon (46' Marcos Antônio), Maycon, Pedrinho, Tetê (46' Marlos), Fernando (74' Mykhailo Mudryk). Coach: Roberto De Zerbi.
Real Madrid CF: Thibaut Courtois, David Alaba, Ferland Mendy (69' Marcelo), Éder Militão (87' Jesús Vallejo), Luka Modric (78' Eduardo Camavinga), Toni Kroos (78' Federico Valverde), Casemiro, Lucas Vázquez, Karim Benzema, Vinícius Júnior, Rodrygo (78' Marco Asensio). Coach: Carlo Ancelotti.
Goals: 37' Sergiy Kryvtsov 0-1 (og), 51', 56' Vinícius Júnior 0-2, 0-3, 65' Rodrygo 0-4, 90+1' Karim Benzema 0-5.
Referee: Srdjan Jovanovic (SRB)   Attendance: 34,037

19.10.21   Stadio Giuseppe Meazza, Milano:
          Internazionale Milano – FC Sheriff Tiraspol 3-1 (1-0)
Internazionale Milano: Samir Handanovic, Stefan de Vrij, Milan Skriniar, Federico Dimarco (53' Alessandro Bastoni), Denzel Dumfries, Ivan Perisic (85' Aleksandar Kolarov), Arturo Vidal (75' Roberto Gagliardini), Marcelo Brozovic (85' Stefano Sensi), Nicolò Barella, Edin Dzeko (75' Alexis Sánchez), Lautaro Martínez. Coach: Simone Inzaghi.
FC Sheriff Tiraspol: Dumitru Celeadnic, Cristiano, Danilo Arboleda, Gustavo Dulanto, Fernando Costanza, Sébastien Thill, Dimitris Kolovos (84' Maxim Cojocaru), Bruno Souza, Edmund Addo (75' Boban Nikolov), Adama Traoré (90' Serafim Cojocari), Frank Castañeda (46' Stjepan Radeljic). Coach: Yuriy Vernydub.
Goals: 34' Edin Dzeko 1-0, 52' Sébastien Thill 1-1, 58' Arturo Vidal 2-1, 67' Stefan de Vrij 3-1.
Referee: Danny Makkelie (HOL)   Attendance: 43,305

03.11.21   Estadio Santiago Bernabéu, Madrid: Real Madrid CF – Shakhtar Donetsk 2-1 (1-1)
Real Madrid CF: Thibaut Courtois, David Alaba, Dani Carvajal (66' Nacho), Ferland Mendy, Éder Militão, Luka Modric, Toni Kroos, Casemiro, Lucas Vázquez, Karim Benzema (79' Luka Jovic), Vinícius Júnior. Coach: Carlo Ancelotti.
Shakhtar Donetsk: Anatoliy Trubin, Ismaily, Marlon, Mykola Matvienko, Dodô, Taras Stepanenko (80' Georgiy Sudakov), Alan Patrick (79' Marcos Antônio), Maycon, Mykhailo Mudryk (71' Manor Solomon), Tetê (80' Marlos), Fernando (86' Dentinho).
Coach: Roberto De Zerbi.
Goals: 14' Karim Benzema 1-0, 39' Fernando 1-1, 61' Karim Benzema 2-1.
Referee: Benoît Bastien (FRA)   Attendance: 38,105

03.11.21   Bolshaya Sportivnaya Arena, Tiraspol:
          FC Sheriff Tiraspol – Internazionale Milano 1-3 (0-0)
FC Sheriff Tiraspol: Georgios Athanasiadis, Cristiano, Danilo Arboleda, Gustavo Dulanto, Fernando Costanza, Sébastien Thill, Dimitris Kolovos (73' Bruno Souza), Jasurbek Yaxshiboyev (82' Keston Julien), Edmund Addo (62' Stjepan Radeljic), Adama Traoré, Frank Castañeda. Coach: Yuriy Vernydub.
Internazionale Milano: Samir Handanovic, Matteo Darmian (46' Denzel Dumfries), Stefan de Vrij (85' Andrea Ranocchia), Milan Skriniar, Federico Dimarco (64' Ivan Perisic), Alessandro Bastoni, Arturo Vidal, Marcelo Brozovic, Nicolò Barella, Edin Dzeko (81' Joaquín Correa), Lautaro Martínez (81' Alexis Sánchez). Coach: Simone Inzaghi.
Goals: 54' Marcelo Brozovic 0-1, 66' Milan Skriniar 0-2, 82' Alexis Sánchez 0-3, 90+2' Adama Traoré 1-3.
Referee: Felix Zwayer (GER)   Attendance: 5,930

24.11.21   Stadio Giuseppe Meazza, Milano:
Internazionale Milano – Shakhtar Donetsk 2-0 (0-0)
Internazionale Milano: Samir Handanovic, Matteo Darmian (79' Danilo D'Ambrosio), Andrea Ranocchia, Milan Skriniar, Alessandro Bastoni, Ivan Perisic (86' Federico Dimarco), Marcelo Brozovic, Hakan Çalhanoglu (86' Stefano Sensi), Nicolò Barella (78' Arturo Vidal), Edin Dzeko, Lautaro Martínez (68' Joaquín Correa). Coach: Simone Inzaghi.
Shakhtar Donetsk: Anatoliy Trubin, Marlon, Mykola Matvienko, Dodô, Vitão, Taras Stepanenko (46' Marcos Antônio), Manor Solomon, Maycon, Pedrinho (73' Artem Bondarenko), Tetê (80' Marlos), Fernando (80' Mykhailo Mudryk). Coach: Roberto De Zerbi.
Goals: 61', 67' Edin Dzeko 1-0, 2-0.
Referee: Ovidiu Alin Hategan (ROM)   Attendance: 46,225

24.11.21   Bolshaya Sportivnaya Arena, Tiraspol:
FC Sheriff Tiraspol – Real Madrid CF 0-3 (0-2)
FC Sheriff Tiraspol: Georgios Athanasiadis, Cristiano, Danilo Arboleda, Gustavo Dulanto, Fernando Costanza, Sébastien Thill, Dimitris Kolovos (60' Boban Nikolov), Bruno Souza (59' Keston Julien), Edmund Addo, Adama Traoré (81' Maxim Cojocaru), Frank Castañeda (60' Momo Yansané). Coach: Yuriy Vernydub.
Real Madrid CF: Thibaut Courtois, David Alaba (65' Nacho), Dani Carvajal (65' Lucas Vázquez), Ferland Mendy (60' Marcelo), Éder Militão, Luka Modric, Toni Kroos, Casemiro (84' Antonio Blanco), Karim Benzema, Vinícius Júnior, Rodrygo (84' Marco Asensio). Coach: Carlo Ancelotti.
Goals: 30' David Alaba 0-1, 45+1' Toni Kroos 0-2, 55' Karim Benzema 0-3.
Referee: Szymon Marciniak (POL)   Attendance: 5,932

07.12.21   NSC Olimpiyskiy, Kyiv: Shakhtar Donetsk – FC Sheriff Tiraspol 1-1 (1-0)
Shakhtar Donetsk: Andriy Pyatov (86' Oleksiy Shevchenko), Sergiy Kryvtsov, Valeriy Bondar, Dodô, Viktor Kornienko (67' Ismaily), Marlos, Manor Solomon, Marcos Antônio, Artem Bondarenko (67' Maycon), Georgiy Sudakov (46' Tetê), Fernando (46' Mykhailo Mudryk). Coach: Roberto De Zerbi.
FC Sheriff Tiraspol: Georgios Athanasiadis, Cristiano, Danilo Arboleda, Gustavo Dulanto, Fernando Costanza, Sébastien Thill, Dimitris Kolovos (46' Boban Nikolov), Bruno Souza, Edmund Addo, Adama Traoré, Momo Yansané. Coach: Yuriy Vernydub.
Goals: 42' Fernando 1-0, 90+3' Boban Nikolov 1-1.
Referee: Donatas Rumsas (LTU)   Attendance: 6,841

07.12.21   Estadio Santiago Bernabéu, Madrid:
Real Madrid CF – Internazionale Milano 2-0 (1-0)
Real Madrid CF: Thibaut Courtois, David Alaba, Dani Carvajal, Ferland Mendy, Éder Militão, Luka Modric, Toni Kroos (78' Federico Valverde), Casemiro (71' Eduardo Camavinga), Luka Jovic (78' Mariano Díaz), Vinícius Júnior (81' Eden Hazard), Rodrygo (78' Marco Asensio). Coach: Carlo Ancelotti.
Internazionale Milano: Samir Handanovic, Danilo D'Ambrosio, Milan Skriniar, Denzel Dumfries (46' Federico Dimarco), Alessandro Bastoni, Ivan Perisic, Marcelo Brozovic (60' Arturo Vidal), Hakan Çalhanoglu (60' Matías Vecino), Nicolò Barella, Edin Dzeko (60' Alexis Sánchez), Lautaro Martínez (66' Roberto Gagliardini). Coach: Simone Inzaghi.
Goals: 17' Toni Kroos 1-0, 79' Marco Asensio 2-0.
Referee: Dr. Felix Brych (GER)   Attendance: 46,887
Sent-off: 64' Nicolò Barella.

45

GROUP E

14.09.21 Camp Nou, Barcelona: FC Barcelona – Bayern München 0-3 (0-1)
FC Barcelona: Marc-André ter Stegen, Piqué, Jordi Alba (74' Álex Baldé), Sergi Roberto (59' Yusuf Demir), Ronald Araújo, Eric García (66' Óscar Mingueza), Sergio Busquets (59' Gavi), Frenkie de Jong, Pedri, Luuk de Jong (66' Philippe Coutinho), Memphis Depay. Coach: Ronald Koeman.
Bayern München: Manuel Neuer, Niklas Süle (82' Josip Stanisic), Benjamin Pavard (66' Lucas Hernández), Dayot Upamecano, Alphonso Davies, Leon Goretzka, Joshua Kimmich, Jamal Musiala (69' Serge Gnabry), Thomas Müller (82' Marcel Sabitzer), Robert Lewandowski, Leroy Sané (82' Kingsley Coman). Coach: Julian Nagelsmann.
Goals: 34' Thomas Müller 0-1, 56', 85' Robert Lewandowski 0-2, 0-3.
Referee: Michael Oliver (ENG)   Attendance: 39,737

14.09.21 NSC Olimpiyskiy, Kyiv: Dynamo Kyiv – SL Benfica 0-0
Dynamo Kyiv: Denis Boyko, Tomasz Kedziora, Vitaliy Mykolenko, Oleksandr Syrota, Ilya Zabarnyi, Sergiy Sydorchuk, Vitaliy Buyalskyi, Carlos de Pena (76' Benjamin Verbic), Viktor Tsygankov (76' Oleksandr Karavayev), Mykola Shaparenko, Ilya Shkurin (60' Denys Garmash). Coach: Mircea Lucescu.
SL Benfica: Odisseas Vlachodimos, Jan Vertonghen, Nicolás Otamendi, Gilberto (59' Valentino Lazaro), Álex Grimaldo, Morato, João Mário (85' Adel Taarabt), Rafa Silva (90' Pizzi), Julian Weigl, Roman Yaremchuk (59' Darwin Núñez), Éverton (59' Nemanja Radonjic). Coach: Jorge Jesus.
Referee: Anthony Taylor (ENG)   Attendance: 21,657

29.09.21 Estádio do Sport Lisboa e Benfica, Lisboa: SL Benfica – FC Barcelona 3-0 (1-0)
SL Benfica: Odisseas Vlachodimos, Jan Vertonghen, Nicolás Otamendi, Álex Grimaldo (75' André Almeida), Lucas Veríssimo, João Mário, Valentino Lazaro (45+1' Gilberto), Rafa Silva (86' Pizzi), Julian Weigl, Roman Yaremchuk (76' Adel Taarabt), Darwin Núñez (86' Gonçalo Ramos). Coach: Jorge Jesus.
FC Barcelona: Marc-André ter Stegen, Piqué (33' Gavi), Sergi Roberto (89' Óscar Mingueza), Ronald Araújo, Eric García, Sergiño Dest, Sergio Busquets (68' Nico González), Frenkie de Jong, Pedri (68' Philippe Coutinho), Luuk de Jong (68' Ansu Fati), Memphis Depay. Coach: Ronald Koeman.
Goals: 3' Darwin Núñez 1-0, 69' Rafa Silva 2-0, 79' Darwin Núñez 3-0 (p).
Referee: Daniele Orsato (ITA)   Attendance: 29,454
Sent-off: 87' Eric García.

29.09.21 Allianz Arena, München: Bayern München – Dynamo Kyiv 5-0 (2-0)
Bayern München: Manuel Neuer, Niklas Süle, Lucas Hernández, Dayot Upamecano, Alphonso Davies (69' Benjamin Pavard), Leon Goretzka (79' Marcel Sabitzer), Serge Gnabry (69' Jamal Musiala), Joshua Kimmich, Thomas Müller, Robert Lewandowski (79' Eric Maxim Choupo-Moting), Leroy Sané (79' Bouna Sarr). Coach: Julian Nagelsmann.
Dynamo Kyiv: Georgiy Bushchan, Artem Shabanov, Oleksandr Tymchyk (46' Tomasz Kedziora), Vitaliy Mykolenko, Ilya Zabarnyi, Sergiy Sydorchuk, Denys Garmash (70' Vladyslav Supryaga), Oleksandr Andrievskyi, Carlos de Pena, Viktor Tsygankov (70' Oleksandr Karavayev), Mykola Shaparenko (46' Volodymyr Shepelyev). Coach: Mircea Lucescu.
Goals: 12', 27' Robert Lewandowski 1-0 (p), 2-0, 68' Serge Gnabry 3-0, 74' Leroy Sané 4-0, 87' Eric Maxim Choupo-Moting 5-0.
Referee: Marco Guida (ITA)   Attendance: 25,000
20.10.21 Camp Nou, Barcelona: FC Barcelona – Dynamo Kyiv 1-0 (1-0)

FC Barcelona: Marc-André ter Stegen, Piqué, Jordi Alba, Clément Lenglet, Óscar Mingueza (46' Philippe Coutinho), Sergiño Dest, Sergio Busquets, Frenkie de Jong, Gavi (69' Sergi Roberto), Luuk de Jong (46' Ansu Fati), Memphis Depay (75' Sergio Agüero). Coach: Ronald Koeman.

Dynamo Kyiv: Georgiy Bushchan, Tomasz Kedziora (78' Oleksandr Tymchyk), Vitaliy Mykolenko, Oleksandr Syrota, Ilya Zabarnyi, Sergiy Sydorchuk, Vitaliy Buyalskyi (85' Eric Ramírez), Carlos de Pena (61' Vitinho), Viktor Tsygankov (85' Oleksandr Karavayev), Mykola Shaparenko, Vladyslav Supryaga (61' Denys Garmash). Coach: Mircea Lucescu.

Goal: FC Barcelona: 36' Piqué 1-0.

Referee: Clément Turpin (FRA)   Attendance: 45,968

20.10.21   Estádio do Sport Lisboa e Benfica, Lisboa: SL Benfica – Bayern München 0-4 (0-0)

SL Benfica: Odisseas Vlachodimos, Jan Vertonghen, Nicolás Otamendi, André Almeida (40' Diogo Gonçalves), Álex Grimaldo, Lucas Veríssimo, João Mário (81' Adel Taarabt), Rafa Silva (80' Pizzi), Julian Weigl, Roman Yaremchuk (76' Éverton), Darwin Núñez (81' Gonçalo Ramos). Coach: Jorge Jesus.

Bayern München: Manuel Neuer, Niklas Süle, Lucas Hernández (85' Omar Richards), Benjamin Pavard (66' Serge Gnabry), Dayot Upamecano, Marcel Sabitzer (86' Corentin Tolisso), Joshua Kimmich, Thomas Müller (77' Josip Stanisic), Robert Lewandowski, Kingsley Coman (86' Jamal Musiala), Leroy Sané. Coach: Julian Nagelsmann.

Goals: 70' Leroy Sané 0-1, 80' Éverton 0-2 (og), 82' Robert Lewandowski 0-3, 84' Leroy Sané 0-4.

Referee: Ovidiu Alin Hategan (ROM)   Attendance: 55,201

02.11.21   Allianz Arena, München: Bayern München – SL Benfica 5-2 (2-1)

Bayern München: Manuel Neuer, Benjamin Pavard, Dayot Upamecano, Alphonso Davies (65' Omar Richards), Tanguy Nianzou Kouassi, Leon Goretzka, Serge Gnabry (85' Bouna Sarr), Joshua Kimmich (72' Marcel Sabitzer), Robert Lewandowski, Kingsley Coman (64' Jamal Musiala), Leroy Sané (72' Thomas Müller). Coach: Julian Nagelsmann.

SL Benfica: Odisseas Vlachodimos, Jan Vertonghen, Gilberto, Álex Grimaldo (77' Gonçalo Ramos), Lucas Veríssimo, Morato, Pizzi (64' Rafa Silva), Soualiho Meïté, João Mário (77' Paulo Bernardo), Roman Yaremchuk (64' Darwin Núñez), Éverton (64' Diogo Gonçalves). Coach: Jorge Jesus.

Goals: 26' Robert Lewandowski 1-0, 32' Serge Gnabry 2-0, 38' Morato 2-1, 49' Leroy Sané 3-1, 61' Robert Lewandowski 4-1, 74' Darwin Núñez 4-2, 84' Robert Lewandowski 5-2.

Referee: Szymon Marciniak (POL)   Attendance: 50,000

Robert Lewandowski missed a penalty kick (45+1').

02.11.21   NSC Olimpiyskiy, Kyiv: Dynamo Kyiv – FC Barcelona 0-1 (0-0)

Dynamo Kyiv: Georgiy Bushchan, Tomasz Kedziora (78' Oleksandr Tymchyk), Vitaliy Mykolenko, Oleksandr Syrota, Ilya Zabarnyi, Sergiy Sydorchuk, Vitaliy Buyalskyi (85' Eric Ramírez), Carlos de Pena (61' Vitinho), Viktor Tsygankov (85' Oleksandr Karavayev), Mykola Shaparenko, Vladyslav Supryaga (61' Denys Garmash). Coach: Mircea Lucescu.

FC Barcelona: Marc-André ter Stegen, Piqué, Jordi Alba, Clément Lenglet, Óscar Mingueza (46' Philippe Coutinho), Sergiño Dest, Sergio Busquets, Frenkie de Jong, Gavi (69' Sergi Roberto), Luuk de Jong (46' Ansu Fati), Memphis Depay (75' Sergio Agüero). Coach: Ronald Koeman.

Goal: 70' Ansu Fati 0-1.

Referee: Ovidiu Alin Hategan (ROM)   Attendance: 31,378

47

23.11.21 NSC Olimpiyskiy, Kyiv: Dynamo Kyiv – Bayern München 1-2 (0-2)
Dynamo Kyiv: Georgiy Bushchan, Tomasz Kedziora (76' Oleksandr Karavayev), Vitaliy
Mykolenko, Oleksandr Syrota, Ilya Zabarnyi, Sergiy Sydorchuk, Vitaliy Buyalskyi, Carlos de
Pena (46' Denys Garmash), Viktor Tsygankov, Mykola Shaparenko, Ilya Shkurin (46'
Vitinho). Coach: Mircea Lucescu.
Bayern München: Manuel Neuer, Lucas Hernández (46' Bouna Sarr), Benjamin Pavard,
Alphonso Davies, Tanguy Nianzou Kouassi (85' Malik Tillman), Leon Goretzka, Corentin
Tolisso, Thomas Müller, Robert Lewandowski, Kingsley Coman (67' Marc Roca), Leroy Sané
(87' Omar Richards). Coach: Julian Nagelsmann.
Goals: 14' Robert Lewandowski 0-1, 42' Kingsley Coman 0-2, 70' Denys Garmash 1-2.
Referee: Halil Umut Meler (TUR) Attendance: 28,732

23.11.21 Camp Nou, Barcelona: FC Barcelona – SL Benfica 0-0
FC Barcelona: Marc-André ter Stegen, Piqué, Jordi Alba, Clément Lenglet (86' Sergiño Dest),
Ronald Araújo (86' Eric García), Sergio Busquets, Frenkie de Jong, Nico González, Gavi,
Memphis Depay, Yusuf Demir (66' Ousmane Dembélé). Coach: Xavi.
SL Benfica: Odisseas Vlachodimos, Jan Vertonghen, Nicolás Otamendi, André Almeida,
Gilberto, Álex Grimaldo (81' Haris Seferovic), João Mário (59' Adel Taarabt), Rafa Silva (70'
Valentino Lazaro), Julian Weigl, Roman Yaremchuk (59' Darwin Núñez), Éverton (70' Pizzi).
Coach: Jorge Jesus.
Referee: Sergey Karasev (RUS) Attendance: 49,572

08.12.21 Allianz Arena, München: Bayern München – FC Barcelona 3-0 (2-0)
Bayern München: Manuel Neuer, Niklas Süle (78' Tanguy Nianzou Kouassi), Benjamin
Pavard, Dayot Upamecano, Alphonso Davies (71' Omar Richards), Corentin Tolisso (60' Marc
Roca), Jamal Musiala, Thomas Müller, Robert Lewandowski (77' Malik Tillman), Kingsley
Coman (71' Bouna Sarr), Leroy Sané. Coach: Julian Nagelsmann.
FC Barcelona: Marc-André ter Stegen, Piqué, Jordi Alba (31' Óscar Mingueza), Clément
Lenglet, Ronald Araújo, Sergiño Dest (46' Nico González), Sergio Busquets, Frenkie de Jong
(73' Riqui Puig), Gavi (86' Yusuf Demir), Memphis Depay, Ousmane Dembélé (73' Philippe
Coutinho). Coach: Xavi.
Goals: 34' Thomas Müller 1-0, 43' Leroy Sané 2-0, 62' Jamal Musiala 3-0.
Referee: Ovidiu Alin Hategan (ROM) Attendance: 0

08.12.21 Estádio do Sport Lisboa e Benfica, Lisboa: SL Benfica – Dynamo Kyiv 2-0 (2-0)
SL Benfica: Odisseas Vlachodimos, Jan Vertonghen, Nicolás Otamendi, André Almeida,
Gilberto (73' Valentino Lazaro), Álex Grimaldo, Pizzi (59' Éverton), João Mário (73' Adel
Taarabt), Rafa Silva (82' Paulo Bernardo), Julian Weigl, Roman Yaremchuk (82' Darwin
Núñez). Coach: Jorge Jesus.
Dynamo Kyiv: Georgiy Bushchan, Oleksandr Tymchyk, Vitaliy Mykolenko, Oleksandr Syrota,
Ilya Zabarnyi, Sergiy Sydorchuk (86' Oleksandr Andriyevskyi), Denys Garmash (79' Eric
Ramírez), Vitaliy Buyalskyi, Benjamin Verbic (64' Carlos de Pena), Viktor Tsygankov (79'
Oleksandr Karavayev), Mykola Shaparenko. Coach: Mircea Lucescu.
Goals: 16' Roman Yaremchuk 1-0, 22' Gilberto 2-0.
Referee: Deniz Aytekin (GER) Attendance: 36,591

GROUP F

14.09.21   Stadion Wankdorf, Bern: BSC Young Boys – Manchester United 2-1 (0-1)
BSC Young Boys: David von Ballmoos, Ulisses Garcia, Silvan Hefti (83' Miralem Sulejmani), Mohamed Ali Camara, Christopher Martins Pereira (82' Fabian Rieder), Nicolas Moumi Ngamaleu, Christian Fassnacht, Vincent Sierro (46' Jordan Siebatcheu), Sandro Lauper (90+2' Cédric Zesiger), Michel Aebischer, Meschack Elia (90+2' Wilfried Kanga).
Coach: David Wagner.
Manchester United: David de Gea, Victor Lindelöf, Harry Maguire, Luke Shaw, Aaron Wan-Bissaka, Paul Pogba, Fred (89' Anthony Martial), Bruno Fernandes (72' Nemanja Matic), Donny van de Beek (46' Raphaël Varane), Cristiano Ronaldo (72' Jesse Lingard), Jadon Sancho (37' Diogo Dalot). Coach: Ole Gunnar Solskjær.
Goals: 13' Cristiano Ronaldo 0-1, 66' Nicolas Moumi Ngamaleu 1-1,
90+5' Jordan Siebatcheu 2-1.
Referee: François Letexier (FRA)   Attendance: 31,120
Sent-off: 35' Aaron Wan-Bissaka.

14.09.21   Estadio de la Cerámica, Villarreal: Villarreal CF – Atalanta Bergamo 2-2 (1-1)
Villarreal CF: Gerónimo Rulli, Raúl Albiol, Pau Torres, Juan Foyth, Étienne Capoue (60' Francis Coquelin), Dani Parejo, Manu Trigueros (60' Moi Gómez), Pedraza (88' Mario Gaspar), Yeremi Pino (72' Alberto Moreno), Gerard Moreno, Boulaye Dia (61' Arnaut Danjuma Groeneveld). Coach: Unai Emery.
Atalanta Bergamo: Juan Musso, Rafael Tolói, José Palomino, Berat Djimsiti (61' Merih Demiral), Davide Zappacosta, Robin Gosens, Marten de Roon (70' Teun Koopmeiners), Remo Freuler, Ruslan Malinovskyi (71' Mario Pasalic), Matteo Pessina (79' Aleksey Miranchuk), Duván Zapata (70' Josip Ilicic). Coach: Gian Piero Gasperini.
Goals: 6' Remo Freuler 0-1, 39' Manu Trigueros 1-1, 73' Arnaut Danjuma Groeneveld 2-1, 83' Robin Gosens 2-2.
Referee: Clément Turpin (FRA)   Attendance: 12,916
Sent-off: 84' Francis Coquelin.

29.09.21   Gewiss Stadium, Bergamo: Atalanta Bergamo – BSC Young Boys 1-0 (0-0)
Atalanta Bergamo: Juan Musso, Rafael Tolói, Berat Djimsiti, Davide Zappacosta (89' Giuseppe Pezzella), Robin Gosens (11' Joakim Mæhle), Merih Demiral, Marten de Roon, Remo Freuler (89' Teun Koopmeiners), Ruslan Malinovskyi (75' Luis Muriel), Matteo Pessina (75' Mario Pasalic), Duván Zapata. Coach: Gian Piero Gasperini.
BSC Young Boys: David von Ballmoos, Ulisses Garcia, Silvan Hefti (83' Quentin Maceiras), Mohamed Ali Camara, Christopher Martins Pereira, Nicolas Moumi Ngamaleu, Vincent Sierro (69' Felix Mambimbi), Sandro Lauper, Michel Aebischer (83' Marvin Spielmann), Jordan Siebatcheu (66' Wilfried Kanga), Meschack Elia (66' Fabian Rieder). Coach: David Wagner.
Goal: 68' Matteo Pessina 1-0.
Referee: Dr. Felix Brych (GER)   Attendance: 8,536

29.09.21 Old Trafford, Manchester: Manchester United – Villarreal CF 2-1 (0-0)
Manchester United: David de Gea, Alex Telles (89' Fred), Victor Lindelöf, Raphaël Varane,
Diogo Dalot, Paul Pogba (75' Edinson Cavani), Bruno Fernandes, Scott McTominay, Cristiano
Ronaldo, Jadon Sancho (75' Nemanja Matic), Mason Greenwood (89' Jesse Lingard).
Coach: Ole Gunnar Solskjær.
Villarreal CF: Gerónimo Rulli, Raúl Albiol (73' Aïssa Mandi), Alberto Moreno (73' Rubén
Peña), Pau Torres, Juan Foyth, Étienne Capoue, Dani Parejo, Manu Trigueros (61' Pervis
Estupiñán), Yeremi Pino (73' Moi Gómez), Paco Alcácer (58' Boulaye Dia), Arnaut Danjuma
Groeneveld. Coach: Unai Emery.
Goals: 53' Paco Alcácer 0-1, 60' Alex Telles 1-1, 90+5' Cristiano Ronaldo 2-1.
Referee: Felix Zwayer (GER) Attendance: 73,130

20.10.21 Old Trafford, Manchester: Manchester United – Atalanta Bergamo 3-2 (0-2)
Manchester United: David de Gea, Victor Lindelöf, Harry Maguire, Luke Shaw, Aaron Wan-
Bissaka, Fred (88' Nemanja Matic), Bruno Fernandes, Scott McTominay (66' Paul Pogba),
Cristiano Ronaldo, Marcus Rashford (67' Edinson Cavani), Mason Greenwood (73' Jadon
Sancho). Coach: Ole Gunnar Solskjær.
Atalanta Bergamo: Juan Musso, José Palomino, Davide Zappacosta, Merih Demiral (46'
Matteo Lovato), Joakim Mæhle, Josip Ilicic (68' Aleksey Miranchuk), Marten de Roon, Remo
Freuler, Mario Pasalic (68' Ruslan Malinovskyi), Teun Koopmeiners (80' Giuseppe Pezzella),
Luis Muriel (56' Duván Zapata). Coach: Gian Piero Gasperini.
Goals: 15' Mario Pasalic 0-1, 29' Merih Demiral 0-2, 53' Marcus Rashford 1-2,
75' Harry Maguire 2-2, 81' Cristiano Ronaldo 3-2.
Referee: Szymon Marciniak (POL) Attendance: 72,279

20.10.21 Stadion Wankdorf, Bern: BSC Young Boys – Villarreal CF 1-4 (0-2)
BSC Young Boys: David von Ballmoos, Jordan Lefort (62' Silvan Hefti), Ulisses Garcia,
Mohamed Ali Camara, Christopher Martins Pereira (70' Fabian Rieder), Nicolas Moumi
Ngamaleu, Christian Fassnacht (90' Felix Mambimbi), Sandro Lauper, Michel Aebischer,
Jordan Siebatcheu (70' Wilfried Kanga), Meschack Elia. Coach: David Wagner.
Villarreal CF: Gerónimo Rulli, Raúl Albiol (83' Aïssa Mandi), Pau Torres, Juan Foyth, Étienne
Capoue, Dani Parejo, Francis Coquelin (69' Alberto Moreno), Pedraza, Yeremi Pino (89' Moi
Gómez), Gerard Moreno, Arnaut Danjuma Groeneveld (90' Samuel Chukwueze).
Coach: Unai Emery.
Goals: 6' Yeremi Pino 0-1 16' Gerard Moreno 0-2, 77' Meschack Elia 1-2,
88' Alberto Moreno 1-3, 90+2' Samuel Chukwueze 1-4.
Referee: Sergey Karasev (RUS) Attendance: 27,398

02.11.21 Gewiss Stadium, Bergamo: Atalanta Bergamo – Manchester United 2-2 (1-1)
Atalanta Bergamo: Juan Musso, José Palomino, Davide Zappacosta, Merih Demiral, Joakim
Mæhle, Josip Ilicic (71' Luis Muriel), Marten de Roon, Remo Freuler, Mario Pasalic (46'
Berat Djimsiti), Teun Koopmeiners, Duván Zapata. Coach: Gian Piero Gasperini.
Manchester United: David de Gea, Raphaël Varane (38' Mason Greenwood), Harry Maguire,
Luke Shaw, Eric Bailly, Aaron Wan-Bissaka, Paul Pogba (69' Nemanja Matic), Bruno
Fernandes (87' Donny van de Beek), Scott McTominay (87' Jadon Sancho), Cristiano
Ronaldo, Marcus Rashford (69' Edinson Cavani). Coach: Ole Gunnar Solskjær.
Goals: 12' Josip Ilicic 1-0, 45+1' Cristiano Ronaldo 1-1, 56' Duván Zapata 2-1, 90+1'
Cristiano Ronaldo 2-2.
Referee: Slavko Vincic (SVN) Attendance: 14,443

50

02.11.21 Estadio de la Cerámica, Villarreal: Villarreal CF – BSC Young Boys 2-0 (1-0)
Villarreal CF: Gerónimo Rulli, Raúl Albiol, Mario Gaspar, Pau Torres, Étienne Capoue, Dani
Parejo (90+2' Moi Gómez), Francis Coquelin (75' Alberto Moreno), Pedraza (75' Pervis
Estupiñán), Yeremi Pino (59' Samuel Chukwueze), Arnaut Danjuma Groeneveld, Boulaye Dia
(59' Manu Trigueros). Coach: Unai Emery.
BSC Young Boys: Guillaume Faivre, Ulisses Garcia (75' Jordan Lefort), Nicolas Bürgy,
Silvan Hefti (75' Quentin Maceiras), Nicolas Moumi Ngamaleu (82' Jordan Siebatcheu),
Christian Fassnacht, Vincent Sierro (75' Felix Mambimbi), Sandro Lauper, Michel Aebischer,
Fabian Rieder, Meschack Elia. Coach: David Wagner.
Goals: 36' Étienne Capoue 1-0, 89' Arnaut Danjuma Groeneveld 2-0.
Referee: Serdar Gözübüyük (HOL) Attendance: 14,890

23.11.21 Estadio de la Cerámica, Villarreal: Villarreal CF – Manchester United 0-2 (0-0)
Villarreal CF: Gerónimo Rulli, Raúl Albiol, Pervis Estupiñán (79' Dani Raba), Juan
Foyth, Étienne Capoue, Dani Parejo, Moi Gómez (84' Boulaye Dia), Manu Trigueros (73'
Alberto Moreno), Yeremi Pino (73' Samuel Chukwueze), Arnaut Danjuma Groeneveld.
Coach: Unai Emery.
Manchester United: David de Gea, Alex Telles, Victor Lindelöf, Harry Maguire, Aaron Wan-
Bissaka, Fred, Donny van de Beek (66' Bruno Fernandes), Scott McTominay, Cristiano
Ronaldo (90+1' Nemanja Matic), Anthony Martial (66' Marcus Rashford), Jadon Sancho
(90+3' Mata). Coach: Michael Carrick.
Goals: 78' Cristiano Ronaldo 0-1, 90' Jadon Sancho 0-2.
Referee: Dr. Felix Brych (GER) Attendance: 20,875

23.11.21 Stadion Wankdorf, Bern: BSC Young Boys – Atalanta Bergamo 3-3 (1-1)
BSC Young Boys: Guillaume Faivre, Ulisses Garcia, Nicolas Bürgy, Silvan Hefti, Christopher
Martins Pereira (88' Wilfried Kanga), Nicolas Moumi Ngamaleu, Sandro Lauper, Michel
Aebischer, Fabian Rieder (67' Vincent Sierro), Jordan Siebatcheu, Meschack Elia (67' Felix
Mambimbi). Coach: David Wagner.
Atalanta Bergamo: Juan Musso, Rafael Tolói, José Palomino, Davide Zappacosta (46'
Giuseppe Pezzella), Merih Demiral (71' Berat Djimsiti), Joakim Mæhle (87' Luis Muriel),
Marten de Roon, Remo Freuler (78' Matteo Pessina), Mario Pasalic (71' Teun Koopmeiners),
Ruslan Malinovskyi, Duván Zapata. Coach: Gian Piero Gasperini.
Goals: 10' Duván Zapata 0-1, 39' Jordan Siebatcheu 1-1, 51' José Palomino 1-2,
80' Vincent Sierro 2-2, 84' Silvan Hefti 3-2, 88' Luis Muriel 3-3.
Referee: Daniel Siebert (GER) Attendance: 31,120

08.12.21 Old Trafford, Manchester: Manchester United – BSC Young Boys 1-1 (1-1)
Manchester United: Dean Henderson (68' Tom Heaton), Luke Shaw (61' Teden Mengi), Eric
Bailly, Aaron Wan-Bissaka, Mata (89' Charlie Savage), Nemanja Matic, Jesse Lingard (89'
Zidane Iqbal), Donny van de Beek, Mason Greenwood, Anthony Elanga, Amad Diallo (68'
Shola Shoretire). Coach: Ralf Rangnick.
BSC Young Boys: Guillaume Faivre, Fabian Lustenberger, Jordan Lefort, Mohamed Camara
(77' Sandro Lauper), Quentin Maceiras, Christopher Martins Pereira, Nicolas Moumi
Ngamaleu, Michel Aebischer (62' Vincent Sierro), Fabian Rieder (62' Silvan Hefti), Jordan
Siebatcheu (62' Wilfried Kanga), Meschack Elia (87' Nico Maier). Coach: David Wagner.
Goals: 9' Mason Greenwood 1-0, 42' Fabian Rieder 1-1.
Referee: Benoît Bastien (FRA) Attendance: 73,156

09.12.21   Gewiss Stadium, Bergamo: Atalanta Bergamo – Villarreal CF 2-3 (0-2)
Atalanta Bergamo: Juan Musso, Rafael Tolói, José Palomino, Hans Hateboer, Merih Demiral
(46' Berat Djimsiti), Joakim Mæhle (90' Davide Zappacosta), Josip Ilicic, Marten de Roon
(54' Luis Muriel), Remo Freuler, Matteo Pessina (46' Ruslan Malinovskyi), Duván Zapata.
Coach: Gian Piero Gasperini.
Villarreal CF: Gerónimo Rulli, Raúl Albiol, Alberto Moreno (88' Pedraza), Pervis Estupiñán,
Pau Torres, Juan Foyth, Étienne Capoue, Dani Parejo (90+3' Manu Trigueros), Moi Gómez
(90+3' Rubén Peña), Gerard Moreno (80' Iborra), Arnaut Danjuma Groeneveld (88' Boulaye
Dia). Coach: Unai Emery.
Goals: 3' Arnaut Danjuma Groeneveld 0-1, 42' Étienne Capoue 0-2,
51' Arnaut Danjuma Groeneveld 0-3, 71' Ruslan Malinovskyi 1-3, 80' Duván Zapata 2-3.
Referee: Anthony Taylor (ENG)   Attendance: 11,690

GROUP G

14.09.21   Estadio Ramón Sánchez Pizjuán, Sevilla: Sevilla FC – Red Bull Salzburg 1-1 (1-1)
Sevilla FC: Yassine "Bono" Bounou, Jesús Navas (87' Gonzalo Montiel), Marcos Acuña,
Diego Carlos, Jules Koundé, Ivan Rakitic (65' Rafa Mir), Alejandro "Papu" Gómez (58' Érik
Lamela), Fernando, Suso (46' Lucas Ocampos), Joan Jordán (46' Thomas Delaney), Youssef
En-Nesyri. Coach: Lopetegui.
Red Bull Salzburg: Philipp Köhn, Andreas Ulmer, Maximilian Wöber (51' Kamil Piatkowski),
Rasmus Kristensen, Oumar Solet, Brenden Aaronson, Nicolas Seiwald (80' Nicolás Capaldo),
Mohamed Camara, Luka Sucic, Karim Adeyemi (80' Noah Okafor), Benjamin Sesko (67'
Chikwubuike Adamu). Coach: Matthias Jaissle.
Goals: 21' Luka Sucic 0-1 (p), 42' Ivan Rakitic 1-1 (p).
Referee: Aleksei Kulbakov (BLS)   Attendance: 18,373
Sent-off: 50' Youssef En-Nesyri.

Karim Adeyemi missed a penalty kick (13').

Luka Sucic missed a penalty kick (37').

14.09.21   Stade Pierre-Mauroy, Villeneuve-d'Ascq: Lille OSC – VfL Wolfsburg 0-0
Lille OSC: Ivo Grbic, José Fonte, Reinildo, Zeki Çelik, Sven Botman, Benjamin André, Xeka
(83' Amadou Onana), Jonathan Ikoné (74' Isaac Lihadji), Angel Gomes (74' Yusuf Yazici),
Burak Yilmaz, Jonathan David. Coach: Jocelyn Gourvennec.
VfL Wolfsburg: Koen Casteels, Jérôme Roussillon (84' Yannick Gerhardt), John Anthony
Brooks, Kevin Mbabu, Ridle Baku (61' Dodi Lukébakio), Maxence Lacroix, Josuha
Guilavogui, Maximilian Arnold, Maximilian Philipp (66' Sebastiaan Bornauw), Renato Steffen
(61' Luca Waldschmidt), Wout Weghorst (66' Lukas Nmecha). Coach: Mark van Bommel.
Referee: Danny Makkelie (HOL)   Attendance: 34,314
Sent-off: 62' John Anthony Brooks.

29.09.21   Red Bull Arena, Wals-Siezenheim: Red Bull Salzburg – Lille OSC 2-1 (1-0)
Red Bull Salzburg: Philipp Köhn, Andreas Ulmer, Jérôme Onguéné, Maximilian Wöber, Rasmus Kristensen, Noah Okafor (62' Benjamin Sesko), Brenden Aaronson, Nicolas Seiwald, Mohamed Camara, Luka Sucic (71' Nicolás Capaldo), Karim Adeyemi (75' Chikwubuike Adamu). Coach: Matthias Jaissle.
Lille OSC: Ivo Grbic, José Fonte, Gabriel Gudmundsson (84' Reinildo), Tiago Djaló, Sven Botman, Benjamin André, Xeka (60' Amadou Onana), Angel Gomes (59' Jonathan Ikoné), Burak Yilmaz, Timothy Weah (59' Jonathan Bamba), Jonathan David (84' Isaac Lihadji). Coach: Jocelyn Gourvennec.
Goals: 35', 53' Karim Adeyemi 1-0 (p), 2-0 (p), 62' Burak Yilmaz 2-1.
Referee: Halil Umut Meler (TUR)   Attendance: 24,207

29.09.21   Volkswagen Arena, Wolfsburg: VfL Wolfsburg – Sevilla FC 1-1 (0-0)
VfL Wolfsburg: Koen Casteels, Jérôme Roussillon, Kevin Mbabu (62' Lukas Nmecha), Ridle Baku, Sebastiaan Bornauw, Maxence Lacroix, Josuha Guilavogui, Maximilian Arnold, Renato Steffen (74' Luca Waldschmidt), Wout Weghorst (90+2' Yannick Gerhardt), Dodi Lukébakio. Coach: Mark van Bommel.
Sevilla FC: Yassine "Bono" Bounou, Jesús Navas, Marcos Acuña (46' Karim Rekik), Diego Carlos, Jules Koundé, Alejandro "Papu" Gómez, Fernando, Lucas Ocampos (74' Munir), Suso (52' Érik Lamela), Joan Jordán (70' Iván Romero), Rafa Mir (53' Ivan Rakitic). Coach: Lopetegui.
Goals: 48' Renato Steffen 1-0, 87' Ivan Rakitic 1-1 (p).
Referee: Georgi Kabakov (BUL)   Attendance: 11,733
Sent-off: 85' Josuha Guilavogui.

20.10.21   Red Bull Arena, Wals-Siezenheim: Red Bull Salzburg – VfL Wolfsburg 3-1 (1-1)
Red Bull Salzburg: Philipp Köhn, Andreas Ulmer (86' Daouda Guindo), Jérôme Onguéné, Maximilian Wöber (72' Bernardo), Rasmus Kristensen, Noah Okafor (87' Roko Simic), Brenden Aaronson, Nicolas Seiwald, Mohamed Camara (66' Nicolás Capaldo), Luka Sucic, Karim Adeyemi (87' Chikwubuike Adamu). Coach: Matthias Jaissle.
VfL Wolfsburg: Koen Casteels, Jérôme Roussillon (70' Paulo Otávio), John Anthony Brooks, Kevin Mbabu, Ridle Baku (70' Felix Nmecha), Maxence Lacroix, Maximilian Arnold, Renato Steffen, Aster Vranckx, Dodi Lukébakio, Lukas Nmecha. Coach: Mark van Bommel.
Goals: 3' Karim Adeyemi 1-0, 15' Lukas Nmecha 1-1, 65', 77' Noah Okafor 2-1, 3-1.
Referee: Daniele Orsato (ITA)   Attendance: 29,520

20.10.21   Stade Pierre-Mauroy, Villeneuve-d'Ascq: Lille OSC – Sevilla FC 0-0
Lille OSC: Ivo Grbic, José Fonte, Reinildo, Zeki Çelik, Tiago Djaló, Benjamin André, Renato Sanches (71' Jonathan Ikoné), Amadou Onana (71' Xeka), Burak Yilmaz, Jonathan Bamba, Jonathan David (82' Timothy Weah). Coach: Jocelyn Gourvennec.
Sevilla FC: Yassine "Bono" Bounou, Jesús Navas, Karim Rekik (57' Joan Jordán), Marcos Acuña (65' Ludwig Augustinsson), Diego Carlos, Fernando, Thomas Delaney, Lucas Ocampos (74' Érik Lamela), Suso (74' Ivan Rakitic), Óliver Torres (64' Alejandro "Papu" Gómez), Rafa Mir. Coach: Lopetegui.
Referee: Michael Oliver (ENG)   Attendance: 34,362

02.11.21   Volkswagen Arena, Wolfsburg: VfL Wolfsburg – Red Bull Salzburg 2-1 (1-1)
VfL Wolfsburg: Koen Casteels, John Anthony Brooks, Paulo Otávio (73' Renato Steffen),
Ridle Baku, Maxence Lacroix, Josuha Guilavogui, Maximilian Arnold, Yannick Gerhardt (73'
Jérôme Roussillon), Aster Vranckx (82' Kevin Mbabu), Wout Weghorst (63' Dodi
Lukébakio), Lukas Nmecha. Coach: Florian Kohfeldt.
Red Bull Salzburg: Philipp Köhn, Andreas Ulmer, Jérôme Onguéné (77' Oumar Solet),
Maximilian Wöber, Rasmus Kristensen, Noah Okafor, Brenden Aaronson, Nicolas Seiwald,
Mohamed Camara (89' Maurits Kjærgaard), Luka Sucic (77' Chikwubuike Adamu), Karim
Adeyemi (63' Benjamin Sesko). Coach: Matthias Jaissle.
Goals: 3' Ridle Baku 1-0, 3-0' Maximilian Wöber 1-1, 60' Lukas Nmecha 2-1.
Referee: Artur Soares Dias (POR)   Attendance: 16,112

02.11.21   Estadio Ramón Sánchez Pizjuán, Sevilla: Sevilla FC – Lille OSC 1-2 (1-1)
Sevilla FC: Yassine "Bono" Bounou, Jesús Navas (65' Gonzalo Montiel), Marcos Acuña,
Diego Carlos, Jules Koundé, Fernando, Thomas Delaney (57' Érik Lamela), Lucas Ocampos,
Suso (57' Joan Jordán), Óliver Torres (72' Munir), Rafa Mir (57' Youssef En-Nesyri).
Coach: Lopetegui.
Lille OSC: Ivo Grbic, José Fonte, Reinildo, Zeki Çelik, Tiago Djaló, Benjamin André, Renato
Sanches (75' Amadou Onana), Jonathan Ikoné, Jonathan Bamba, Timothy Weah (72' Yusuf
Yazici), Jonathan David (86' Xeka). Coach: Jocelyn Gourvennec.
Goals: 15' Lucas Ocampos 1-0, 43' Jonathan David 1-1 (p), 51' Jonathan Ikoné 1-2.
Referee: István Kovács (ROM)   Attendance: 29,369

23.11.21   Estadio Ramón Sánchez Pizjuán, Sevilla: Sevilla FC – VfL Wolfsburg 2-0 (1-0)
Sevilla FC: Yassine "Bono" Bounou, Marcos Acuña, Diego Carlos (90+4' Ludwig
Augustinsson), Gonzalo Montiel, Jules Koundé, Ivan Rakitic (90+3' Karim Rekik), Alejandro
"Papu" Gómez (80' Óliver Torres), Fernando, Lucas Ocampos, Joan Jordán (82' Thomas
Delaney), Munir (80' Rafa Mir). Coach: Lopetegui.
VfL Wolfsburg: Pavao Pervan, Jérôme Roussillon (75' Paulo Otávio), John Anthony Brooks
(88' Daniel Ginczek), Ridle Baku (75' Kevin Mbabu), Maxence Lacroix, Josuha Guilavogui,
Maximilian Arnold, Yannick Gerhardt (66' Maximilian Philipp), Aster Vranckx (75' Dodi
Lukébakio), Wout Weghorst, Lukas Nmecha. Coach: Florian Kohfeldt.
Goals: 12' Joan Jordán 1-0, 90+7' Rafa Mir 2-0.
Referee: Cüneyt Çakir (TUR)   Attendance: 28,663

23.11.21   Stade Pierre-Mauroy, Villeneuve-d'Ascq: Lille OSC – Red Bull Salzburg 1-0 (1-0)
Lille OSC: Ivo Grbic, José Fonte, Reinildo, Zeki Çelik, Tiago Djaló, Renato Sanches, Xeka,
Burak Yilmaz (70' Amadou Onana), Jonathan Bamba, Timothy Weah (84' Yusuf Yazici),
Jonathan David (90+3' Isaac Lihadji). Coach: Jocelyn Gourvennec.
Red Bull Salzburg: Philipp Köhn, Andreas Ulmer, Jérôme Onguéné, Maximilian Wöber,
Rasmus Kristensen, Brenden Aaronson (85' Maurits Kjærgaard), Nicolas Seiwald (85'
Bernardo), Mohamed Camara, Luka Sucic (59' Nicolás Capaldo), Karim Adeyemi, Benjamin
Sesko (59' Chikwubuike Adamu). Coach: Matthias Jaissle.
Goal: 31' Jonathan David 1-0.
Referee: Anthony Taylor (ENG)   Attendance: 33,573

08.12.21   Volkswagen Arena, Wolfsburg: VfL Wolfsburg – Lille OSC 1-3 (0-1)
VfL Wolfsburg: Koen Casteels, Paulo Otávio (63' Jérôme Roussillon), Kevin Mbabu (63'
Ridle Baku), Sebastiaan Bornauw, Maxence Lacroix, Josuha Guilavogui (75' Felix Nmecha),
Maximilian Arnold, Yannick Gerhardt (46' Dodi Lukébakio), Aster Vranckx, Wout Weghorst,
Luca Waldschmidt (74' Renato Steffen). Coach: Florian Kohfeldt.
Lille OSC: Ivo Grbic, José Fonte, Reinildo, Zeki Çelik (83' Tiago Djaló), Gabriel
Gudmundsson (68' Angel Gomes), Sven Botman, Benjamin André, Renato Sanches, Jonathan
Ikoné (84' Yusuf Yazici), Burak Yilmaz (75' Amadou Onana), Jonathan David.
Coach: Jocelyn Gourvennec.
Goals: 11' Burak Yilmaz 0-1, 72' Jonathan David 0-2, 78' Angel Gomes 0-3,
89' Renato Steffen 1-3.
Referee: Daniele Orsato (ITA)   Attendance: 6,544

08.12.21   Red Bull Arena, Wals-Siezenheim: Red Bull Salzburg – Sevilla FC 1-0 (0-0)
Red Bull Salzburg: Philipp Köhn, Andreas Ulmer, Jérôme Onguéné, Rasmus Kristensen,
Oumar Solet, Noah Okafor (84' Chikwubuike Adamu), Brenden Aaronson, Nicolas Seiwald,
Mohamed Camara, Luka Sucic (75' Nicolás Capaldo), Karim Adeyemi (66' Benjamin Sesko).
Coach: Matthias Jaissle.
Sevilla FC: Yassine "Bono" Bounou, Ludwig Augustinsson (53' Rafa Mir), Diego Carlos,
Gonzalo Montiel (68' Karim Rekik), Jules Koundé, Ivan Rakitic (68' Óliver Torres), Alejandro
"Papu" Gómez (68' Óscar Rodríguez), Fernando, Lucas Ocampos, Joan Jordán, Munir.
Coach: Lopetegui.
Goal: 50' Noah Okafor 1-0.
Referee: Slavko Vincic (SVN)   Attendance: 0
Sent-off: 64' Joan Jordán.

GROUP H

14.09.21   Stamford Bridge, London: Chelsea FC – Zenit Saint Petersburg 1-0 (0-0)
Chelsea FC: Edouard Mendy, Azpilicueta (83' Thiago Silva), Marcos Alonso (83' Ben
Chilwell), Antonio Rüdiger, Andreas Christensen, Reece James, Mateo Kovacic, Jorginho,
Hakim Ziyech (63' Kai Havertz), Mason Mount (90+3' Ruben Loftus-Cheek), Romelu
Lukaku. Coach: Thomas Tuchel.
Zenit Saint Petersburg: Stanislav Kritsyuk, Yaroslav Rakitskiy (88' Danil Krugovoy), Douglas
Santos, Dmitri Chistyakov, Wilmar Barrios, Daler Kuzyaev (82' Kirill Kravtsov), Aleksey
Sutormin, Claudinho (88' Andrey Mostovoy), Wendel (76' Aleksandr Erokhin), Sardar
Azmoun, Malcom (75' Artem Dzyuba). Coach: Sergey Semak.
Goal: 69' Romelu Lukaku 1-0.
Referee: Bartosz Frankowski (POL)   Attendance: 39,252

14.09.21   Eleda Stadion, Malmö: Malmö FF – Juventus FC 0-3 (0-3)
Malmö FF: Ismael Diawara, Lasse Nielsen, Franz Brorsson, Anel Ahmedhodzic, Søren Rieks
(75' Martin Olsson), Anders Christiansen, Jo Inge Berget, Erdal Rakip (59' Adi Nalic), Bonke
Innocent (75' Sebastian Nanasi), Veljko Birmancevic (59' Malik Abubakari), Antonio Colak.
Coach: Jon Dahl Tomasson.
Juventus FC: Wojciech Szczesny, Leonardo Bonucci, Danilo, Alex Sandro, Matthijs de Ligt
(87' Daniele Rugani), Juan Cuadrado (82' Dejan Kulusevski), Adrien Rabiot, Manuel
Locatelli, Rodrigo Bentancur (68' Weston McKennie), Morata (67' Moise Kean), Paulo
Dybala (82' Aaron Ramsey). Coach: Massimiliano Allegri.
Goals: 23' Alex Sandro 0-1, 45' Paulo Dybala 0-2 (p), 45+1' Morata 0-3.
Referee: Artur Soares Dias (POR)   Attendance: 5,832

29.09.21 Krestovsky Stadium, Saint Petersburg: Zenit Saint Petersburg – Malmö FF 4-0 (1-0)
Zenit Saint Petersburg: Stanislav Kritsyuk, Yaroslav Rakitskiy, Douglas Santos (84' Danil Krugovoy), Dmitri Chistyakov, Wilmar Barrios, Daler Kuzyaev (75' Sardar Azmoun), Aleksey Sutormin (83' Kirill Kravtsov), Claudinho (75' Aleksandr Erokhin), Wendel, Artem Dzyuba (84' Andrey Mostovoy), Malcom. Coach: Sergey Semak.
Malmö FF: Johan Dahlin, Eric Larsson, Lasse Nielsen, Franz Brorsson (87' Noah Eile), Anel Ahmedhodzic, Anders Christiansen, Jo Inge Berget, Erdal Rakip (55' Martin Olsson), Bonke Innocent (62' Sergio Peña), Veljko Birmancevic (88' Adi Nalic), Antonio Colak (63' Malik Abubakari). Coach: Jon Dahl Tomasson.
Goals: 9' Claudinho 1-0, 49' Daler Kuzyaev 2-0, 80' Aleksey Sutormin 3-0, 90+4' Wendel 4-0.
Referee: Anastasios Sidiropoulos (GRE) Attendance: 15,339
Sent-off: 53' Anel Ahmedhodzic.

29.09.21 Allianz Stadium, Torino: Juventus FC – Chelsea FC 1-0 (0-0)
Juventus FC: Wojciech Szczesny, Leonardo Bonucci, Danilo, Alex Sandro, Matthijs de Ligt, Juan Cuadrado, Adrien Rabiot (76' Weston McKennie), Manuel Locatelli, Rodrigo Bentancur (83' Giorgio Chiellini), Federico Bernardeschi (65' Dejan Kulusevski), Federico Chiesa (77' Moise Kean). Coach: Massimiliano Allegri.
Chelsea FC: Edouard Mendy, Thiago Silva, Azpilicueta (62' Ruben Loftus-Cheek), Marcos Alonso (46' Ben Chilwell), Antonio Rüdiger, Andreas Christensen (75' Ross Barkley), Mateo Kovacic, Jorginho (62' Trevoh Chalobah), Hakim Ziyech (62' Callum Hudson-Odoi), Kai Havertz, Romelu Lukaku. Coach: Thomas Tuchel.
Goal: 46' Federico Chiesa 1-0.
Referee: Jesús Gil Manzano (ESP) Attendance: 19,934

20.10.21 Krestovsky Stadium, Saint Petersburg:
          Zenit Saint Petersburg – Juventus FC 0-1 (0-0)
Zenit Saint Petersburg: Stanislav Kritsyuk, Dejan Lovren, Yaroslav Rakitskiy, Vyacheslav Karaveav (61' Aleksey Sutormin), Douglas Santos, Dmitri Chistyakov (88' Danil Krugovoy), Wilmar Barrios, Claudinho (88' Aleksandr Erokhin), Wendel, Artem Dzyuba (60' Sardar Azmoun), Malcom (69' Daler Kuzyaev). Coach: Sergey Semak.
Juventus FC: Wojciech Szczesny, Leonardo Bonucci, Alex Sandro (58' Juan Cuadrado), Mattia De Sciglio, Matthijs de Ligt, Manuel Locatelli (58' Arthur), Rodrigo Bentancur (84' Aaron Ramsey), Weston McKennie, Morata (76' Moise Kean), Federico Bernardeschi (58' Dejan Kulusevski), Federico Chiesa. Coach: Massimiliano Allegri.
Goal: 86' Dejan Kulusevski 0-1.
Referee: Sandro Schärer (SUI) Attendance: 18,717

20.10.21 Stamford Bridge, London: Chelsea FC – Malmö FF 4-0 (1-0)
Chelsea FC: Edouard Mendy, Thiago Silva, Azpilicueta (66' Reece James), Antonio Rüdiger, Andreas Christensen, Ben Chilwell (66' Marcos Alonso), Jorginho, N'Golo Kanté (65' Saúl), Mason Mount, Romelu Lukaku (23' Kai Havertz), Timo Werner (44' Callum Hudson-Odoi). Coach: Thomas Tuchel.
Malmö FF: Johan Dahlin (46' Ismael Diawara), Martin Olsson, Eric Larsson, Lasse Nielsen, Franz Brorsson, Anders Christiansen (58' Adi Nalic), Jo Inge Berget (84' Niklas Moisander), Sergio Peña (59' Erdal Rakip), Bonke Innocent, Veljko Birmancevic (46' Malik Abubakari), Antonio Colak. Coach: Jon Dahl Tomasson.
Goals: 9' Andreas Christensen 1-0, 21' Jorginho 2-0 (p), 48' Kai Havertz 3-0, 57' Jorginho 4-0 (p).
Referee: François Letexier (FRA) Attendance: 39,095

02.11.21   Eleda Stadion, Malmö: Malmö FF – Chelsea FC 0-1 (0-0)
Malmö FF: Johan Dahlin, Lasse Nielsen, Franz Brorsson, Anel Ahmedhodzic, Søren Rieks (57' Martin Olsson), Jo Inge Berget (86' Eric Larsson), Sergio Peña (58' Oscar Lewicki), Erdal Rakip (86' Veljko Birmancevic), Bonke Innocent, Sebastian Nanasi (74' Adi Nalic), Antonio Colak. Coach: Jon Dahl Tomasson.
Chelsea FC: Edouard Mendy, Thiago Silva, Azpilicueta, Marcos Alonso, Antonio Rüdiger, Andreas Christensen, Jorginho, Hakim Ziyech (74' Ross Barkley), Ruben Loftus-Cheek, Kai Havertz, Callum Hudson-Odoi (74' Christian Pulisic). Coach: Thomas Tuchel.
Goal: 56' Hakim Ziyech 0-1.
Referee: Dr. Felix Brych (GER)   Attendance: 19,551

02.11.21   Allianz Stadium, Torino: Juventus FC – Zenit Saint Petersburg 4-2 (1-1)
Juventus FC: Wojciech Szczesny, Leonardo Bonucci (85' Daniele Rugani), Danilo, Alex Sandro, Matthijs de Ligt, Manuel Locatelli (80' Arthur), Weston McKennie, Morata, Paulo Dybala (85' Dejan Kulusevski), Federico Bernardeschi (80' Adrien Rabiot), Federico Chiesa. Coach: Massimiliano Allegri.
Zenit Saint Petersburg: Stanislav Kritsyuk, Dejan Lovren, Yaroslav Rakitskiy (74' Artem Dzyuba), Vyacheslav Karaveav (59' Malcom), Dmitri Chistyakov, Wilmar Barrios, Aleksey Sutormin, Claudinho (74' Aleksandr Erokhin), Andrey Mostovoy (58' Danil Krugovoy), Wendel (88' Daniil Kuznetsov), Sardar Azmoun. Coach: Sergey Semak.
Goals: 11' Paulo Dybala 1-0, 26' Leonardo Bonucci 1-1 (og), 58' Paulo Dybala 2-1 (p), 73' Federico Chiesa 3-1, 82' Morata 4-1, 90+2' Sardar Azmoun 4-2.
Referee: Alejandro Hernández Hernández (ESP)   Attendance: 20,053

23.11.21   Stamford Bridge, London: Chelsea FC – Juventus FC 4-0 (1-0)
Chelsea FC: Edouard Mendy, Thiago Silva, Antonio Rüdiger, Ben Chilwell (71' Azpilicueta), Reece James, Jorginho (76' Saúl), N'Golo Kanté (37' Ruben Loftus-Cheek), Hakim Ziyech, Trevoh Chalobah, Christian Pulisic (72' Timo Werner), Callum Hudson-Odoi (76' Mason Mount). Coach: Thomas Tuchel.
Juventus FC: Wojciech Szczesny, Leonardo Bonucci, Alex Sandro, Matthijs de Ligt, Juan Cuadrado (80' Koni De Winter), Adrien Rabiot, Manuel Locatelli (67' Arthur), Rodrigo Bentancur (59' Paulo Dybala), Weston McKennie, Morata (67' Moise Kean), Federico Chiesa (80' Dejan Kulusevski). Coach: Massimiliano Allegri.
Goals: 25' Trevoh Chalobah 1-0, 55' Reece James 2-0, 58' Callum Hudson-Odoi 3-0, 90+5' Timo Werner 4-0.
Referee: Srdjan Jovanovic (SRB)   Attendance: 39,513

23.11.21   Eleda Stadion, Malmö: Malmö FF – Zenit Saint Petersburg 1-1 (1-0)
Malmö FF: Johan Dahlin, Niklas Moisander, Eric Larsson, Franz Brorsson, Anel Ahmedhodzic, Søren Rieks, Oscar Lewicki, Sergio Peña (78' Erdal Rakip), Bonke Innocent, Veljko Birmancevic (69' Martin Olsson), Antonio Colak. Coach: Jon Dahl Tomasson.
Zenit Saint Petersburg: Mikhail Kerzhakov, Dejan Lovren (46' Aleksandr Erokhin), Yaroslav Rakitskiy, Vyacheslav Karaveav, Douglas Santos, Dmitri Chistyakov, Wilmar Barrios, Claudinho (46' Andrey Mostovoy), Wendel, Artem Dzyuba, Malcom (90+3' Danil Krugovoy). Coach: Sergey Semak.
Goals: 28' Søren Rieks 1-0, 90+2' Yaroslav Rakitskiy 1-1 (p).
Referee: Andris Treimanis (LAT)   Attendance: 15,520
Sent-off: 86' Dmitri Chistyakov.

Artem Dzyuba missed a penalty kick (53').

08.12.21   Krestovsky Stadium, Saint Petersburg:
Zenit Saint Petersburg – Chelsea FC 3-3 (2-1)
Zenit Saint Petersburg: Mikhail Kerzhakov, Dejan Lovren, Yaroslav Rakitskiy (66' Danil Krugovoy), Vyacheslav Karaveav, Douglas Santos, Wilmar Barrios, Daler Kuzyaev (80' Magomed Ozdoev), Claudinho, Wendel (51' Andrey Mostovoy), Sardar Azmoun (79' Artem Dzyuba), Malcom (80' Aleksandr Erokhin). Coach: Sergey Semak.
Chelsea FC: Kepa, Azpilicueta, Andreas Christensen, Malang Sarr, Reece James, Saúl (76' Marcos Alonso), Ross Barkley (64' Hakim Ziyech), Mason Mount, Romelu Lukaku (73' Kai Havertz), Timo Werner, Callum Hudson-Odoi (65' Christian Pulisic). Coach: Thomas Tuchel.
Goals: 2' Timo Werner 0-1, 38' Claudinho 1-1, 41' Sardar Azmoun 2-1, 62' Romelu Lukaku 2-2, 85' Timo Werner 2-3, 90+4' Magomed Ozdoev 3-3.
Referee: Serdar Gözübüyük (HOL)   Attendance: 29,349

08.12.21   Allianz Stadium, Torino: Juventus FC – Malmö FF 1-0 (1-0)
Juventus FC: Mattia Perin, Leonardo Bonucci, Alex Sandro, Daniele Rugani, Koni De Winter (71' Mattia De Sciglio), Adrien Rabiot, Arthur, Rodrigo Bentancur (90' Fabio Miretti), Paulo Dybala (46' Morata), Federico Bernardeschi (82' Juan Cuadrado), Moise Kean (90' Cosimo Da Graca). Coach: Massimiliano Allegri.
Malmö FF: Ismael Diawara, Martin Olsson, Niklas Moisander, Lasse Nielsen, Anel Ahmedhodzic, Anders Christiansen, Jo Inge Berget, Erdal Rakip (30' Sergio Peña), Bonke Innocent (89' Adi Nalic), Veljko Birmancevic, Antonio Colak (78' Malik Abubakari). Coach: Jon Dahl Tomasson.
Goal: 18' Moise Kean 1-0.
Referee: Irfan Peljto (BIH)   Attendance: 17,501

KNOCKOUT PHASE

ROUND OF 16

15.02.22   Estádio José Alvalade, Lisboa: Sporting CP – Manchester City 0-5 (0-4)
Sporting CP: Antonio Adán, Sebastián Coates, Ricardo Esgaio, Matheus Reis, Pedro Porro (82' Luís Carlos Neto), Gonçalo Inácio, Pablo Sarabia (75' Bruno Tabata), João Palhinha, Pedro Gonçalves "Pote" (51' Manuel Ugarte), Matheus Nunes, Paulinho (75' Islam Slimani). Coach: Rúben Amorim.
Manchester City: Ederson Moraes, João Cancelo, Aymeric Laporte (85' Nathan Aké), John Stones (61' Oleksandr Zinchenko), Rúben Dias, Kevin De Bruyne, Bernardo Silva (85' Liam Delap), Rodri (73' Fernandinho), Phil Foden (61' Ilkay Gündogan), Riyad Mahrez, Raheem Sterling. Coach: Pep Guardiola.
Goals: 7' Riyad Mahrez 0-1, 17' Bernardo Silva 0-2, 32' Phil Foden 0-3, 44' Bernardo Silva 0-4, 58' Raheem Sterling 0-5.
Referee: Srdjan Jovanovic (SRB)   Attendance: 48,129

15.02.22   Parc des Princes, Paris: Paris Saint-Germain – Real Madrid CF 1-0 (0-0)
Paris Saint-Germain: Gianluigi Donnarumma, Marquinhos, Presnel Kimpembe, Achraf Hakimi, Nuno Mendes, Ángel Di María (73' Neymar), Marco Verratti, Danilo Pereira (87' Idrissa Gueye), Leandro Paredes, Lionel Messi, Kylian Mbappé. Coach: Mauricio Pochettino.
Real Madrid CF: Thibaut Courtois, David Alaba, Dani Carvajal (72' Lucas Vázquez), Ferland Mendy, Éder Militão, Luka Modric (82' Federico Valverde), Toni Kroos, Casemiro, Karim Benzema (87' Gareth Bale), Marco Asensio (72' Rodrygo), Vinícius Júnior (82' Eden Hazard). Coach: Carlo Ancelotti.
Goal: 90+4' Kylian Mbappé 1-0.
Referee: Daniele Orsato (ITA)   Attendance: 47,443

Leonel Messi missed a penalty kick (62').

16.02.22   Red Bull Arena, Salzburg: Red Bull Salzburg – Bayern München 1-1 (1-0)
Red Bull Salzburg: Philipp Köhn, Andreas Ulmer, Max Wöber, Rasmus Kristensen, Oumar Solet, Noah Okafor (12' Chikwubuike Adamu), Brenden Aaronson, Nicolas Seiwald (80' Luka Sucic), Mohamed Camara, Nicolás Capaldo, Karim Adeyemi (87' Maurits Kjærgaard). Coach: Matthias Jaissle.
Bayern München: Sven Ulreich, Niklas Süle, Lucas Hernández, Benjamin Pavard, Serge Gnabry (77' Eric Maxim Choupo-Moting), Corentin Tolisso (80' Marcel Sabitzer), Joshua Kimmich, Thomas Müller, Robert Lewandowski, Kingsley Coman, Leroy Sané. Coach: Julian Nagelsmann.
Goals: 21' Chikwubuike Adamu 1-0, 90' Kingsley Coman 1-1.
Referee: Michael Oliver (ENG)   Attendance: 29,520

16.02.22   Stadio Giuseppe Meazza, Milano: Internazionale Milano – Liverpool FC 0-2 (0-0)
Internazionale Milano: Samir Handanovic, Stefan de Vrij (87' Andrea Ranocchia), Milan Skriniar, Denzel Dumfries (87' Matteo Darmian), Alessandro Bastoni (90+1' Federico Dimarco), Ivan Perisic, Arturo Vidal (87' Roberto Gagliardini), Marcelo Brozovic, Hakan Çalhanoglu, Edin Dzeko, Lautaro Martínez (71' Alexis Sánchez). Coach: Simone Inzaghi.
Liverpool FC: Alisson, Virgil van Dijk, Andrew Robertson, Trent Alexander-Arnold, Ibrahima Konaté, Thiago Alcântara (86' James Milner), Fabinho (60' Jordan Henderson), Harvey Elliott (59' Naby Keïta), Mohamed Salah, Sadio Mané (59' Luis Díaz), Diogo Jota (46' Roberto Firmino). Coach: Jürgen Klopp.
Goals: 75' Roberto Firmino 0-1, 83' Mohamed Salah 0-2.
Referee: Szymon Marciniak (POL)   Attendance: 37,918

22.02.22   Stamford Bridge, London: Chelsea FC – Lille OSC 2-0 (1-0)
Chelsea FC: Édouard Mendy, Thiago Silva, Azpilicueta, Marcos Alonso (80' Malang Sarr), Antonio Rüdiger, Andreas Christensen, Mateo Kovacic (51' Ruben Loftus-Cheek), N'Golo Kanté, Hakim Ziyech (60' Saúl), Christian Pulisic (80' Timo Werner), Kai Havertz. Coach: Thomas Tuchel.
Lille OSC: Léo Jardim, José Fonte, Zeki Çelik, Tiago Djaló (76' Gabriel Gudmundsson), Sven Botman, Benjamin André, Renato Sanches (81' Hatem Ben Arfa), Xeka, Amadou Onana (65' Burak Yilmaz), Jonathan Bamba, Jonathan David (81' Edon Zhegrova). Coach: Jocelyn Gourvennec.
Goals: 8' Kai Havertz 1-0, 63' Christian Pulisic 2-0.
Referee: Jesús Gil Manzano (ESP)   Attendance: 38,832

22.02.22   Estadio de la Cerámica, Villarreal: Villarreal CF – Juventus FC 1-1 (0-1)
Villarreal CF: Gerónimo Rulli, Raúl Albiol, Alberto Moreno (79' Manu Trigueros), Pau
Torres, Juan Foyth, Étienne Capoue, Dani Parejo, Giovani Lo Celso, Pedraza (79' Pervis
Estupiñán), Arnaut Danjuma Groeneveld (90' Boulaye Dia), Samuel Chukwueze (90' Yeremi
Pino). Coach: Unai Emery.
Juventus FC: Wojciech Szczesny, Danilo, Alex Sandro (46' Leonardo Bonucci), Mattia De
Sciglio (87' Luca Pellegrini), Matthijs de Ligt, Juan Cuadrado, Adrien Rabiot, Manuel
Locatelli (71' Arthur), Weston McKennie (81' Denis Zakaria), Morata, Dusan Vlahovic.
Coach: Massimiliano Allegri.
Goals: 1' Dusan Vlahovic 0-1, 66' Dani Parejo 1-1.
Referee: Daniel Siebert (GER)   Attendance: 17,686

23.02.22   Estádio do Sport Lisboa e Benfica, Lisboa: SL Benfica – AFC Ajax 2-2 (1-2)
SL Benfica: Odisseas Vlachodimos, Jan Vertonghen, Nicolás Otamendi, Gilberto (90+1'
Diogo Gonçalves), Álex Grimaldo, Adel Taarabt (85' Paulo Bernardo), Rafa Silva, Julian
Weigl, Éverton (62' Roman Yaremchuk), Darwin Núñez (90' Valentino Lazaro), Gonçalo
Ramos. Coach: Nélson Veríssimo.
AFC Ajax: Remko Pasveer, Daley Blind (73' Nico Tagliafico), Noussair Mazraoui (90+2'
Devyne Rensch), Lisandro Martínez, Jurriën Timber, Edson Álvarez, Ryan Gravenberch (73'
Davy Klaassen), Dusan Tadic, Steven Berghuis, Sébastien Haller, Antony.
Coach: Erik ten Hag.
Goals: 18' Dusan Tadic 0-1, 26' Sébastien Haller 1-1 (og), 29' Sébastien Haller 1-2,
72' Roman Yaremchuk 2-2.
Referee: Slavko Vincic (SVN)   Attendance: 54,760

23.02.22   Estadio Wanda Metropolitano, Madrid:
            Atlético Madrid – Manchester United 1-1 (1-0)
Atlético Madrid: Jan Oblak, Sime Vrsaljko, Stefan Savic, José Giménez, Reinildo, Renan Lodi
(76' Thomas Lemar), Héctor Herrera, Geoffrey Kondogbia, Marcos Llorente, Ángel Correa,
João Félix (76' Antoine Griezmann). Coach: Diego Simeone.
Manchester United: David de Gea, Victor Lindelöf (66' Aaron Wan-Bissaka), Raphaël Varane,
Harry Maguire, Luke Shaw (67' Alex Telles), Paul Pogba (66' Nemanja Matic), Fred, Bruno
Fernandes, Cristiano Ronaldo, Marcus Rashford (75' Anthony Elanga), Jadon Sancho (82'
Jesse Lingard). Coach: Ralf Rangnick.
Goals: 7' João Félix 1-0, 80' Anthony Elanga 1-1.
Referee: Ovidiu Hategan (ROM)   Attendance: 63,273

08.03.22   Allianz Arena, München: Bayern München – Red Bull Salzburg 7-1 (4-0)
Bayern München: Manuel Neuer, Niklas Süle (66' Tanguy Nianzou Kouassi), Lucas
Hernández (60' Dayot Upamecano), Benjamin Pavard, Serge Gnabry (46' Bouna Sarr), Joshua
Kimmich, Jamal Musiala (66' Marc Roca), Thomas Müller, Robert Lewandowski, Kingsley
Coman (66' Eric Maxim Choupo-Moting), Leroy Sané. Coach: Julian Nagelsmann.
Red Bull Salzburg: Philipp Köhn, Andreas Ulmer, Max Wöber, Rasmus Kristensen, Oumar
Solet (46' Kamil Piatkowski), Brenden Aaronson, Nicolas Seiwald (46' Luka Sucic),
Mohamed Camara (67' Samson Tijani), Nicolás Capaldo, Chikwubuike Adamu (61' Maurits
Kjærgaard), Karim Adeyemi (62' Benjamin Sesko). Coach: Matthias Jaissle.
Goals: 12', 21' 23' Robert Lewandowski 1-0 (p), 2-0 (p), 3-0, 31' Serge Gnabry 4-0,
54' Thomas Müller 5-0, 70' Maurits Kjærgaard 5-1, 83' Thomas Müller 6-1,
85' Leroy Sané 7-1.
Referee: Clément Turpin (FRA)   Attendance: 25,000

60

08.03.22   Anfield, Liverpool: Liverpool FC – Internazionale Milano 0-1 (0-0)
Liverpool FC: Alisson, Joel Matip, Virgil van Dijk, Andrew Robertson, Trent Alexander-
Arnold, Thiago Alcântara (65' Jordan Henderson), Fabinho, Curtis Jones (65' Naby Keïta),
Mohamed Salah, Sadio Mané, Diogo Jota (83' Luis Díaz). Coach: Jürgen Klopp.
Internazionale Milano: Samir Handanovic, Stefan de Vrij (46' Danilo D'Ambrosio), Milan
Skriniar, Denzel Dumfries (75' Matteo Darmian), Alessandro Bastoni, Ivan Perisic, Arturo
Vidal, Marcelo Brozovic (75' Roberto Gagliardini), Hakan Çalhanoglu (83' Matías Vecino),
Alexis Sánchez, Lautaro Martínez (75' Joaquín Correa). Coach: Simone Inzaghi.
Goal: 61' Lautaro Martínez 0-1.
Referee: Antonio Mateu Lahoz (ESP)   Attendance: 51,747
Sent-off: 63' Alexis Sánchez.

09-03-22   Etihad Stadium, Manchester: Manchester City – Sporting CP 0-0
Manchester City: Ederson Moraes (73' Scott Carson), Aymeric Laporte (84' Luke Mbete-
Tabu), John Stones, Conrad Jonathan Egan-Riley, Fernandinho, Ilkay Gündogan, Oleksandr
Zinchenko, Bernardo Silva (46' Riyad Mahrez), Phil Foden (46' James McAtee), Raheem
Sterling, Gabriel Jesus. Coach: Pep Guardiola.
Sporting CP: Antonio Adán, Luís Carlos Neto (89' Zouhair Feddal), Sebastián Coates,
Matheus Reis, Pedro Porro (78' Ricardo Esgaio), Gonçalo Inácio, Pablo Sarabia (58' Marcus
Edwards), Manuel Ugarte, Islam Slimani (89' Rodrigo Ribeiro), Paulinho (78' Nuno Santos),
Bruno Tabata. Coach: Rúben Amorim.
Referee: Halil Umut Meler (TUR)   Attendance: 51,213

09.03.22   Estadio Santiago Bernabéu, Madrid:
                Real Madrid CF – Paris Saint-Germain 3-1 (0-1)
Real Madrid CF: Thibaut Courtois, David Alaba, Nacho, Dani Carvajal (66' Lucas Vázquez),
Éder Militão, Luka Modric, Toni Kroos (57' Eduardo Camavinga), Federico Valverde, Karim
Benzema, Marco Asensio (57' Rodrygo), Vinícius Júnior. Coach: Carlo Ancelotti.
Paris Saint-Germain: Gianluigi Donnarumma, Marquinhos, Presnel Kimpembe, Achraf Hakimi
(88' Julian Draxler), Nuno Mendes, Marco Verratti, Danilo Pereira (81' Ángel Di María),
Leandro Paredes (71' Idrissa Gueye), Lionel Messi, Neymar, Kylian Mbappé.
Coach: Mauricio Pochettino.
Goals: 39' Kylian Mbappé 0-1, 61', 76', 78' Karim Benzema 1-1, 2-1, 3-1.
Referee: Danny Makkelie (HOL)   Attendance: 59,895

15.03.22   Johan Cruyff Arena, Amsterdam: AFC Ajax – SL Benfica 0-1 (0-0)
AFC Ajax: André Onana, Daley Blind, Noussair Mazraoui, Lisandro Martínez, Jurriën Timber
(90+6' Mohammed Kudus), Edson Álvarez (81' Brian Brobbey), Ryan Gravenberch, Dusan
Tadic, Steven Berghuis (81' Davy Klaassen), Sébastien Haller, Antony. Coach: Erik ten Hag.
SL Benfica: Odisseas Vlachodimos, Jan Vertonghen, Nicolás Otamendi, Gilberto (90+1'
Valentino Lazaro), Álex Grimaldo, Adel Taarabt (46' Soualiho Meïté), Rafa Silva, Julian
Weigl, Éverton (72' Roman Yaremchuk), Darwin Núñez (81' Diogo Gonçalves), Gonçalo
Ramos (90+1' Paulo Bernardo). Coach: Nélson Veríssimo.
Goal: 77' Darwin Núñez 0-1.
Referee: Carlos del Cerro Grande (ESP)   Attendance: 54,066

15.03.22   Old Trafford, Manchester: Manchester United – Atlético Madrid 0-1 (0-1)
Manchester United: David de Gea, Alex Telles, Raphaël Varane, Harry Maguire (84' Mata),
Diogo Dalot, Fred (75' Edinson Cavani), Bruno Fernandes (67' Paul Pogba), Scott
McTominay (67' Nemanja Matic), Cristiano Ronaldo, Jadon Sancho, Anthony Elanga (67'
Marcus Rashford). Coach: Ralf Rangnick.
Atlético Madrid: Jan Oblak, Stefan Savic, José Giménez, Reinildo, Renan Lodi, Héctor
Herrera, Koke (80' Geoffrey Kondogbia), Rodrigo De Paul, Marcos Llorente, Antoine
Griezmann (90+3' Ángel Correa), João Félix (90' Felipe Monteiro). Coach: Diego Simeone.
Goal: 41' Renan Lodi 0-1.
Referee: Slavko Vincic (SVN)   Attendance: 73,008

16.03.22   Stade Pierre-Mauroy, Villeneuve-d'Ascq: Lille OSC – Chelsea FC 1-2 (1-1)
Lille OSC: Léo Jardim, José Fonte, Zeki Çelik (58' Timothy Weah), Gabriel Gudmundsson
(77' Domagoj Bradaric), Tiago Djaló, Sven Botman (58' Amadou Onana), Benjamin André,
Xeka, Burak Yilmaz, Jonathan Bamba (78' Angel Gomes), Jonathan David (77' Hatem Ben
Arfa). Coach: Jocelyn Gourvennec.
Chelsea FC: Édouard Mendy, Thiago Silva, Azpilicueta, Marcos Alonso, Antonio Rüdiger,
Andreas Christensen (33' Trevoh Chalobah), Mateo Kovacic (46' Mason Mount), Jorginho
(74' Ruben Loftus-Cheek), N'Golo Kanté, Christian Pulisic (74' Romelu Lukaku), Kai
Havertz (83' Hakim Ziyech). Coach: Thomas Tuchel.
Goals: 38' Burak Yilmaz 1-0 (p), 45+3' Christian Pulisic 1-1, 71' Azpilicueta 1-2.
Referee: Davide Massa (ITA)   Attendance: 49,048

16.03.22   Allianz Stadium, Torino: Juventus FC – Villarreal CF 0-3 (0-0)
Juventus FC: Wojciech Szczesny, Danilo, Mattia De Sciglio, Daniele Rugani (79' Paulo
Dybala), Matthijs de Ligt, Juan Cuadrado, Adrien Rabiot, Arthur, Manuel Locatelli (83'
Federico Bernardeschi), Morata (86' Moise Kean), Dusan Vlahovic.
Coach: Massimiliano Allegri.
Villarreal CF: Gerónimo Rulli, Raúl Albiol, Serge Aurier, Pervis Estupiñán, Pau Torres,
Étienne Capoue, Dani Parejo (86' Pedraza), Manu Trigueros (64' Francis Coquelin), Giovani
Lo Celso (74' Gerard Moreno), Yeremi Pino (65' Samuel Chukwueze), Arnaut Danjuma
Groeneveld. Coach: Unai Emery.
Goals: 78' Gerard Moreno 0-1 (p), 85' Pau Torres 0-2,
90+2' Arnaut Danjuma Groeneveld 0-3 (p).
Referee: Szymon Marciniak (POL)   Attendance: 30,385

QUARTER-FINALS

05.04.22   Etihad Stadium, Manchester: Manchester City – Atlético Madrid 1-0 (0-0)
Manchester City: Ederson Moraes, João Cancelo, Aymeric Laporte, Nathan Aké, John Stones,
Ilkay Gündogan (68' Jack Grealish), Kevin De Bruyne, Bernardo Silva, Rodri, Riyad Mahrez
(68' Phil Foden), Raheem Sterling (68' Gabriel Jesus). Coach: Pep Guardiola.
Atlético Madrid: Jan Oblak, Sime Vrsaljko, Stefan Savic, Felipe Monteiro, Reinildo, Renan
Lodi, Geoffrey Kondogbia, Koke (60' Rodrigo De Paul), Marcos Llorente (60' Matheus
Cunha), Antoine Griezmann (60' Ángel Correa), João Félix (81' Thomas Lemar).
Coach: Diego Simeone.
Goal: 70' Kevin De Bruyne 1-0.
Referee: István Kovács (ROM)   Attendance: 52,018

05.04.22 Estádio do Sport Lisboa e Benfica, Lisboa: SL Benfica – Liverpool FC 1-3 (0-2)
SL Benfica: Odisseas Vlachodimos, Jan Vertonghen, Nicolás Otamendi, Gilberto, Álex
Grimaldo, Adel Taarabt (70' Soualiho Meïté), Rafa Silva, Julian Weigl, Éverton (82' Roman
Yaremchuk), Darwin Núñez, Gonçalo Ramos (87' João Mário). Coach: Nélson Veríssimo.
Liverpool FC: Alisson, Virgil van Dijk, Andrew Robertson, Trent Alexander-Arnold (89' Joe
Gomez), Ibrahima Konaté, Thiago Alcântara (61' Jordan Henderson), Fabinho, Naby Keïta
(89' James Milner), Mohamed Salah (61' Diogo Jota), Sadio Mané (61' Roberto Firmino),
Luis Díaz. Coach: Jürgen Klopp.
Goals: 17' Ibrahima Konaté 0-1, 34' Sadio Mané 0-2, 49' Darwin Núñez 1-2,
87' Luis Díaz 1-3.
Referee: Jesús Gil Manzano (ESP) Attendance: 59,633

06.04.22 Stamford Bridge, London: Chelsea FC – Real Madrid CF 1-3 (1-2)
Chelsea FC: Édouard Mendy, Thiago Silva, Azpilicueta, Antonio Rüdiger, Andreas
Christensen (46' Mateo Kovacic), Reece James, Jorginho (64' Ruben Loftus-Cheek), N'Golo
Kanté (46' Hakim Ziyech), Mason Mount, Christian Pulisic (64' Romelu Lukaku), Kai
Havertz. Coach: Thomas Tuchel.
Real Madrid CF: Thibaut Courtois, David Alaba, Dani Carvajal, Ferland Mendy, Éder Militão
(64' Nacho), Luka Modric, Toni Kroos (74' Eduardo Camavinga), Casemiro, Federico
Valverde (86' Dani Ceballos), Karim Benzema (86' Gareth Bale), Vinícius Júnior.
Coach: Carlo Ancelotti.
Goals: 21', 24' Karim Benzema 0-1, 0-2, 40' Kai Havertz 1-2, 46' Karim Benzema 1-3.
Referee: Clément Turpin (FRA) Attendance: 38,689

06.04.22 Estadio de la Cerámica, Villarreal: Villarreal CF – Bayern München 1-0 (1-0)
Villarreal CF: Gerónimo Rulli, Raúl Albiol, Pervis Estupiñán, Pau Torres, Juan Foyth (81'
Serge Aurier), Étienne Capoue, Dani Parejo, Francis Coquelin (59' Pedraza), Giovani Lo
Celso, Gerard Moreno, Arnaut Danjuma Groeneveld (81' Samuel Chukwueze).
Coach: Unai Emery.
Bayern München: Manuel Neuer, Lucas Hernández, Benjamin Pavard (71' Niklas Süle), Dayot
Upamecano, Alphonso Davies, Serge Gnabry (62' Leroy Sané), Joshua Kimmich, Jamal
Musiala, Thomas Müller (62' Leon Goretzka, 90+4' Marc Roca), Robert Lewandowski,
Kingsley Coman. Coach: Julian Nagelsmann.
Goal: 8' Arnaut Danjuma Groeneveld 1-0.
Referee: Anthony Taylor (ENG) Attendance: 21,626

12.04.22 Estadio Santiago Bernabéu, Madrid:
          Real Madrid CF – Chelsea FC 2-3 (0-1,1-3) (AET)
Real Madrid CF: Thibaut Courtois, David Alaba, Nacho (88' Lucas Vázquez), Dani Carvajal,
Ferland Mendy (78' Marcelo), Luka Modric, Toni Kroos (73' Eduardo Camavinga), Casemiro
(78' Rodrygo), Federico Valverde, Karim Benzema, Vinícius Júnior (115' Dani Ceballos).
Coach: Carlo Ancelotti.
Chelsea FC: Édouard Mendy, Thiago Silva, Marcos Alonso, Antonio Rüdiger, Reece James,
Mateo Kovacic (106' Jorginho), N'Golo Kanté (99' Hakim Ziyech), Ruben Loftus-Cheek
(106' Saúl), Mason Mount, Kai Havertz, Timo Werner (83' Christian Pulisic).
Coach: Thomas Tuchel.
Goals: 15' Mason Mount 0-1, 51' Antonio Rüdiger 0-2, 75' Timo Werner 0-3,
80' Rodrygo 1-3, 96' Karim Benzema 2-3.
Referee: Szymon Marciniak (POL) Attendance: 59,839

12.04.22   Allianz Arena, München: Bayern München – Villarreal CF 1-1 (0-0)
Bayern München: Manuel Neuer, Lucas Hernández (87' Alphonso Davies), Benjamin Pavard, Dayot Upamecano, Leon Goretzka, Joshua Kimmich, Jamal Musiala (82' Serge Gnabry), Thomas Müller (90' Eric Maxim Choupo-Moting), Robert Lewandowski, Kingsley Coman, Leroy Sané. Coach: Julian Nagelsmann.
Villarreal CF: Gerónimo Rulli, Raúl Albiol, Pervis Estupiñán, Pau Torres, Juan Foyth, Étienne Capoue, Dani Parejo (90+3' Serge Aurier), Francis Coquelin (84' Samuel Chukwueze), Giovani Lo Celso, Gerard Moreno, Arnaut Danjuma Groeneveld (84' Pedraza).
Coach: Unai Emery.
Goals: 52' Robert Lewandowski 1-0, 88' Samuel Chukwueze 1-1.
Referee: Slavko Vincic (SVN)   Attendance: 70,000

13.04.22   Estadio Wanda Metropolitano, Madrid: Atlético Madrid – Manchester City 0-0
Atlético Madrid: Jan Oblak, Stefan Savic, Felipe Monteiro, Reinildo, Renan Lodi (70' Ángel Correa), Geoffrey Kondogbia, Koke (69' Rodrigo De Paul), Thomas Lemar (82' Luis Suárez), Marcos Llorente, Antoine Griezmann (69' Yannick Carrasco), João Félix (82' Matheus Cunha). Coach: Diego Simeone.
Manchester City: Ederson Moraes, Kyle Walker (73' Nathan Aké), João Cancelo, Aymeric Laporte, John Stones, Ilkay Gündogan, Kevin De Bruyne (65' Raheem Sterling), Bernardo Silva (79' Fernandinho), Rodri, Phil Foden, Riyad Mahrez. Coach: Pep Guardiola.
Referee: Daniel Siebert (GER)   Attendance: 65,675
Sent-off: 90+1' Felipe Monteiro.

13.04.22   Anfield, Liverpool: Liverpool FC – SL Benfica 3-3 (1-1)
Liverpool FC: Alisson, Joel Matip, Joe Gomez, Kostas Tsimikas, Ibrahima Konaté, James Milner (58' Thiago Alcântara, Jordan Henderson (58' Fabinho), Naby Keïta, Roberto Firmino (90+1' Divock Origi), Diogo Jota (57' Mohamed Salah), Luis Díaz (66' Sadio Mané).
Coach: Jürgen Klopp.
SL Benfica: Odisseas Vlachodimos, Jan Vertonghen, Nicolás Otamendi, Gilberto (90+1' Gil Dias), Álex Grimaldo, Adel Taarabt (66' João Mário), Julian Weigl, Diogo Gonçalves (46' Roman Yaremchuk), Éverton (90+1' André Almeida), Darwin Núñez, Gonçalo Ramos (78' Paulo Bernardo). Coach: Nélson Veríssimo.
Goals: 21' Ibrahima Konaté 1-0, 32' Gonçalo Ramos 1-1, 55', 65' Roberto Firmino 2-1, 3-1, 73' Roman Yaremchuk 3-2, 82' Darwin Núñez 3-3.
Referee: Serdar Gözübüyük (HOL)   Attendance: 51,373

SEMI-FINALS

26.04.22   Etihad Stadium, Manchester: Manchester City – Real Madrid CF 4-3 (2-1)
Manchester City: Ederson Moraes, Aymeric Laporte, John Stones (36' Fernandinho), Rúben Dias, Kevin De Bruyne, Oleksandr Zinchenko, Bernardo Silva, Rodri, Phil Foden, Riyad Mahrez, Gabriel Jesus (83' Raheem Sterling). Coach: Pep Guardiola.
Real Madrid CF: Thibaut Courtois, David Alaba (46' Nacho), Dani Carvajal, Ferland Mendy, Éder Militão, Luka Modric (79' Dani Ceballos), Toni Kroos, Federico Valverde, Karim Benzema, Vinícius Júnior (88' Marco Asensio), Rodrygo (70' Eduardo Camavinga).
Coach: Carlo Ancelotti.
Goals: 2' Kevin De Bruyne 1-0, 11' Gabriel Jesus 2-0, 33' Karim Benzema 2-1, 53' Phil Foden 3-1, 55' Vinícius Júnior 3-2, 74' Bernardo Silva 4-2, 82' K. Benzema 4-3 (p).
Referee: István Kovács (ROM)   Attendance: 52,217

27.04.22 Anfield, Liverpool: Liverpool FC – Villarreal CF 2-0 (0-0)
Liverpool FC: Alisson, Virgil van Dijk, Andrew Robertson, Trent Alexander-Arnold (81' Joe Gomez), Ibrahima Konaté, Jordan Henderson (72' Naby Keïta), Thiago Alcântara, Fabinho, Mohamed Salah, Sadio Mané (73' Diogo Jota), Luis Díaz (81' Divock Origi).
Coach: Jürgen Klopp.
Villarreal CF: Gerónimo Rulli, Raúl Albiol, Pervis Estupiñán (72' Manu Trigueros), Pau Torres, Juan Foyth, Étienne Capoue, Dani Parejo (71' Serge Aurier), Francis Coquelin (57' Pedraza), Giovani Lo Celso, Arnaut Danjuma Groeneveld (86' Paco Alcácer), Samuel Chukwueze (72' Boulaye Dia). Coach: Unai Emery.
Goals: 53' Pervis Estupiñán 1-0 (og), 55' Sadio Mané 2-0.
Referee: Szymon Marciniak (POL) Attendance: 51,586

03.05.22 Estadio de la Cerámica, Villarreal: Villarreal CF – Liverpool FC 2-3 (2-0)
Villarreal CF: Gerónimo Rulli, Raúl Albiol (79' Serge Aurier), Pervis Estupiñán (79' Manu Trigueros), Pau Torres, Juan Foyth, Étienne Capoue, Dani Parejo, Francis Coquelin (68' Pedraza), Giovani Lo Celso, Gerard Moreno (68' Samuel Chukwueze), Boulaye Dia (79' Paco Alcácer). Coach: Unai Emery.
Liverpool FC: Alisson, Virgil van Dijk, Andrew Robertson (79' Kostas Tsimikas), Trent Alexander-Arnold, Ibrahima Konaté, Thiago Alcântara (80' Curtis Jones), Fabinho (84' James Milner), Naby Keïta (79' Jordan Henderson), Mohamed Salah, Sadio Mané, Diogo Jota (46' Luis Díaz). Coach: Jürgen Klopp.
Goals: 3' Boulaye Dia 1-0, 41' Francis Coquelin 2-0, 62' Fabinho 2-1, 67' Luis Díaz 2-2, 74' Sadio Mané 2-3.
Referee: Danny Makkelie (HOL) Attendance: 23,665
Sent-off: 86' Étienne Capoue.

04.05.22 Estadio Santiago Bernabéu, Madrid:
         Real Madrid CF – Manchester City 3-1 (0-0,2-1) (AET)
Real Madrid CF: Thibaut Courtois, Nacho, Dani Carvajal, Ferland Mendy, Éder Militão (115' Jesús Vallego), Luka Modric (75' Eduardo Camavinga), Toni Kroos (68' Rodrygo), Casemiro (75' Marco Asensio), Federico Valverde, Karim Benzema (104' Dani Ceballos), Vinícius Júnior (115' Lucas Vázquez). Coach: Carlo Ancelotti.
Manchester City: Ederson Moraes, Kyle Walker (72' Oleksandr Zinchenko), João Cancelo, Aymeric Laporte, Rúben Dias, Kevin De Bruyne (72' Ilkay Gündogan), Bernardo Silva, Rodri (99' Raheem Sterling), Phil Foden, Riyad Mahrez (85' Fernandinho), Gabriel Jesus (78' Jack Grealish). Coach: Pep Guardiola.
Goals: 73' Riyad Mahrez 0-1, 90', 90+1' Rodrygo 1-1, 2-1, 95' Karim Benzema 3-1 (p).
Referee: Daniele Orsato (ITA) Attendance: 61,416

FINAL

28.05.22 Stade de France, Saint-Denis: Liverpool FC – Real Madrid CF 0-1 (0-0)
Liverpool FC: Alisson, Virgil van Dijk, Andrew Robertson, Trent Alexander-Arnold, Ibrahima Konaté, Jordan Henderson (77' Naby Keïta), Thiago Alcântara (77' Roberto Firmino), Fabinho, Mohamed Salah, Sadio Mané, Luis Díaz (65' Diogo Jota). Coach: Jürgen Klopp.
Real Madrid CF: Thibaut Courtois, David Alaba, Dani Carvajal, Ferland Mendy, Éder Militão, Luka Modric (90' Dani Ceballos), Toni Kroos, Casemiro, Federico Valverde (86' Eduardo Camavinga), Karim Benzema, Vinícius Júnior (90+3' Rodrygo). Coach: Carlo Ancelotti.
Goal: 59' Vinícius Júnior 0-1.
Referee: Clément Turpin (FRA) Attendance: 75,000

UEFA CHAMPIONS LEAGUE
2022-2023

PRELIMINARY ROUND

Semi-Final Round

21.06.22   Vikingsvöllur, Reykjavík: SP La Fiorita – Inter Club d'Escaldes 1-2 (1-0)
SP La Fiorita: Gianluca Vivan, Andrea Grandoni, Manuel Miori, Moises Sanchez (71' Mattia
Anastasi), Lorenzo Fatica, Danilo Rinaldi, Armando Amati (90+2' Davide Vaierani), Nicola
Palazzi (71' David Tomassini), Andrea Grassi, Martin Lago (63' Sami Abouzziane), Francesco
Cinotti. Coach: Oscar Lasagni.
Inter Club d'Escaldes: Jesús Coca, Adrià Gallego, Chus Rubio (88' Jordi Rubio), Iván de
Nova, Raul Feher, Jordi Roca, Viti Martínez (69' Sergi Moreno), Víctor Casadesús (69' Ángel
Pérez), Aridai Cabrera (60' Ahmed Belhadji), Genís Soldevila (88' Ildefons Lima), Sascha.
Coach: Raul Obiols Rodriguez.
Goals: 45+2' Danilo Rinaldi 1-0, 55', 66' Genís Soldevila 1-1, 1-2.
Referee: Rohit Saggi (NOR)   Attendance: 39.

21.06.22   Vikingsvöllur, Reykjavík: FCI Levadia – Víkingur Reykjavík 1-6 (1-3)
FCI Levadia: Karl Vallner, Maximiliano Uggè, Milan Mitrovic, Artur Pikk (54' Liliu), Rasmus
Peetson, Marko Putincanin (74' Ilja Antonov), Zakaria Beglarishvili (74' Karl Oigus), Brent
Lepistu, Mark Roosnupp, Ernest Agyiri (81' Murad Velijev), Robert Kirss.
Coach: Vladimir Vassiljev.
Víkingur Reykjavík: Thórdur Ingason, Halldór Sigurdsson, Davíd Atlason (74' Karl
Gunnarsson), Oliver Ekroth, Kyle McLagan, Pablo Punyed (74' Logi Tómasson), Júlíus
Magnússon, Viktor Örlygur Andrason, Nikolaj Hansen (68' Ari Sigurpálsson), Erlingur
Agnarsson (68' Helgi Gudjónsson), Kristall Máni Ingason (78' Birnir Snær Ingason).
Coach: Arnar Gunnlaugsson.
Goals: 5' Zakaria Beglarishvili 1-0 (p), 10' Kyle McLagan 1-1, 27' Kristall Máni Ingason 1-2,
45+1' Halldór Sigurdsson 1-3, 49' Nikolaj Hansen 1-4, 71' Helgi Gudjónsson 1-5,
77' Júlíus Magnússon 1-6.
Referee: Tomasz Musial (POL)   Attendance: 725.

Final Round

24.06.22   Vikingsvöllur, Reykjavík: Inter Club d'Escaldes – Víkingur Reykjavík 0-1 (0-0)
Inter Club d'Escaldes: Jesús Coca, Adrià Gallego, Chus Rubio (86' Ildefons Lima), Iván de
Nova, Raul Feher, Jordi Rubio (65' Genís Soldevila), Jordi Roca, Ahmed Belhadji (75' Jordi
Betriu), Viti Martínez (86' Víctor Casadesús), Aridai Cabrera (75' Ángel Pérez), Sascha.
Coach: Raul Obiols Rodriguez.
Víkingur Reykjavík: Thórdur Ingason, Halldór Sigurdsson (55' Logi Tómasson), Davíd
Atlason (55' Karl Gunnarsson), Oliver Ekroth, Kyle McLagan, Pablo Punyed (67' Birnir Snær
Ingason), Júlíus Magnússon, Viktor Örlygur Andrason (80' Helgi Gudjónsson), Nikolaj
Hansen, Erlingur Agnarsson (67' Ari Sigurpálsson), Kristall Máni Ingason.
Coach: Arnar Gunnlaugsson.
Goal: Vikingur Reykjavik: 68' Kristall Máni Ingason 0-1.
Referee: Urs Schnyder (SUI)   Attendance: 925.

FIRST QUALIFYING ROUND

05.07.22   Vazgen Sargsyan anvan Hanrapetakan Marzadasht, Yerevan:
              Pyunik Erevan FC – CFR Cluj 0-0
Pyunik Erevan FC: David Yurchenko, Alexander González (90+3' Gevorg Najaryan), Anton
Bratkov, Sergiy Vakulenko, Mikhail Kovalenko, Juninho, Artak Dashyan, Renzo Zambrano
(90+3' Yuri Gareginyan), Eugeniu Cociuc (77' Hovhannes Harutyunyan), David Davidyan
(46' Uros Nenadovic), Yusuf Otubanjo (77' Nemanja Mladenovic). Coach: Eghishe Melikyan.
CFR Cluj: Cristian Balgradean, Camora, Denis Kolinger, Andrei Burca, Cristian Manea,
Ciprian Deac (90+1' Adrian Paun), Vito Hammershøy-Mistrati (64' Jefté Betancor), Nana
Adjei-Boateng (82' Mihai Bordeianu), Lovro Cvek, Roger Junio (82' Claudiu Petrila), Gabriel
Debeljuh (90+1' Marko Dugandzic). Coach: Dan Petrescu.
Referee: Bastian Dankert (GER)   Attendance: 8,000.

05.07.22   Eleda Stadion, Malmö: Malmö FF – Víkingur Reykjavík 3-2 (2-1)
Malmö FF: Johan Dahlin, Martin Olsson (71' Jonas Knudsen), Niklas Moisander (56' Felix
Beijmo), Lasse Nielsen, Dennis Hadzikadunic, Anders Christiansen (71' Sebastian Nanasi), Jo
Inge Berget, Sergio Peña, Erdal Rakip (80' Hugo Larsson), Veljko Birmancevic, Ola Toivonen
(71' Patriot Sejdiu). Coach: Milos Milojevic.
Víkingur Reykjavík: Thórdur Ingason, Halldór Sigurdsson, Oliver Ekroth, Logi Tómasson (57'
Davíd Atlason), Karl Gunnarsson, Pablo Punyed, Júlíus Magnússon, Viktor Örlygur Andrason,
Nikolaj Hansen (80' Helgi Gudjónsson), Erlingur Agnarsson (78' Ari Sigurpálsson), Kristall
Máni Ingason. Coach: Arnar Gunnlaugsson.
Goals: 16' Martin Olsson 1-0, 38' Kristall Máni Ingason 1-1, 42' Ola Toivonen 2-1,
84' Veljko Birmancevic 3-1, 90+3' Helgi Gudjónsson 3-2.
Referee: Dumitri Muntean (MOL)   Attendance: 11,830.
Sent off: 39' Kristall Máni Ingason.

05.07.22   Huvepharma Arena, Razgrad:
PFC Ludogorets Razgrad – FK Sutjeska Niksic 2-0 (0-0)
PFC Ludogorets Razgrad: Sergio Padt, Cicinho, Igor Plastun, Anton Nedyalkov, Olivier Verdon, Claude Gonçalves, Alex Santana, Dominik Yankov (79' Spas Delev), Pieros Sotiriou (84' Matías Tissera), Bernard Tekpetey (67' Cauly), Rick (84' Kiril Despodov).
Coach: Ante Simundza.
FK Sutjeska Niksic: Vladan Giljen, Nikola Stijepovic, Ilija Tucevic, Dragan Grivic, Adrijan Rudovic, Milos Drincic, Srdjan Krstovic, Novica Erakovic, Marko Matanovic (90+3' Milos Kalezic), Yulian Nenov (85' Igor Pajovic), Zakaria Al Harish (75' Tyrone Conraad).
Coach: Milija Savovic.
Goals: 74' Alex Santana 1-0, 90+1' Matías Tissera 2-0.
Referee: Vítor Ferreira (POR)   Attendance: 3,963.

05.07.22   Stadiumi Fadil Vokrri, Pristina: KF Ballkani – FK Zalgiris 1-1 (1-1)
KF Ballkani: Stivi Frashëri, Bajram Jashanica (79' Leonit Abazi), Astrit Thaqi, Armend Thaçi, Lumbardh Dellova, Edvin Kuc, Meriton Korenica (85' Dilivio Hoffman), Lindon Emërllahu, Nazmi Gripshi (72' Albion Rrahmani), Albin Berisha (72' Qendrim Zyba), Ermal Krasniqi.
Coach: Ilir Daja.
FK Zalgiris: Edvinas Gertmonas, Saulius Mikoliūnas, Mario Pavelic, Petar Mamic, Nemanja Ljubisavljevic, Nicolás Gorobsov, Oliver Buff (65' Marko Milickovic), Fabien Ourega, Francis Kyeremeh (86' Gustas Jarusevicius), Josip Tadic (65' Mathias Oyewusi), Renan Oliveira (81' Donatas Kazlauskas). Coach: Vladimir Cherubin.
Goals: 15' Nazmi Gripshi 1-0, 25' Oliver Buff 1-1.
Referee: Robert Harwey (IRL)   Attendance: 4,000.

KF Ballkani played their home match at Stadiumi Fadil Vokrri, Pristina, instead of their regular stadium Suva Reka City Stadium, Suhareka, which did not meet UEFA requirements.

05.07.22   Park Hall Stadium, Oswestry: The New Saints – Linfield FC 1-0 (0-0)
The New Saints: Connor Roberts, Chris Marriott, Keston Davies, Daniel Davies, Ryan Astles, Jon Routledge, Daniel Redmond (90+1' Ben Clack), Ryan Brobbel, Leo Smith, Declan McManus, Jordan Williams (76' Adrian Cieslewicz). Coach: Anthony Limbrick.
Linfield FC: Chris Johns, Matthew Clarke, Ben Hall, Sam Roscoe-Byrne, Danny Finlayson, Jamie Mulgrew (67' Kyle McClean), Chris Shields, Kirk Millar (73' Jordan Stewart), Stephen Fallon, Joel Cooper, Robbie McDaid (79' Chris McKee). Coach: David Healy.
Goal: 57' Ryan Brobbel 1-0.
Referee: Andrei Chivulete (ROM)   Attendance: 1,034.

05.07.22   Stadion Poznan, Poznan: Lech Poznan – Qarabag FK 1-0 (1-0)
Lech Poznan: Artur Rudko, Antonio Milic, Lubomir Satka, Pedro Rebocho, Joel Pereira, Jesper Karlström, Radoslaw Murawski (83' Alan Czerwinski), João Amaral (62' Filip Szymczak), Michal Skóras, Kristoffer Velde (62' Adriel Ba Loua), Mikael Ishak (80' Nika Kvekveskiri). Coach: John van den Brom.
Qarabag FK: Sahrudin Mahammadaliyev, Marko Vesovic, Maksim Medvedev, Qara Qarayev, Kevin Medina, Richard Almeyda (62' Marko Jankovic), Abdellah Zoubir, Kady (82' Owusu Kwabena), Elvin Cafarquliyev (82' Tural Bayramov), Leandro Andrade (62' Filip Ozobic), Ibrahima Wadji (62' Ramil Sheydaev). Coach: Qurban Qurbanov.
Goal: 41' Mikael Ishak 1-0.
Referee: José Luis Munuera (ESP)   Attendance: 25,118.

05.07.22   Tallaght Stadium, Dublin: Shamrock Rovers – Hibernians FC 3-0 (2-0)
Shamrock Rovers: Alan Mannus, Roberto Lopes, Sean Hoare, Lee Grace, Andy Lyons, Ronan Finn (81' Sean Gannon), Chris McCann, Gary O'Neill, Dylan Watts (81' Richie Towell), Rory Gaffney (85' Justin Ferizaj), Aaron Greene (67' Aidomo Emakhu). Coach: Stephen Bradley.
Hibernians FC: Ibrahim Koné, Joseph Zerafa (90' Lorenzo Fonseca), Rodolfo Soares, Gonzalo Llerena, Zachary Grech (90' Lucas Caruana), Gabriel Izquier, Dunstan Vella, Ali Diakité, Jurgen Degabriele, Thaylor Lubanzadio (81' Ayrton Attard), Gabriel Mensah (46' Terence Groothusen). Coach: Stefano Sanderra.
Goals: 25' Ronan Finn 1-0, 40' Dylan Watts 2-0, 78' Rory Gaffney 3-0.
Referee: Morten Krogh (DEN)   Attendance: 7,019.

05.07.22   Tose Proeski Arena, Skopje: KF Shkupi – Lincoln Red Imps 3-0 (2-0)
KF Shkupi: Kristijan Naumovski, Vladica Brdarovski, Gagi Margvelashvili, Faustin Senghor, Blerton Sheji, Freddy Álvarez, Queven, Mamadou Danfa (76' Aleks Zlatkov), Walid Hamidi (89' Pepi Georgiev), Sunday Adetunji, Renaldo Cephas (59' Melos Bajrami). Coach: Goce Sedloski.
Lincoln Red Imps: Dayle Coleing, Scott Wiseman, Nano, Bernardo Lopes, Roy Chipolina (76' Kian Ronan), Ethan Britto, Juampe Rico (46' Graeme Torrilla), Liam Walker, Mustapha Yahaya, Marco Rosa (65' Kike Gómez), Juanfri (78' Lee Casciaro). Coach: Raúl Castillo.
Goals: 11' Mamadou Danfa 1-0, 28' Sunday Adetunji 2-0, 62' Scott Wiseman 3-0 (og).
Referee: Sebastian Gishamer (AUT)   Attendance: 2,500.
Sent off: 54' Gagi Margvelashvili.

KF Shkupi played their home match at Tose Proeski Arena, Skopje, instead of their regular stadium Cair Stadium, Skopje, which did not meet UEFA requirements.

06.07.22   Ortaliq Stadion, Kostanay: Tobol Kostanay – Ferencvárosi TC 0-0
Tobol Kostanay: Aleksandr Mokin, Zarko Tomasevic, Sergiy Maliy, Aleksa Amanovic, Bagdat Kairov, Zoran Tosic, Rúben Brígido (64' Igor Sergeev), Askhat Tagybergen, Dusan Jovancic, Samat Zharynbetov (69' Serikzhan Muzhikov), Aybar Zhaksylykov (76' Miljan Vukadinovic). Coach: Milan Milanovic.
Ferencvárosi TC: Dénes Dibusz, Endre Botka (77' Henry Wingo), Adnan Kovacevic, Eldar Civic, Samy Mmaee, Bálint Vécsei (51' Anderson Esiti), Kristoffer Zachariassen (62' Marquinhos), Aïssa Laïdouni, Tokmac Nguen, Franck Boli (62' Fortune Bassey), Adama Traoré (I). Coach: Stanislav Cherchesov.
Referee: Dario Bel (CRO)   Attendance: 8,420.

06.07.22   Bolt Arena, Helsinki: HJK Helsinki – Rīgas Futbola skola 1-0 (1-0)
HJK Helsinki: Conor Hazard, Jukka Raitala, Miro Tenho, Murilo, Arttu Hoskonen, Matti Peltola, Pyry Soiri (84' Casper Terho), Manuel Martic (75' Përparim Hetemaj), Santeri Väänänen, Anthony Olusanya, Bojan Radulovic. Coach: Toni Koskela.
Rīgas Futbola skola: Vytautas Cerniauskas, Vitalijs Jagodinskis, Vladislavs Sorokins, Ziga Lipuscek, Artūrs Zjuzins (79' Ismael Diomandé), Tomislav Saric, Petr Mares, Stefan Panic, Kevin Friesenbichler (90+2' Renārs Varslavāns), Emerson Deocleciano, Andrej Ilic. Coach: Viktors Morozs.
Goal: 11' Manuel Martic 1-0.
Referee: Juxhin Xhaja (ALB)   Attendance: 3,874.

06.07.22   Aspmyra Stadion, Bodø: FK Bodø/Glimt – KÍ Klaksvík 3-0 (2-0)
FK Bodø/Glimt: Nikita Haikin, Marius Høibråten, Brede Moe (63' Japhet Sery), Brice
Wembangomo, Alfons Sampsted, Ulrik Saltnes, Amahl Pellegrino (46' Sondre Sørli), Hugo
Vetlesen (85' Anders Konradsen), Elias Hagen, Ola Solbakken (46' Joel Mvuka), Victor
Boniface (76' Runar Espejord). Coach: Kjetil Knutsen.
KÍ Klaksvík: Mathias Rosenørn, Heini Vatnsdal, Jesper Brinck, Patrick da Silva, Claes
Kronberg (73' Anders Holvad), René Joensen, Deni Pavlovic, Jákup Andreasen, Jóannes
Bjartalíd (90+2' Jóannes Danielsen), Mads Mikkelsen, Páll Klettskard (85' Árni
Frederiksberg). Coach: Mikkjal Thomassen.
Goals: 11', 31', 58' Victor Boniface 1-0, 2-0, 3-0 (p).
Referee: Mohammed Al-Hakim (SWE)   Attendance: 4,227.

06.07.22   Stade Jos Nosbaum, Dudelange: F91 Dudelange – KF Tiranë 1-0 (0-0)
F91 Dudelange: Lucas Fox, Manuel da Costa, Jules Diouf, Mehdi Kirch, Dejvid Sinani (82'
Hugo Antunes), Eliot Gashi (60' Sylvio Ouassiero), Filip Bojic (76' Vova), Aldin
Skenderovic, Charles Morren, Samir Hadji (60' Chris Stumpf), Mohcine Hassan Nader (82'
Ninte Junior). Coach: Fangueiro.
KF Tiranë: Visar Bekaj, Kristijan Tosevski, Marsel Ismajlgeci, Jocelin Behiratche, Filip
Najdovski, Albano Aleksi, Ennur Totre (85' Klevi Qefalija), Vesel Limaj, Taulant Seferi,
Devid (77' Florent Hasani), Redon Xhixha. Coach: Orges Shehi.
Goal: 71' Mohcine Hassan Nader 1-0.
Referee: Rohit Saggi (NOR)   Attendance: 1,555.
Sent off: 54' Mehdi Kirch, 68' Vesel Limaj.

06.07.22   Stadion pod Bijelim Brijegom, Mostar: Zrinjski Mostar – FC Sheriff Tiraspol 0-0
Zrinjski Mostar: Josip Condric, Mario Ticinovic (90+1' Matija Malekinusic), Almir Bekic (72'
Kerim Memija), Hrvoje Barisic, Marin Magdic, Josip Corluka, Ivan Jukic (71' Nikola
Mandic), Mario Cuze, Igor Savic (72' Damir Zlomislic), Nemanja Bilbija, Petar Sucic (46'
Karlo Kamenar). Coach: Sergej Jakirovic.
FC Sheriff Tiraspol: Razak Abalora, Patrick Kpozo, Stjepan Radeljic, Gaby Kiki, Renan
Guedes, Regi Lushkja, Abou Ouattara (78' Iyayi Atiemwen, 86' Keston Julien), Cédric
Badolo, Moussa Kyabou, Momo Yansané, Ibrahim Rasheed (74' Pernambuco).
Coach: Stjepan Tomas.
Referee: Fabio Maresca (ITA)   Attendance: 5,400.

06.07.22   Ljudski vrt, Maribor: NK Maribor – Shakhter Soligorsk 0-0
NK Maribor: Menno Bergsen, Martin Milec, Nemanja Mitrovic, Gregor Sikosek, Max Watson,
Jan Repas, Antoine Makoumbou, Nino Zugelj (67' Rok Kronaveter), Marko Bozic, Roko
Baturina (74' Rok Sirk), Ivan Brnic (74' Ignacio Guerrico). Coach: Radovan Karanovic.
Shakhter Soligorsk: Maksim Plotnikov, Sergey Politevich, Nikola Antic, Milos Satara, Roman
Yuzepchuk (46' Igor Ivanovic), Gleb Shevchenko, Valon Ahmedi, Ardit Krymi, Zaim
Divanovic (90+2' Nikita Korzun), Vitor Feijão, Dembo Darboe (85' Euloge Placca Fessou).
Coach: Sergey Tashuev.
Referee: Anastasios Papapetrou (GRE)   Attendance: 6,450.

06.07.22 Stadión Tehelné pole, Bratislava: Slovan Bratislava – Dinamo Batumi 0-0
Slovan Bratislava: Adrián Chovan, Guram Kashia, Vernon De Marco (58' Giorgi
Chakvetadze), Jurij Medvedev, Myenty Abena, Juraj Kucka (86' Dávid Holman), Jaba
Kankava, Vladimír Weiss (78' Aleksandar Cavric), Jaromír Zmrhal, Tigran Barseghyan (58'
Andre Green), Eric Ramírez (58' Iván Saponjic). Coach: Vladimir Weiss.
Dinamo Batumi: Lazare Kupatadze, Mamuka Kobakhidze, Oleksandr Azatskyi, Grigol
Chabradze, Irakli Azarov, Benjamin Teidi, Vladimer Manuchashvili, Irakli Bidzinashvili (44'
Giorgi Rekhviashvili), Sandro Altunashvili (86' Giorgi Navalovski), Zuriko Davitashvili (72'
Mate Vatsadze), Flamarion (72' Milán Rádin). Coach: George Geguchadze.
Referee: David Coote (ENG) Attendance: 10,589.
Sent off: 42' Mamuka Kobakhidze.

12.07.22 Slokas Stadionā, Jūrmala: Rīgas Futbola skola – HJK Helsinki 2-1 (0-0,2-1) (AET)
Rīgas Futbola skola: Pāvels Steinbors, Vitalijs Jagodinskis, Ziga Lipuscek, Jovan Vlalukin,
Artūrs Zjuzins (56' Kevin Friesenbichler), Tomislav Saric, Petr Mares, Stefan Panic,
Alfusainey Jatta, Emerson Deocleciano, Andrej Ilic (105' Elvis Stuglis).
Coach: Viktors Morozs.
HJK Helsinki: Conor Hazard, Jukka Raitala, Miro Tenho, Murilo, Arttu Hoskonen, Matti
Peltola (54' Santeri Hostikka), Përparim Hetemaj, Pyry Soiri (19' Anthony Olusanya, 76'
Fabian Serrarens), Santeri Väänänen, David Browne (100' Casper Terho), Bojan Radulovic.
Coach: Toni Koskela.
Goals: 48' Artūrs Zjuzins 1-0, 56' Stefan Panic 2-0, 75' Murilo 2-1.
Referee: David Fuxman (ISR) Attendance: 1,631

HJK Helsinki won after extra time on penalties (5:4).

*Penalties: Jagodinskis 1-0, Väänänen 1-1, Saric 2-1, Murilo 2-2, Panic missed, Radulovic 2-3,
Lipuscek 3-3, Serrarens 3-4, Mares 4-4, Terho 4-5.*

*Rīgas Futbola skola played their home match at Slokas Stadionā, Jūrmala, instead of their
regular stadium LNK Sports Parks, Riga, which did not meet UEFA requirements.*

12.07.22 Vilniaus LFF stadionas, Vilnius: FK Zalgiris – KF Ballkani 1-0 (0-0,0-0) (AET)
FK Zalgiris: Edvinas Gertmonas, Saulius Mikoliūnas (90+4' Joël Fey d'Or Bopesu), Mario
Pavelic, Petar Mamic, Nemanja Ljubisavljevic, Nicolás Gorobsov (90+4' Mantas Kuklys),
Oliver Buff (62' Mathias Oyewusi), Fabien Ourega (105' Josip Tadic), Francis Kyeremeh (62'
Gustas Jarusevicius), Marko Milickovic, Renan Oliveira (90' Donatas Kazlauskas).
Coach: Vladimir Cherubin.
KF Ballkani: Stivi Frashëri, Bajram Jashanica (107' Leonit Abazi), Astrit Thaqi, Armend
Thaçi, Lumbardh Dellova, Edvin Kuc (107' Lucas), Meriton Korenica, Lindon Emërllahu (94'
Qendrim Zyba), Nazmi Gripshi, Albin Berisha (56' Dilivio Hoffman, 119' Theophilus
Solomon), Ermal Krasniqi (94' Albion Rrahmani). Coach: Ilir Daja.
Goal: 97' Mathias Oyewusi 1-0.
Referee: Kristoffer Hagenes (NOR) Attendance: 3,542.

FK Zalgiris won after extra time.

71

12.07.22   Tofiq Bahramov adina Respublika stadionu, Baku:
Qarabag FK – Lech Poznan 5-1 (2-1)
Qarabag FK: Sahrudin Mahammadaliyev, Marko Vesovic (76' Abbas Hüseynov), Maksim
Medvedev, Kevin Medina, Richard Almeyda, Filip Ozobic (77' Owusu Kwabena), Abdellah
Zoubir, Kady, Elvin Cafarquliyev (76' Tural Bayramov), Marko Jankovic (83' Ismayil
Ibrahimli), Ibrahima Wadji (66' Ramil Sheydaev). Coach: Qurban Qurbanov.
Lech Poznan: Artur Rudko, Antonio Milic, Lubomír Satka, Pedro Rebocho (85' Barry
Douglas), Joel Pereira, Jesper Karlström (85' Nika Kvekveskiri), Radoslaw Murawski (85'
Filip Marchwinski), João Amaral (72' Georgiy Tsitaishvili), Michal Skóras (72' Filip
Szymczak), Kristoffer Velde, Mikael Ishak. Coach: John van den Brom.
Goals: 1' Kristoffer Velde 0-1, 14' Kady 1-1, 42' Filip Ozobic 2-1, 56' Kevin Medina 3-1,
74' Kady 4-1, 77' Abbas Hüseynov 5-1.
Referee: Andrew Madley (ENG)   Attendance: 27,652.

12.07.22   Victoria Stadium, Gibraltar: Lincoln Red Imps – KF Shkupi 2-0 (1-0)
Lincoln Red Imps: Dayle Coleing, Scott Wiseman, Nano, Bernardo Lopes, Jesús Toscano (68'
Ethan Britto), Jack Sergeant, Liam Walker, Marco Rosa (46' Kian Ronan), Graeme Torrilla,
Juanfri (78' Juampe Rico), Kike Gómez (61' Lee Casciaro). Coach: Raúl Castillo.
KF Shkupi: Kristijan Naumovski, Vladica Brdarovski, Dzhelil Abdula, Faustin Senghor,
Blerton Sheji, Freddy Álvarez, Queven, Aleks Zlatkov (46' Kristijan Trapanovski), Mamadou
Danfa (90+1' Melos Bajrami), Sunday Adetunji, Renaldo Cephas (65' Antonio Kalanoski).
Coach: Goce Sedloski.
Goals: 32' Juanfri 1-0, 69' Lee Casciaro 2-0.
Referee: Filip Glova (SVK)   Attendance: 896.

12.07.22   Stadionul Zimbru, Chisinau: FC Sheriff Tiraspol – Zrinjski Mostar 1-0 (1-0)
FC Sheriff Tiraspol: Razak Abalora, Patrick Kpozo, Stjepan Radeljic, Gaby Kiki, Renan
Guedes, Regi Lushkja (90+3' Serafim Cojocari), Abou Ouattara (85' Stefanos Evangelou),
Cédric Badolo, Moussa Kyabou, Momo Yansané, Ibrahim Rasheed (76' Pernambuco).
Coach: Stjepan Tomas.
Zrinjski Mostar: Josip Condric, Mario Ticinovic (73' Ivan Jukic), Almir Bekic (46' Kerim
Memija), Hrvoje Barisic, Marin Magdic, Damir Zlomislic (46' Karlo Kamenar), Josip Corluka,
Mario Cuze (46' Nikola Mandic), Igor Savic, Niko Jankovic (85' Franko Sabljic), Nemanja
Bilbija. Coach: Sergej Jakirovic.
Goal: 22' Igor Savic 1-0 (og).
Referee: Radu Petrescu (ROM)   Attendance: 4,242.

*FC Sheriff Tiraspol played their home match at Stadionul Zimbru, Chisinau, instead of their
regular stadium Sheriff Stadium, Tiraspol.*

12.07.22   Air Albania Stadium, Tirana: KF Tiranë – F91 Dudelange 1-2 (0-0)
KF Tiranë: Visar Bekaj, Kristijan Tosevski (59' Florjan Pergjoni), Marsel Ismajlgeci, Jocelin Behiratche, Filip Najdovski, Ardit Hila (58' Klevi Qefalija), Albano Aleksi, Ennur Totre (63' Florent Hasani), Taulant Seferi, Devid, Redon Xhixha. Coach: Orges Shehi.
F91 Dudelange: Lucas Fox, Manuel da Costa, Jules Diouf, Chris Stumpf (85' Edis Agovic), Dejvid Sinani, Eliot Gashi (49' Sylvio Ouassiero), Filip Bojic (73' Vova), Aldin Skenderovic (73' Vincent Decker), Charles Morren, Samir Hadji, Mohcine Hassan Nader (85' Ninte Junior). Coach: Fangueiro.
Goals: 49' Filip Bojic 0-1, 61' Dejvid Sinani 0-2, 78' Redon Xhixha 1-2.
Referee: César Soto Grado (ESP)   Attendance: 6,000.

Fangueiro was sent to the stands (78').

KF Tiranë played their home match at Air Albania Stadium, Tirana, instead of their regular stadium Selman Stërmasi Stadium, Tirana, which did not meet UEFA requirements.

12.07.22   MFA Centenary Stadium, Ta'Qali: Hibernians FC – Shamrock Rovers 0-0
Hibernians FC: Ibrahim Koné, Rodolfo Soares (84' Lorenzo Fonseca), Gonzalo Llerena (84' Andreas Bækskov Laursen), Zachary Grech (76' Gabriel Mensah), Gabriel Izquier (68' Joseph Zerafa), Dunstan Vella, Jake Grech, Ali Diakité, Jurgen Degabriele, Terence Groothusen, Ayrton Attard (68' Thaylor Lubanzadio). Coach: Andrea Pisanu.
Shamrock Rovers: Alan Mannus, Roberto Lopes, Sean Hoare, Lee Grace, Andy Lyons, Ronan Finn (77' Sean Gannon), Chris McCann (77' Sean Kavanagh), Gary O'Neill, Dylan Watts (77' Jack Byrne), Rory Gaffney (81' Aidomo Emakhu), Aaron Greene (59' Richie Towell). Coach: Stephen Bradley.
Referee: Manfredas Lukjancukas (LTU)   Attendance: 979.

Hibernians FC played their home match at MFA Centenary Stadium, Ta'Qali, instead of their regular stadium Hibernians Stadium, Paola, which did not meet UEFA requirements.

12.07.22   DG Arena, Podgorica: FK Sutjeska Niksic – PFC Ludogorets Razgrad 0-1 (0-0)
FK Sutjeska Niksic: Vladan Giljen, Nikola Stijepovic, Dragan Grivic, Adrijan Rudovic, Milos Drincic, Srdjan Krstovic (74' Ilija Tucevic), Novica Erakovic, Marko Matanovic (80' Nikola Djurkovic), Yulian Nenov (79' Fahd Saad Mohamed), Zakaria Al Harish (80' Dusan Vukovic), Vuk Strikovic (65' Tyrone Conraad). Coach: Milija Savovic.
PFC Ludogorets Razgrad: Sergio Padt, Igor Plastun, Anton Nedyalkov (90' Danny Gruper), Olivier Verdon, Zan Karnicnik, Cauly, Alex Santana, Show (74' Dominik Yankov), Spas Delev (65' Rick), Pieros Sotiriou (74' Igor Thiago), Kiril Despodov (66' Bernard Tekpetey). Coach: Ante Simundza.
Goal: 53' Pieros Sotiriou 0-1.
Referee: Gergö Bogár (HUN)   Attendance: 1,000.

FK Sutjeska Niksic played their home match at DG Arena, Podgorica, instead of their regular stadium Gradski stadion, Niksic, which did not meet UEFA requirements.

12.07.22   Víkingsvöllur, Reykjavík: Víkingur Reykjavík – Malmö FF 3-3 (1-2)
Víkingur Reykjavík: Ingvar Jónsson, Halldór Sigurdsson (44' Davíd Atlason), Oliver Ekroth, Logi Tómasson (46' Ari Sigurpálsson), Karl Gunnarsson, Pablo Punyed, Júlíus Magnússon, Viktor Örlygur Andrason, Nikolaj Hansen, Erlingur Agnarsson, Helgi Gudjónsson (64' Birnir Snær Ingason). Coach: Arnar Gunnlaugsson.
Malmö FF: Johan Dahlin, Martin Olsson, Niklas Moisander, Lasse Nielsen (46' Dennis Hadzikadunic), Felix Beijmo, Anders Christiansen (62' Ola Toivonen), Jo Inge Berget, Sergio Peña, Veljko Birmancevic (87' Eric Larsson), Hugo Larsson, Isaac Kiese Thelin (62' Erdal Rakip). Coach: Milos Milojevic.
Goals: 15' Karl Gunnarsson 1-0, 34' Veljko Birmancevic 1-1, 44' Felix Beijmo 1-2, 47' Anders Christiansen 1-3, 56' Nikolaj Hansen 2-3, 74' Karl Gunnarsson 3-3.
Referee: John Beaton (SCO)   Attendance: 1,080.

13.07.22   Yeni Sakarya Atatürk Stadyumu, Adapazari (TUR):
Shakhter Soligorsk – NK Maribor 0-2 (0-1)
Shakhter Soligorsk: Maksim Plotnikov, Nikola Antic, Milos Satara, Roman Yuzepchuk, Gleb Shevchenko (46' Euloge Placca Fessou), Valon Ahmedi (59' Nikita Korzun), Igor Ivanovic, Ardit Krymi, Zaim Divanovic, Vitor Feijão (61' Maksim Skavysh), Dembo Darboe. Coach: Sergey Tashuev.
NK Maribor: Menno Bergsen, Martin Milec, Nemanja Mitrovic, Gregor Sikosek, Max Watson, Jan Repas, Antoine Makoumbou (86' Aljaz Antolin), Nino Zugelj (63' Ignacio Guerrico), Marko Bozic (86' Aleks Pihler), Roko Baturina (71' Rok Sirk), Ivan Brnic (63' Rok Kronaveter). Coach: Radovan Karanovic.
Goals: 12', 56' Roko Baturina 0-1, 0-2.
Referee: Enea Jorgji (ALB)   Attendance: 0

Due to the country's involvement in the Russian invasion of Ukraine, Belarusian teams were required to play their home matches at neutral venues and behind closed doors until further notice.

13.07.22   Vid Djúpumýrar, Klaksvík: KÍ Klaksvík – FK Bodø/Glimt 3-1 (2-0)
KÍ Klaksvík: Mathias Rosenørn, Heini Vatnsdal, Jesper Brinck, Patrick da Silva, Claes Kronberg (76' Anders Holvad), René Joensen, Deni Pavlovic, Jákup Andreasen, Jóannes Bjartalíd, Mads Mikkelsen, Páll Klettskard. Coach: Mikkjal Thomassen.
FK Bodø/Glimt: Nikita Haikin, Marius Høibråten, Brice Wembangomo, Alfons Sampsted, Isak Amundsen, Ulrik Saltnes, Hugo Vetlesen, Elias Hagen, Joel Mvuka, Gilbert Koomson, Victor Boniface. Coach: Kjetil Knutsen.
Goals: 12' Mads Mikkelsen 1-0, 20' Jákup Andreasen 2-0, 55' Victor Boniface 2-1 (p), 85' Jákup Andreasen 3-1.
Referee: Horatiu Fesnic (ROM)   Attendance: 883.

Match was originally scheduled for 12th July 2022, but was rescheduled to the following day, as FK Bodø/Glimt's flight to the Faroe Islands arrived late due to adverse weather conditions.

13.07.22   Batumi Arena, Batumi: Dinamo Batumi – Slovan Bratislava 1-2 (0-0,0-0) (AET)
Dinamo Batumi: Lazare Kupatadze, Giorgi Rekhviashvili, Oleksandr Azatskyi, Grigol
Chabradze (85' Mate Vatsadze), Irakli Azarov (105' Giorgi Navalovski), Benjamin Teidi (85'
Guga Palavandishvili), Vladimer Manuchashvili, Irakli Bidzinashvili (62' Jaba Jigauri), Sandro
Altunashvili (113' Milán Rádin), Zuriko Davitashvili, Flamarion. Coach: George Geguchadze.
Slovan Bratislava: Adrián Chovan, Guram Kashia, Lukás Pauschek (105' Eric Ramírez), Jurij
Medvedev (114' Andre Green), Myenty Abena, Juraj Kucka (114' Alen Mustafic), Jaba
Kankava, Vladimír Weiss, Dávid Holman (46' Iván Saponjic), Giorgi Chakvetadze (62' Tigran
Barseghyan), Aleksandar Cavric (67' Jaromír Zmrhal). Coach: Vladimir Weiss.
Goals: 104' Zuriko Davitashvili 1-0, 115' Tigran Barseghyan 1-1, 120+3' Vladimír Weiss 1-2.
Referee: António Nobre (POR)   Attendance: 20,022.

Slovan Bratislava won after extra time.

13.07.22   Groupama Aréna, Budapest: Ferencvárosi TC – Tobol Kostanay 5-1 (3-1)
Ferencvárosi TC: Dénes Dibusz, Adnan Kovacevic (83' Mats Knoester), Eldar Civic, Henry
Wingo, Samy Mmaee, Anderson Esiti (75' Stjepan Loncar), Kristoffer Zachariassen (83'
Xavier Mercier), Aïssa Laïdouni, Tokmac Nguen (68' Carlos Auzqui), Franck Boli (69'
Fortune Bassey), Adama Traoré (I). Coach: Stanislav Cherchesov.
Tobol Kostanay: Aleksandr Mokin, Zarko Tomasevic, Sergiy Maliy, Aleksa Amanovic,
Bagdat Kairov, Zoran Tosic (78' Aybar Zhaksylykov), Rúben Brígido (75' Miljan
Vukadinovic), Askhat Tagybergen, Dusan Jovancic, Samat Zharynbetov (68' Serikzhan
Muzhikov), Igor Sergeev (75' Serge Deblé). Coach: Milan Milanovic.
Goals: 4', 17' Adama Traoré 1-0, 2-0, 21' Aïssa Laïdouni 3-0, 23' Igor Sergeev 3-1,
74', 90+1' Fortune Bassey 4-1, 5-1.
Referee: Krzysztof Jakubik (POL)   Attendance: 17,347.
Sent off: 81' Serikzhan Muzhikov.

13.07.22   Stadionul Dr. Constantin Radulescu, Cluj-Napoca:
          CFR Cluj – Pyunik Erevan FC 2-2 (1-0,1-1) (AET)
CFR Cluj: Cristian Balgradean, Camora, Daniel Graovac, Andrei Burca, Cristian Manea,
Ciprian Deac (114' Karlo Muhar), Adrian Paun (71' Claudiu Petrila), Nana Adjei-Boateng
(114' Yuri Matias), Lovro Cvek (87' Mihai Bordeianu), Roger Junio (96' Emmanuel Damoah
Yeboah), Gabriel Debeljuh (87' Marko Dugandzic). Coach: Dan Petrescu.
Pyunik Erevan FC: David Yurchenko, Zoran Gajic, Alexander González (64' Nemanja
Mladenovic), Sergiy Vakulenko (90+2' Gevorg Najaryan), Mikhail Kovalenko, Juninho (103'
Artur Avagyan), Artak Dashyan, Renzo Zambrano (64' Hovhannes Harutyunyan), Eugeniu
Cociuc, Yusuf Otubanjo (85' David Davidyan), Uros Nenadovic (46' Luka Juricic).
Coach: Eghishe Melikyan.
Goals: 6' Nana Adjei-Boateng 1-0, 89' Zoran Gajic 1-1, 94' Claudiu Petrila 2-1,
119' Zoran Gajic 2-2.
Referee: Michael Fabbri (ITA)   Attendance: 7,017.

Pyunik Erevan FC won after extra time on penalties (4:3).

Penalties: Dudandzic 1-0, Cociuc 1-1, Petrila missed, Dashyan 1-2, Burca 2-2,
*   Harutyunyan 2-3, Muhar 3-3, Avagyan 3-4, Camora missed.*

75

13.07.22   Windsor Park, Belfast: Linfield FC – The New Saints 2-0 (0-0,1-0) (AET)
Linfield FC: Chris Johns, Matthew Clarke, Ben Hall (78' Jamie Mulgrew), Sam Roscoe-Byrne, Danny Finlayson (67' Chris McKee), Chris Shields, Kirk Millar (100' Conor Pepper), Stephen Fallon (100' Cammy Palmer), Joel Cooper, Kyle McClean (67' Jordan Stewart), Robbie McDaid (78' Ethan Devine). Coach: David Healy.
The New Saints: Connor Roberts, Chris Marriott, Keston Davies (111' Blaine Hudson), Daniel Davies (83' Josh Pask), Ryan Astles, Jon Routledge, Daniel Redmond (68' Ben Clack), Ryan Brobbel, Leo Smith (105' Joshua Daniels), Declan McManus, Jordan Williams (78' Adrian Cieslewicz). Coach: Anthony Limbrick.
Goals: 90+4' Jamie Mulgrew 1-0, 95' Ethan Devine 2-0.
Referee: Duje Strukan (CRO)   Attendance: 2,971.

Linfield FC won after extra time.

SECOND QUALIFYING ROUND

(Champions Path)

19.07.22   Tofiq Bahramov adina Republika stadionu, Baku:
           Qarabag FK – FC Zürich 3-2 (2-0)
Qarabag FK: Sahrudin Mahammadaliyev, Marko Vesovic (78' Abbas Hüseynov), Maksim Medvedev, Kevin Medina, Richard Almeyda, Filip Ozobic (59' Ramil Sheydaev), Abdellah Zoubir, Kady, Elvin Cafarquliyev (71' Tural Bayramov), Marko Jankovic (71' Ismayil Ibrahimli), Ibrahima Wadji (78' Owusu Kwabena). Coach: Qurban Qurbanov.
FC Zürich: Yanick Brecher, Marc Hornschuh (46' Cheick Conde), Nikola Boranijasevic, Fidan Aliti, Mirlind Kryeziu, Adrián Guerrero, Lindrit Kamberi, Blerim Dzemaili (75' Ole Selnæs), Antonio Marchesano (76' Bledian Krasniqi), Fabian Rohner (76' Aiyegun Tosin), Wilfried Gnonto (90' Jonathan Okita). Coach: Franco Foda.
Goals: 17' Kady 1-0, 36' Ibrahima Wadji 2-0, 65' Lindrit Kamberi 2-1, 66' Ibrahima Wadji 3-1, 85' Mirlind Kryeziu 3-2 (p).
Referee: Irfan Peljto (BIH)   Attendance: 30,782.

19.07.22   Vilniaus LFF stadionas, Vilnius: FK Zalgiris – Malmö FF 1-0 (0-0)
FK Zalgiris: Edvinas Gertmonas, Mario Pavelic, Petar Mamic, Joël Fey d'Or Bopesu, Nemanja Ljubisavljevic, Nicolás Gorobsov, Oliver Buff (82' Mantas Kuklys), Fabien Ourega (73' Gustas Jarusevicius), Marko Milickovic (90+5' Josip Tadic), Renan Oliveira (82' Donatas Kazlauskas), Mathias Oyewusi (73' Francis Kyeremeh). Coach: Vladimir Cherubin.
Malmö FF: Johan Dahlin, Martin Olsson (74' Niklas Moisander), Lasse Nielsen, Dennis Hadzikadunic, Felix Beijmo (70' Eric Larsson), Anders Christiansen (70' Ola Toivonen), Jo Inge Berget, Sergio Peña (70' Hugo Larsson), Veljko Birmancevic (46' Moustafa Zeidan), Mahamé Siby, Isaac Kiese Thelin. Coach: Milos Milojevic.
Goal: 49' Fabien Ourega 1-0.
Referee: Georgi Kabakov (BUL)   Attendance: 4,918.

19.07.22   Vazgen Sargsyan anvan Hanrapetakan Marzadasht, Yerevan:
Pyunik Erevan FC – F91 Dudelange 0-1 (0-0)
Pyunik Erevan FC: David Yurchenko, Zoran Gajic, Alexander González (84' Gevorg
Najaryan), Mikhail Kovalenko, Juninho, Artak Dashyan, Eugeniu Cociuc (84' André
Mensalão), Hovhannes Harutyunyan (64' Renzo Zambrano), David Davidyan (74' Nemanja
Mladenovic), Yusuf Otubanjo, Luka Juricic (64' Uros Nenadovic). Coach: Eghishe Melikyan.
F91 Dudelange: Lucas Fox, Manuel da Costa, Jules Diouf, Mehdi Kirch, Sylvio Ouassiero (79'
Chris Stumpf), Dejvid Sinani (85' Bruno Frere), Filip Bojic (79' Edis Agovic), Aldin
Skenderovic, Charles Morren, Samir Hadji, Mohcine Hassan Nader (90+1' Ninte Junior).
Coach: Fangueiro.
Goal: 72' Samir Hadji 0-1 (p).
Referee: Craig Pawson (ENG)   Attendance: 9,000.

19.07.22   Huvepharma Arena, Razgrad:
PFC Ludogorets Razgrad – Shamrock Rovers 3-0 (2-0)
PFC Ludogorets Razgrad: Sergio Padt, Cicinho, Igor Plastun, Anton Nedyalkov, Olivier
Verdon, Cauly (89' Igor Thiago), Alex Santana, Show, Pieros Sotiriou (89' Matías Tissera),
Bernard Tekpetey (71' Kiril Despodov), Rick (78' Spas Delev). Coach: Ante Simundza.
Shamrock Rovers: Alan Mannus, Roberto Lopes, Sean Hoare, Lee Grace, Andy Lyons, Ronan
Finn (76' Sean Gannon), Chris McCann, Richie Towell (78' Sean Kavanagh), Gary O'Neill,
Dylan Watts (61' Graham Burke), Rory Gaffney. Coach: Stephen Bradley.
Goals: 26', 35' Pieros Sotiriou 1-0, 2-0, 90+4' Igor Thiago 3-0.
Referee: João Pedro Pinheiro (POR)   Attendance: 4,983.

19.07.22   Windsor Park, Belfast: Linfield FC – FK Bodø/Glimt 1-0 (0-0)
Linfield FC: Chris Johns, Matthew Clarke, Ben Hall, Sam Roscoe-Byrne, Danny Finlayson,
Jamie Mulgrew (64' Kyle McClean), Chris Shields, Kirk Millar, Stephen Fallon, Robbie
McDaid (64' Eetu Vertainen), Jordan Stewart (89' Niall Quinn). Coach: David Healy.
FK Bodø/Glimt: Nikita Haikin, Marius Høibråten, Brice Wembangomo, Alfons Sampsted, Isak
Amundsen, Ulrik Saltnes, Hugo Vetlesen, Elias Hagen (86' Anders Konradsen), Joel Mvuka
(86' Gilbert Koomson), Runar Espejord (66' Victor Boniface), Sondre Sørli (66' Amahl
Pellegrino). Coach: Kjetil Knutsen.
Goal: 83' Kirk Millar 1-0.
Referee: Andris Treimanis (LAT)   Attendance: 3,168.

19.07.22   Stadion Maksimir, Zagreb: Dinamo Zagreb – KF Shkupi 2-2 (1-1)
Dinamo Zagreb: Dominik Livakovic, Dino Peric, Sadegh Moharrami (77' Stefan Ristovski),
Josip Sutalo (17' Kévin Théophile-Catherine), Arijan Ademi, Josip Misic (64' Martin
Baturina), Luka Ivanusec, Robert Ljubicic, Josip Drmic (64' Mislav Orsic), Bruno Petkovic,
Dario Spikic (46' Luka Menalo). Coach: Ante Cacic.
KF Shkupi: Kristijan Naumovski, Vladica Brdarovski, Dzhelil Abdula, Gagi Margvelashvili,
Faustin Senghor, Blerton Sheji (69' Angelce Timovski), Freddy Álvarez (87' Renaldo
Cephas), Queven, Mamadou Danfa (78' Kristijan Trapanovski), Walid Hamidi (69' Pepi
Georgiev), Sunday Adetunji (87' Ali Adem). Coach: Goce Sedloski.
Goals: 25' Queven 0-1, 44' Arijan Ademi 1-1, 86' Bruno Petkovic 2-1,
89' Renaldo Cephas 2-2.
Referee: Radu Petrescu (ROM)   Attendance: 7,912.

20.07.22   Bolt Arena, Helsinki: HJK Helsinki – Viktoria Plzen 1-2 (0-1)
HJK Helsinki: Conor Hazard, Jukka Raitala, Miro Tenho (72' Matti Peltola), Murilo (79' Pyry Soiri), Arttu Hoskonen, Përparim Hetemaj (79' Johannes Yli-Kokko), Santeri Väänänen, David Browne, Santeri Hostikka (71' Nassim Boujellab), Bojan Radulovic, Malik Abubakari. Coach: Toni Koskela.
Viktoria Plzen: Jindrich Stanek, Radim Rezník, Lukás Hejda, Ludek Pernica, Milan Havel, Jan Kopic (85' Libor Holík), Jan Sýkora (85' Kristi Qose), Jhon Mosquera, Lukás Kalvach, Pavel Bucha, Tomás Chorý (81' René Dedic). Coach: Michal Bílek.
Goals: 6' Tomás Chorý 0-1 (p), 50' Bojan Radulovic 1-1, 57' Jan Kopic 1-2.
Referee: Nikola Dabanovic (MNE)   Attendance: 5,236.

20.07.22   Sammy Ofer Stadium, Haifa: Maccabi Haifa – Olympiakos Piraeus 1-1 (0-1)
Maccabi Haifa: Josh Cohen, Daniel Sundgren, Bogdan Planic, Shon Goldberg, Pierre Cornud (79' Sun Menachem), Tjaronn Chery, Ali Muhammad, Neta Lavi (61' Mohammad Abu Fani), Dolev Haziza, Omer Atzili (50' Nikita Rukavytsya), Din David (60' Frantzdy Pierrot). Coach: Barak Bakhar.
Olympiakos Piraeus: Tomás Vaclík, Kostas Manolas, Sime Vrsaljko (81' Sokratis Papastathopoulos), Pape Cissé, Oleg Reabciuk, Yann M'Vila (72' Andreas Bouchalakis), Georgios Masouras (81' Pipa Ávila), Mamadou Kané, Aguibou Camara (46' Mady Camara), Tiquinho Soares, Philip Zinckernagel (46' Aboubakar Kamara). Coach: Pedro Martins.
Goals: 7' Philip Zinckernagel 0-1, 90+2' Dolev Haziza 1-1.
Referee: Sascha Stegemann (GER)   Attendance: 29.654.

20.07.22   Groupama Aréna, Budapest: Ferencvárosi TC – Slovan Bratislava 1-2 (0-0)
Ferencvárosi TC: Dénes Dibusz, Adnan Kovacevic, Eldar Civic, Henry Wingo, Samy Mmaee, Anderson Esiti, Kristoffer Zachariassen, Aïssa Laïdouni (72' Xavier Mercier), Tokmac Nguen (80' Carlos Auzqui), Franck Boli (72' Fortune Bassey), Adama Traoré (I) (57' Stjepan Loncar). Coach: Stanislav Cherchesov.
Slovan Bratislava: Adrián Chovan, Guram Kashia, Lukás Pauschek (73' Aleksandar Cavric), Vernon De Marco, Jurij Medvedev, Myenty Abena, Juraj Kucka (90+3' Dávid Holman), Jaba Kankava, Vladimír Weiss (73' Giorgi Chakvetadze), Tigran Barseghyan (90+3' Uche Agbo), Iván Saponjic (69' Eric Ramírez). Coach: Vladimir Weiss.
Goals: 70' Kristoffer Zachariassen 1-0, 81' Guram Kashia 1-1, 86' Tigran Barseghyan 1-2
Referee: Ricardo de Burgos Bengoetxea (ESP)   Attendance: 20,459.

20.07.22   Ljudski vrt, Maribor: NK Maribor – FC Sheriff Tiraspol 0-0
NK Maribor: Menno Bergsen, Martin Milec, Nemanja Mitrovic, Gregor Sikosek, Max Watson, Aleks Pihler (67' Aljaz Antolin), Jan Repas, Nino Zugelj (82' Rok Kronaveter), Danijel Sturm (82' Ignacio Guerrico), Roko Baturina, Ivan Brnic. Coach: Radovan Karanovic.
FC Sheriff Tiraspol: Razak Abalora, Patrick Kpozo, Stjepan Radeljic, Gaby Kiki, Renan Guedes, Regi Lushkja, Cédric Badolo, Moussa Kyabou, Momo Yansané (65' Kay Tejan), Pernambuco, Ibrahim Rasheed (77' Abou Ouattara). Coach: Stjepan Tomas.
Referee: Harald Lechner (AUT)   Attendance: 7,150.

26.07.22 Doosan Arena, Plzen: Viktoria Plzen – HJK Helsinki 5-0 (3-0)
Viktoria Plzen: Jindrich Stanek, Radim Rezník (46' Libor Holík), Lukás Hejda (63' Filip Kasa), Ludek Pernica, Milan Havel, Jan Kopic (77' Matej Trusa), Jan Sýkora, Jhon Mosquera (70' Václav Pilar), Lukás Kalvach, Pavel Bucha, Tomás Chorý (63' Jan Kliment). Coach: Michal Bílek.
HJK Helsinki: Conor Hazard, Jukka Raitala, Miro Tenho, Murilo (58' Pyry Soiri), Arttu Hoskonen, Matti Peltola (72' Johannes Yli-Kokko), Pĕrparim Hetemaj, David Browne, Santeri Hostikka (81' Casper Terho), Bojan Radulovic (46' Paulus Arajuuri), Malik Abubakari (58' Fabian Serrarens). Coach: Toni Koskela.
Goals: 11' Ludek Pernica 1-0, 21' Jan Sýkora 2-0, 31' Lukás Hejda 3-0, 73' Jan Sýkora 4-0, 84' Jan Kliment 5-0.
Referee: Aleksandar Stavrev (MKD)   Attendance: 10,810.

26.07.22 Stadionul Zimbru, Chisinau: FC Sheriff Tiraspol – NK Maribor 1-0 (0-0)
FC Sheriff Tiraspol: Razak Abalora, Patrick Kpozo, Stjepan Radeljic, Gaby Kiki, Renan Guedes, Regi Lushkja (90+3' Stefanos Evangelou), Cédric Badolo, Moussa Kyabou, Kay Tejan (85' Momo Yansané), Pernambuco (69' Abou Ouattara), Ibrahim Rasheed. Coach: Stjepan Tomas.
NK Maribor: Menno Bergsen, Nemanja Mitrovic, Gregor Sikosek, Max Watson (90+2' Danijel Sturm), Sven Karic, Jan Repas, Nino Zugelj (45' Ignacio Guerrico, 90+2' Zan Vipotnik), Aljaz Antolin (73' Luka Uskokovic), Rok Sirk (73' Rok Kronaveter), Roko Baturina, Ivan Brnic. Coach: Radovan Karanovic.
Goal: 88' Momo Yansané 1-0.
Referee: Tamás Bognár (HUN)   Attendance: 6,738.

FC Sheriff Tiraspol played their home match at Stadionul Zimbru, Chisinau, instead of their regular stadium Sheriff Stadium, Tiraspol, due to Transnistria's involvement in the Russian invasion of Ukraine.

26.07.22 Stade Jos Nosbaum, Dudelange: F91 Dudelange – Pyunik Erevan FC 1-4 (1-1)
F91 Dudelange: Lucas Fox, Manuel da Costa, Jules Diouf, Mehdi Kirch (82' Chris Stumpf), Sylvio Ouassiero (90' Ninte Junior), Dejvid Sinani, Filip Bojic (60' Vova), Aldin Skenderovic (81' Edis Agovic), Charles Morren (90' Bruno Frere), Samir Hadji, Mohcine Hassan Nader. Coach: Fangueiro.
Pyunik Erevan FC: David Yurchenko, Zoran Gajic, Mikhail Kovalenko, Juninho, Artak Dashyan, André Mensalão (46' Eugeniu Cociuc), Renzo Zambrano (77' Yuri Gareginyan), Hovhannes Harutyunyan, David Davidyan (67' Alexander González), Yusuf Otubanjo (87' Gevorg Najaryan), Uros Nenadovic (46' Luka Juricic). Coach: Eghishe Melikyan.
Goals: 21' Mohcine Hassan Nader 1-0, 24' Juninho 1-1, 53' Luka Juricic 1-2, 76' Yusuf Otubanjo 1-3, 85' Luka Juricic 1-4.
Referee: José Luis Munuera Montero (ESP)   Attendance: 1,495.

26.07.22   Tose Proeski Arena, Skopje: KF Shkupi – Dinamo Zagreb 0-1 (0-0)
KF Shkupi: Kristijan Naumovski, Vladica Brdarovski (83' Kristijan Trapanovski), Dzhelil
Abdula (60' Ali Adem), Gagi Margvelashvili, Faustin Senghor, Blerton Sheji, Freddy Álvarez,
Queven, Walid Hamidi (38' Pepi Georgiev), Sunday Adetunji, Renaldo Cephas.
Coach: Goce Sedloski.
Dinamo Zagreb: Dominik Livakovic, Stefan Ristovski (90+3' Sadegh Moharrami), Dino Peric,
Rasmus Lauritsen, Arijan Ademi (80' Martin Baturina), Josip Misic, Luka Ivanusec, Robert
Ljubicic, Mislav Orsic (90+6' Amer Gojak), Bruno Petkovic, Dario Spikic (46' Luka Menalo).
Coach: Ante Cacic.
Goal: 47' Arijan Ademi 0-1.
Referee: Jakob Kehlet (DEN)   Attendance: 12,500.

*KF Shkupi played their home match at Tose Proeski Arena, Skopje, instead of their regular
stadium Cair Stadium, Skopje, which did not meet UEFA requirements.*

26.07.22   Tallaght Stadium, Dublin: Shamrock Rovers – PFC Ludogorets Razgrad 2-1 (1-0)
Shamrock Rovers: Alan Mannus, Sean Gannon, Sean Hoare, Lee Grace, Andy Lyons, Ronan
Finn (71' Neil Farrugia), Chris McCann (83' Justin Ferizaj), Richie Towell (78' Aidomo
Emakhu), Gary O'Neill (71' Rory Gaffney), Aaron Greene, Graham Burke (71' Dylan Watts).
Coach: Stephen Bradley.
PFC Ludogorets Razgrad: Sergio Padt, Igor Plastun, Anton Nedyalkov, Olivier Verdon, Zan
Karnicnik, Cauly (90+2' Georgi Terziev), Alex Santana, Show, Pieros Sotiriou (86' Igor
Thiago), Kiril Despodov (46' Rick), Bernard Tekpetey (46' Spas Delev).
Coach: Ante Simundza.
Goals: 21' Aaron Greene 1-0, 88' Aidomo Emakhu 2-0, 90+1' Cauly 2-1.
Referee: Fabio Maresca (ITA)   Attendance: 6,322.
Sent off: 51' Show.

27.07.22   Aspmyra Stadion, Bodø: FK Bodø/Glimt – Linfield FC 8-0 (4-0)
FK Bodø/Glimt: Nikita Haikin, Marius Høibråten, Brice Wembangomo (46' Ask Tjærandsen-
Skau), Alfons Sampsted, Isak Amundsen, Ulrik Saltnes (46' Anders Konradsen), Amahl
Pellegrino (69' Sondre Sørli), Hugo Vetlesen, Elias Hagen, Joel Mvuka (64' Gilbert
Koomson), Victor Boniface (46' Runar Espejord). Coach: Kjetil Knutsen.
Linfield FC: Chris Johns, Matthew Clarke (75' Joshua Archer), Ben Hall, Sam Roscoe-Byrne,
Danny Finlayson, Jamie Mulgrew (56' Kyle McClean), Chris Shields, Kirk Millar, Stephen
Fallon (56' Andrew Clarke), Robbie McDaid (61' Niall Quinn), Jordan Stewart (56' Cammy
Palmer). Coach: David Healy.
Goals: 7' Hugo Vetlesen 1-0, 21' Victor Boniface 2-0 (p), 24' Amahl Pellegrino 3-0,
28' Ulrik Saltnes 4-0, 52' Runar Espejord 5-0, 54' Amahl Pellegrino 6-0 (p),
73' Alfons Sampsted 7-0, 88' Runar Espejord 8-0.
Referee: Roi Reinshreiber (ISR)   Attendance: 5,110.
Sent off: 20' Kirk Millar.

27.07.22   Stadion Letzigrund, Zürich: FC Zürich – Qarabag FK 2-2 (1-0,2-1) (AET)
FC Zürich: Yanick Brecher, Nikola Boranijasevic, Fidan Aliti, Mirlind Kryeziu, Adrián
Guerrero (70' Jonathan Okita), Lindrit Kamberi, Antonio Marchesano (79' Ivan Santini), Ole
Selnæs (71' Marc Hornschuh), Fabian Rohner (70' Aiyegun Tosin), Cheick Conde (119' Becir
Omeragic), Wilfried Gnonto (105+1' Bledian Krasniqi). Coach: Franco Foda.
Qarabag FK: Sahrudin Mahammadaliyev, Marko Vesovic (117' Abbas Hüseynov), Maksim
Medvedev (90+1' Bahlul Mustafazade), Kevin Medina (45' Badavi Hüseynov), Richard
Almeyda (66' Qara Qarayev), Abdellah Zoubir, Kady, Elvin Cafarquliyev (46' Tural
Bayramov), Marko Jankovic, Ramil Sheydaev, Ibrahima Wadji (67' Owusu Kwabena).
Coach: Qurban Qurbanov.
Goals: 4' Maksim Medvedev 1-0 (og), 55' Kady 1-1, 90+5' Ivan Santini 2-1,
98' Owusu Kwabena 2-2.
Referee: Allard Lindhout (HOL)   Attendance: 10,237.

Qarabag FK won after extra time.

27.07.22   Eleda Stadion, Malmö: Malmö FF – FK Zalgiris 0-2 (0-1)
Malmö FF: Johan Dahlin, Niklas Moisander, Lasse Nielsen, Jonas Knudsen (57' Søren Rieks),
Felix Beijmo (71' Eric Larsson), Anders Christiansen, Jo Inge Berget (57' Patriot Sejdiu),
Sergio Peña (76' Hugo Larsson), Moustafa Zeidan, Veljko Birmancevic (46' Isaac Kiese
Thelin), Ola Toivonen. Coach: Milos Milojevic.
FK Zalgiris: Edvinas Gertmonas, Mario Pavelic, Petar Mamic, Joël Fey d'Or Bopesu, Nemanja
Ljubisavljevic, Nicolás Gorobsov, Oliver Buff (81' Saulius Mikoliūnas), Fabien Ourega (71'
Gustas Jarusevicius), Marko Milickovic, Renan Oliveira (71' Donatas Kazlauskas), Mathias
Oyewusi (57' Francis Kyeremeh). Coach: Vladimir Cherubin.
Goals: 34' Mathias Oyewusi 0-1, 52' Renan Oliveira 0-2.
Referee: Kristo Tohver (EST)   Attendance: 17,234.
Sent off: 77' Anders Christiansen.

27.07.22   Stadión Tehelné pole, Bratislava: Slovan Bratislava – Ferencvárosi TC 1-4 (0-2)
Slovan Bratislava: Adrián Chovan, Guram Kashia, Lukás Pauschek (87' Vladimír Weiss,
90+3' Dávid Holman), Vernon De Marco, Jurij Medvedev (11' Andre Green), Myenty Abena,
Juraj Kucka, Jaba Kankava (90+2' Uche Agbo), Giorgi Chakvetadze, Tigran Barseghyan, Iván
Saponjic (87' Aleksandar Cavric). Coach: Vladimir Weiss.
Ferencvárosi TC: Dénes Dibusz, Endre Botka, Eldar Civic, Samy Mmaee, Mats Knoester,
Anderson Esiti, Kristoffer Zachariassen, Aïssa Laïdouni, Tokmac Nguen (90+3' Rasmus
Thelander), Franck Boli (63' Bálint Vécsei), Adama Traoré (I). Coach: Stanislav Cherchesov.
Goals: 20' Franck Boli 0-1, 30' Kristoffer Zachariassen 0-2, 70' Vernon De Marco 1-2,
89' Adama Traoré (I) 1-3, 90+5' Aïssa Laïdouni 1-4.
Referee: Marco Di Bello (ITA)   Attendance: 21,500.

81

27.07.22   Stadio Georgios Karaiskáki, Piraeus:
Olympiakos Piraeus – Maccabi Haifa 0-4 (0-1)
Olympiakos Piraeus: Tomás Vaclík, Kostas Manolas, Sime Vrsaljko, Pape Cissé, Oleg Reabciuk, Andreas Bouchalakis (46' João Carvalho), Georgios Masouras (68' Mathieu Valbuena), Mady Camara (77' Yann M'Vila), Mamadou Kané (62' Youssef El-Arabi), Tiquinho Soares, Philip Zinckernagel (63' Pierre Kunde Malong). Coach: Pedro Martins.
Maccabi Haifa: Josh Cohen, Daniel Sundgren, Bogdan Planic, Shon Goldberg, Pierre Cornud (72' Sun Menachem), Tjaronn Chery (78' Omer Atzili), Ali Muhammad, Neta Lavi, Dolev Haziza (72' Ofri Arad), Din David (78' Mohammad Abu Fani), Frantzdy Pierrot (86' Nikita Rukavytsya). Coach: Barak Bakhar.
Goals: 5' Tjaronn Chery 0-1, 61', 65' Frantzdy Pierrot 0-2, 0-3, 86' Mohammad Abu Fani 0-4.
Referee: Daniel Stefanski (POL)   Attendance: 21,705.

(League Path)

19.07.22   MCH Arena, Herning: FC Midtjylland – AEK Larnaca 1-1 (0-0)
FC Midtjylland: Elías Ólafsson, Erik Sviatchenko, Henrik Dalsgaard, Joel Andersson (60' Mads Thychosen), Paulinho (60' Nikolas Dyhr), Juninho, Anders Dreyer, Evander (44' Charles), Gustav Isaksen (75' Sory Kaba), Edward Chilufya (59' Victor Lind), Raphael Onyedika. Coach: Bo Henriksen.
AEK Larnaca: Kenan Piric, Nenad Tomovic, Oier, Ángel García, Kypros Christoforou (72' Roberto Rosales), Gus Ledes, Hrvoje Milicevic, Ádám Gyurcsó (90' Mikel González), Ivan Trickovski (82' Omri Altman), Imad Faraj (83' Rafail Mamas), Victor Olatunji (72' Rafael Lopes). Coach: José Luis Oltra.
Goals: 81' Ádám Gyurcsó 0-1, 84' Erik Sviatchenko 1-1.
Referee: Novak Simovic (SRB)   Attendance: 7,008.

20.07.22   Stadion Miejski im. Wladyslawa Króla, Lódz (POL):
Dynamo Kyiv – Fenerbahçe 0-0
Dynamo Kyiv: Georgiy Bushchan, Tomasz Kedziora, Vladyslav Dubinchak, Denys Popov (83' Oleksandr Syrota), Ilya Zabarnyi, Sergiy Sydorchuk, Vitaliy Buyalskyi (77' Denys Garmash), Benjamin Verbic (83' Vladyslav Vanat), Viktor Tsygankov (88' Oleksandr Karavayev), Mykola Shaparenko, Artem Besedin. Coach: Mircea Lucescu.
Fenerbahçe: Altay Bayindir, Serdar Aziz (46' Marcel Tisserand), Attila Szalai, Willian Arão, Irfan Kahveci (63' Bruma), Bright Osayi-Samuel, Ferdi Kadioglu, Ismail Yüksek, Joshua King (63' Lincoln), Enner Valencia (72' Serdar Dursun), Diego Rossi (72' Arda Güler).
Coach: Jorge Jesus.
Referee: Glenn Nyberg (SWE)   Attendance: 11,603.

Due to the Russian invasion of Ukraine, Ukrainian teams were required to play their home matches at neutral venues until further notice.

26.07.22   AEK Arena – George Karapatakis, Larnaca:
            AEK Larnaca – FC Midtjylland 1-1 (1-1,1-1) (AET)
AEK Larnaca: Kenan Piric, Roberto Rosales (88' Kypros Christoforou), Nenad Tomovic, Oier,
Ángel García, Gus Ledes, Hrvoje Milicevic, Ádám Gyurcsó (83' Bruno Gama), Ivan
Trickovski (90' José Romo), Imad Faraj (65' Omri Altman), Victor Olatunji (65' Rafael Lopes,
118' Rafail Mamas). Coach: José Luis Oltra.
FC Midtjylland: Elías Ólafsson, Erik Sviatchenko, Henrik Dalsgaard, Joel Andersson, Paulinho
(46' Nikolas Dyhr), Juninho (72' Mads Thychosen), Anders Dreyer, Charles (84' Oliver
Sørensen), Gustav Isaksen (83' Sory Kaba), Edward Chilufya (46' Pione Sisto), Raphael
Onyedika (114' Chris Kouakou). Coach: Bo Henriksen.
Goals: 9' Victor Olatunji 1-0, 12' Henrik Dalsgaard 1-1.
Referee: István Vad (II) (HUN)   Attendance: 6,163.

FC Midtjylland won on penalties after extra time (4:3).

*Penalties: Dreyer 1-0, Altman missed, Sisto 2-0, Milicevic 2-1, Sørensen 3-1, Romo 3-2,
Dyhr 4-2, Bruno Gama 4-3, Kaba missed, Gus Ledes missed.*

27.07.22   Ülker Stadyumu Fenerbahçe Sükrü Saracoglu Spor Kompleksi, Istanbul:
            Fenerbahçe – Dynamo Kyiv 1-2 (0-0,1-1) (AET)
Fenerbahçe: Altay Bayindir, Marcel Tisserand (85' Lincoln), Attila Szalai, Willian Arão (95'
Filip Novák), Irfan Kahveci (46' Emre Mor, 77' Bruma), Bright Osayi-Samuel, Ferdi
Kadioglu, Ismail Yüksek, Joshua King (63' Miguel Crespo), Enner Valencia (77' Serdar
Dursun), Diego Rossi. Coach: Jorge Jesus.
Dynamo Kyiv: Georgiy Bushchan, Tomasz Kedziora (90' Oleksandr Karavayev), Vladyslav
Dubinchak (105' Kostiantyn Vivcharenko), Denys Popov, Ilya Zabarnyi, Sergiy Sydorchuk
(105' Oleksnadr Andriyevskyi), Vitaliy Buyalskyi (67' Denys Garmash), Benjamin Verbic
(37' Vladyslav Vanat), Viktor Tsygankov, Mykola Shaparenko, Artem Besedin (67'
Volodymyr Shepelyev). Coach: Mircea Lucescu.
Goals: 57' Vitaliy Buyalskyi 0-1, 88' Attila Szalai 1-1, 114' Oleksandr Karavayev 1-2.
Referee: Massimiliano Irrati (ITA)   Attendance: 40,000.
Sent off: 53' Ismail Yüksek.

Enner Valencia missed a penalty kick (70').

Dynamo Kyiv won after extra time.

83

THIRD QUALIFYING ROUND

(Champions Path)

02.08.22   Stadionul Zimbru, Chisinau: FC Sheriff Tiraspol – Viktoria Plzen 1-2 (1-1)
FC Sheriff Tiraspol: Razak Abalora, Patrick Kpozo, Stjepan Radeljic, Gaby Kiki, Renan
Guedes, Regi Lushkja (72' Giannis Botos), Cédric Badolo, Moussa Kyabou, Kay Tejan,
Pernambuco, Ibrahim Rasheed (89' Abou Ouattara). Coach: Stjepan Tomas.
Viktoria Plzen: Jindrich Stanek, Lukás Hejda, Ludek Pernica, Milan Havel, Jan Kopic, Jan
Sýkora, Jhon Mosquera (75' Libor Holík), Lukás Kalvach, Pavel Bucha (90+2' Kristi Qose),
Tomás Chorý (66' René Dedic), Jan Kliment (75' Matej Trusa). Coach: Michal Bílek.
Goals: 36' Ibrahim Rasheed 1-0 (p), 41' Tomás Chorý 1-1 (p), 55' Pavel Bucha 1-2.
Referee: Danny Makkelie (HOL)   Attendance: 8,153.

*FC Sheriff Tiraspol played their home match at Stadionul Zimbru, Chisinau, instead of their
regular stadium Sheriff Stadium, Tiraspol, due to Transnistria's involvement in the Russian
invasion of Ukraine.*

02.08.22   Huvepharma Arena, Razgrad: PFC Ludogorets Razgrad – Dinamo Zagreb 1-2 (1-2)
PFC Ludogorets Razgrad: Sergio Padt (46' Simon Sluga), Cicinho, Igor Plastun, Anton
Nedyalkov, Olivier Verdon, Cauly (46' Dominik Yankov), Jakub Piotrowski, Ivan Yordanov,
Pieros Sotiriou (79' Igor Thiago), Bernard Tekpetey (73' Kiril Despodov), Rick (79' Spas
Delev). Coach: Ante Simundza.
Dinamo Zagreb: Dominik Livakovic, Stefan Ristovski, Dino Peric, Rasmus Lauritsen, Arijan
Ademi, Josip Misic, Luka Ivanusec (46' Dario Spikic), Robert Ljubicic, Martin Baturina (86'
Bosko Sutalo), Mislav Orsic (71' Luka Menalo), Josip Drmic (60' Bruno Petkovic).
Coach: Ante Cacic.
Goals: 6' Dino Peric 0-1, 9' Sergio Padt 0-2 (og), 22' Bernard Tekpetey 1-2.
Referee: Cüneyt Çakir (TUR)   Attendance: 7,505.

03.08.22   Tofiq Bahramov adina Respublika stadionu, Baku:
            Qarabag FK – Ferencvárosi TC 1-1 (1-1)
Qarabag FK: Sahrudin Mahammadaliyev, Marko Vesovic, Qara Qarayev, Badavi Hüseynov,
Bahlul Mustafazade, Filip Ozobic (79' Ramil Sheydaev), Abdellah Zoubir, Tural Bayramov,
Marko Jankovic (83' Júlio Romão), Ibrahima Wadji (90+3' Leandro Andrade), Owusu
Kwabena. Coach: Qurban Qurbanov.
Ferencvárosi TC: Dénes Dibusz, Endre Botka, Eldar Civic, Samy Mmaee (57' Rasmus
Thelander), Mats Knoester (68' Adnan Kovacevic), Anderson Esiti, Kristoffer Zachariassen,
Aïssa Laïdouni (88' Muhamed Besic), Tokmac Nguen, Franck Boli (68' Bálint Vécsei),
Adama Traoré (I). Coach: Stanislav Cherchesov.
Goals: 17' Franck Boli 0-1, 34' Owusu Kwabena 1-1.
Referee: Andreas Ekberg (SWE)   Attendance: 31,200.

03.08.22 Aspmyra Stadion, Bodø: FK Bodø/Glimt – FK Zalgiris 5-0 (2-0)
FK Bodø/Glimt: Nikita Haikin, Marius Høibråten, Brede Moe (19' Isak Amundsen), Brice Wembangomo, Alfons Sampsted, Ulrik Saltnes, Amahl Pellegrino (80' Sondre Sørli), Hugo Vetlesen, Elias Hagen, Joel Mvuka (88' Gilbert Koomson), Lars-Jørgen Salvesen (80' Runar Espejord). Coach: Kjetil Knutsen.
FK Zalgiris: Edvinas Gertmonas, Mario Pavelic, Petar Mamic, Joël Fey d'Or Bopesu (68' Donatas Kazlauskas), Nemanja Ljubisavljevic, Nicolás Gorobsov, Oliver Buff (88' Mantas Kuklys), Fabien Ourega (68' Gustas Jarusevicius), Marko Milickovic, Renan Oliveira (88' Francis Kyeremeh), Mathias Oyewusi (68' Saulius Mikoliūnas). Coach: Vladimir Cherubin.
Goals: 33' Hugo Vetlesen 1-0 (p), 36' Amahl Pellegrino 2-0, 58' Lars-Jørgen Salvesen 3-0, 61' Marius Høibråten 4-0, 90+3' Runar Espejord 5-0.
Referee: István Vad (II) (HUN) Attendance: 6,117.

03.08.22 Sammy Ofer Stadium, Haifa: Maccabi Haifa – Apollon Limassol 4-0 (1-0)
Maccabi Haifa: Josh Cohen, Daniel Sundgren, Bogdan Planic, Shon Goldberg, Pierre Cornud (74' Sun Menachem), Tjaronn Chery, Ali Muhammad (74' Mohammad Abu Fani), Neta Lavi, Dolev Haziza (80' Mavis Tchibota), Din David (65' Omer Atzili), Frantzdy Pierrot (80' Nikita Rukavytsya). Coach: Barak Bakhar.
Apollon Limassol: Aleksandar Jovanovic, Valentin Roberge, Mathieu Peybernes, Vukasin Jovanovic, Amine Khammas (90+3' Ido Shahar), Nicolas Diguiny (64' Euclides Cabral), Israel Coll, Danilo Spoljaric (45' Chambos Kyriakou), Hervin Ongenda (45' Vá), Andreas Panayiotou (64' Rangelo Janga), Ioannis Pittas. Coach: Alexander Zorniger.
Goals: 38' Mathieu Peybernes 1-0 (og), 54', 62' Ali Muhammad 2-0, 3-0, 79' Frantzdy Pierrot 4-0.
Referee: Maurizio Mariani (ITA) Attendance: 29,876.
Sent off: 61' Vukasin Jovanovic.

03.08.22 Stadion Rajko Mitic, Beograd:
Crvena Zvezda Beograd – Pyunik Erevan FC 5-0 (3-0)
Crvena Zvezda Beograd: Milan Borjan, Aleksandar Dragovic, Nemanja Milunovic, Milan Rodic, Strahinja Erakovic, Aleksandar Katai (67' Slavoljub Srnic), Guélor Kanga (76' Sékou Sanogo), Mirko Ivanic (76' Stefan Mitrovic), Kings Kangwa, Aleksandar Pesic (69' Milan Pavkov), Osman Bukari (76' Ibrahim Mustapha). Coach: Dejan Stankovic.
Pyunik Erevan FC: David Yurchenko, Zoran Gajic, Mikhail Kovalenko, Juninho, Artak Dashyan, Renzo Zambrano, Eugeniu Cociuc (88' Gevorg Najaryan), Hovhannes Harutyunyan (66' Uros Nenadovic), David Davidyan (46' Alexander González), Yusuf Otubanjo (56' Marjan Radeski), Luka Juricic (88' Nemanja Mladenovic). Coach: Eghishe Melikyan.
Goals: 29' Osman Bukari 1-0, 33' Kings Kangwa 2-0, 44', 70' Osman Bukari 3-0, 4-0, 77' Stefan Mitrovic 5-0.
Referee: Artur Soares Dias (POR) Attendance: 40,456.
Sent off: 89' Milan Rodic.

09.08.22   Vilniaus LFF stadionas, Vilnius: FK Zalgiris – FK Bodø/Glimt 1-1 (1-0)
FK Zalgiris: Edvinas Gertmonas, Saulius Mikoliūnas, Mario Pavelic, Petar Mamic, Nemanja
Ljubisavljevic (82' Kipras Kazukolovas), Nicolás Gorobsov, Oliver Buff, Fabien Ourega (64'
Joël Fey d'Or Bopesu), Francis Kyeremeh (64' Mathias Oyewusi), Marko Milickovic, Renan
Oliveira (76' Donatas Kazlauskas). Coach: Vladimir Cherubin.
FK Bodø/Glimt: Nikita Haikin (15' Julian Lund), Marius Høibråten, Alfons Sampsted, Isak
Amundsen, Ulrik Saltnes, Amahl Pellegrino (63' Sondre Sørli), Hugo Vetlesen (81' Anders
Konradsen), Elias Hagen, Ask Tjærandsen-Skau, Joel Mvuka (63' Gilbert Koomson), Lars-
Jørgen Salvesen (63' Runar Espejord). Coach: Kjetil Knutsen.
Goals: 39' Francis Kyeremeh 1-0, 51' Joel Mvuka 1-1.
Referee: Sandro Schärer (SUI)   Attendance: 4,629.
Sent off: 57' Petar Mamic.

09.08.22   Neo GSP Stadium, Nicosia: Apollon Limassol – Maccabi Haifa 2-0 (2-0)
Apollon Limassol: Aleksandar Jovanovic, Valentin Roberge (73' Panagiotis Artymatas),
Mathieu Peybernes, Chambos Kyriakou (73' Vá), Amine Khammas, Euclides Cabral, Nicolas
Diguiny, Israel Coll, Rangelo Janga (57' Bagaliy Dabo), Hervin Ongenda (73' Ido Shahar),
Ioannis Pittas. Coach: Alexander Zorniger.
Maccabi Haifa: Josh Cohen, Daniel Sundgren, Bogdan Planic, Shon Goldberg, Sun Menachem
(60' Pierre Cornud), Ofri Arad (46' Ali Muhammad), Neta Lavi, Mohammad Abu Fani, Omer
Atzili (60' Dolev Haziza), Din David (76' Maor Levi), Frantzdy Pierrot (90+3' Nikita
Rukavytsya). Coach: Barak Bakhar.
Goals: 19' Hervin Ongenda 1-0, 26' Israel Coll 2-0.
Referee: Felix Zwayer (GER)   Attendance: 3,936.

*Apollon Limassol played their home match at GSP Stadium, Nicosia, instead of their regular
stadium Tsirio Stadium, Limassol, which did not meet UEFA requirements.*

09.08.22   Doosan Aréna, Plzen: Viktoria Plzen – FC Sheriff Tiraspol 2-1 (1-0)
Viktoria Plzen: Jindrich Stanek, Lukás Hejda, Ludek Pernica, Milan Havel, Jan Kopic, Jan
Sýkora (90' Matej Trusa), Jhon Mosquera (90' Václav Pilar), Lukás Kalvach, Pavel Bucha,
Tomás Chorý (73' René Dedic), Jan Kliment (59' Libor Holík). Coach: Michal Bílek.
FC Sheriff Tiraspol: Razak Abalora, Stefanos Evangelou, Patrick Kpozo, Gaby Kiki, Renan
Guedes, Abou Ouattara (80' Keston Julien), Cédric Badolo (70' Giannis Botos), Salifu
Mudasiru, Moussa Kyabou, Pernambuco (46' Kay Tejan), Ibrahim Rasheed.
Coach: Stjepan Tomas.
Goals: 10' Jan Kliment 1-0, 47' Ibrahim Rasheed 1-1 (p), 62' Jhon Mosquera 2-1.
Referee: Orel Grinfeld (ISR)   Attendance: 10,770.
Sent off: 85' Stefanos Evangelou.

Tomás Chorý missed a penalty kick (27').

09.08.22   Vazgen Sargsyan anvan Hanrapetakan Marzadasht, Yerevan:
Pyunik Erevan FC – Crvena Zvezda Beograd 0-2 (0-1)
Pyunik Erevan FC: Stanislav Buchnev, Artur Avagyan (78' Gevorg Najaryan), Alexander
González, Anton Bratkov (78' Yuri Gareginyan), Mikhail Kovalenko, Juninho, Artak Dashyan,
Eugeniu Cociuc, Hovhannes Harutyunyan (79' Alan Aussi), Yusuf Otubanjo (62' Marjan
Radeski), Luka Juricic (83' Nemanja Mladenovic). Coach: Eghishe Melikyan.
Crvena Zvezda Beograd: Milan Borjan, Aleksandar Dragovic, Nemanja Milunovic, Marko
Gobeljic, Strahinja Erakovic (64' Nikola Stankovic), Aleksandar Katai (64' El Fardou Ben
Mohamed), Sékou Sanogo (46' Stefan Mitrovic), Guélor Kanga (77' Slavoljub Srnic), Kings
Kangwa, Milan Pavkov, Osman Bukari (69' Ibrahim Mustapha). Coach: Dejan Stankovic.
Goals: 44' Guélor Kanga 0-1 (p), 60' Milan Pavkov 0-2.
Referee: William Collum (SCO)   Attendance: 6,000.

Aleksandar Katai missed a penalty kick (29').

09.08.22   Groupama Aréna, Budapest: Ferencvárosi TC – Qarabag FK 1-3 (0-1)
Ferencvárosi TC: Dénes Dibusz, Rasmus Thelander, Endre Botka, Adnan Kovacevic (51' Mats
Knoester), Eldar Civic (84' Lóránd Pászka), Anderson Esiti (51' Bálint Vécsei), Kristoffer
Zachariassen, Aïssa Laïdouni, Tokmac Nguen (84' Marquinhos), Franck Boli (61' Ryan
Mmaee), Adama Traoré (I). Coach: Stanislav Cherchesov.
Qarabag FK: Sahrudin Mahammadaliyev, Marko Vesovic, Qara Qarayev (86' Júlio Romão),
Badavi Hüseynov, Bahlul Mustafazade, Abdellah Zoubir (86' Leandro Andrade), Kady, Tural
Bayramov, Marko Jankovic (58' Richard Almeida), Ramil Sheydaev, Ibrahima Wadji (82'
Owusu Kwabena). Coach: Qurban Qurbanov.
Goals: 7' Abdellah Zoubir 0-1, 54', 78' Ibrahima Wadji 0-2, 0-3, 86' Adama Traoré (I) 1-3.
Referee: Carlos del Cerro Grande (ESP)   Attendance: 18,875.

09.08.22   Stadion Maksimir, Zagreb: Dinamo Zagreb – PFC Ludogorets Razgrad 4-2 (3-1)
Dinamo Zagreb: Dominik Livakovic, Stefan Ristovski (46' Sadegh Moharrami), Dino Peric,
Bosko Sutalo, Arijan Ademi, Josip Misic (46' Amer Gojak), Robert Ljubicic, Martin Baturina
(46' Luka Ivanusec), Mislav Orsic, Josip Drmic (71' Bruno Petkovic), Dario Spikic (90+1'
Luka Menalo). Coach: Ante Cacic.
PFC Ludogorets Razgrad: Simon Sluga, Cicinho (46' Zan Karnicnik), Igor Plastun (46' Spas
Delev), Anton Nedyalkov, Olivier Verdon, Jakub Piotrowski, Show (46' Ivan Yordanov),
Dominik Yankov, Kiril Despodov (85' Jorghinho), Rick, Igor Thiago (66' Matías Tissera).
Coach: Ante Simundza.
Goals: 13' Josip Drmic 1-0, 27', 44' Mislav Orsic 2-0 (p), 3-0,
45+4', 49' Kiril Despodov 3-1, 3-2 (p), 87' Bruno Petkovic 4-2 (p).
Referee: Benoît Bastien (FRA)   Attendance: 13,658.
Sent off: 17' Dominik Yankov, 73' Rick, 87' Zan Karnicnik.

87

(League Path)

02.08.22   Stade Louis II, Monaco: AS Monaco – PSV Eindhoven 1-1 (0-1)
AS Monaco: Alexander Nübel, Guillermo Maripán, Axel Disasi, Vanderson, Aleksandr
Golovin (76' Breel Embolo), Youssouf Fofana, Eliot Matazo, Kevin Volland (76' Gelson
Martins), Wissam Ben Yedder (84' Sofiane Diop), Takumi Minamino (67' Krépin Diatta),
Ismail Jakobs. Coach: Philippe Clement.
PSV Eindhoven: Walter Benítez, Phillipp Mwene (76' Fredrik Oppegård), Philipp Max (61'
André Ramalho), Armando Obispo, Jordan Teze, Ibrahim Sangaré (78' Marco van Ginkel),
Guus Til (62' Érick Gutiérrez), Joey Veerman, Ismael Saibari (76' Xavi Simons), Luuk de
Jong, Cody Gakpo. Coach: Ruud van Nistelrooij.
Goals: 38' Joey Veerman 0-1, 80' Axel Disasi 1-1.
Referee: Davide Massa (ITA)   Attendance: 10,802.

02.08.22   King Power at Den Dreef, Heverlee:
          Union Saint-Gilloise – Glasgow Rangers FC 2-0 (1-0)
Union Saint-Gilloise: Anthony Moris, Bart Nieuwkoop, Christian Burgess, Siebe Van Der
Heyden, Ross Sykes, Teddy Teuma (90+2' Cameron Puertas), Senne Lynen, Jean Amani,
Dante Vanzeir (90+2' Guillaume François), Loïc Lapoussin, Simon Adingra (85' Ilyes Ziani).
Coach: Karel Geraerts.
Glasgow Rangers FC: Jon McLaughlin, James Tavernier, Connor Goldson, Borna Barisic (67'
Ridvan Yilmaz), Ryan Jack (67' Ben Davies), John Lundstram, Glen Kamara, James Sands,
Antonio Colak, Rabbi Matondo (77' Tom Lawrence), Malik Tillman (77' Scott Wright).
Coach: Giovanni van Bronckhorst.
Goals: 27' Teddy Teuma 1-0, 76' Dante Vanzeir 2-0 (p).
Referee: Irfan Peljto (BIH)   Attendance: 1,100.

*Union Saint-Gilloise played their home match at King Power at Den Dreef, Heverlee, instead
of their regular stadium Joseph Marien Stadium, Brussels, which did not meet UEFA
requirements.*

02.08.22   Estádio do Sport Lisboa e Benfica, Lisboa: SL Benfica – FC Midtjylland 4-1 (3-0)
SL Benfica: Odisseas Vlachodimos, Nicolás Otamendi, Gilberto, Álex Grimaldo, Morato, João
Mário, Rafa Silva (78' Henrique Araújo), Florentino Luís, Enzo Fernández, David Neres (87'
Chiquinho), Gonçalo Ramos (79' Roman Yaremchuk). Coach: Roger Schmidt.
FC Midtjylland: Elías Ólafsson, Erik Sviatchenko, Henrik Dalsgaard, Joel Andersson (67'
Mads Thychosen), Juninho, Nikolas Dyhr (62' Paulinho), Pione Sisto, Anders Dreyer (46'
Edward Chilufya), Charles (79' Chris Kouakou), Oliver Sørensen, Sory Kaba (67' Gustav
Isaksen). Coach: Henrik Jensen.
Goals: 17', 33' Gonçalo Ramos 1-0, 2-0, 40' Enzo Fernández 3-0, 61' Gonçalo Ramos 4-0,
78' Pione Sisto 4-1 (p).
Referee: Alejandro Hernández Hernández (ESP)   Attendance: 53,346.

03.08.22   Stadion Miejski im. Wladyslawa Króla, Lódz (POL):
Dynamo Kyiv – Sturm Graz 1-0 (1-0)
Dynamo Kyiv: Georgiy Bushchan, Tomasz Kedziora, Oleksandr Karavayev, Vladyslav Dubinchak (71' Kostiantyn Vivcharenko), Denys Popov, Ilya Zabarnyi, Sergiy Sydorchuk, Vitaliy Buyalskyi, Mykola Shaparenko, Volodymyr Shepelyev (71' Denys Garmash), Artem Besedin (83' Vladyslav Vanat). Coach: Mircea Lucescu.
Sturm Graz: Jörg Siebenhandl, Jon Gorenc-Stankovic, Gregory Wüthrich, Jusuf Gazibegovic, David Affengruber, Amadou Dante (68' David Schnegg), Stefan Hierländer (67' Ivan Ljubic), Tomi Horvat, Alexander Prass (78' Vesel Demaku), Manprit Sarkaria, Rasmus Højlund (89' Christoph Lang). Coach: Christian Ilzer.
Goal: 28' Oleksandr Karavayev 1-0.
Referee: François Letexier (FRA)   Attendance: 6,092.

Due to the Russian invasion of Ukraine, Ukrainian teams were required to play their home matches at neutral venues until further notice.

09.08.22   Cepheus Park Randers, Randers: FC Midtjylland – SL Benfica 1-3 (0-1)
FC Midtjylland: Elías Ólafsson, Henrik Dalsgaard, Joel Andersson, Mads Thychosen, Paulinho (87' Nikolas Dyhr), Juninho, Pione Sisto (77' Edward Chilufya), Anders Dreyer (70' Gustav Isaksen), Evander (46' Oliver Sørensen), Raphael Onyedika, Sory Kaba (70' Júnior Brumado). Coach: Henrik Jensen.
SL Benfica: Odisseas Vlachodimos, Nicolás Otamendi, Gilberto (76' Alexander Bah), Álex Grimaldo, Morato, João Mário (89' Diego Moreira), Rafa Silva (46' Henrique Araújo), Chiquinho (79' Diogo Gonçalves), Florentino Luís, Enzo Fernández, Gonçalo Ramos (46' Roman Yaremchuk). Coach: Roger Schmidt.
Goals: 23' Enzo Fernández 0-1, 56' Henrique Araújo 0-2, 63' Pione Sisto 1-2, 88' Diogo Gonçalves 1-3.
Referee: Srdjan Jovanovic (SRB)   Attendance: 5,111.

FC Midtjylland played their home match at Cepheus Park Randers, Randers, as their regular stadium, the MCH Arena, Herning, was being used for the 2022 FEI World Equestrian Games.

09.08.22   Philips Stadion, Eindhoven: PSV Eindhoven – AS Monaco 3-2 (1-0,2-2) (AET)
PSV Eindhoven: Walter Benítez, Phillipp Mwene (77' Johan Bakayoko), Philipp Max (77' Fredrik Oppegård), Armando Obispo (88' Marco van Ginkel), Jordan Teze, Ibrahim Sangaré, Guus Til (65' Érick Gutiérrez), Joey Veerman (107' Jarrad Branthwaite), Ismael Saibari (65' André Ramalho), Luuk de Jong, Cody Gakpo. Coach: Ruud van Nistelrooij.
AS Monaco: Alexander Nübel, Guillermo Maripán, Axel Disasi, Vanderson, Aleksandr Golovin (53' Krépin Diatta), Youssouf Fofana, Eliot Matazo (105' Jean Lucas), Kevin Volland (46' Breel Embolo), Wissam Ben Yedder (82' Sofiane Diop), Takumi Minamino (68' Gelson Martins), Ismail Jakobs (53' Caio Henrique). Coach: Philippe Clement.
Goals: 21' Joey Veerman 1-0, 58' Guillermo Maripán 1-1, 70' Wissam Ben Yedder 1-2, 89' Érick Gutiérrez 2-2, 109' Luuk de Jong 3-2.
Referee: Jesús Gil Manzano (ESP)   Attendance: 33,000.

PSV Eindhoven won after extra time.

09.08.22   Merkur Arena, Graz: Sturm Graz – Dynamo Kyiv 1-2 (1-0,1-0) (AET)
Sturm Graz: Jörg Siebenhandl, Jon Gorenc-Stankovic (102' Mohammed Fuseini), Gregory
Wüthrich, Jusuf Gazibegovic, David Affengruber, Amadou Dante (102' David Schnegg),
Stefan Hierländer (103' Vesel Demaku), Tomi Horvat (84' Christoph Lang), Alexander Prass
(115' Moritz Wels), Manprit Sarkaria, Rasmus Højlund (75' Ivan Ljubic).
Coach: Christian Ilzer.
Dynamo Kyiv: Georgiy Bushchan, Tomasz Kedziora (71' Oleksandr Karavayev), Vladyslav
Dubinchak (71' Kostiantyn Vivcharenko), Oleksandr Syrota, Ilya Zabarnyi, Sergiy Sydorchuk,
Vitaliy Buyalskyi, Viktor Tsygankov, Mykola Shaparenko, Volodymyr Shepelyev (82' Denys
Garmash, 99' Oleksandr Andriyevskyi), Artem Besedin (76' Vladyslav Vanat).
Coach: Mircea Lucescu.
Goals: 27' Rasmus Højlund 1-0, 97' Kostiantyn Vivcharenko 1-1, 112' Viktor Tsyhankov 1-2.
Referee: Ivan Kruzliak (SVK)   Attendance: 14,007.
Sent-off: 105' Manprit Sarkaria.

Dynamo Kyiv won after extra time.

09.08.22   Ibrox Stadium, Glasgow: Glasgow Rangers FC – Union Saint-Gilloise 3-0 (1-0)
Glasgow Rangers FC: Jon McLaughlin, James Tavernier, Connor Goldson, Borna Barisic,
Scott Arfield (64' Rabbi Matondo), Tom Lawrence (87' Glen Kamara), John Lundstram,
James Sands (79' Ben Davies), Antonio Colak (79' Alfredo Morelos), Ryan Kent, Malik
Tillman. Coach: Giovanni van Bronckhorst.
Union Saint-Gilloise: Anthony Moris, Bart Nieuwkoop (77' Guillaume François), Christian
Burgess, Siebe Van Der Heyden, Ross Sykes (83' Dennis Eckert-Ayensa), Teddy Teuma,
Senne Lynen (87' Cameron Puertas), Jean Amani, Dante Vanzeir, Loïc Lapoussin, Simon
Adingra. Coach: Karel Geraerts.
Goals: 45' James Tavernier 1-0 (p), 58' Antonio Colak 2-0, 78' Malik Tillman 3-0.
Referee: Anastasios Sidiropoulos (GRE)   Attendance: 48,454.
Sent-off: 90+4' Jean Amani.

PLAY-OFF ROUND

The winners of the ties advanced to the Group Stage.

The losers were transferred to the UEFA Europa League Group Stage.

(Champions Path)

16.08.22   Aspmyra Stadion, Bodø: FK Bodø/Glimt – Dinamo Zagreb 1-0 (1-0)
FK Bodø/Glimt: Nikita Haikin, Marius Høibråten, Alfons Sampsted, Isak
Amundsen, Ulrik Saltnes, Hugo Vetlesen, Elias Hagen (82' Albert Grønbæk Erlykke), Amahl
Pellegrino, Lars-Jørgen Salvesen (68' Runar Espejord), Joel Mvuka (81' Gilbert Koomson).
Coach: Kjetil Knutsen.
Dinamo Zagreb: Dominik Livakovic, Stefan Ristovski, Rasmus Lauritsen, Bosko Sutalo,
Arijan Ademi, Josip Misic, Robert Ljubicic, Martin Baturina (77' Amer Gojak), Mislav Orsic
(69' Mahir Emreli), Josip Drmic (46' Bruno Petkovic), Dario Spikic (46' Luka Ivanusec).
Coach: Ante Cacic.
Goal: 37' Amahl Pellegrino 1-0.
Referee: Danny Makkelie (HOL)   Attendance: 7,762.

16.08.22   Telia Parken, København: FC København – Trabzonspor 2-1 (1-0)
FC København: Mathew Ryan, Davit Khocholava, Denis Vavro, Kevin Diks (81' Peter Ankersen), Victor Kristiansen, Rasmus Falk (89' Marko Stamenic), Zeca, Victor Claesson, Lukas Lerager, Pep Biel (81' Ísak Bergmann Jóhannesson), Hákon Haraldsson (67' William Bøving). Coach: Jess Thorup.
Trapzonspor: Ugurcan Çakir, Jens Stryger Larsen, Vitor Hugo, Stefano Denswil (58' Marc Bartra), Eren Elmali, Anastasios Bakasetas, Manolis Siopis (58' Enis Bardhi), Trézéguet, Abdülkadir Ömür (89' Dorukhan Toköz), Jean Kouassi (46' Djaniny), Andreas Cornelius. Coach: Abdullah Avci.
Goals: 9' Victor Claesson 1-0, 48' Lukas Lerager 2-0, 79' Anastasios Bakasetas 2-1.
Referee: Michael Oliver (ENG)   Attendance: 27,520.

17.08.22   Tofiq Bahramov adina Respublika stadionu, Baku:
           Qarabag FK – Viktoria Plzen 0-0
Qarabag FK: Sahrudin Mahammadaliyev, Marko Vesovic, Qara Qarayev, Badavi Hüseynov, Bahlul Mustafazade, Abdellah Zoubir, Kady, Tural Bayramov, Marko Jankovic (73' Richard Almeida), Ramil Sheydaev (62' Filip Ozobic), Ibrahima Wadji (73' Owusu Kwabena). Coach: Qurban Qurbanov.
Viktoria Plzen: Jindrich Stanek, Lukás Hejda, Ludek Pernica, Milan Havel, Václav Jemelka, Jan Kopic (90+1' Libor Holík), Jan Sýkora (71' Erik Jirka), Jhon Mosquera (59' Václav Pilar), Lukás Kalvach, Pavel Bucha, Tomás Chorý (71' Jan Kliment). Coach: Michal Bílek.
Referee: Slavko Vincic (SVN)   Attendance: 31,150.

17.08.22   Sammy Ofer Stadium, Haifa: Maccabi Haifa – Crvena Zvezda Beograd 3-2 (1-2)
Maccabi Haifa: Josh Cohen, Daniel Sundgren, Bogdan Planic, Shon Goldberg, Pierre Cornud (62' Sun Menachem), Tjaronn Chery, Ali Muhammad, Neta Lavi, Dolev Haziza (76' Mohammad Abu Fani), Din David (62' Omer Atzili), Frantzdy Pierrot (70' Nikita Rukavytsya). Coach: Barak Bakhar.
Crvena Zvezda Beograd: Milan Borjan, Aleksandar Dragovic, Nemanja Milunovic, Milan Rodic, Strahinja Erakovic, Aleksandar Katai (56' Slavoljub Srnic), Guélor Kanga, Mirko Ivanic (72' Sékou Sanogo), Kings Kangwa, Aleksandar Pesic (72' El Fardou Ben Mohamed), Osman Bukari (60' Stefan Mitrovic). Coach: Dejan Stankovic.
Goals: 18' Frantzdy Pierrot 1-0, 27' Aleksandar Pesic 1-1, 39' Guélor Kanga 1-2, 51' Frantzdy Pierrot 2-2, 61' Tjaronn Chery 3-2.
Referee: Carlos del Cerro Grande (ESP)   Attendance: 29,132.

23.08.22   Doosan Aréna, Plzen: Viktoria Plzen – Qarabag FK 2-1 (0-1)
Viktoria Plzen: Jindrich Stanek, Ludek Pernica, Milan Havel, Libor Holík, Václav Jemelka, Jan Kopic (90+4' Filip Cihák), Jan Sýkora (46' Jan Kliment, 74' Erik Jirka), Jhon Mosquera, Lukás Kalvach, Pavel Bucha, Tomás Chorý (86' René Dedic). Coach: Michal Bílek.
Qarabag FK: Sahrudin Mahammadaliyev, Marko Vesovic, Qara Qarayev, Badavi Hüseynov, Bahlul Mustafazade, Richard Almeida (54' Marko Jankovic), Filip Ozobic (70' Ramil Sheydaev), Abdellah Zoubir, Kady, Tural Bayramov, Ibrahima Wadji (81' Owusu Kwabena). Coach: Qurban Qurbanov.
Goals: 38' Filip Ozobic 0-1, 58' Jan Kopic 1-1, 73' Jan Kliment 2-1.
Referee: Artur Soares Dias (POR)   Attendance: 10,963.

91

23.08.22   Stadion Rajko Mitic, Beograd: Crvena Zvezda Beograd – Maccabi Haifa 2-2 (2-1)
Crvena Zvezda Beograd: Milan Borjan, Aleksandar Dragovic, Nemanja Milunovic, Milan
Rodic (84' Sékou Sanogo), Strahinja Erakovic, Aleksandar Katai, Slavoljub Srnic, Guélor
Kanga (53' Kings Kangwa), Mirko Ivanic, Aleksandar Pesic (78' Milan Pavkov), Osman
Bukari (84' Ibrahim Mustapha). Coach: Dejan Stankovic.
Maccabi Haifa: Josh Cohen, Daniel Sundgren, Bogdan Planic, Shon Goldberg, Pierre Cornud,
Tjaronn Chery (90+3' Rami Gershon), Ali Muhammad, Neta Lavi, Dolev Haziza, Din David
(72' Omer Atzili), Frantzdy Pierrot. Coach: Barak Bakhar.
Goals: 27' Aleksandar Pesic 1-0, 43' Mirko Ivanic 2-0, 45+5' Daniel Sundgren 2-1,
90' Milan Pavkov 2-2 (og).
Referee: Anthony Taylor (ENG)   Attendance: 47,731.

Dolev Haziza missed a penalty kick (45+4').

24.08.22   Stadion Maksimir, Zagreb: Dinamo Zagreb – FK Bodø/Glimt 4-1 (2-0,2-1)
Dinamo Zagreb: Dominik Livakovic, Stefan Ristovski (91' Sadegh Moharrami), Dino Peric
(71' Emir Dilaver), Bosko Sutalo, Arijan Ademi (91' Petar Bockaj), Luka Ivanusec, Robert
Ljubicic, Martin Baturina (60' Amer Gojak), Mislav Orsic (82' Josip Drmic), Bruno Petkovic,
Dario Spikic (60' Mahir Emreli). Coach: Ante Cacic.
FK Bodø/Glimt: Nikita Haikin, Marius Høibråten, Brice Wembangomo (111' Ask Tjærandsen-
Skau), Alfons Sampsted, Isak Amundsen (106' Gaute Vetti), Ulrik Saltnes, Hugo Vetlesen
(106' Anders Konradsen), Elias Hagen (63' Albert Grønbæk Erlykke), Amahl Pellegrino, Lars-
Jørgen Salvesen (63' Runar Espejord), Joel Mvuka (104' Gilbert Koomson).
Coach: Kjetil Knutsen.
Goals: 4' Mislav Orsic 1-0, 35' Bruno Petkovic 2-0, 70' Albert Grønbæk Erlykke 2-1,
116' Josip Drmic 3-1, 120' Petar Bockaj 4-1.
Referee: Antonio Mateu Lahoz (ESP)   Attendance: 18,349.

24.08.22   Senol Günes Spor Kompleksi, Trabzon: Trabzonspor – FC København 0-0
Trapzonspor: Ugurcan Çakir, Jens Stryger Larsen, Marc Bartra, Stefano Denswil, Eren Elmali,
Manolis Siopis, Enis Bardhi, Dorukhan Toköz (73' Jean Kouassi), Abdülkadir Ömür (66'
Trézéguet), Djaniny (78' Anastasios Bakasetas), Andreas Cornelius. Coach: Abdullah Avci.
FC København: Mathew Ryan, Davit Khocholava, Denis Vavro, Kevin Diks, Victor
Kristiansen, Rasmus Falk, Zeca, Victor Claesson (78' Hákon Haraldsson), Lukas Lerager (85'
Valdemar Lund Jensen), Pep Biel (79' Mamoudou Karamoko), Mohamed Daramy (63' Paul
Mukairu). Coach: Jess Thorup.
Referee: Danny Makkelie (HOL)   Attendance: 36,128.

(League Path)

16.08.22   Ibrox Stadium, Glasgow: Glasgow Rangers FC – PSV Eindhoven 2-2 (1-1)
Glasgow Rangers FC: Jon McLaughlin, James Tavernier, Connor Goldson, Borna Barisic,
Steven Davis (71' Glen Kamara), John Lundstram, James Sands, Tom Lawrence, Antonio
Colak, Ryan Kent, Malik Tillman (71' Scott Wright). Coach: Giovanni van Bronckhorst.
PSV Eindhoven: Walter Benítez, André Ramalho, Philipp Max, Armando Obispo (79' Jarrad
Branthwaite), Jordan Teze, Érick Gutiérrez, Ibrahim Sangaré, Joey Veerman, Luuk de Jong,
Cody Gakpo, Ismael Saibari. Coach: Ruud van Nistelrooij.
Goals: 37' Ibrahim Sangaré 0-1, 40' Antonio Colak 1-1, 70' Tom Lawrence 2-1,
78' Armando Obispo 2-2.
Referee: Daniele Orsato (ITA)   Attendance: 49,097.

17.08.22   Stadion Miejski LKS Lodz, Lódz (POL): Dynamo Kyiv – SL Benfica 0-2 (0-2)
Dynamo Kyiv: Georgiy Bushchan, Tomasz Kedziora, Vladyslav Dubinchak (63' Kostiantyn Vivcharenko), Denys Popov (80' Oleksandr Syrota), Ilya Zabarnyi, Vitaliy Buyalskyi, Oleksandr Andriyevskyi, Viktor Tsygankov (64' Oleksandr Karavayev), Mykola Shaparenko, Volodymyr Shepelyev (73' Anton Tsarenko), Artem Besedin (74' Vladyslav Vanat). Coach: Mircea Lucescu.
SL Benfica: Odisseas Vlachodimos, Nicolás Otamendi, Gilberto (69' Alexander Bah), Álex Grimaldo, Morato, João Mário, Rafa Silva (84' Chiquinho), Florentino Luís, Enzo Fernández, David Neres (63' Henrique Araújo), Gonçalo Ramos (63' Roman Yaremchuk). Coach: Roger Schmidt.
Goals: 9' Gilberto 0-1, 37' Gonçalo Ramos 0-2.
Referee: Felix Zwayer (GER)   Attendance: 16,450.

Due to the Russian invasion of Ukraine, Ukrainian teams were required to play their home matches at neutral venues until further notice.

23.08.22   Estádio do Sport Lisboa e Benfica, Lisboa: SL Benfica – Dynamo Kyiv 3-0 (3-0)
SL Benfica: Odisseas Vlachodimos, Nicolás Otamendi, Gilberto, Álex Grimaldo, Morato, João Mário, Rafa Silva (70' Henrique Araújo), Florentino Luís (70' Julian Weigl), Enzo Fernández (90' Paulo Bernardo), David Neres (70' Diogo Gonçalves), Gonçalo Ramos (52' Petar Musa). Coach: Roger Schmidt.
Dynamo Kyiv: Georgiy Bushchan, Tomasz Kedziora, Oleksandr Karavayev (87' Oleksandr Tymchyk), Oleksandr Syrota, Kostiantyn Vivcharenko (63' Vladyslav Dubinchak), Ilya Zabarnyi, Sergiy Sydorchuk, Vitaliy Buyalskyi (90+3' Oleksandr Yatsyk), Mykola Shaparenko, Volodymyr Shepelyev (87' Anton Tsarenko), Artem Besedin (63' Vladyslav Vanat). Coach: Mircea Lucescu.
Goals: 27' Nicolás Otamendi 1-0, 40' Rafa Silva 2-0, 42' David Neres 3-0.
Referee: Clément Turpin (FRA)   Attendance: 58,705.

24.08.22   Philips Stadion, Eindhoven: PSV Eindhoven – Glasgow Rangers FC 0-1 (0-0)
PSV Eindhoven: Walter Benítez, André Ramalho (62' Phillipp Mwene), Philipp Max (85' Marco van Ginkel), Armando Obispo, Jordan Teze, Érick Gutiérrez (62' Guus Til), Ibrahim Sangaré, Joey Veerman, Luuk de Jong (46' Xavi Simons), Cody Gakpo, Ismael Saibari (76' Carlos Vinícius). Coach: Ruud van Nistelrooij.
Glasgow Rangers FC: Jon McLaughlin, James Tavernier, Connor Goldson, Borna Barisic, John Lundstram, Glen Kamara (73' Scott Arfield), James Sands, Tom Lawrence (73' Scott Wright), Antonio Colak (90+2' Fashion Sakala), Ryan Kent, Malik Tillman. Coach: Giovanni van Bronckhorst.
Goal: 60' Antonio Colak 0-1.
Referee: Szymon Marciniak (POL)   Attendance: 34,893.

GROUP STAGE

The top two teams of each group advanced to the Round of 16.
The third-placed teams will be transferred to the UEFA Europa League Knockout Round Play-offs.

GROUP A

SSC Napoli	6	5	0	1	20 -	6	15
Liverpool FC	6	5	0	1	17 -	6	15
AFC Ajax	6	2	0	4	11 -	15	6
Glasgow Rangers FC	6	0	0	6	2 -	22	0

GROUP B

FC Porto	6	4	0	2	12 -	7	12
Club Brugge KV	6	3	2	1	7 -	4	11
Bayer Leverkusen	6	1	2	3	4 -	8	5
Atlético Madrid	6	1	2	3	5 -	9	5

GROUP C

Bayern München	6	6	0	0	18 -	2	18
Internazionale Milano	6	3	1	2	10 -	7	10
FC Barcelona	6	2	1	3	12 -	12	7
Viktoria Plzen	6	0	0	6	5 -	24	0

GROUP D

Tottenham Hotspur	6	3	2	1	8 -	6	11
Eintracht Frankfurt	6	3	1	2	7 -	8	10
Sporting CP	6	2	1	3	8 -	9	7
Olympique Marseille	6	2	0	4	8 -	8	6

GROUP E

Chelsea FC	6	4	1	1	10 -	4	13
AC Milan	6	3	1	2	12 -	7	10
Red Bull Salzburg	6	1	3	2	5 -	9	6
Dinamo Zagreb	6	1	1	4	4 -	11	4

GROUP F

Real Madrid CF	6	4	1	1	15 -	6	13
RB Leipzig	6	4	0	2	13 -	9	12
Shakhtar Donetsk	6	1	3	2	8 -	10	6
Celtic FC	6	0	2	6	6 -	15	2

GROUP G

Manchester City	6	4	2	0	14	-	2	14
Borussia Dortmund	6	2	3	1	19	-	5	9
Sevilla FC	6	1	2	3	6	-	12	5
FC København	6	0	3	3	1	-	12	3

GROUP H

SL Benfica	6	4	2	0	16	-	7	14
Paris Saint-Germain	6	4	2	0	16	-	7	14
FC Juventus	6	1	0	5	6	-	13	3
Maccabi Haifa	6	1	0	5	7	-	21	3

GROUP A

07.09.22   Johan Cruijff ArenA, Amsterdam: AFC Ajax – Glasgow Rangers FC 4-0 (3-0)
AFC Ajax: Remko Pasveer, Daley Blind (81' Youri Baas), Calvin Bassey, Jurriën Timber, Devyne Rensch, Edson Álvarez (88' Jorge Sánchez), Kenneth Taylor, Mohammed Kudus (89' Brian Brobbey), Dusan Tadic, Steven Berghuis (81' Davy Klaassen), Steven Bergwijn (81' Lucas Ocampos). Coach: Alfred Schreuder.
Glasgow Rangers FC: Jon McLaughlin, James Tavernier (46' Leon King), Connor Goldson, Borna Barisic, John Lundstram, Glen Kamara (78' Steven Davis), Scott Wright (46' Rabbi Matondo), James Sands, Antonio Colak, Ryan Kent, Malik Tillman (46' Ryan Jack). Coach: Giovanni van Bronckhorst.
Goals: 17' Edson Álvarez 1-0, 32' Steven Berghuis 2-0, 33' Mohammed Kudus 3-0, 80' Steven Bergwijn 4-0.
Referee: Tobias Stieler (GER)   Attendance: 52,862.

07.09.22   Stadio Diego Armando Maradona, Napoli: SSC Napoli – Liverpool FC 4-1 (3-0)
SSC Napoli: Alex Meret, Giovanni Di Lorenzo, Amir Rrahmani, Mathías Olivera (74' Mário Rui), Kim Min-Jae, Piotr Zielinski (74' Eljif Elmas), Stanislav Lobotka, Frank Zambo Anguissa, Matteo Politano (58' Hirving Lozano), Victor Osimhen (41' Giovanni Simeone), Khvicha Kvaratskhelia (57' Alessio Zerbin). Coach: Luciano Spalletti.
Liverpool FC: Alisson, Virgil van Dijk, Andy Robertson, Joe Gomez (46' Joe Matip), Trent Alexander-Arnold, James Milner (62' Thiago Alcântara), Fabinho, Harvey Elliott (77' Arthur), Roberto Firmino (62' Darwin Núñez), Mohamed Salah (62' Diogo Jota), Luis Díaz. Coach: Jürgen Klopp.
Goals: 5' Piotr Zielinski 1-0 (p), 31' Frank Zambo Anguissa 2-0, 44' Giovanni Simeone 3-0, 47' Piotr Zielinski 4-0, 49' Luis Díaz 4-1.
Referee: Carlos del Cerro Grande (ESP)   Attendance: 51,793.

Victor Osimhen missed a penalty kick (18').

95

13.09.22   Anfield, Liverpool: Liverpool FC – AFC Ajax 2-1 (1-1)
Liverpool FC: Alisson, Joe Matip, Virgil van Dijk, Kostas Tsimikas, Trent Alexander-Arnold,
Thiago Alcântara (90+4' Stefan Bajcatic), Fabinho, Harvey Elliott (66' Roberto Firmino),
Mohamed Salah, Diogo Jota (66' Darwin Núñez), Luis Díaz (90+2' James Milner).
Coach: Jürgen Klopp.
AFC Ajax: Remko Pasveer, Daley Blind, Calvin Bassey, Jurriën Timber, Devyne Rensch (68'
Jorge Sánchez), Edson Álvarez, Kenneth Taylor (80' Florian Grillitsch), Mohammed Kudus
(86' Brian Brobbey), Dusan Tadic, Steven Berghuis, Steven Bergwijn.
Coach: Alfred Schreuder.
Goals: 17' Mohamed Salah 1-0, 27' Mohammed Kudus 1-1, 89' Joe Matip 2-1.
Referee: Artur Soares Dias (POR)   Attendance: 52,387.

14.09.22   Ibrox Stadium, Glasgow: Glasgow Rangers FC – SSC Napoli 0-3 (0-0)
Glasgow Rangers FC: Allan McGregor, James Tavernier (82' Glen Kamara), Connor Goldson,
Borna Barisic, Steven Davis (82' Malik Tillman), Scott Arfield (72' Rabbi Matondo), Ryan
Jack (63' Leon King), John Lundstram, James Sands, Alfredo Morelos (72' Antonio Colak),
Ryan Kent. Coach: Giovanni van Bronckhorst.
SSC Napoli: Alex Meret, Mário Rui (77' Mathías Olivera), Giovanni Di Lorenzo, Amir
Rrahmani, Kim Min-Jae, Piotr Zielinski (83' Tanguy Ndombèlé), Stanislav Lobotka, Frank
Zambo Anguissa, Matteo Politano (77' Alessio Zerbin), Giovanni Simeone (77' Giacomo
Raspadori), Khvicha Kvaratskhelia (90' Eljif Elmas). Coach: Luciano Spalletti.
Goals: 68' Matteo Politano 0-1 (p), 85' Giacomo Raspadori 0-2, 90+1' Tanguy Ndombèlé 0-3.
Referee: Antonio Mateu Lahoz (ESP)   Attendance: 50,121.
Sent off: 55' James Sands.

Piotr Zielinski missed a penalty kick (60').

*The match was originally scheduled to be played on 13th September 2022, but was rescheduled
to the following day following the death of Queen Elizabeth II.*

04.10.22   Anfield, Liverpool: Liverpool FC – Glasgow Rangers FC 2-0 (1-0)
Liverpool FC: Alisson, Joe Matip, Virgil van Dijk, Kostas Tsimikas, Trent Alexander-Arnold
(90+3' Joe Gomez), Jordan Henderson (70' Fabinho), Thiago Alcântara (81' James Milner),
Mohamed Salah, Diogo Jota (69' Roberto Firmino), Luis Díaz, Darwin Núñez (80' Harvey
Elliott). Coach: Jürgen Klopp.
Glasgow Rangers FC: Allan McGregor, James Tavernier, Connor Goldson, Ben Davies (81'
Glen Kamara), Borna Barisic, Leon King, Steven Davis (66' Ryan Jack), John Lundstram,
Alfredo Morelos (73' Antonio Colak), Ryan Kent (81' Rabbi Matondo), Malik Tillman (66'
Fashion Sakala). Coach: Giovanni van Bronckhorst.
Goals: 7' Trent Alexander-Arnold 1-0, 53' Mohamed Salah 2-0 (p).
Referee: Clément Turpin (FRA)   Attendance: 49,512.

04.10.22   Johan Cruijff ArenA, Amsterdam: AFC Ajax – SSC Napoli 1-6 (1-3)
AFC Ajax: Remko Pasveer, Daley Blind, Calvin Bassey, Jurriën Timber (80' Florian
Grillitsch), Devyne Rensch (84' Youri Baas), Edson Álvarez, Kenneth Taylor (72' Davy
Klaassen), Mohammed Kudus, Dusan Tadic, Steven Berghuis (72' Brian Brobbey), Steven
Bergwijn. Coach: Alfred Schreuder.
SSC Napoli: Alex Meret, Giovanni Di Lorenzo (84' Alessandro Zanoli), Amir Rrahmani,
Mathías Olivera, Kim Min-Jae, Piotr Zielinski (46' Tanguy Ndombèlé), Stanislav Lobotka (80'
Gianluca Gaetano), Frank Zambo Anguissa, Hirving Lozano, Khvicha Kvaratskhelia (64' Eljif
Elmas), Giacomo Raspadori (64' Giovanni Simeone). Coach: Luciano Spalletti.
Goals: 9' Mohammed Kudus 1-0, 18' Giacomo Raspadori 1-1, 33' Giovanni Di Lorenzo 1-2,
45' Piotr Zielinski 1-3, 47' Giacomo Raspadori 1-4, 63' Khvicha Kvaratskhelia 1-5,
81' Giovanni Simeone 1-6.
Referee: François Letexier (FRA)   Attendance: 52,896.
Sent off: 73' Dusan Tadic.

12.10.22   Stadio Diego Armando Maradona, Napoli: SSC Napoli – AFC Ajax 4-2 (2-0)
SSC Napoli: Alex Meret, Juan Jesus, Giovanni Di Lorenzo, Mathías Olivera, Kim Min-Jae,
Piotr Zielinski (89' Gianluca Gaetano), Stanislav Lobotka, Frank Zambo Anguissa (49'
Tanguy Ndombèlé), Hirving Lozano (77' Matteo Politano), Khvicha Kvaratskhelia (77' Eljif
Elmas), Giacomo Raspadori (50' Victor Osimhen). Coach: Luciano Spalletti.
AFC Ajax: Remko Pasveer, Daley Blind, Jorge Sánchez (65' Youri Baas), Calvin Bassey,
Jurriën Timber, Davy Klaassen, Edson Álvarez, Kenneth Taylor (64' Florian Grillitsch),
Mohammed Kudus (65' Brian Brobbey), Steven Berghuis (84' Francisco Conceição), Steven
Bergwijn (84' Lucas Ocampos). Coach: Alfred Schreuder.
Goals: 4' Hirving Lozano 1-0, 16' Giacomo Raspadori 2-0, 49' Dany Klaassen 2-1,
62' Khvicha Kvaratskhelia 3-1 (p), 83' Steven Bergwijn 3-2 (p), 89' Victor Osimhen 4-2.
Referee: Felix Zwayer (GER)   Attendance: 52,229.

12.10.22   Ibrox Stadium, Glasgow: Glasgow Rangers FC – Liverpool FC 1-7 (1-1)
Glasgow Rangers FC: Allan McGregor, James Tavernier, Connor Goldson (45' Leon King),
Ben Davies, Borna Barisic, Scott Arfield, Ryan Jack (60' Steven Davis), John Lundstram,
Antonio Colak (76' Alfredo Morelos), Ryan Kent (76' Scott Wright), Fashion Sakala (76'
Rabbi Matondo). Coach: Giovanni van Bronckhorst.
Liverpool FC: Alisson, Virgil van Dijk, Joe Gomez, Kostas Tsimikas (67' Andy Robertson),
Ibrahima Konaté (79' James Milner), Jordan Henderson (67' Thiago Alcântara), Fabinho,
Fábio Carvalho, Harvey Elliott, Roberto Firmino (73' Diogo Jota), Darwin Núñez (68'
Mohamed Salah). Coach: Jürgen Klopp.
Goals: 17' Scott Arfield 1-0, 24', 55' Roberto Firmino 1-1, 1-2, 66' Darwin Núñez 1-3,
76', 80', 81' Mohamed Salah 1-4, 1-5, 1-6, 87' Harvey Elliott 1-7.
Referee: Slavko Vincic (SVN)   Attendance: 48,820.

26.10.22   Stadio Diego Armando Maradona, Napoli:
SSC Napoli – Glasgow Rangers FC 3-0 (2-0)
SSC Napoli: Alex Meret, Mário Rui, Giovanni Di Lorenzo (86' Alessandro Zanoli), Leo
Østigård, Kim Min-Jae, Stanislav Lobotka (83' Piotr Zielinski), Tanguy Ndombèlé, Eljif Elmas
(73' Gianluca Gaetano), Matteo Politano (73' Hirving Lozano), Giovanni Simeone, Giacomo
Raspadori (83' Alessio Zerbin). Coach: Luciano Spalletti.
Glasgow Rangers FC: Allan McGregor, James Tavernier, Ben Davies, Ridvan Yilmaz, Leon
King (76' Borna Barisic), John Lundstram, Scott Wright (46' Fashion Sakala), James Sands,
Alfredo Morelos (68' Antonio Colak), Ryan Kent, Malik Tillman (67' Scott Arfield).
Coach: Giovanni van Bronckhorst.
Goals: 11', 16' Giovanni Simeone 1-0, 2-0, 80' Leo Østigård 3-0.
Referee: Halil Umut Meler (TUR)   Attendance: 39,835.

26.10.22   Johan Cruijff ArenA, Amsterdam: AFC Ajax – Liverpool FC 0-3 (0-1)
AFC Ajax: Remko Pasveer, Daley Blind (58' Owen Wijndal), Jorge Sánchez, Calvin Bassey,
Jurriën Timber, Davy Klaassen (58' Mohammed Kudus), Edson Álvarez (85' Florian
Grillitsch), Dusan Tadic, Steven Berghuis (85' Francisco Conceição), Steven Bergwijn, Brian
Brobbey (63' Kenneth Taylor). Coach: Alfred Schreuder.
Liverpool FC: Alisson, Virgil van Dijk, Andy Robertson (87' Kostas Tsimikas), Joe Gomez,
Trent Alexander-Arnold, Jordan Henderson (70' James Milner), Fabinho (71' Stefan Bajcetic),
Harvey Elliott (71' Fábio Carvalho), Roberto Firmino, Mohamed Salah, Darwin Núñez (63'
Curtis Jones). Coach: Jürgen Klopp.
Goals: 42' Mohamed Salah 0-1, 49' Darwin Núñez 0-2, 52' Harvey Elliott 0-3.
Referee: José María Sánchez Martínez (ESP)   Attendance: 53,327.

01.11.22   Anfield, Liverpool: Liverpool FC – SSC Napoli 2-0 (0-0)
Liverpool FC: Alisson, Virgil van Dijk, Kostas Tsimikas, Trent Alexander-Arnold (87' Calvin
Ramsay), Ibrahima Konaté, James Milner (48' Harvey Elliott), Thiago Alcântara (87' Stefan
Bajcetic), Fabinho, Curtis Jones (73' Darwin Núñez), Roberto Firmino (87' Fábio Carvalho),
Mohamed Salah. Coach: Jürgen Klopp.
SSC Napoli: Alex Meret, Giovanni Di Lorenzo, Mathías Olivera, Leo Østigård, Kim Min-Jae,
Stanislav Lobotka (83' Piotr Zielinski), Tanguy Ndombèlé (87' Giacomo Raspadori), Frank
Zambo Anguissa, Matteo Politano (70' Hirving Lozano), Victor Osimhen (87' Giovanni
Simeone), Khvicha Kvaratskhelia (83' Eljif Elmas). Coach: Luciano Spalletti.
Goals: 85' Mohamed Salah 1-0, 90+8' Darwin Núñez 2-0.
Referee: Tobias Stieler (GER)   Attendance: 52,077.

01.11.22   Ibrox Stadium, Glasgow: Glasgow Rangers FC – AFC Ajax 1-3 (0-2)
Glasgow Rangers FC: Allan McGregor, James Tavernier, Borna Barisic, Leon King, Steven
Davis (60' Glen Kamara), Scott Arfield (83' Alex Lowry), James Sands, Antonio Colak (60'
Alfredo Morelos), Ryan Kent (83' Rabbi Matondo), Fashion Sakala, Malik Tillman (60' Scott
Wright). Coach: Giovanni van Bronckhorst.
AFC Ajax: Remko Pasveer, Jorge Sánchez, Owen Wijndal (44' Devyne Rensch), Calvin
Bassey, Jurriën Timber, Edson Álvarez, Kenneth Taylor (87' Florian Grillitsch), Mohammed
Kudus, Dusan Tadic, Steven Berghuis (55' Davy Klaassen), Steven Bergwijn (88' Francisco
Conceição). Coach: Alfred Schreuder.
Goals: 4' Steven Berghuis 0-1, 29' Mohammed Kudus 0-2, 87' James Tavernier 1-2 (p),
89' Francisco Conceição 1-3.
Referee: Glenn Nyberg (SWE)   Attendance: 48,817.

GROUP B

07.09.22   Estádio Cívitas Metropolitano, Madrid: Atlético Madrid – FC Porto 2-1 (0-0)
Atlético Madrid: Jan Oblak, José Giménez, Reinildo, Nahuel Molina (46' Rodrigo de Paul),
Axel Witsel, Saúl (61' Antoine Griezmann), Koke, Yannick Carrasco (46' Thomas Lemar),
Marcos Llorente, Álvaro Morata (68' Mario Hermoso), João Félix (71' Ángel Correa).
Coach: Diego Simeone.
FC Porto: Diogo Costa, Pepe, Zaidu Sanusi, David Carmo, Mateus Uribe, Otávio (77' Bruno
Costa), Stephen Eustáquio, Mehdi Taremi, Galeno (88' Gabriel Veron), Pepê Aquino (62' João
Mário), Evanilson (78' Toni Martínez). Coach: Sérgio Conceição.
Goals: 90+2' Mario Hermoso 1-0, 90+6' Mateus Uribe 1-1 (p),
90+11' Antoine Griezmann 2-1.
Referee: Szymon Marciniak (POL)   Attendance: 51,777.
Sent off: 81' Mehdi Taremi.

07.09.22   Jan Breydelstadion, Brugge: Club Brugge KV – Bayer Leverkusen 1-0 (1-0)
Club Brugge KV: Simon Mignolet, Denis Odoi, Brandon Mechele, Bjorn Meijer, Abakar
Sylla, Hans Vanaken, Casper Nielsen, Raphael Onyedika (83' Éder Balanta), Andreas Skov
Olsen (83' Cisse Sandra), Kamal Sowah (89' Eduard Sobol), Ferrán Jutglà (64' Roman
Yaremchuk). Coach: Carl Hoefkens.
Bayer Leverkusen: Lukás Hrádecký, Jonathan Tah, Jeremie Frimpong (86' Sardar Azmoun),
Mitchel Bakker (67' Adam Hlozek), Odilon Kossounou, Piero Hincapié, Charles Aránguiz (46'
Exequiel Palacios), Robert Andrich (67' Kerem Demirbay), Callum Hudson-Odoi (86' Nadiem
Amiri), Patrik Schick, Moussa Diaby. Coach: Gerardo Seoane.
Goal: 42' Abakar Sylla 1-0.
Referee: Irfan Peljto (BIH)   Attendance: 21,235.

13.09.22   Estádio do Dragão, Porto: FC Porto – Club Brugge KV 0-4 (0-1)
FC Porto: Diogo Costa, Pepe, Zaidu Sanusi (76' Wendell), João Mário (46' Daniel Namaso
Loader), David Carmo, Mateus Uribe, Otávio (61' Gonçalo Borges), Stephen Eustáquio,
Galeno (61' Gabriel Veron), Pepê Aquino, Evanilson (46' Toni Martínez).
Coach: Sérgio Conceição.
Club Brugge KV: Simon Mignolet, Denis Odoi, Brandon Mechele, Bjorn Meijer (75' Eduard
Sobol), Abakar Sylla (65' Dedryck Boyata), Hans Vanaken, Casper Nielsen, Raphael
Onyedika, Andreas Skov Olsen (71' Roman Yaremchuk), Kamal Sowah, Ferrán Jutglà (75'
Antonio Nusa). Coach: Carl Hoefkens.
Goals: 15' Ferrán Jutglà 0-1 (p), 47' Kamal Sowah 0-2, 52' Andreas Skov Olsen 0-3,
89' Antonio Nusa 0-4.
Referee: Anastasios Sidiropoulos (GRE)   Attendance: 39,225.

13.09.22 BayArena, Leverkusen: Bayer Leverkusen – Atlético Madrid 2-0 (0-0)
Bayer Leverkusen: Lukás Hrádecký, Jonathan Tah, Edmond Tapsoba (89' Mitchel Bakker), Odilon Kossounou, Piero Hincapié, Kerem Demirbay, Robert Andrich, Callum Hudson-Odoi (90+1' Nadiem Amiri), Patrik Schick (89' Charles Aránguiz), Moussa Diaby (89' Sardar Azmoun), Adam Hlozek (69' Jeremie Frimpong). Coach: Gerardo Seoane.
Atlético Madrid: Ivo Grbic, Felipe Monteiro, Reinildo (62' Yannick Carrasco), Mario Hermoso, Nahuel Molina (63' Antoine Griezmann), Axel Witsel, Saúl (46' Rodrigo de Paul), Koke, Marcos Llorente, Álvaro Morata (73' Matheus Cunha), João Félix (73' Ángel Correa). Coach: Diego Simeone.
Goals: 84' Robert Andrich 1-0, 87' Moussa Diaby 2-0.
Referee: Michael Oliver (ENG)   Attendance: 25,825.

04.10.22   Estádio do Dragão, Porto: FC Porto – Bayer Leverkusen 2-0 (0-0)
FC Porto: Diogo Costa, Pepe, Wendell (63' Zaidu Sanusi), João Mário (63' Galeno), David Carmo, Mateus Uribe (83' Marko Grujic), Bruno Costa (46' Otávio), Stephen Eustáquio, Mehdi Taremi, Pepê Aquino, Evanilson (71' Toni Martínez). Coach: Sérgio Conceição.
Bayer Leverkusen: Lukás Hrádecký, Jonathan Tah, Jeremie Frimpong, Edmond Tapsoba, Piero Hincapié, Charles Aránguiz (79' Nadiem Amiri), Robert Andrich (72' Kerem Demirbay), Callum Hudson-Odoi (86' Timothy Fosu-Mensah), Patrik Schick, Moussa Diaby, Adam Hlozek (72' Amine Adli). Coach: Gerardo Seoane.
Goals: 69' Zaidu Sanusi 1-0, 87' Galeno 2-0.
Referee: Anthony Taylor (ENG)   Attendance: 42,399.
Sent off: 88' Jeremie Frimpong.

Patrik Schick missed a penalty kick (45').

04.10.22   Jan Breydelstadion, Brugge: Club Brugge KV – Atlético Madrid 2-0 (1-0)
Club Brugge KV: Simon Mignolet, Denis Odoi, Brandon Mechele, Bjorn Meijer (78' Eduard Sobol), Abakar Sylla (89' Jorne Spileers), Hans Vanaken, Casper Nielsen, Raphael Onyedika, Tajon Buchanan (79' Éder Balanta), Kamal Sowah, Ferrán Jutglà (86' Antonio Nusa). Coach: Carl Hoefkens.
Atlético Madrid: Jan Oblak, Stefan Savic, José Giménez (46' Geoffrey Kondogbia), Reinildo, Nahuel Molina, Axel Witsel, Koke, Yannick Carrasco (80' João Félix), Marcos Llorente (33' Ángel Correa), Antoine Griezmann, Álvaro Morata (65' Matheus Cunha). Coach: Diego Simeone.
Goals: 36' Kamal Sowah 1-0, 62' Ferrán Jutglà 2-0.
Referee: István Kovács (ROM)   Attendance: 25,667.

Antoine Griezmann missed a penalty kick (76').

12.10.22   Estádio Cívitas Metropolitano, Madrid: Atlético Madrid – Club Brugge KV 0-0
Atlético Madrid: Jan Oblak, Stefan Savic, José Giménez, Reinildo, Nahuel Molina, Saúl (73'
Matheus Cunha), Geoffrey Kondogbia, Koke (60' Rodrigo de Paul), Thomas Lemar (60'
Álvaro Morata), Antoine Griezmann (79' Axel Witsel), Ángel Correa (60' Yannick Carrasco).
Coach: Diego Simeone.
Club Brugge KV: Simon Mignolet, Denis Odoi, Brandon Mechele, Abakar Sylla, Hans
Vanaken, Casper Nielsen, Raphael Onyedika, Andreas Skov Olsen (50' Bjorn Meijer), Tajon
Buchanan (83' Clinton Mata), Kamal Sowah, Ferrán Jutglà (73' Éder Balanta).
Coach: Carl Hoefkens.
Referee: Danny Makkelie (HOL)   Attendance: 60,810.
Sent off: 82' Kamal Sowah.

12.10.22   BayArena, Leverkusen: Bayer Leverkusen – FC Porto 0-3 (0-1)
Bayer Leverkusen: Lukás Hrádecký, Jonathan Tah, Mitchel Bakker, Odilon Kossounou (69'
Edmond Tapsoba), Piero Hincapié, Charles Aránguiz, Kerem Demirbay, Callum Hudson-Odoi
(69' Adam Hlozek), Patrik Schick, Moussa Diaby (88' Timothy Fosu-Mensah), Amine Adli
(57' Paulinho). Coach: Xabi Alonso.
FC Porto: Diogo Costa, Fábio Cardoso, Zaidu Sanusi, João Mário (46' Evanilson), David
Carmo, Mateus Uribe (85' Bernardo Folha), Otávio, Stephen Eustáquio (90+2' Toni Martínez),
Mehdi Taremi (90+2' Daniel Namaso Loader), Galeno (85' Gonçalo Borges), Pepê Aquino.
Coach: Sérgio Conceição.
Goals: 6' Galeno 0-1, 53', 64' Mehdi Taremi 0-2 (p), 0-3 (p).
Referee: István Kovács (ROM)   Attendance: 30,210.

Kerem Demirbay missed a penalty kick (16').

26.10.22   Jan Breydelstadion, Brugge: Club Brugge KV – FC Porto 0-4 (0-1)
Club Brugge KV: Simon Mignolet, Denis Odoi (71' Bjorn Meijer), Brandon Mechele, Abakar
Sylla (71' Dedryck Boyata), Hans Vanaken, Casper Nielsen (80' Lynnt Audoor), Noa Lang,
Raphael Onyedika (81' Éder Balanta), Andreas Skov Olsen (71' Antonio Nusa), Tajon
Buchanan, Ferrán Jutglà. Coach: Carl Hoefkens.
FC Porto: Diogo Costa, Fábio Cardoso, Zaidu Sanusi (76' Wendell), David Carmo, Mateus
Uribe, Otávio, Stephen Eustáquio (77' Bruno Costa), Mehdi Taremi, Galeno (77' Gabriel
Veron), Pepê Aquino (88' Toni Martínez), Evanilson (88' Rodrigo Conceição).
Coach: Sérgio Conceição.
Goals: 33' Mehdi Taremi 0-1, 57' Evanilson 0-2, 60' Stephen Eustáquio 0-3,
70' Mehdi Taremi 0-4.
Referee: Michael Oliver (ENG)   Attendance: 26,144.

Noa Lang missed a penalty kick (51').

26.10.22   Estádio Cívitas Metropolitano, Madrid:
Atlético Madrid – Bayer Leverkusen 2-2 (1-2)
Atlético Madrid: Jan Oblak, José Giménez (87' João Félix), Reinildo, Mario Hermoso (46'
Saúl), Nahuel Molina, Axel Witsel, Geoffrey Kondogbia, Yannick Carrasco, Antoine
Griezmann, Álvaro Morata (61' Matheus Cunha), Ángel Correa (46' Rodrigo de Paul).
Coach: Diego Simeone.
Bayer Leverkusen: Lukás Hrádecký, Jeremie Frimpong, Mitchel Bakker, Edmond Tapsoba
(61' Jonathan Tah), Odilon Kossounou, Piero Hincapié, Robert Andrich, Nadiem Amiri,
Callum Hudson-Odoi (60' Amine Adli), Moussa Diaby (76' Paulinho), Adam Hlozek (89'
Timothy Fosu-Mensah). Coach: Xabi Alonso.
Goals: 9' Moussa Diaby 0-1, 22' Yannick Carrasco 1-1, 29' Callum Hudson-Odoi 1-2,
50' Rodrigo de Paul 2-2.
Referee: Clément Turpin (FRA)   Attendance: 63,803.

Yannick Carrasco missed a penalty kick (90+9').

01.11.22   Estádio do Dragão, Porto: FC Porto – Atlético Madrid 2-1 (2-0)
FC Porto: Diogo Costa, Iván Marcano, Fábio Cardoso, Zaidu Sanusi (53' Wendell), Otávio
(89' Gonçalo Borges), Marko Grujic, Stephen Eustáquio, Mehdi Taremi, Galeno (89' Bernardo
Folha), Pepê Aquino (89' Rodrigo Conceição), Evanilson (81' Toni Martínez).
Coach: Sérgio Conceição.
Atlético Madrid: Jan Oblak, Stefan Savic, José Giménez, Reinildo, Nahuel Molina, Axel
Witsel, Saúl (60' Yannick Carrasco), Rodrigo de Paul, Antoine Griezmann, Ángel Correa (85'
Pablo Barrios), João Félix (61' Matheus Cunha). Coach: Diego Simeone.
Goals: 5' Mehdi Taremi 1-0, 24' Stephen Eustáquio 2-0, 90+5' Iván Marcano 2-1 (og).
Referee: Daniele Orsato (ITA)   Attendance: 47,546.

01.11.22   BayArena, Leverkusen: Bayer Leverkusen – Club Brugge KV 0-0
Bayer Leverkusen: Lukás Hrádecký, Jonathan Tah, Jeremie Frimpong, Mitchel Bakker,
Edmond Tapsoba, Odilon Kossounou, Robert Andrich, Exequiel Palacios (46' Kerem
Demirbay), Callum Hudson-Odoi (76' Nadiem Amiri), Patrik Schick (89' Adam Hlozek),
Moussa Diaby (76' Amine Adli). Coach: Xabi Alonso.
Club Brugge KV: Simon Mignolet, Dedryck Boyata, Eduard Sobol (79' Cyle Larin), Brandon
Mechele, Bjorn Meijer, Hans Vanaken, Casper Nielsen, Noa Lang (67' Andreas Skov Olsen),
Tajon Buchanan, Kamal Sowah, Ferrán Jutglà (87' Roman Yaremchuk).
Coach: Carl Hoefkens.
Referee: Maurizio Mariani (ITA)   Attendance: 30,210.

GROUP C

07.09.22   Spotify Camp Nou, Barcelona: FC Barcelona – Viktoria Plzen 5-1 (3-1)
FC Barcelona: Marc-André ter Stegen, Jordi Alba, Sergi Roberto (46' Piqué), Andreas
Christensen, Jules Koundé, Franck Kessié (81' Pablo Torre), Frenkie de Jong, Pedri (75'
Gavi), Robert Lewandowski, Ousmane Dembélé (75' Memphis Depay), Ansu Fati (66' Ferrán
Torres). Coach: Xavi.
Viktoria Plzen: Jindrich Stanek, Lukás Hejda, Ludek Pernica, Milan Havel, Václav Jemelka
(86' Libor Holík), Jan Sýkora (79' Václav Pilar), Jhon Mosquera (79' Erik Jirka), Adam
Vlkanova (78' Ales Cermák), Lukás Kalvach, Pavel Bucha, Tomás Chorý (66' Fortune
Bassey). Coach: Michal Bílek.
Goals: 13' Franck Kessié 1-0, 34' Robert Lewandowski 2-0, 44' Jan Sýkora 2-1,
45+3', 67' Robert Lewandowski 3-1, 4-1, 71' Ferrán Torres 5-1).
Referee: Lawrence Visser (BEL)   Attendance: 77,411.

07.09.22   Stadio Giuseppe Meazza, Milan:
Internazionale Milano – Bayern München 0-2 (0-1)
Internazionale Milano: André Onana, Danilo D'Ambrosio, Milan Skriniar (72' Stefan de Vrij), Robin Gosens, Denzel Dumfries (71' Matteo Darmian), Alessandro Bastoni (72' Federico Dimarco), Henrikh Mkhitaryan, Marcelo Brozovic, Hakan Çalhanoglu (81' Roberto Gagliardini), Edin Dzeko (71' Joaquín Correa), Lautaro Martínez. Coach: Simone Inzaghi.
Bayern München: Manuel Neuer, Lucas Hernández (84' Josip Stanisic), Benjamin Pavard, Matthijs de Ligt (75' Dayot Upamecano), Alphonso Davies, Marcel Sabitzer (61' Leon Goretzka), Joshua Kimmich, Thomas Müller, Sadio Mané, Kingsley Coman (75' Serge Gnabry), Leroy Sané (84' Jamal Musiala). Coach: Julian Nagelsmann.
Goals: 25' Leroy Sané 0-1, 66' Danilo D'Ambrosio 0-2 (og).
Referee: Clément Turpin (FRA)   Attendance: 58,951.

13.09.22   Doosan Aréna, Plzen: Viktoria Plzen – Internazionale Milano 0-2 (0-1)
Viktoria Plzen: Jindrich Stanek, Lukás Hejda, Ludek Pernica, Milan Havel (76' Libor Holík), Václav Jemelka, Jan Sýkora (71' Erik Jirka), Jhon Mosquera, Adam Vlkanova (84' Ales Cermák), Lukás Kalvach (76' Modou N'Diaye), Pavel Bucha, Tomás Chorý (71' Fortune Bassey). Coach: Michal Bílek.
Internazionale Milano: André Onana, Francesco Acerbi, Milan Skriniar, Robin Gosens, Denzel Dumfries, Alessandro Bastoni (64' Danilo D'Ambrosio), Henrikh Mkhitaryan (72' Hakan Çalhanoglu), Marcelo Brozovic (84' Kristjan Asllani), Nicolò Barella (72' Roberto Gagliardini), Edin Dzeko, Joaquín Correa (72' Lautaro Martínez). Coach: Simone Inzaghi.
Goals: 20' Edin Dzeko 0-1, 71' Denzel Dumfries 0-2.
Referee: Sandro Schärer (SUI)   Attendance: 11,252.
Sent off: 61' Pavel Bucha.

13.09.22   Allianz Arena, München: Bayern München – FC Barcelona 2-0 (0-0)
Bayern München: Manuel Neuer, Lucas Hernández, Benjamin Pavard (21' Noussair Mazraoui), Dayot Upamecano, Alphonso Davies, Marcel Sabitzer (46' Leon Goretzka), Joshua Kimmich, Thomas Müller, Sadio Mané (70' Serge Gnabry), Leroy Sané (79' Mathys Tel), Jamal Musiala (80' Ryan Gravenberch). Coach: Julian Nagelsmann.
FC Barcelona: Marc-André ter Stegen, Marcos Alonso, Andreas Christensen (70' Eric García), Jules Koundé, Ronald Araújo, Sergio Busquets (80' Franck Kessié), Pedri, Gavi (61' Frenkie de Jong), Robert Lewandowski, Ousmane Dembélé (80' Ansu Fati), Raphinha (61' Ferrán Torres). Coach: Xavi.
Goals: 51' Lucas Hernández 1-0, 54' Leroy Sané 2-0.
Referee: Danny Makkelie (HOL)   Attendance: 75,000.

04.10.22   Allianz Arena, München: Bayern München – Viktoria Plzen 5-0 (3-0)
Bayern München: Manuel Neuer, Noussair Mazraoui, Dayot Upamecano (72' Benjamin Pavard), Matthijs de Ligt, Alphonso Davies (46' Josip Stanisic), Leon Goretzka (73' Marcel Sabitzer), Ryan Gravenberch, Sadio Mané, Serge Gnabry, Leroy Sané (58' Mathys Tel), Jamal Musiala (46' Eric Maxim Choupo-Moting). Coach: Julian Nagelsmann.
Viktoria Plzen: Marián Tvrdon (63' Mohamed Tijani), Lukás Hejda, Ludek Pernica, Milan Havel, Libor Holík, Jan Kopic (58' Erik Jirka), Jhon Mosquera (86' Václav Pilar), Adam Vlkanova (46' Václav Jemelka), Lukás Kalvach, Modou N'Diaye, Tomás Chorý (58' Fortune Bassey). Coach: Michal Bílek.
Goals: 7' Leroy Sané 1-0, 13' Serge Gnabry 2-0, 21' Sadio Mané 3-0, 50' Leroy Sané 4-0, 59' Eric Maxim Choupo-Moting 5-0.
Referee: Nikola Dabanovic (MNE)   Attendance: 75,000.

103

04.10.22 Stadio Giuseppe Meazza, Milan: Internazionale Milano – FC Barcelona 1-0 (1-0)
Internazionale Milano: André Onana, Matteo Darmian (77' Robin Gosens), Stefan de Vrij (77' Francesco Acerbi), Milan Skriniar, Federico Dimarco (76' Denzel Dumfries), Alessandro Bastoni, Henrikh Mkhitaryan, Hakan Çalhanoglu (85' Kristjan Asllani), Nicolò Barella, Joaquín Correa (56' Edin Dzeko), Lautaro Martínez. Coach: Simone Inzaghi.
FC Barcelona: Marc-André ter Stegen, Sergi Roberto, Marcos Alonso (64' Álex Baldé), Andreas Christensen (58' Piqué), Eric García, Sergio Busquets, Pedri, Gavi (83' Franck Kessié), Robert Lewandowski, Ousmane Dembélé, Raphinha (63' Ansu Fati). Coach: Xavi.
Goal: 45+2' Hakan Çalhanoglu 1-0.
Referee: Slavko Vincic (SVN)   Attendance: 71,368.

12.10.22 Spotify Camp Nou, Barcelona: FC Barcelona – Internazionale Milano 3-3 (1-0)
FC Barcelona: Marc-André ter Stegen, Piqué, Sergi Roberto (72' Franck Kessié), Marcos Alonso (72' Álex Baldé), Eric García, Sergio Busquets (63' Frenkie de Jong), Pedri, Gavi (82' Ferrán Torres), Robert Lewandowski, Ousmane Dembélé, Raphinha (64' Ansu Fati). Coach: Xavi.
Internazionale Milano: André Onana, Stefan de Vrij, Milan Skriniar, Federico Dimarco (67' Matteo Darmian), Denzel Dumfries, Alessandro Bastoni (85' Francesco Acerbi), Henrikh Mkhitaryan, Hakan Çalhanoglu (76' Robin Gosens), Nicolò Barella (85' Kristjan Asllani), Edin Dzeko (76' Raoul Bellanova), Lautaro Martínez. Coach: Simone Inzaghi.
Goals: 40' Ousmane Dembélé 1-0, 50' Nicolò Barella 1-1, 63' Lautaro Martínez 1-2, 82' Robert Lewandowski 2-2, 89' Robin Gosens 2-3, 90+2' Robert Lewandowski 3-3.
Referee: Szymon Marciniak (POL)   Attendance: 92,302.

12.10.22 Doosan Aréna, Plzen: Viktoria Plzen – Bayern München 2-4 (0-4)
Viktoria Plzen: Jindrich Stanek, Lukás Hejda, Milan Havel (46' Libor Holík), Václav Jemelka (46' Ludek Pernica), Mohamed Tijani, Jan Kopic (25' Erik Jirka), Jhon Mosquera, Adam Vlkanova (81' Václav Pilar), Lukás Kalvach, Pavel Bucha, Tomás Chorý (46' Jan Kliment). Coach: Michal Bílek.
Bayern München: Sven Ulreich, Benjamin Pavard, Noussair Mazraoui, Dayot Upamecano (70' Paul Wanner), Josip Stanisic, Leon Goretzka (56' Ryan Gravenberch), Joshua Kimmich, Thomas Müller (28' Mathys Tel), Sadio Mané, Kingsley Coman (46' Eric Maxim Choupo-Moting), Leroy Sané (70' Marcel Sabitzer). Coach: Julian Nagelsmann.
Goals: 10' Sadio Mané 0-1, 14' Thomas Müller 0-2, 25', 35' Leon Goretzka 0-3, 0-4, 62' Adam Vlkanova 1-4, 75' Jan Kliment 2-4.
Referee: Bartosz Frankowski (POL)   Attendance: 11,326.

26.10.22 Stadio Giuseppe Meazza, Milan: Internazionale Milano – Viktoria Plzen 4-0 (2-0)
Internazionale Milano: André Onana, Francesco Acerbi, Milan Skriniar, Federico Dimarco (77' Robin Gosens), Denzel Dumfries, Alessandro Bastoni, Henrikh Mkhitaryan (83' Roberto Gagliardini), Hakan Çalhanoglu (71' Kristjan Asllani), Nicolò Barella, Edin Dzeko (71' Joaquín Correa), Lautaro Martínez (83' Romelu Lukaku). Coach: Simone Inzaghi.
Viktoria Plzen: Jindrich Stanek, Lukás Hejda, Ludek Pernica, Milan Havel, Mohamed Tijani (51' Václav Jemelka), Jhon Mosquera, Adam Vlkanova (84' Václav Pilar), Lukás Kalvach (70' Modou N'Diaye), Erik Jirka (46' Libor Holík), Pavel Bucha, Fortune Bassey (46' Tomás Chorý). Coach: Michal Bílek.
Goals: 35' Henrikh Mkhitaryan 1-0, 42', 66' Edin Dzeko 2-0, 3-0, 87' Romelu Lukaku 4-0.
Referee: Andreas Ekberg (SWE)   Attendance: 71,849.

26.10.22 Spotify Camp Nou, Barcelona: FC Barcelona – Bayern München 0-3 (0-2)
FC Barcelona: Marc-André ter Stegen, Marcos Alonso, Héctor Bellerín, Jules Koundé (67'
Eric García), Álex Baldé, Sergio Busquets (58' Ferrán Torres), Franck Kessié, Frenkie de Jong,
Pedri (58' Raphinha), Robert Lewandowski (82' Pablo Torre), Ousmane Dembélé (68' Ansu
Fati). Coach: Xavi.
Bayern München: Sven Ulreich, Noussair Mazraoui (79' Josip Stanisic), Dayot Upamecano
(63' Benjamin Pavard), Matthijs de Ligt, Alphonso Davies, Leon Goretzka (46' Marcel
Sabitzer), Joshua Kimmich, Eric Maxim Choupo-Moting (63' Thomas Müller), Sadio Mané,
Serge Gnabry, Jamal Musiala (67' Ryan Gravenberch). Coach: Julian Nagelsmann.
Goals: 10' Sadio Mané 0-1, 31' Eric Maxim Choupo-Moting 0-2, 90+5' Benjamin Pavard 0-3.
Referee: Anthony Taylor (ENG)   Attendance: 84,016.

01.11.22 Allianz Arena, München: Bayern München – Internazionale Milano 2-0 (1-0)
Bayern München: Sven Ulreich, Benjamin Pavard, Noussair Mazraoui (65' Jamal Musiala),
Dayot Upamecano (46' Alphonso Davies), Josip Stanisic, Marcel Sabitzer, Joshua Kimmich,
Ryan Gravenberch, Eric Maxim Choupo-Moting (73' Mathys Tel), Sadio Mané (66' Serge
Gnabry), Kingsley Coman (76' Paul Wanner). Coach: Julian Nagelsmann.
Internazionale Milano: André Onana, Matteo Darmian, Stefan de Vrij (76' Milan Skriniar),
Francesco Acerbi, Robin Gosens, Raoul Bellanova, Roberto Gagliardini (60' Hakan
Çalhanoglu), Nicolò Barella (60' Henrikh Mkhitaryan), Kristjan Asllani, Joaquín Correa (76'
Valentin Carboni), Lautaro Martínez (60' Edin Dzeko). Coach: Simone Inzaghi.
Goals: 32' Benjamin Pavard 1-0, 72' Eric Maxim Choupo-Moting 2-0.
Referee: Ivan Kruzliak (SVK)   Attendance: 75,000.

01.11.22 Doosan Aréna, Plzen: Viktoria Plzen – FC Barcelona 2-4 (0-2)
Viktoria Plzen: Jindrich Stanek, Lukás Hejda, Ludek Pernica, Libor Holík, Václav Jemelka
(57' Milan Havel), Václav Pilar (88' Adam Kronus), Adam Vlkanova, Lukás Kalvach (78'
Ales Cermák), Erik Jirka, Modou N'Diaye (57' Pavel Bucha), Tomás Chorý (79' Fortune
Bassey). Coach: Michal Bílek.
FC Barcelona: Iñaki Peña, Piqué, Jordi Alba (57' Álex Baldé), Marcos Alonso, Héctor
Bellerín, Franck Kessié (67' Marc Casadó), Gavi, Pablo Torre (77' Álvaro Sanz), Ferrán
Torres, Raphinha (78' Ousmane Dembélé), Ansu Fati. Coach: Xavi.
Goals: 6' Marcos Alonso 0-1, 44' Ferrán Torres 0-2, 51' Tomás Chorý 1-2 (p),
54' Ferrán Torres 1-3, 63' Tomás Chorý 2-3, 75' Pablo Torre 2-4.
Referee: Radu Petrescu (ROM)   Attendance: 11,258.

GROUP D

07.09.22 Deutsche Bank Park, Frankfurt am Main:
          Eintracht Frankfurt – Sporting CP 0-3 (0-0)
Eintracht Frankfurt: Kevin Trapp, Christopher Lenz (46' Luca Pellegrini), Evan Ndicka, Tuta,
Mario Götze, Djibril Sow, Daichi Kamada (84' Makoto Hasebe), Kristijan Jakic (83' Ansgar
Knauff), Éric Dina-Ebimbe (66' Rafael Borré), Jesper Lindstrøm (74' Lucas Alario), Randal
Kolo Muani. Coach: Oliver Glasner.
Sporting CP: Antonio Adán, Sebastián Coates, Matheus Reis, Jerry St. Juste (52' Luís Carlos
Neto), Pedro Porro, Gonçalo Inácio, Manuel Ugarte, Pedro Gonçalves "Pote" (79' Nuno
Santos), Hidemasa Morita, Marcus Edwards (73' Rochinha), Trincão (79' Paulinho).
Coach: Rúben Amorim.
Goals: 65' Marcus Edwards 0-1, 67' Trincão 0-2, 82' Nuno Santos 0-3.
Referee: Orel Grinfeld (ISR)   Attendance: 50,500.

105

07.09.22   Tottenham Hotspur Stadium, London:
Tottenham Hotspur – Olympique Marseille 2-0 (0-0)
Tottenham Hotspur: Hugo Lloris, Clément Lenglet (73' Ben Davies), Eric Dier, Cristian
Romero (73' Japhet Tanganga), Emerson Royal (61' Dejan Kulusevski), Ivan Perisic, Pierre-
Emile Højbjerg, Rodrigo Bentancur (85' Yves Bissouma), Heung-Min Son (86' Matt Doherty),
Harry Kane, Richarlison. Coach: Antonio Conte.
Olympique Marseille: Pau López, Jonathan Clauss (70' Sead Kolasinac), Chancel Mbemba,
Samuel Gigot (87' Cengiz Ünder), Eric Bailly, Nuno Tavares, Jordan Veretout (87' Pape
Gueye), Valentin Rongier, Gerson (50' Leonardo Balerdi), Mattéo Guendouzi, Luis Suárez
(71' Amine Harit). Coach: Igor Tudor.
Goals: 76', 81' Richarlison 1-0, 2-0.
Referee: Slavko Vincic (SVN)   Attendance: 57,367.
Sent off: 47' Chancel Mbemba.

13.09.22   Estádio José Alvalade, Lisboa: Sporting CP – Tottenham Hotspur 2-0 (0-0)
Sporting CP: Antonio Adán, Sebastián Coates, Matheus Reis, Pedro Porro, Gonçalo Inácio,
Nuno Santos (90+2' Ricardo Esgaio), Manuel Ugarte, Pedro Gonçalves "Pote", Hidemasa
Morita (71' Sotirios Alexandropoulos), Marcus Edwards (90+2' Arthur Gomes), Trincão (76'
Paulinho). Coach: Rúben Amorim.
Tottenham Hotspur: Hugo Lloris, Ben Davies, Eric Dier, Cristian Romero, Emerson Royal,
Ivan Perisic, Pierre-Emile Højbjerg, Rodrigo Bentancur, Heung-Min Son (72' Dejan
Kulusevski), Harry Kane, Richarlison. Coach: Antonio Conte.
Goals: 90' Paulinho 1-0, 90+3' Arthur Gomes 2-0.
Referee: Srdjan Jovanovic (SRB)   Attendance: 39,899.

13.09.22   Stade Orange Vélodrome, Marseille:
Olympique Marseille – Eintracht Frankfurt 0-1 (0-1)
Olympique Marseille: Pau López, Jonathan Clauss, Sead Kolasinac (82' Issa Kaboré), Eric
Bailly (65' Mattéo Guendouzi), Nuno Tavares, Leonardo Balerdi, Dimitri Payet (60' Cengiz
Ünder), Jordan Veretout, Valentin Rongier, Gerson (59' Amine Harit), Alexis Sánchez (59'
Luis Suárez). Coach: Igor Tudor.
Eintracht Frankfurt: Kevin Trapp, Makoto Hasebe, Evan Ndicka, Tuta, Mario Götze (71'
Sebastian Rode), Djibril Sow, Daichi Kamada (88' Éric Dina-Ebimbe), Kristijan Jakic (79'
Timothy Chandler), Jesper Lindstrøm (79' Rafael Borré), Randal Kolo Muani (88' Lucas
Alario), Ansgar Knauff. Coach: Oliver Glasner.
Goal: 43' Jesper Lindstrøm 0-1.
Referee: José María Sánchez Martínez (ESP)   Attendance: 62,500.

04.10.22   Stade Orange Vélodrome, Marseille: Olympique Marseille – Sporting CP 4-1 (3-1)
Olympique Marseille: Pau López, Jonathan Clauss (32' Issa Kaboré), Chancel Mbemba, Eric
Bailly (77' Samuel Gigot), Nuno Tavares, Leonardo Balerdi, Jordan Veretout (62' Valentin
Rongier), Amine Harit (77' Gerson), Mattéo Guendouzi, Alexis Sánchez, Cengiz Ünder (62'
Pape Gueye). Coach: Igor Tudor.
Sporting CP: Antonio Adán, Ricardo Esgaio, Matheus Reis, Jerry St. Juste (46' José Martínez
Marsà), Gonçalo Inácio, Nuno Santos (46' Paulinho), Manuel Ugarte (46' Flávio Nazinho),
Pedro Gonçalves "Pote" (46' Sotirios Alexandropoulos), Hidemasa Morita, Marcus Edwards
(26' Franco Israel *goalkeeper*), Trincão. Coach: Rúben Amorim.
Goals: 1' Trincão 0-1, 13' Alexis Sánchez 1-1, 16' Amine Harit 2-1, 28' Leonardo Balerdi 3-1,
84' Chancel Mbemba 4-1.
Referee: Davide Massa (ITA)   Attendance: 618.
Sent off: 23' Antonio Adán.

04.10.22   Deutsche Bank Park, Frankfurt am Main:
            Eintracht Frankfurt – Tottenham Hotspur 0-0
Eintracht Frankfurt: Kevin Trapp, Makoto Hasebe, Evan Ndicka, Tuta, Sebastian Rode (71'
Luca Pellegrini), Djibril Sow, Daichi Kamada, Kristijan Jakic, Jesper Lindstrøm (87' Éric
Dina-Ebimbe), Randal Kolo Muani (57' Rafael Borré), Ansgar Knauff. Coach: Oliver Glasner.
Tottenham Hotspur: Hugo Lloris, Clément Lenglet (78' Ben Davies), Eric Dier, Cristian
Romero, Emerson Royal, Ivan Perisic (71' Ryan Sessegnon), Pierre-Emile Højbjerg, Rodrigo
Bentancur, Heung-Min Son, Harry Kane, Richarlison (79' Bryan Gil). Coach: Antonio Conte.
Referee: Daniele Orsato (ITA)   Attendance: 50,500.

12.10.22   Tottenham Hotspur Stadium, London:
            Tottenham Hotspur – Eintracht Frankfurt 3-2 (3-1)
Tottenham Hotspur: Hugo Lloris, Clément Lenglet, Eric Dier (78' Davinson Sánchez), Cristian
Romero, Emerson Royal, Pierre-Emile Højbjerg (85' Bryan Gil), Rodrigo Bentancur (67' Yves
Bissouma), Ryan Sessegnon, Heung-Min Son (86' Lucas Moura), Harry Kane, Richarlison
(67' Oliver Skipp). Coach: Antonio Conte.
Eintracht Frankfurt: Kevin Trapp, Makoto Hasebe (69' Éric Dina-Ebimbe), Christopher Lenz
(70' Faride Alidou), Evan Ndicka, Tuta, Sebastian Rode (69' Hrvoje Smolcic), Djibril Sow,
Daichi Kamada (78' Mario Götze), Kristijan Jakic, Jesper Lindstrøm, Randal Kolo Muani (69'
Rafael Borré). Coach: Oliver Glasner.
Goals: 14' Daichi Kamada 0-1, 19' Heung-Min Son 1-1, 28' Harry Kane 2-1 (p),
36' Heung-Min Son 3-1, 87' Faride Alidou 3-2.
Referee: Carlos del Cerro Grande (ESP)   Attendance: 55,180.
Sent off: 59' Tuta.

Harry Kane missed a penalty kick (90+2').

12.10.22 Estádio José Alvalade, Lisboa: Sporting CP – Olympique Marseille 0-2 (0-2)
Sporting CP: Franco Israel, Sebastián Coates (35' José Martínez Marsà), Ricardo Esgaio,
Matheus Reis, Gonçalo Inácio, Nuno Santos (59' Pedro Porro), Manuel Ugarte, Pedro
Gonçalves "Pote", Hidemasa Morita (22' Abdul Fatawu Issahaku), Marcus Edwards (35'
Sotirios Alexandropoulos), Trincão (46' Flávio Nazinho). Coach: Rúben Amorim.
Olympique Marseille: Pau López, Jonathan Clauss (64' Issa Kaboré), Chancel Mbemba, Eric
Bailly (64' Samuel Gigot), Nuno Tavares, Leonardo Balerdi, Jordan Veretout (87' Pape
Gueye), Valentin Rongier, Amine Harit (72' Dimitri Payet), Mattéo Guendouzi (64' Cengiz
Ünder), Alexis Sánchez. Coach: Igor Tudor.
Goals: 20' Mattéo Guendouzi 0-1 (p), 30' Alexis Sánchez 0-2.
Referee: Alejandro José Hernández Hernández (ESP)   Attendance: 38,126.
Sent off: 19' Ricardo Esgaio, 61' Pedro Gonçalves "Pote".

26.10.22 Tottenham Hotspur Stadium, London: Tottenham Hotspur – Sporting CP 1-1 (0-1)
Tottenham Hotspur: Hugo Lloris, Matt Doherty (71' Bryan Gil), Ben Davies (81' Clément
Lenglet), Eric Dier, Cristian Romero, Ivan Perisic, Pierre-Emile Højbjerg, Rodrigo Bentancur,
Heung-Min Son, Lucas Moura (81' Emerson Royal), Harry Kane. Coach: Antonio Conte.
Sporting CP: Antonio Adán, Sebastián Coates, Matheus Reis, Pedro Porro, Gonçalo Inácio,
Nuno Santos (61' Flávio Nazinho), Manuel Ugarte, Hidemasa Morita (61' Mateus Fernandes),
Paulinho (75' Jerry St. Juste), Marcus Edwards (71' Abdul Fatawu Issahaku), Trincão (71'
Arthur Gomes). Coach: Rúben Amorim.
Goals: 22' Marcus Edwards 0-1, 80' Rodrigo Bentancur 1-1.
Referee: Danny Makkelie (HOL)   Attendance: 59,588.

26.10.22 Deutsche Bank Park, Frankfurt am Main:
          Eintracht Frankfurt – Olympique Marseille 2-1 (2-1)
Eintracht Frankfurt: Kevin Trapp, Christopher Lenz (45' Luca Pellegrini), Evan Ndicka,
Hrvoje Smolcic, Mario Götze, Djibril Sow, Daichi Kamada, Kristijan Jakic, Éric Dina-Ebimbe
(79' Faride Alidou), Jesper Lindstrøm (69' Sebastian Rode), Randal Kolo Muani (79' Rafael
Borré). Coach: Oliver Glasner.
Olympique Marseille: Pau López, Jonathan Clauss (86' Luis Suárez), Chancel Mbemba,
Samuel Gigot (60' Sead Kolasinac), Nuno Tavares, Leonardo Balerdi, Jordan Veretout,
Valentin Rongier, Amine Harit, Mattéo Guendouzi (60' Cengiz Ünder), Alexis Sánchez.
Coach: Igor Tudor.
Goals: 3' Daichi Kamada 1-0, 22' Mattéo Guendouzi 1-1, 27' Randal Kolo Muani 2-1.
Referee: Jesús Gil Manzano (ESP)   Attendance: 48,700.

01.11.22 Estádio José Alvalade, Lisboa: Sporting CP – Eintracht Frankfurt 1-2 (1-0)
Sporting CP: Antonio Adán, Sebastián Coates, Jerry St. Juste (78' Jovane Cabral), Pedro
Porro, Gonçalo Inácio, Nuno Santos (32' Matheus Reis), Arthur Gomes, Manuel Ugarte (63'
Dário Essugo), Pedro Gonçalves "Pote", Paulinho, Marcus Edwards (63' Trincão).
Coach: Rúben Amorim.
Eintracht Frankfurt: Kevin Trapp, Luca Pellegrini, Evan Ndicka, Tuta, Mario Götze (90' Faride
Alidou), Djibril Sow, Daichi Kamada, Kristijan Jakic (81' Hrvoje Smolcic), Éric Dina-Ebimbe
(69' Ansgar Knauff), Jesper Lindstrøm (46' Sebastian Rode), Randal Kolo Muani (80' Rafael
Borré). Coach: Oliver Glasner.
Goals: 39' Arthur Gomes 1-0, 62' Daichi Kamada 1-1 (p), 72' Randal Kolo Muani 1-2.
Referee: Slavko Vincic (SVN)   Attendance: 41,744.

01.11.22   Stade Orange Vélodrome, Marseille:
Olympique Marseille – Tottenham Hotspur 1-2 (1-0)
Olympique Marseille: Pau López, Jonathan Clauss (74' Issa Kaboré), Chancel Mbemba, Eric
Bailly (9' Samuel Gigot, 73' Sead Kolasinac), Nuno Tavares, Leonardo Balerdi, Jordan
Veretout (74' Cengiz Ünder), Valentin Rongier (83' Luis Suárez), Amine Harit, Mattéo
Guendouzi, Alexis Sánchez. Coach: Igor Tudor.
Tottenham Hotspur: Hugo Lloris, Ben Davies, Clément Lenglet, Eric Dier, Ivan Perisic, Pierre-
Emile Højbjerg, Rodrigo Bentancur (84' Oliver Skipp), Ryan Sessegnon (46' Emerson Royal),
Heung-Min Son (29' Yves Bissouma), Lucas Moura (90+3' Bryan Gil), Harry Kane.
Coach: Antonio Conte.
Goals: 45+2' Chancel Mbemba 1-0, 54' Clément Lenglet 1-1,
90+5' Pierre-Emile Højbjerg 1-2.
Referee: Szymon Marciniak (POL)   Attendance: 50,768.

GROUP E

06.09.22   Stadion Maksimir, Zagreb: Dinamo Zagreb – Chelsea FC 1-0 (1-0)
Dinamo Zagreb: Dominik Livakovic, Stefan Ristovski, Dino Peric, Sadegh Moharrami (76'
Rasmus Lauritsen), Josip Sutalo, Arijan Ademi (88' Martin Baturina), Josip Misic, Luka
Ivanusec, Robert Ljubicic, Mislav Orsic (76' Dario Spikic), Bruno Petkovic (90+8' Josip
Drmic). Coach: Ante Cacic.
Chelsea FC: Kepa, César Azpilicueta (46' Hakim Ziyech), Kalidou Koulibaly, Ben Chilwell
(71' Marc Cucurella), Reece James, Wesley Fofana, Mateo Kovacic (59' Jorginho), Mason
Mount, Kai Havertz, Pierre-Emerick Aubameyang (59' Armando Broja), Raheem Sterling (75'
Christian Pulisic). Coach: Thomas Tuchel.
Goal: 13' Mislav Orsic 1-0.
Referee: István Kovács (ROM)   Attendance: 20,607.

06.09.22   Red Bull Arena, Wals-Siezenheim: Red Bull Salzburg – AC Milan 1-1 (1-1)
Red Bull Salzburg: Philipp Köhn, Andreas Ulmer, Oumar Solet (42' Bernardo), Strahinja
Pavlovic, Amar Dedic, Nicolas Seiwald, Nicolás Capaldo, Maurits Kjærgaard, Dijon Kameri
(65' Lucas Gourna-Douath), Noah Okafor (90+3' Junior Chikwubuike Adamu), Fernando (65'
Benjamin Sesko). Coach: Matthias Jaissle.
AC Milan: Mike Maignan, Davide Calabria (57' Sergiño Dest), Fikayo Tomori, Theo
Hernández, Pierre Kalulu, Ismaél Bennacer (57' Tommaso Pobega), Alexis Saelemaekers (80'
Junior Messias), Sandro Tonali, Charles De Ketelaere (70' Brahim Díaz), Olivier Giroud (57'
Divock Origi), Rafael Leão. Coach: Stefano Pioli.
Goals: 28' Noah Okafor 1-0, 40' Alexis Saelemaekers 1-1.
Referee: Srdjan Jovanovic (SRB)   Attendance: 29,520.

14.09.22   Stadio Giuseppe Meazza, Milano: AC Milan – Dinamo Zagreb 3-1 (1-0)
AC Milan: Mike Maignan, Davide Calabria, Fikayo Tomori, Theo Hernández, Pierre Kalulu,
Ismaël Bennacer (78' Rade Krunic), Brahim Díaz (78' Sergiño Dest), Alexis Saelemaekers
(78' Junior Messias), Sandro Tonali (67' Tommaso Pobega), Olivier Giroud (68' Charles De
Ketelaere), Rafael Leão. Coach: Stefano Pioli.
Dinamo Zagreb: Dominik Livakovic, Stefan Ristovski (78' Josip Drmic), Dino Peric, Sadegh
Moharrami (63' Dario Spikic), Josip Sutalo, Arijan Ademi, Josip Misic, Luka Ivanusec, Robert
Ljubicic, Mislav Orsic (84' Antonio Marin), Bruno Petkovic (84' Martin Baturina).
Coach: Ante Cacic.
Goals: 45' Olivier Giroud 1-0 (p), 47' Alexis Saelemaekers 2-0, 56' Mislav Orsic 2-1,
77' Tommaso Pobega 3-1.
Referee: Jesús Gil Manzano (ESP)   Attendance: 61,341.

14.09.22 Stamford Bridge, London: Chelsea FC – Red Bull Salzburg 1-1 (0-0)
Chelsea FC: Kepa, Thiago Silva, César Azpilicueta (81' Hakim Ziyech), Marc Cucurella, Reece James, Mateo Kovacic (81' Conor Gallagher), Jorginho, Mason Mount, Kai Havertz (66' Ruben Loftus-Cheek), Pierre-Emerick Aubameyang (66' Armando Broja), Raheem Sterling (84' Christian Pulisic). Coach: Graham Potter.
Red Bull Salzburg: Philipp Köhn, Andreas Ulmer, Bernardo, Strahinja Pavlovic, Amar Dedic, Nicolas Seiwald, Luka Sucic (70' Dijon Kameri), Nicolás Capaldo, Maurits Kjærgaard (46' Lucas Gourna-Douath), Noah Okafor (85' Sékou Koïta), Benjamin Sesko (70' Junior Chikwubuike Adamu). Coach: Matthias Jaissle.
Goals: 48' Raheem Sterling 1-0, 75' Noah Okafor 1-1.
Referee: Ivan Kruzliak (SVK)   Attendance: 38,818.

05.10.22 Red Bull Arena, Wals-Siezenheim: Red Bull Salzburg – Dinamo Zagreb 1-0 (0-0)
Red Bull Salzburg: Philipp Köhn, Andreas Ulmer (79' Max Wöber), Oumar Solet, Strahinja Pavlovic, Amar Dedic, Nicolas Seiwald, Luka Sucic (90+2' Lucas Gourna-Douath), Nicolás Capaldo, Maurits Kjærgaard, Noah Okafor (79' Junior Chikwubuike Adamu), Benjamin Sesko. Coach: Matthias Jaissle.
Dinamo Zagreb: Dominik Livakovic, Kévin Théophile-Catherine (76' Josip Drmic), Dino Peric, Sadegh Moharrami (80' Petar Bockaj), Josip Sutalo, Arijan Ademi, Josip Misic, Luka Ivanusec (87' Martin Baturina), Robert Ljubicic, Mislav Orsic (80' Dario Spikic), Bruno Petkovic. Coach: Ante Cacic.
Goal: 71' Noah Okafor 1-0 (p).
Referee: Andris Treimanis (LAT)   Attendance: 28,864.

05.10.22 Stamford Bridge, London: Chelsea FC – AC Milan 3-0 (1-0)
Chelsea FC: Kepa, Thiago Silva, Kalidou Koulibaly, Ben Chilwell, Reece James, Wesley Fofana (38' Trevoh Chalobah), Mateo Kovacic (66' Jorginho), Ruben Loftus-Cheek, Mason Mount (74' Kai Havertz), Pierre-Emerick Aubameyang (65' Conor Gallagher), Raheem Sterling (75' Armando Broja). Coach: Graham Potter.
AC Milan: Ciprian Tatarusanu, Fodé Ballo-Touré, Fikayo Tomori, Sergiño Dest, Pierre Kalulu, Rade Krunic (65' Matteo Gabbia), Ismaël Bennacer (73' Tommaso Pobega), Sandro Tonali, Charles De Ketelaere (64' Ante Rebic), Olivier Giroud (73' Divock Origi), Rafael Leão (72' Brahim Díaz). Coach: Stefano Pioli.
Goals: 24' Wesley Fofana 1-0, 56' Pierre-Emerick Aubameyang 2-0, 62' Reece James 3-0.
Referee: Danny Makkelie (HOL)   Attendance: 39,537.

11.10.22 Stadion Maksimir, Zagreb: Dinamo Zagreb – Red Bull Salzburg 1-1 (1-1)
Dinamo Zagreb: Dominik Livakovic, Stefan Ristovski (79' Sadegh Moharrami), Dino Peric, Josip Sutalo, Arijan Ademi (67' Josip Drmic), Josip Misic (86' Marko Bulat), Luka Ivanusec (80' Martin Baturina), Robert Ljubicic, Mislav Orsic, Bruno Petkovic, Dario Spikic (80' Petar Bockaj). Coach: Ante Cacic.
Red Bull Salzburg: Philipp Köhn, Andreas Ulmer, Oumar Solet, Strahinja Pavlovic, Amar Dedic, Nicolas Seiwald, Luka Sucic, Maurits Kjærgaard, Lucas Gourna-Douath, Noah Okafor (62' Junior Chikwubuike Adamu), Benjamin Sesko (86' Roko Simic). Coach: Matthias Jaissle.
Goals: 12' Nicolas Seiwald 0-1, 40' Robert Ljubicic 1-1.
Referee: Tobias Stieler (GER)   Attendance: 20,779.

110

11.10.22 Stadio Giuseppe Meazza, Milano: AC Milan – Chelsea FC 0-2 (0-2)
AC Milan: Ciprian Tatarusanu, Fikayo Tomori, Theo Hernández (80' Fodé Ballo-Touré),
Matteo Gabbia, Pierre Kalulu, Rade Krunic, Ismaël Bennacer (62' Tommaso Pobega), Brahim
Díaz (37' Sergiño Dest), Sandro Tonali, Olivier Giroud (62' Ante Rebic), Rafael Leão (80'
Divock Origi). Coach: Stefano Pioli.
Chelsea FC: Kepa, Thiago Silva, Kalidou Koulibaly, Trevoh Chalobah, Ben Chilwell (89'
Marc Cucurella), Reece James (62' César Azpilicueta), Mateo Kovacic, Jorginho, Mason
Mount (46' Conor Gallagher), Pierre-Emerick Aubameyang (79' Kai Havertz), Raheem
Sterling (62' Ruben Loftus-Cheek). Coach: Graham Potter.
Goals: 21' Jorginho 0-1 (p), 34' Pierre-Emerick Aubameyang 0-2.
Referee: Daniel Siebert (GER)   Attendance: 75,051.
Sent off: 18' Fikayo Tomori.

25.10.22 Red Bull Arena, Wals-Siezenheim: Red Bull Salzburg – Chelsea FC 1-2 (0-1)
Red Bull Salzburg: Philipp Köhn, Bernardo, Max Wöber (78' Andreas Ulmer), Strahinja
Pavlovic, Amar Dedic, Nicolas Seiwald, Luka Sucic (61' Benjamin Sesko), Maurits
Kjærgaard, Lucas Gourna-Douath, Noah Okafor (78' Roko Simic), Junior Chikwubuike
Adamu (82' Dijon Kameri). Coach: Matthias Jaissle.
Chelsea FC: Kepa, Thiago Silva, Marc Cucurella, Trevoh Chalobah, Mateo Kovacic (68'
Ruben Loftus-Cheek), Jorginho, Christian Pulisic (75' César Azpilicueta), Kai Havertz, Conor
Gallagher (88' Hakim Ziyech), Pierre-Emerick Aubameyang (75' Armando Broja), Raheem
Sterling (88' Mason Mount). Coach: Graham Potter.
Goals: 23' Mateo Kovacic 0-1, 49' Junior Chikwubuike Adamu 1-1, 64' Kai Havertz 1-2.
Referee: Sandro Schärer (SUI)   Attendance: 29,520.

25.10.22 Stadion Maksimir, Zagreb: Dinamo Zagreb – AC Milan 0-4 (0-1)
Dinamo Zagreb: Dominik Livakovic, Stefan Ristovski (58' Dario Spikic), Dino Peric, Sadegh
Moharrami, Josip Sutalo, Arijan Ademi (57' Martin Baturina), Josip Misic (75' Marko Bulat),
Luka Ivanusec, Robert Ljubicic, Mislav Orsic (75' Petar Bockaj), Bruno Petkovic (58' Josip
Drmic). Coach: Ante Cacic.
AC Milan: Ciprian Tatarusanu, Simon Kjær, Theo Hernández (70' Fodé Ballo-Touré), Matteo
Gabbia, Pierre Kalulu, Ismaël Bennacer (70' Tommaso Pobega), Sandro Tonali, Charles De
Ketelaere (52' Rade Krunic), Olivier Giroud (81' Divock Origi), Ante Rebic, Rafael Leão (70'
Junior Messias). Coach: Stefano Pioli.
Goals: 39' Matteo Gabbia 0-1, 49' Rafael Leão 0-2, 59' Olivier Giroud 0-3 (p),
69' Robert Ljubicic 0-4 (og).
Referee: Szymon Marciniak (POL)   Attendance: 20,572.

02.11.22 Stamford Bridge, London: Chelsea FC – Dinamo Zagreb 2-1 (2-1)
Chelsea FC: Édouard Mendy, César Azpilicueta, Kalidou Koulibaly (65' Thiago Silva),
Trevoh Chalobah, Ben Chilwell, Jorginho, Mason Mount, Denis Zakaria (71' Ruben Loftus-
Cheek), Kai Havertz (64' Conor Gallagher), Pierre-Emerick Aubameyang (65' Armando
Broja), Raheem Sterling (83' Christian Pulisic). Coach: Graham Potter.
Dinamo Zagreb: Dominik Livakovic, Stefan Ristovski (69' Mahir Emreli), Dino Peric, Sadegh
Moharrami, Josip Sutalo, Arijan Ademi (83' Marko Bulat), Josip Misic, Luka Ivanusec, Robert
Ljubicic, Mislav Orsic (89' Dario Spikic), Bruno Petkovic (83' Josip Drmic).
Coach: Ante Cacic.
Goals: 7' Bruno Petkovic 0-1, 18' Raheem Sterling 1-1, 30' Denis Zakaria 2-1.
Referee: François Letexier (FRA)   Attendance: 39,392.

02.11.22   Stadio Giuseppe Meazza, Milano: AC Milan – Red Bull Salzburg 4-0 (1-0)
AC Milan: Ciprian Tatarusanu, Simon Kjær, Fikayo Tomori, Theo Hernández (78' Fodé Ballo-Touré), Pierre Kalulu (86' Matteo Gabbia), Rade Krunic (78' Charles De Ketelaere), Ismaël Bennacer (69' Tommaso Pobega), Sandro Tonali, Olivier Giroud, Ante Rebic, Rafael Leão (69' Junior Messias). Coach: Stefano Pioli.
Red Bull Salzburg: Philipp Köhn, Max Wöber (77' Andreas Ulmer), Oumar Solet (46' Bernardo), Strahinja Pavlovic, Amar Dedic, Nicolas Seiwald, Luka Sucic, Maurits Kjærgaard, Lucas Gourna-Douath (64' Dijon Kameri), Noah Okafor (77' Sékou Koïta), Junior Chikwubuike Adamu (62' Benjamin Sesko). Coach: Matthias Jaissle.
Goals: 14' Olivier Giroud 1-0, 46' Rade Krunic 2-0, 57' Olivier Giroud 3-0, 90+1' Junior Messias 4-0.
Referee: Antonio Mateu Lahoz (ESP)   Attendance: 74,292.

GROUP F

06.09.22   Celtic Park, Glasgow: Celtic FC – Real Madrid CF 0-3 (0-0)
Celtic FC: Joe Hart, Cameron Carter-Vickers, Josip Juranovic, Greg Taylor, Moritz Jenz, Callum McGregor, Matt O'Riley (72' Aaron Mooy), Reo Hatate (72' David Turnbull), Georgios Giakoumakis (72' Kyogo Furuhashi), Jota (82' Sead Haksabanovic), Liel Abada (46' Daizen Maeda). Coach: Ange Postecoglou.
Real Madrid CF: Thibaut Courtois, David Alaba, Dani Carvajal, Ferland Mendy, Éder Militão (46' Antonio Rüdiger), Luka Modric (81' Marco Asensio), Toni Kroos, Federico Valverde, Aurélien Tchouaméni (71' Eduardo Camavinga), Karim Benzema (30' Eden Hazard), Vinícius Júnior (80' Rodrygo). Coach: Carlo Ancelotti.
Goals: 56' Vinícius Júnior 0-1, 60' Luka Modric 0-2, 77' Eden Hazard 0-3.
Referee: Sandro Schärer (SUI)   Attendance: 57,057.

06.09.22   Red Bul Arena, Leipzig: RB Leipzig – Shakhtar Donetsk 1-4 (0-1)
RB Leipzig: Péter Gulácsi, Marcel Halstenberg (46' David Raum), Willi Orbán, Abdou Diallo, Mohamed Simakan, Konrad Laimer (82' Amadou Haïdara), Xaver Schlager (70' Benjamin Henrichs), Dominik Szoboszlai, André Silva, Timo Werner (70' Emil Forsberg), Christopher Nkunku. Coach: Domenico Tedesco.
Shakhtar Donetsk: Anatoliy Trubin, Mykola Matvienko, Lucas Taylor, Valeriy Bondar, Yukhym Konoplya, Taras Stepanenko (86' Sergiy Kryvtsov), Artem Bondarenko (62' Neven Djurasek), Mykhaylo Mudryk, Georgiy Sudakov, Oleksandr Zubkov (70' Lassina Traoré), Marian Shved (61' Ivan Petryak). Coach: Igor Jovicevic.
Goals: 16' Marian Shved 0-1, 57' Mohamed Simakan 1-1, 58' Marian Shved 1-2, 76' Mykhaylo Mudryk 1-3, 85' LassinaTraoré 1-4.
Referee: João Pedro Pinheiro (POR)   Attendance: 41,591.

14.09.22   Stadion Wojska Polskiego, Warszawa (POL):
Shakhtar Donetsk – Celtic FC 1-1 (1-1)
Shakhtar Donetsk: Anatoliy Trubin, Mykola Matvienko, Lucas Taylor, Valeriy Bondar, Yukhym Konoplya, Taras Stepanenko, Artem Bondarenko (74' Neven Djurasek), Mykhaylo Mudryk, Georgiy Sudakov (78' Oleh Ocheretko), Oleksandr Zubkov (61' Lassina Traoré), Marian Shved (60' Ivan Petryak). Coach: Igor Jovicevic.
Celtic FC: Joe Hart, Cameron Carter-Vickers, Josip Juranovic, Greg Taylor, Moritz Jenz, Callum McGregor, Sead Haksabanovic (46' Daizen Maeda), Matt O'Riley (68' Aaron Mooy), Reo Hatate (68' David Turnbull), Jota (86' Liel Abada), Kyogo Furuhashi (68' Georgios Giakoumakis). Coach: Ange Postecoglou.
Goals: 10' Artem Bondarenko 0-1 (og), 29' Mykhaylo Mudryk 1-1.
Referee: Glenn Nyberg (SWE)   Attendance: 20,697.

Due to the Russian invasion of Ukraine, Ukrainian teams were required to play their home matches at neutral venues until further notice. Therefore, Shakhtar Donetsk played at Stadion Wosjka Polskiego, Warszawa, Poland, unstead of their regular stadium Donbass Arena, Donetsk.

14.09.22   Estadio Santiago Bernabéu, Madrid: Real Madrid CF – RB Leipzig 2-0 (0-0)
Real Madrid CF: Thibaut Courtois, David Alaba (81' Ferland Mendy), Nacho, Dani Carvajal, Antonio Rüdiger, Luka Modric (81' Toni Kroos), Federico Valverde, Aurélien Tchouaméni, Eduardo Camavinga (64' Marco Asensio), Vinícius Júnior (85' Dani Ceballos), Rodrygo (85' Mariano Díaz). Coach: Carlo Ancelotti.
RB Leipzig: Péter Gulácsi, Willi Orbán, Abdou Diallo, David Raum, Mohamed Simakan (75' Benjamin Henrichs), Emil Forsberg (81' Yussuf Poulsen), Xaver Schlager, Amadou Haïdara (75' Kevin Kampl), Dominik Szoboszlai, Timo Werner (81' André Silva), Christopher Nkunku. Coach: Marco Rose.
Goals: 80' Federico Valverde 1-0, 90+1' Marco Asensio 2-0.
Referee: Maurizio Mariani (ITA)   Attendance: 54.289.

05.10.22   Red Bull Arena, Leipzig: RB Leipzig – Celtic FC 3-1 (1-0)
RB Leipzig: Péter Gulácsi (13' Janis Blaswich), Willi Orbán, David Raum (81' Marcel Halstenberg), Mohamed Simakan, Josko Gvardiol, Kevin Kampl (71' Amadou Haïdara), Xaver Schlager, Dominik Szoboszlai (82' Yussuf Poulsen), André Silva, Timo Werner (71' Emil Forsberg), Christopher Nkunku. Coach: Marco Rose.
Celtic FC: Joe Hart, Josip Juranovic, Greg Taylor, Stephen Welsh, Moritz Jenz, Callum McGregor (37' Oliver Abildgaard), Matt O'Riley (75' Sead Haksabanovic), Reo Hatate (82' James McCarthy), Jota, Daizen Maeda (75' James Forrest), Kyogo Furuhashi (82' Georgios Giakoumakis). Coach: Ange Postecoglou.
Goals: 27' Christopher Nkunku 1-0, 47' Jota 1-1, 64', 77' André Silva 2-1, 3-1.
Referee: Espen Eskås (NOR)   Attendance: 45,228.

05.10.22   Estadio Santiago Bernabéu, Madrid: Real Madrid CF – Shakhtar Donetsk 2-1 (2-1)
Real Madrid CF: Andriy Lunin, David Alaba, Dani Carvajal, Ferland Mendy, Éder Militão,
Toni Kroos, Federico Valverde, Aurélien Tchouaméni (75' Eduardo Camavinga), Karim
Benzema, Vinícius Júnior, Rodrygo (80' Marco Asensio). Coach: Carlo Ancelotti.
Shakhtar Donetsk: Anatoliy Trubin, Mykola Matvienko, Bogdan Mykhaylichenko, Valeriy
Bondar, Yukhym Konoplya, Taras Stepanenko (88' Lassina Traoré), Artem Bondarenko,
Mykhaylo Mudryk, Georgiy Sudakov (88' Neven Djurasek), Oleksandr Zubkov (67' Danylo
Sikan), Marian Shved (67' Ivan Petryak). Coach: Igor Jovicevic.
Goals: 13' Rodrygo 1-0, 28' Vinícius Júnior 2-0, 39' Oleksandr Zubkov 2-1.
Referee: Ivan Kruzliak (SVK)   Attendance: 56,011.

11.10.22   Stadion Wojska Polskiego, Warszawa (POL):
            Shakhtar Donetsk – Real Madrid CF 1-1 (0-0)
Shakhtar Donetsk: Anatoliy Trubin, Mykola Matvienko, Bogdan Mykhaylichenko, Valeriy
Bondar, Yukhym Konoplya, Taras Stepanenko, Artem Bondarenko, Mykhaylo Mudryk (85'
Ivan Petryak), Georgiy Sudakov (81' Neven Djurasek), Oleksandr Zubkov (82' Lucas Taylor),
Lassina Traoré (77' Danylo Sikan). Coach: Igor Jovicevic.
Real Madrid CF: Andriy Lunin, Nacho, Antonio Rüdiger, Ferland Mendy (68' David Alaba),
Toni Kroos, Lucas Vázquez, Federico Valverde (68' Eduardo Camavinga), Aurélien
Tchouaméni (57' Luka Modric), Karim Benzema, Eden Hazard (57' Vinícius Júnior), Rodrygo
(68' Marco Asensio). Coach: Carlo Ancelotti.
Goals: 46' Oleksandr Zubkov 1-0, 90+5' Antonio Rüdiger 1-1.
Referee: Orel Grinfeld (ISR)   Attendance: 29,030.

11.10.22   Celtic Park, Glasgow: Celtic FC – RB Leipzig 0-2 (0-0)
Celtic FC: Joe Hart, Cameron Carter-Vickers, Josip Juranovic, Greg Taylor, Moritz Jenz, Sead
Haksabanovic (66' David Turnbull), Matt O'Riley, Reo Hatate (66' Aaron Mooy), Daizen
Maeda (80' Alexandro Bernabei), Kyogo Furuhashi (66' Georgios Giakoumakis), Liel Abada
(42' James Forrest). Coach: Ange Postecoglou.
RB Leipzig: Janis Blaswich, Willi Orbán, David Raum, Mohamed Simakan (76' Benjamin
Henrichs), Josko Gvardiol, Xaver Schlager, Amadou Haïdara (84' Abdou Diallo), Dominik
Szoboszlai (76' Emil Forsberg), André Silva (77' Yussuf Poulsen), Timo Werner, Christopher
Nkunku (88' Hugo Novoa). Coach: Marco Rose.
Goals: 75' Timo Werner 0-1, 84' Emil Forsberg 0-2.
Referee: Halil Umut Meler (TUR)   Attendance: 57,565.

25.10.22   Celtic Park, Glasgow: Celtic FC – Shakhtar Donetsk 1-1 (1-0)
Celtic FC: Joe Hart, Cameron Carter-Vickers, Josip Juranovic, Greg Taylor, Moritz Jenz, Sead
Haksabanovic (66' Daizen Maeda), Matt O'Riley, Reo Hatate (84' David Turnbull), Georgios
Giakoumakis, Kyogo Furuhashi (65' Aaron Mooy), Liel Abada (65' James Forrest).
Coach: Ange Postecoglou.
Shakhtar Donetsk: Anatoliy Trubin, Mykola Matvienko, Bogdan Mykhaylichenko, Lucas
Taylor, Valeriy Bondar, Taras Stepanenko, Artem Bondarenko, Mykhaylo Mudryk (90' Ivan
Petryak), Georgiy Sudakov (90' Sergiy Kryvtsov), Oleksandr Zubkov, Lassina Traoré (57'
Danylo Sikan). Coach: Igor Jovicevic.
Goals: 34' Georgios Giakoumakis 1-0, 58' Mykhaylo Mudryk 1-1.
Referee: Serdar Gözübüyük (HOL)   Attendance: 57,478.

25.10.22   Red Bull Arena, Leipzig: RB Leipzig – Real Madrid CF 3-2 (2-1)
RB Leipzig: Janis Blaswich, Willi Orbán, David Raum (69' Abdou Diallo), Mohamed Simakan (89' Benjamin Henrichs), Josko Gvardiol, Emil Forsberg (69' Dani Olmo), Xaver Schlager, Amadou Haïdara (84' Kevin Kampl), Dominik Szoboszlai, André Silva (69' Timo Werner), Christopher Nkunku. Coach: Marco Rose.
Real Madrid CF: Thibaut Courtois, Nacho (68' David Alaba), Antonio Rüdiger, Éder Militão, Toni Kroos (76' Eden Hazard), Lucas Vázquez (68' Dani Carvajal), Aurélien Tchouaméni, Eduardo Camavinga, Marco Asensio, Vinícius Júnior, Rodrygo. Coach: Carlo Ancelotti.
Goals: 13' Josko Gvardiol 1-0, 18' Christopher Nkunku 2-0, 44' Vinícius Júnior 2-1, 81' Timo Werner 3-1, 90+4' Rodrygo 3-2 (p).
Referee: Daniele Orsato (ITA)   Attendance: 45,228.

02.11.22   Estadio Santiago Bernabéu, Madrid: Real Madrid CF – Celtic FC 5-1 (2-0)
Real Madrid CF: Thibaut Courtois, David Alaba (66' Nacho), Dani Carvajal (64' Lucas Vázquez), Ferland Mendy, Éder Militão (73' Jesús Vallejo), Luka Modric (66' Dani Caballos), Toni Kroos, Federico Valverde, Marco Asensio, Vinícius Júnior (63' Karim Benzema), Rodrygo. Coach: Carlo Ancelotti.
Celtic FC: Joe Hart, Carl Starfelt, Josip Juranovic, Greg Taylor, Moritz Jenz, Aaron Mooy (63' David Turnbull), Matt O'Riley, Reo Hatate (82' Oliver Abildgaard), Daizen Maeda (63' Sead Haksabanovic), Kyogo Furuhashi (62' Georgios Giakoumakis), Liel Abada (63' Jota). Coach: Ange Postecoglou.
Goals: 6' Luka Modric 1-0 (p), 21' Rodrygo 2-0 (p), 51' Marco Asensio 3-0, 61' Vinícius Júnior 4-0, 71' Federico Valverde 5-0, 84' Jota 5-1.
Referee: Stéphanie Frappart (FRA)   Attendance: 52,511.

Josip Juranovic missed a penalty kick (35').

02.11.22   Stadion Wojska Polskiego, Warszawa (POL):
          Shakhtar Donetsk – RB Leipzig 0-4 (0-1)
Shakhtar Donetsk: Anatoliy Trubin, Mykola Matvienko, Bogdan Mykhaylichenko, Valeriy Bondar, Yukhym Konoplya (59' Lucas Taylor), Taras Stepanenko, Ivan Petryak, Artem Bondarenko (81' Dmytro Kryskiv), Mykhaylo Mudryk (74' Andriy Totovytskyi), Georgiy Sudakov (59' Neven Djurasek), Lassina Traoré (59' Danylo Sikan). Coach: Igor Jovicevic.
RB Leipzig: Janis Blaswich, Willi Orbán, David Raum (67' Marcel Halstenberg), Mohamed Simakan (67' Benjamin Henrichs), Josko Gvardiol, Kevin Kampl, Xaver Schlager (74' Abdou Diallo), Dominik Szoboszlai (67' Dani Olmo), André Silva, Timo Werner (19' Emil Forsberg), Christopher Nkunku. Coach: Marco Rose.
Goals: 10' Christopher Nkunku 0-1, 50' André Silva 0-2, 62' Dominik Szoboszlai 0-3, 68' Valeriy Bondar 0-4 (og).
Referee: Michael Oliver (ENG)   Attendance: 26,045.

GROUP G

06.09.22   SIGNAL IDUNA PARK, Dortmund:
Borussia Dortmund – FC København 3-0 (2-0)
Borussia Dortmund: Alexander Meyer, Thomas Meunier, Raphaël Guerreiro (86' Tom Rothe), Niklas Süle, Nico Schlotterbeck, Marco Reus (86' Marius Wolf), Thorgan Hazard (23' Gio Reyna), Julian Brandt, Salih Özcan (66' Emre Can), Jude Bellingham, Anthony Modeste (67' Youssoufa Moukoko). Coach: Edin Terzic.
FC København: Mathew Ryan, Davit Khocholava (81' Nicolai Boilesen), Denis Vavro, Kevin Diks (81' Elias Jelert), Victor Kristiansen, Rasmus Falk, Zeca Rodrigues (72' Christian Sørensen), Victor Claesson, Lukas Lerager, Andreas Cornelius, Mohamed Daramy (60' Hákon Haraldsson). Coach: Jess Thorup.
Goals: 35' Marco Reus 1-0, 42' Raphaël Guerreiro 2-0, 83' Jude Bellingham 3-0.
Referee: François Letexier (FRA)   Attendance: 81,365.

06.09.22   Estadio Ramón Sánchez Pizjuán, Sevilla: Sevilla FC – Manchester City 0-4 (0-1)
Sevilla FC: Yassine Bounou "Bono", Jesús Navas, Alex Telles (57' Kasper Dolberg), Marcos Acuña, Tanguy Nianzou, José Ángel Carmona, Ivan Rakitic (46' Rafa Mir), Papu Gómez (73' Suso), Thomas Delaney (46' Joan Jordán), Nemanja Gudelj, Isco (78' Adnan Januzaj). Coach: Lopetegui.
Manchester City: Ederson, João Cancelo, Rúben Dias, Manuel Akanji, Kevin De Bruyne (78' Riyad Mahrez), Jack Grealish (62' Ilkay Gündogan), Bernado Silva, Rodri (78' Kalvin Phillips), Phil Foden (70' Cole Palmer), Sergio Gómez, Erling Haaland (70' Julián Álvarez). Coach: Pep Guardiola.
Goals: 20' Erling Haaland 0-1, 58' Phil Foden 0-2, 67' Erling Haaland 0-3, 90+2' Rúben Dias 0-4.
Referee: Davide Massa (ITA)   Attendance: 38,764.

14.09.22   Etihad Stadium, Manchester: Manchester City – Borussia Dortmund 2-1 (0-0)
Manchester City: Ederson, João Cancelo, Nathan Aké, John Stones, Manuel Akanji, Ilkay Gündogan (58' Bernardo Silva), Kevin De Bruyne, Jack Grealish (58' Phil Foden), Rodri, Riyad Mahrez (58' Julián Álvarez), Erling Haaland (90+2' Kalvin Phillips). Coach: Pep Guardiola.
Borussia Dortmund: Alexander Meyer, Mats Hummels, Thomas Meunier, Raphaël Guerreiro, Niklas Süle, Marco Reus (88' Youssoufa Moukoko), Emre Can, Salih Özcan (88' Karim Adeyemi), Gio Reyna (62' Donyell Malen), Jude Bellingham, Anthony Modeste (78' Nico Schlotterbeck). Coach: Edin Terzic.
Goals: 56' Jude Bellingham 0-1, 80' John Stones 1-1, 84' Erling Haaland 2-1.
Referee: Daniele Orsato (ITA)   Attendance: 50,441.

14.09.22   Telia Parken, København: FC København – Sevilla FC 0-0
FC København: Mathew Ryan, Davit Khocholava, Denis Vavro, Kevin Diks, Victor Kristiansen, Rasmus Falk (79' Lukas Lerager), Zeca Rodrigues, Victor Claesson (79' Hákon Haraldsson), Ísak Bergmann Jóhannesson (87' Christian Sørensen), Marko Stamenic, Mohamed Daramy (73' Paul Mukairu). Coach: Jess Thorup.
Sevilla FC: Marko Dmitrovic, Alex Telles, José Ángel Carmona, Kike Salas, Ivan Rakitic (67' Joan Jordán), Fernando, Érik Lamela (73' Suso), Thomas Delaney (67' Papu Gómez), Nemanja Gudelj, Isco (84' Adnan Januzaj), Youssef En-Nesyri (74' Kasper Dolberg). Coach: Lopetegui.
Referee: Irfan Peljto (BIH)   Attendance: 34,910.

05.10.22 Etihad Stadium, Manchester: Manchester City – FC København 5-0 (3-0)
Manchester City: Ederson, João Cancelo (57' Rico Lewis), Aymeric Laporte, Rúben Dias,
Ilkay Gündogan, Jack Grealish, Bernardo Silva (66' Josh Wilson-Esbrand), Sergio Gómez,
Riyad Mahrez, Erling Haaland (46' Cole Palmer), Julián Álvarez. Coach: Pep Guardiola.
FC København: Kamil Grabara, Davit Khocholava, Denis Vavro, Kevin Diks (66' Peter
Ankersen), Victor Kristiansen, Victor Claesson (66' Paul Mukairu), Lukas Lerager (79'
Christian Sørensen), Ísak Bergmann Jóhannesson, Marko Stamenic, Mamoudou Karamoko
(46' Valdemar Lund Jensen), Mohamed Daramy (56' Hákon Haraldsson).
Coach: Jacob Neestrup.
Goals: 7', 33' Erling Haaland 1-0, 2-0, 39' Davit Khocholava 3-0 (og),
55' Riyad Mahrez 4-0 (p), 76' Julián Álvarez 5-0.
Referee: Donatas Rumsas (LTU) Attendance: 51,765.

05.10.22 Estadio Ramón Sánchez Pizjuán, Sevilla: Sevilla FC – Borussia Dortmund 1-4 (0-3)
Sevilla FC: Yassine Bounou "Bono", Jesús Navas (46' Gonzalo Montiel), Alex Telles, José
Ángel Carmona, Kike Salas, Ivan Rakitic (62' Thomas Delaney), Nemanja Gudelj, Isco (62'
Papu Gómez), Suso (46' Érik Lamela), Joan Jordán (77' Kasper Dolberg), Youssef En-Nesyri.
Coach: Lopetegui.
Borussia Dortmund: Alexander Meyer, Thomas Meunier, Raphaël Guerreiro (80' Tom Rothe),
Niklas Süle, Nico Schlotterbeck, Emre Can, Julian Brandt (85' Thorgan Hazard), Salih Özcan
(85' Antonios Papadopoulos), Jude Bellingham, Karim Adeyemi (64' Donyell Malen),
Youssoufa Moukoko (80' Anthony Modeste). Coach: Edin Terzic.
Goals: 6' Raphaël Guerreiro 0-1, 41' Jude Bellingham 0-2, 43' Karim Adeyemi 0-3,
51' Youssef En-Nesyri 1-3, 75' Julian Brandt 1-4.
Referee: Maurizio Mariani (ITA) Attendance: 34,596.

11.10.22 Telia Parken , København: FC København – Manchester City 0-0
FC København: Kamil Grabara, Nicolai Boilesen, Davit Khocholava (80' Kevin Diks), Victor
Kristiansen, Valdemar Lund Jensen, Elias Jelert, Victor Claesson, Lukas Lerager, Hákon
Haraldsson (59' Ísak Bergmann Jóhannesson), Marko Stamenic (90+3' Paul Mukairu),
Mohamed Daramy. Coach: Jacob Neestrup.
Manchester City: Ederson, João Cancelo, Aymeric Laporte (88' Nathan Aké), Manuel Akanji,
Ilkay Gündogan, Kevin De Bruyne (77' Bernardo Silva), Jack Grealish (77' Phil Foden),
Rodri, Sergio Gómez, Riyad Mahrez (32' Rúben Dias), Julián Álvarez. Coach: Pep Guardiola.
Referee: Artur Soares Dias (POR) Attendance: 35,447.
Sent off: 30' Sergio Gómez.

Riyad Mahrez missed a penalty kick (25').

11.10.22 SIGNAL IDUNA PARK, Dortmund: Borussia Dortmund – Sevilla FC 1-1 (1-1)
Borussia Dortmund: Gregor Kobel, Mats Hummels, Thomas Meunier (83' Nico
Schlotterbeck), Niklas Süle, Tom Rothe (46' Raphaël Guerreiro), Julian Brandt, Salih Özcan,
Jude Bellingham, Anthony Modeste (64' Youssoufa Moukoko), Donyell Malen (71' Gio
Reyna), Karim Adeyemi (71' Thorgan Hazard). Coach: Edin Terzic.
Sevilla FC: Yassine Bounou "Bono", Jesús Navas (90+1' Gonzalo Montiel), Marcus Acuña
(71' Alex Telles), Marcão (90+1' Joan Jordán), Tanguy Nianzou, José Ángel Carmona, Ivan
Rakitic, Érik Lamela, Nemanja Gudelj, Suso (59' Adnan Januzaj), Youssef En-Nesyri (59'
Isco). Coach: Jorge Sampaoli.
Goals: 18' Tanguy Nianzou 0-1, 35' Jude Bellingham 1-1.
Referee: Srdjan Jovanovic (SRB) Attendance: 81,000.

117

25.10.22 Estadio Ramón Sánchez Pizjuán, Sevilla: Sevilla FC – FC København 3-0 (0-0)
Sevilla FC: Marko Dmitrovic, Alex Telles, Marcão, Gonzalo Montiel, Ivan Rakitic, Papu
Gómez (77' Marcus Acuña), Nemanja Gudelj, Isco, Suso (55' Érik Lamela), Joan Jordán,
Kasper Dolberg (46' Youssef En-Nesyri, 70' Rafa Mir). Coach: Jorge Sampaoli.
FC København: Kamil Grabara, Davit Khocholava, Victor Kristiansen, Valdemar Lund Jensen
(80' Kevin Diks), Elias Jelert (81' Christian Sørensen), Victor Claesson, Lukas Lerager, Ísak
Bergmann Jóhannesson (63' Roony Bardghji), Hákon Haraldsson (72' Andreas Cornelius),
William Clem (81' Orri Óskarsson), Mohamed Daramy. Coach: Jacob Neestrup.
Goals: 61' Youssef En-Nesyri 1-0, 88' Isco 2-0, 90+2' Gonzalo Montiel 3-0.
Referee: Benoît Bastien (FRA) Attendance: 29,884.
Send off: 90+5' Davit Khocholava.

25.10.22 SIGNAL IDUNA PARK, Dortmund: Borussia Dortmund – Manchester City 0-0
Borussia Dortmund: Gregor Kobel, Mats Hummels, Niklas Süle, Nico Schlotterbeck, Thorgan
Hazard (82' Marius Wolf), Emre Can, Julian Brandt, Gio Reyna (87' Antonios Papadopoulos),
Jude Bellingham, Karim Adeyemi (73' Donyell Malen), Youssoufa Moukoko (82' Anthony
Modeste). Coach: Edin Terzic.
Manchester City: Stefan Ortega, João Cancelo (46' Manuel Akanji), Nathan Aké, John Stones,
Rúben Dias, Ilkay Gündogan, Rodri, Phil Foden (81' Jack Grealish), Riyad Mahrez (88' Cole
Palmer), Erling Haaland (46' Bernardo Silva), Julián Álvarez. Coach: Pep Guardiola.
Referee: Davide Massa (ITA) Attendance: 81,000.

Riyad Mahrez missed a penalty kick (58').

02.11.22 Etihad Stadium, Manchester: Manchester City – Sevilla FC 3-1 (0-1)
Manchester City: Stefan Ortega, Aymeric Laporte, Rúben Dias, Rico Lewis (85' João
Cancelo), Ilkay Gündogan (57' Bernardo Silva), Jack Grealish (46' Rodri), Phil Foden, Sergio
Gómez (70' Josh Wilson-Esbrand), Cole Palmer (70' Kevin De Bruyne), Riyad Mahrez, Julián
Álvarez. Coach: Pep Guardiola.
Sevilla FC: Yassine Bounou "Bono", Karim Rekik, Marcus Acuña (46' Alex Telles), Marcão
(45+1' Nemanja Gudelj), Gonzalo Montiel, José Ángel Carmona, Ivan Rakitic (67' Joan
Jordán), Papu Gómez (46' Suso), Thomas Delaney, Isco (57' Érik Lamela), Rafa Mir.
Coach: Jorge Sampaoli.
Goals: 31' Rafa Mir 0-1, 52' Rico Lewis 1-1, 73' Julián Álvarez 2-1, 83' Riyad Mahrez 3-1.
Referee: Orel Grinfeld (ISR) Attendance: 51,610.

02.11.22 Telia Parken , København: FC København – Borussia Dortmund 1-1 (1-1)
FC København: Kamil Grabara, Christian Sørensen (58' Victor Kristiansen), Denis Vavro,
Kevin Diks (79' Elias Jelert), Valdemar Lund Jensen, Victor Claesson (70' Rasmus Falk),
Lukas Lerager, Hákon Haraldsson, Roony Bardghji (70' Ísak Bergmann Jóhannesson),
William Clem, Mohamed Daramy (79' Orri Óskarsson). Coach: Jacob Neestrup.
Borussia Dortmund: Gregor Kobel (46' Alexander Meyer), Mats Hummels (46' Niklas Süle),
Nico Schlotterbeck, Thorgan Hazard (72' Soumaïla Coulibaly), Emre Can, Felix Passlack,
Salih Özcan (63' Youssoufa Moukoko), Gio Reyna (63' Julian Brandt), Anthony Modeste,
Donyell Malen, Karim Adeyemi. Coach: Edin Terzic.
Goals: 23' Thorgan Hazard 0-1, 41' Hákon Haraldsson 1-1.
Referee: Aliyar Aghayev (AZE) Attendance: 31,900.

GROUP H

06.09.22   Parc des Princes, Paris: Paris Saint-Germain – FC Juventus 2-1 (2-0)
Paris Saint-Germain: Gianluigi Donnarumma, Sergio Ramos, Marquinhos, Presnel Kimpembe, Achraf Hakimi (78' Nordi Mukiele), Nuno Mendes, Marco Verratti (87' Renato Sanches), Vitinha (78' Danilo Pereira), Lionel Messi (84' Carlos Soler), Neymar, Kylian Mbappé.
Coach: Christophe Galtier.
FC Juventus: Mattia Perin, Leonardo Bonucci, Danilo, Bremer, Juan Cuadrado (74' Mattia De Sciglio), Filip Kostic, Leandro Paredes, Adrien Rabiot (87' Moise Kean), Fabio Miretti (46' Weston McKennie), Arkadiusz Milik (68' Manuel Locatelli), Dusan Vlahovic.
Coach: Massimiliano Allegri.
Goals: 5', 22' Kylian Mbappé 1-0, 2-0, 53' Weston McKennie 2-1.
Referee: Anthony Taylor (ENG)   Attendance: 47,415.

06.09.22   Estádio da Luz, Lisboa: SL Benfica – Maccabi Haifa 2-0 (0-0)
SL Benfica: Odisseas Vlachodimos, Nicolás Otamendi, Ález Grimaldo, Alexander Bah, António Silva, João Mário (79' Chiquinho), Rafa Silva (79' Diogo Gonçalves), Florentino, Enzo Fernández, David Neres (65' Fredrik Aursnes), Gonçalo Ramos (46' Petar Musa).
Coach: Roger Schmidt.
Maccabi Haifa: Josh Cohen, Daniel Sundgren, Shon Goldberg, Dylan Batubinsika, Abdoulaye Seck (67' Suf Podgoreanu, 78' Sun Menachem), Tjaronn Chery, Ali Muhammad (31' Mohammad Abu Fani), Neta Lavi, Dolev Haziza, Din David (46' Omer Atzili), Frantzdy Pierrot (78' Nikita Rukavytsya). Coach: Barak Bakhar.
Goals: 49' Rafa Silva 1-0, 54' Álex Grimaldo 2-0.
Referee: Andreas Ekberg (SWE)   Attendance: 55,130.

14.09.22   Allianz Stadium, Torino: FC Juventus – SL Benfica 1-2 (1-1)
FC Juventus: Mattia Perin, Leonardo Bonucci, Danilo, Bremer, Juan Cuadrado (58' Mattia De Sciglio), Filip Kostic (70' Moise Kean), Leandro Paredes, Weston McKennie, Fabio Miretti (58' Ángel Di María), Arkadiusz Milik (70' Nicolò Fagioli), Dusan Vlahovic.
Coach: Massimiliano Allegri.
SL Benfica: Odisseas Vlachodimos, Nicolás Otamendi, Álex Grimaldo, Alexander Bah, António Silva, João Mário (86' Julian Draxler), Rafa Silva (86' Diogo Gonçalves), Florentino, Enzo Fernández (81' Fredrik Aursnes), David Neres (81' Chiquinho), Gonçalo Ramos (81' Petar Musa). Coach: Roger Schmidt.
Goals: 4' Arkadiusz Milik 1-0, 43' João Mário 1-1 (p), 55' David Neres 1-2.
Referee: Felix Zwayer (GER)   Attendance: 34,015.

14.09.22   Sammy Ofer Stadium, Haifa: Maccabi Haifa – Paris Saint-Germain 1-3 (1-1)
Maccabi Haifa: Josh Cohen, Daniel Sundgren (55' Abdoulaye Seck), Shon Goldberg, Dylan Batubinsika, Pierre Cornud (90+1' Mavis Tchibota), Tjaronn Chery, Neta Lavi, Dolev Haziza, Mohammad Abu Fani, Omer Atzili (76' Din David), Frantzdy Pierrot (90+1' Nikita Rukavytsya). Coach: Barak Bakhar.
Paris Saint-Germain: Gianluigi Donnarumma, Sergio Ramos, Marquinhos, Nordi Mukiele (83' Achraf Hakimi), Nuno Mendes, Marco Verratti, Danilo Pereira, Vitinha (74' Fabián Ruiz), Lionel Messi, Neymar (90+1' Carlos Soler), Kylian Mbappé. Coach: Christophe Galtier.
Goals: 24' Tjaronn Chery 1-0, 37' Lionel Messi 1-1, 69' Kylian Mbappé 1-2, 88' Neymar 1-3.
Referee: Daniel Siebert (GER)   Attendance: 30,421.

05.10.22   Allianz Stadium, Torino: FC Juventus – Maccabi Haifa 3-1 (1-0)
FC Juventus: Wojciech Szczesny, Danilo, Mattia De Sciglio (46' Alex Sandro), Bremer, Ángel Di María, Juan Cuadrado (67' Leonardo Bonucci), Filip Kostic (66' Manuel Locatelli), Leandro Paredes (85' Fabio Miretti), Adrien Rabiot, Weston McKennie, Dusan Vlahovic (73' Moise Kean). Coach: Massimiliano Allegri.
Maccabi Haifa: Josh Cohen, Daniel Sundgren, Shon Goldberg, Dylan Batubinsika, Pierre Cornud (60' Dolev Haziza), Abdoulaye Seck, Tjaronn Chery, Ali Muhammad (84' Nikita Rukavytsya), Mohammad Abu Fani (72' Neta Lavi), Mavis Tchibota (59' Omer Atzili), Frantzdy Pierrot (72' Din David). Coach: Barak Bakhar.
Goals: 35' Adrien Rabiot 1-0, 50' Dusan Vlahovic 2-0, 75' Din David 2-1, 83' Adrien Rabiot 3-1.
Referee: Sandro Schärer (SUI)   Attendance: 28,498.

05.10.22   Estádio da Luz, Lisboa: SL Benfica – Paris Saint-Germain 1-1 (1-1)
SL Benfica: Odisseas Vlachodimos, Nicolás Otamendi, Álex Grimaldo, Alexander Bah, António Silva, João Mário, Rafa Silva, Florentino, Enzo Fernández (78' Fredrik Aursnes), David Neres (90+1' Rodrigo Pinho), Gonçalo Ramos (78' Julian Draxler).
Coach: Roger Schmidt.
Paris Saint-Germain: Gianluigi Donnarumma, Sergio Ramos, Marquinhos, Achraf Hakimi, Nuno Mendes (67' Juan Bernat), Marco Verratti, Danilo Pereira, Vitinha (87' Fabián Ruiz), Lionel Messi (81' Pablo Sarabia), Neymar, Kylian Mbappé. Coach: Christophe Galtier.
Goals: 22' Lionel Messi 0-1, 42' Danilo Pereira 1-1 (og).
Referee: Jesús Gil Manzano (ESP)   Attendance: 62,295.

11.10.22   Sammy Ofer Stadium, Haifa: Maccabi Haifa – FC Juventus 2-0 (2-0)
Maccabi Haifa: Josh Cohen, Daniel Sundgren, Shon Goldberg, Dylan Batubinsika, Pierre Cornud (71' Sun Menachem), Tjaronn Chery, Ali Muhammad (86' Mavis Tchibota), Neta Lavi, Omer Atzili (66' Abdoulaye Seck), Din David (72' Mohammad Abu Fani), Frantzdy Pierrot (86' Nikita Rukavytsya). Coach: Barak Bakhar.
FC Juventus: Wojciech Szczesny, Leonardo Bonucci, Danilo (68' Moise Kean), Alex Sandro (74' Matías Soulé), Daniele Rugani, Ángel Di María (24' Arkadiusz Milik), Juan Cuadrado, Leandro Paredes (46' Manuel Locatelli), Adrien Rabiot, Weston McKennie (46' Filip Kostic), Dusan Vlahovic. Coach: Massimiliano Allegri.
Goals: 7', 42' Omer Atzili 1-0, 2-0.
Referee: Antonio Mateu Lahoz (ESP)   Attendance: 30,074.

11.10.22   Parc des Princes, Paris: Paris Saint-Germain – SL Benfica 1-1 (1-0)
Paris Saint-Germain: Gianluigi Donnarumma, Sergio Ramos, Marquinhos, Juan Bernat (85' Nordi Mukiele), Achraf Hakimi, Marco Verratti, Pablo Sarabia (74' Hugo Ekitike), Danilo Pereira, Vitinha (85' Fabián Ruiz), Neymar, Kylian Mbappé (90' Carlos Soler).
Coach: Christophe Galtier.
SL Benfica: Odisseas Vlachodimos, Nicolás Otamendi, Álex Grimaldo, Alexander Bah (63' Gilberto), António Silva, João Mário (90+3' Chiquinho), Fredrik Aursnes, Rafa Silva (78' Julian Draxler), Florentino (78' Diogo Gonçalves), Enzo Fernández, Gonçalo Ramos (77' Rodrigo Pinho). Coach: Roger Schmidt.
Goals: 39' Kylian Mbappé 1-0 (p), 62' João Mário 1-1 (p).
Referee: Michael Oliver (ENG)   Attendance: 46,435.

120

25.10.22 Parc des Princes, Paris: Paris Saint-Germain – Maccabi Haifa 7-2 (4-1)
Paris Saint-Germain: Gianluigi Donnarumma, Sergio Ramos, Marquinhos (79' Presnel
Kimpembe), Juan Bernat, Achraf Hakimi, Renato Sanches (68' Carlos Soler), Fabián Ruiz (83'
Pablo Sarabia), Vitinha (79' Warren Zaïre-Emery), Lionel Messi, Neymar, Kylian Mbappé
(79' Hugo Ekitike). Coach: Christophe Galtier.
Maccabi Haifa: Josh Cohen, Shon Goldberg, Dylan Batubinsika, Pierre Cornud (70' Sun
Menachem), Abdoulaye Seck, Tjaronn Chery, Ali Muhammad (83' Ofri Arad), Neta Lavi,
Mohammad Abu Fani (71' Raz Meir), Omer Atzili (65' Din David), Frantzdy Pierrot (83'
Nikita Rukavytsya). Coach: Barak Bakhar.
Goals: 19' Lionel Messi 1-0, 32' Kylian Mbappé 2-0, 35' Neymar 3-0,
38' Abdoulaye Seck 3-1, 44' Lionel Messi 4-1, 50' Abdoulaye Seck 4-2,
64' Kylian Mbappé 5-2, 67' Shon Goldberg 6-2 (og), 84' Carlos Soler 7-2.
Referee: Felix Zwayer (FER) Attendance: 46,435.

25.10.22 Estádio da Luz, Lisboa: SL Benfica – FC Juventus 4-3 (3-1)
SL Benfica: Odisseas Vlachodimos, Nicolás Otamendi, Álex Grimaldo, Alexander Bah (81'
Gilberto), António Silva, João Mário (90+4' Chiquinho), Fredrik Aursnes, Rafa Silva (87'
Petar Musa), Florentino, Enzo Fernández, Gonçalo Ramos (87' David Neres).
Coach: Roger Schmidt.
FC Juventus: Wojciech Szczesny, Leonardo Bonucci (60' Alex Sandro), Danilo, Federico
Gatti, Juan Cuadrado (60' Fabio Miretti), Filip Kostic (70' Samuel Iling-Junior), Adrien
Rabiot, Manuel Locatelli, Weston McKennie, Moise Kean (46' Arkadiusz Milik), Dusan
Vlahovic (70' Matías Soulé). Coach: Massimiliano Allegri.
Goals: 17' António Silva 1-0, 21' Moise Kean 1-1, 28' João Mário 2-1 (p),
35', 50' Rafa Silva 3-1, 4-1, 77' Arkadiusz Milik 4-2, 79' Weston McKennie 4-3.
Referee: Srdjan Jovanovic (SRB) Attendance: 60,131.

02.11.22 Allianz Stadium, Torino: FC Juventus – Paris Saint-Germain 1-2 (1-1)
FC Juventus: Wojciech Szczesny, Leonardo Bonucci, Alex Sandro, Federico Gatti, Juan
Cuadrado (88' Enzo Barrenechea), Filip Kostic, Adrien Rabiot, Manuel Locatelli (85' Matías
Soulé), Nicolò Fagioli (88' Tommaso Barbieri), Fabio Miretti (74' Federico Chiesa),
Arkadiusz Milik. Coach: Massimiliano Allegri.
Paris Saint-Germain: Gianluigi Donnarumma, Sergio Ramos, Marquinhos, Juan Bernat (68'
Nuno Mendes), Achraf Hakimi, Marco Verratti (88' Danilo Pereira), Fabián Ruiz (21' Renato
Sanches), Carlos Soler (68' Hugo Ekitike), Vitinha, Lionel Messi, Kylian Mbappé.
Coach: Christophe Galtier.
Goals: 13' Kylian Mbappé 0-1, 39' Leonardo Bonucci 1-1, 69' Nuno Mendes 1-2.
Referee: Carlos del Cerro Grande (ESP) Attendance: 41,089.

02.11.22 Sammy Ofer Stadium, Haifa: Maccabi Haifa – SL Benfica 1-6 (1-1)
Maccabi Haifa: Josh Cohen, Shon Goldberg, Pierre Cornud (85' Sun Menachem), Abdoulaye
Seck, Tjaronn Chery, Raz Meir (63' Omer Atzili), Ali Muhammad (77' Ofri Arad), Neta Lavi,
Mohammad Abu Fani, Din David (63' Mavis Tchibota), Frantzdy Pierrot (77' Nikita
Rukavytsya). Coach: Barak Bakhar.
SL Benfica: Odisseas Vlachodimos, Nicolás Otamendi, Álex Grimaldo, Alexander Bah,
António Silva (88' Lucas Veríssimo), João Mário, Fredrik Aursnes (32' Chiquinho), Rafa Silva
(82' Henrique Araújo), Florentino, David Neres (82' Diogo Gonçalves), Gonçalo Ramos (32'
Petar Musa). Coach: Roger Schmidt.
Goals: 20' Gonçalo Ramos 0-1, 26' Tjaronn Chery 1-1 (p), 59' Petar Musa 1-2,
69' Álex Grimaldo 1-3, 73' Rafa Silva 1-4, 88' Henrique Araújo 1-5, 90+2' João Mário 1-6.
Referee: Anthony Taylor (ENG) Attendance: 30,464.

121

KNOCKOUT PHASE

ROUND OF 16

14.02.23   Stadio Giuseppe Meazza, Milano: AC Milan – Tottenham Hotspur 1-0 (1-0)
AC Milan: Ciprian Tatarusanu, Simon Kjær, Theo Hernández, Pierre Kalulu, Malick Thiaw, Rade Krunic, Brahim Díaz (77' Charles De Ketelaere), Alexis Saelemaekers (77' Junior Messias), Sandro Tonali (86' Tommaso Pobega), Olivier Giroud, Rafael Leão (90+1' Ante Rebic). Coach: Stefano Pioli.
Tottenham Hotspur: Fraser Forster, Clément Lenglet (81' Ben Davies), Eric Dier, Cristian Romero, Emerson Royal, Ivan Perisic, Oliver Skipp, Dejan Kulusevski (70' Richarlison), Pape Sarr, Heung-Min Son (81' Arnaut Danjuma), Harry Kane. Coach: Antonio Conte.
Goal: 7' Brahim Díaz 1-0.
Referee: Sandro Schärer (SUI)   Attendance: 74,320.

14.02.23   Parc des Princes, Paris: Paris Saint-Germain – Bayern München 0-1 (0-0)
Paris Saint-Germain: Gianluigi Donnarumma, Sergio Ramos, Marquinhos, Achraf Hakimi (46' Presnel Kimpembe), Nuno Mendes, Marco Verratti, Danilo Pereira (75' Vitinha), Carlos Soler (57' Kylian Mbappé), Warren Zaïre-Emery (57' Fabián Ruiz), Lionel Messi, Neymar. Coach: Christophe Galtier.
Bayern München: Yann Sommer, João Cancelo (46' Alphonso Davies), Benjamin Pavard, Dayot Upamecano, Matthijs de Ligt, Leon Goretzka, Joshua Kimmich, Eric Maxim Choupo-Moting (76' Thomas Müller), Kingsley Coman (75' Serge Gnabry), Leroy Sané (90' Josip Stanisic), Jamal Musiala (87' Ryan Gravenberch). Coach: Julian Nagelsmann.
Goal: 53' Kingsley Coman 0-1.
Referee: Michael Oliver (ENG)   Attendance: 46,435.
Send off: 90+2' Benjamin Pavard.

15.02.23   Jan Breydelstadion, Brugge: Club Brugge KV – SL Benfica 0-2 (0-0)
Club Brugge KV: Simon Mignolet, Denis Odoi (65' Casper Nielsen), Clinton Mata, Brandon Mechele, Jack Hendry, Bjorn Meijer, Hans Vanaken, Noa Lang, Raphael Onyedika, Tajon Buchanan, Kamal Sowah (79' Ferrán Jutglà). Coach: Scott Parker.
SL Benfica: Odisseas Vlachodimos, Nicolás Otamendi, Álex Grimaldo, Alexander Bah, António Silva, João Mário (90+4' João Neves), Fredrik Aursnes, Rafa Silva (65' David Neres), Chiquinho, Florentino, Gonçalo Ramos (65' Gonçalo Guedes). Coach: Roger Schmidt.
Goals: 51' João Mário 0-1 (p), 88' David Neres 0-2.
Referee: Davide Massa (ITA)   Attendance: 24,136.

15.02.23   Signal Iduna Park, Dortmund: Borussia Dortmund – Chelsea FC 1-0 (0-0)
Borussia Dortmund: Gregor Kobel, Raphaël Guerreiro, Niklas Süle, Nico Schlotterbeck, Emre Can, Julian Brandt, Marius Wolf (73' Julian Ryerson), Salih Özcan, Jude Bellingham, Sébastien Haller (68' Anthony Modeste), Karim Adeyemi (79' Jamie Bynoe-Gittens). Coach: Edin Terzic.
Chelsea FC: Kepa, Thiago Silva, Kalidou Koulibaly, Ben Chilwell (71' Marc Cucurella), Reece James, Hakim Ziyech, Ruben Loftus-Cheek, Kai Havertz, Mykhaylo Mudryk (71' Mason Mount), Enzo Fernández, João Félix. Coach: Graham Potter.
Goal: 63' KarimAdeyemi 1-0.
Referee: Jesús Gil Manzano (ESP)   Attendance: 81,365.

21.02.23   Anfield, Liverpool: Liverpool FC – Real Madrid CF 2-5 (2-2)
Liverpool FC: Alisson, Virgil van Dijk, Andy Robertson, Joe Gomez (73' Joe Matip), Trent
Alexander-Arnold, Stefan Bajcetic (85' Harvey Elliott), Jordan Henderson (73' James Milner),
Fabinho, Mohamed Salah, Cody Gakpo (64' Roberto Firmino), Darwin Núñez (64' Diogo
Jota). Coach: Jürgen Klopp.
Real Madrid CF: Thibaut Courtois, David Alaba (27' Nacho), Dani Carvajal, Antonio Rüdiger,
Éder Militão, Luka Modric (87' Toni Kroos), Federico Valverde, Eduardo Camavinga, Karim
Benzema (87' Marco Asensio), Vinícius Júnior, Rodrygo (81' Dani Caballos).
Coach: Carlo Ancelotti.
Goals: 4' Darwin Núñez 1-0 14' Mohamed Salah 2-0, 21', 36' Vinícius Júnior 1-2, 2-2,
47' Éder Militão 2-3, 55', 67' Karim Benzema 2-4, 2-5.
Referee: István Kovács (ROM)   Attendance: 52,337.

21.02.23   Deutsche Bank Park, Frankfurt am Main:
            Eintracht Frankfurt – SSC Napoli 0-2 (0-1)
Eintracht Frankfurt: Kevin Trapp, Philipp Max (90+2' Christopher Lenz), Aurélio Buta (69'
Ansgar Knauff), Evan Ndicka, Tuta, Mario Götze (81' Faride Alidou), Djibril Sow, Daichi
Kamada, Kristijan Jakic, Jesper Lindstrøm (69' Rafael Borré), Randal Kolo Muani.
Coach: Oliver Glasner.
SSC Napoli: Alex Meret, Giovanni Di Lorenzo, Amir Rrahmani, Mathías Olivera, Kim Min-
Jae, Piotr Zielinski, Stanislav Lobotka, Frank Zambo Anguissa (80' Tanguy Ndombèlé),
Hirving Lozano (80' Eljif Elmas), Victor Osimhen (84' Giovanni Simeone), Khvicha
Kvaratskhelia (84' Matteo Politano). Coach: Luciano Spalletti.
Goals: 40' Victor Osimhen 0-1, 65' Giovanni Di Lorenzo 0-2.
Referee: Artur Soares Dias (POR)   Attendance: 47,500.
Send off: 58' Randal Kolo Muani.

Khvicha Kvaratskhelia missed a penalty kick (36').

22.02.23   Red Bull Arena, Leipzig: RB Leipzig – Manchester City 1-1 (0-1)
RB Leipzig: Janis Blaswich, Marcel Halstenberg (89' David Raum), Willi Orbán, Lukas
Klostermann (46' Benjamin Henrichs), Josko Gvardiol, Emil Forsberg (66' Christopher
Nkunku), Konrad Laimer, Xaver Schlager (82' Amadou Haïdara), Dominik Szoboszlai, André
Silva (82' Yussuf Poulsen), Timo Werner. Coach: Marco Rose.
Manchester City: Ederson, Kyle Walker, Nathan Aké, Rúben Dias, Manuel Akanji, Ilkay
Gündogan, Jack Grealish, Bernardo Silva, Rodri, Riyad Mahrez, Erling Haaland.
Coach: Pep Guardiola.
Goals: 27' Riyad Mahrez 0-1, 70' Josko Gvardiol 1-1.
Referee: Serdar Gözübüyük (HOL)   Attendance: 45,228.

22.02.23   Stadio Giuseppe Meazza, Milano: Internazionale Milano – FC Porto 1-0 (0-0)
Internazionale Milano: André Onana, Matteo Darmian, Francesco Acerbi, Milan Skriniar (81'
Denzel Dumfries), Federico Dimarco (58' Robin Gosens), Alessandro Bastoni, Henrikh
Mkhitaryan (72' Marcelo Brozovic), Hakan Çalhanoglu, Nicolò Barella, Edin Dzeko (58'
Romelu Lukaku), Lautaro Martínez. Coach: Simone Inzaghi.
FC Porto: Diogo Costa, Pepe, Iván Marcano, Zaidu Sanusi, João Mário (90+2' Gonçalo
Borges), Mateus Uribe, Otávio, Marko Grujic, Mehdi Taremi (83' Wendell), Galeno (51'
Evanilson), Pepê Aquino. Coach: Sérgio Conceição.
Goal: 86' Romelu Lukaku 1-0.
Referee: Srdjan Jovanovic (SRB)   Attendance: 75,374.
Send off: 78' Otávio.

07.03.23   Estádio da Luz, Lisboa: SL Benfica – Club Brugge 5-1 (2-0)
SL Benfica: Odisseas Vlachodimos, Nicolás Otamendi (74' Morato), Álex Grimaldo, Alexander Bah (63' Gilberto), António Silva (88' Lucas Veríssimo), João Mário (74' João Neves), Fredrik Aursnes, Rafa Silva, Chiquinho (63' David Neres), Florentino, Gonçalo Ramos. Coach: Roger Schmidt.
Club Brugge KV: Simon Mignolet, Clinton Mata (62' Denis Odoi), Brandon Mechele, Bjorn Meijer, Abakar Sylla, Hans Vanaken (74' Mats Rits), Casper Nielsen, Noa Lang (46' Raphael Onyedika), Roman Yaremchuk (62' Ferrán Jutglà), Tajon Buchanan, Kamal Sowah (75' Antonio Nusa). Coach: Scott Parker.
Goals: 38' Rafa Silva 1-0, 45+2', 57' Gonçalo Ramos 2-0, 3-0, 71' João Mário 4-0 (p), 78' David Neres 5-0, 87' Bjorn Meijer 5-1.
Referee: Halil Umut Meler (TUR)   Attendance: 60,960.

07.03.23   Stamford Bridge, London: Chelsea FC – Borussia Dortmund 2-0 (1-0)
Chelsea FC: Kepa, Kalidou Koulibaly, Marc Cucurella, Ben Chilwell, Reece James, Wesley Fofana, Mateo Kovacic (83' Christian Pulisic), Kai Havertz, Enzo Fernández (87' Denis Zakaria), Raheem Sterling (82' Ruben Loftus-Cheek), João Félix (67' Conor Gallagher). Coach: Graham Potter.
Borussia Dortmund: Alexander Meyer, Raphaël Guerreiro, Niklas Süle, Nico Schlotterbeck, Marco Reus, Emre Can, Julian Brandt (5' Gio Reyna), Marius Wolf, Salih Özcan (64' Jamie Bynoe-Gittens), Jude Bellingham, Sébastien Haller (77' Donyell Malen). Coach: Edin Terzic.
Goals: 43' Raheem Sterling 1-0, 53' Kai Havertz 2-0 (p).
Referee: Danny Makkelie (HOL)   Attendance: 38,882.

08.03.23   Allianz Arena, München: Bayern München – Paris Saint-Germain 2-0 (0-0)
Bayern München: Yann Sommer, Dayot Upamecano, Matthijs de Ligt, Josip Stanisic, Leon Goretzka, Joshua Kimmich, Eric Maxim Choupo-Moting (68' Leroy Sané), Thomas Müller (86' João Cancelo), Kingsley Coman (86' Serge Gnabry), Alphonso Davies, Jamal Musiala (82' Sadio Mané). Coach: Julian Nagelsmann.
Paris Saint-Germain: Gianluigi Donnarumma, Sergio Ramos, Marquinhos (36' Nordi Mukiele, 46' El Chadaïlle Bitshiabu), Achraf Hakimi, Nuno Mendes (82' Juan Bernat), Marco Verratti, Danilo Pereira, Fabián Ruiz (76' Warren Zaïre-Emery), Vitinha (81' Hugo Ekitike), Lionel Messi, Kylian Mbappé. Coach: Christophe Galtier.
Goals: 61' Eric Maxim Choupo-Moting 1-0, 89' Serge Gnabry 2-0.
Referee: Daniele ORSATO (ITA)   Attendance: 75,000.

08.03.23   Tottenham Hotspur Stadium, London: Tottenham Hotspur – AC Milan 0-0
Tottenham Hotspur: Fraser Forster, Ben Davies, Clément Lenglet, Cristian Romero, Emerson Royal (70' Richarlison), Ivan Perisic (53' Pedro Porro), Pierre-Emile Højbjerg, Oliver Skipp, Dejan Kulusevski (83' Davinson Sánchez), Heung-Min Son, Harry Kane.
Coach: Antonio Conte.
AC Milan: Mike Maignan, Fikayo Tomori, Theo Hernández, Pierre Kalulu, Malick Thiaw, Rade Krunic, Brahim Díaz (81' Ismaël Bennacer), Sandro Tonali, Olivier Giroud (81' Divock Origi), Rafael Leão (89' Ante Rebic), Junior Messias (56' Alexis Saelemaekers).
Coach: Stefano Pioli.
Referee: Clément Turpin (FRA)   Attendance: 61,602.
Send off: 77' Cristian Romero.

14.03.23 Etihad Stadium, Manchester: Manchester City – RB Leipzig 7-0 (3-0)
Manchester City: Ederson, Nathan Aké, John Stones (64' Sergio Gómez), Rúben Dias, Manuel Akanji, Ilkay Gündogan (55' Riyad Mahrez), Kevin De Bruyne, Jack Grealish (55' Phil Foden), Bernardo Silva, Rodri (64' Kalvin Phillips), Erling Haaland (63' Julián Álvarez). Coach: Pep Guardiola.
RB Leipzig: Janis Blaswich, Willi Orbán, Benjamin Henrichs (80' Lukas Klostermann), David Raum, Josko Gvardiol, Emil Forsberg (62' André Silva), Kevin Kampl, Konrad Laimer, Amadou Haïdara (63' Mohamed Simakan), Dominik Szoboszlai (72' Dani Olmo), Timo Werner (62' Yussuf Poulsen). Coach: Marco Rose.
Goals: 22', 24', 45+2' Erling Haaland 1-0 (p), 2-0, 3-0, 49' Ilkay Gündogan 4-0, 53', 57' Erling Haaland 5-0, 6-0, 90+2' Kevin De Bruyne 7-0.
Referee: Slavko Vincic (SVN)   Attendance: 52,038.

14.03.23   Estádio do Dragão, Porto: FC Porto – Internazionale Milano 0-0
FC Porto: Diogo Costa, Iván Marcano, Fábio Cardoso, Zaidu Sanusi (85' Wendell), Mateus Uribe (85' Danny Namaso Loader), Marko Grujic, Stephen Eustáquio (70' André Franco), Mehdi Taremi, Galeno, Pepê Aquino, Evanilson (71' Toni Martínez).
Coach: Sérgio Conceição.
Internazionale Milano: André Onana, Matteo Darmian (80' Milan Skriniar), Francesco Acerbi, Federico Dimarco (70' Danilo D'Ambrosio), Denzel Dumfries, Alessandro Bastoni (74' Stefan de Vrij), Henrikh Mkhitaryan, Hakan Çalhanoglu, Nicolò Barella (80' Marcelo Brozovic), Edin Dzeko (70' Romelu Lukaku), Lautaro Martínez. Coach: Simone Inzaghi.
Referee: Szymon Marciniak (POL)   Attendance: 48,015.
Send off: 90+7' Pepê Aquino.

15.03.23   Estadio Santiago Bernabéu, Madrid: Real Madrid CF – Liverpool FC 1-0 (0-0)
Real Madrid CF: Thibaut Courtois, Nacho, Dani Carvajal (86' Lucas Vázquez), Antonio Rüdiger, Éder Militão, Luka Modric (82' Dani Caballos), Toni Kroos (84' Aurélien Tchouaméni), Federico Valverde, Eduardo Camavinga, Karim Benzema (82' Rodrygo), Vinícius Júnior (84' Marco Asensio). Coach: Carlo Ancelotti.
Liverpool FC: Alisson, Virgil van Dijk, Andy Robertson (90+1' Kostas Tsimikas), Trent Alexander-Arnold, Ibrahima Konaté, James Milner (73' Alex Oxlade-Chamberlain), Fabinho, Mohamed Salah, Diogo Jota (57' Harvey Elliott), Cody Gakpo (90+1' Fábio Carvalho), Darwin Núñez (57' Roberto Firmino). Coach: Jürgen Klopp.
Goal: 78' Karim Benzema 1-0.
Referee: Felix Zwayer (GER)   Attendance: 63,127.

15.03.23   Stadio Diego Armando Maradona, Napoli:
SSC Napoli – Eintracht Frankfurt 3-0 (1-0)
SSC Napoli: Alex Meret, Mário Rui, Giovanni Di Lorenzo, Amir Rrahmani, Kim Min-Jae (66' Juan Jesus), Piotr Zielinski (74' Tanguy Ndombèlé), Stanislav Lobotka, Frank Zambo Anguissa, Matteo Politano (67' Hirving Lozano), Victor Osimhen (81' Giovanni Simeone), Khvicha Kvaratskhelia (74' Eljif Elmas). Coach: Luciano Spalletti.
Eintracht Frankfurt: Kevin Trapp, Christopher Lenz (67' Philipp Max), Aurélio Buta, Evan Ndicka, Tuta, Sebastian Rode (74' Kristijan Jakic), Mario Götze, Djibril Sow, Daichi Kamada, Rafael Borré, Ansgar Knauff (62' Faride Alidou). Coach: Oliver Glasner.
Goals: 45+2', 53' Victor Osimhen 1-0, 2-0, 64' Piotr Zielinski 3-0 (p).
Referee: Anthony Taylor (ENG)   Attendance: 49,082.

125

QUARTER-FINALS

11.04.23   Estádio da Luz, Lisboa: SL Benfica – Internazionale Milano 0-2 (0-0)
SL Benfica: Odisseas Vlachodimos, Gilberto, Álex Grimaldo, Morato, António Silva, João Mário, Fredrik Aursnes, Rafa Silva, Chiquinho, Florentino (64' David Neres), Gonçalo Ramos. Coach: Roger Schmidt.
Internazionale Milano: André Onana, Matteo Darmian, Francesco Acerbi, Federico Dimarco (63' Robin Gosens), Denzel Dumfries (87' Danilo D'Ambrosio), Alessandro Bastoni (90+1' Stefan de Vrij), Henrikh Mkhitaryan, Marcelo Brozovic, Nicolò Barella, Edin Dzeko (63' Romelu Lukaku), Lautaro Martínez (63' Joaquín Correa). Coach: Simone Inzaghi.
Goals: 51' Nicolò Barella 0-1, 82' Romelu Lukaku 0-2 (p).
Referee: Michael Oliver (ENG)   Attendance: 62,594.

11.04.23   Etihad Stadium, Manchester: Manchester City – Bayern München 3-0 (1-0)
Manchester City: Ederson, Nathan Aké, John Stones, Rúben Dias, Manuel Akanji, Ilkay Gündogan, Kevin De Bruyne (68' Julián Álvarez), Jack Grealish, Bernardo Silva, Rodri, Erling Haaland. Coach: Pep Guardiola.
Bayern München: Yann Sommer, Benjamin Pavard, Dayot Upamecano, Matthijs de Ligt, Leon Goretzka, Joshua Kimmich, Serge Gnabry (80' Thomas Müller), Kingsley Coman, Leroy Sané, Alphonso Davies (80' João Cancelo), Jamal Musiala (69' Sadio Mané).
Coach: Thomas Tuchel.
Goals: 27' Rodri 1-0, 70' Bernardo Silva 2-0, 76' Erling Haaland 3-0.
Referee: Jesús Gil Manzano (ESP)   Attendance: 52,257.

12.04.23   Estadio Santiago Bernabéu, Madrid: Real Madrid CF – Chelsea FC 2-0 (1-0)
Real Madrid CF: Thibaut Courtois, David Alaba, Dani Carvajal, Éder Militão, Luka Modric (81' Dani Ceballos), Toni Kroos (84' Aurélien Tchouaméni), Federico Valverde, Eduardo Camavinga (71' Antonio Rüdiger), Karim Benzema, Vinícius Júnior, Rodrygo (71' Marco Asensio). Coach: Carlo Ancelotti.
Chelsea FC: Kepa, Thiago Silva (76' Mason Mount), Kalidou Koulibaly (55' Marc Cucurella), Ben Chilwell, Reece James, Wesley Fofana, Mateo Kovacic, N'Golo Kanté (75' Conor Gallagher), Enzo Fernández, Raheem Sterling (65' Kai Havertz), João Félix (65' Trevoh Chalobah). Coach: Frank Lampard.
Goals: 21' Karim Benzema 1-0, 74' Marco Asencio 2-0.
Referee: François Letexier (FRA)   Attendance: 63,142.
Send off: 59' Ben Chilwell.

12.04.23   Stadio Giuseppe Meazza, Milano: AC Milan – SSC Napoli 1-0 (1-0)
AC Milan: Mike Maignan, Simon Kjær, Davide Calabria, Fikayo Tomori, Theo Hernández, Rade Krunic, Ismaël Bennacer (67' Alexis Saelemaekers), Brahim Díaz (80' Ante Rebic), Sandro Tonali, Olivier Giroud, Rafael Leão. Coach: Stefano Pioli.
SSC Napoli: Alex Meret, Mário Rui (81' Mathías Olivera), Giovanni Di Lorenzo, Amir Rrahmani, Kim Min-Jae, Piotr Zielinski (80' Tanguy Ndombèlé), Stanislav Lobotka, Frank Zambo Anguissa, Eljif Elmas, Hirving Lozano (69' Giacomo Raspadori), Khvicha Kvaratskhelia (81' Matteo Politano). Coach: Luciano Spalletti.
Goal: 40' Ismaël Bennacer 1-0.
Referee: István Kovács (ROM)   Attendance: 74,742.
Send off: 74' Frank Zambo Anguissa.

18.04.23   Stamford Bridge, London: Chelsea FC – Real Madrid CF 0-2 (0-0)
Chelsea FC: Kepa, Thiago Silva, Marc Cucurella (68' Mykhaylo Mudryk), Trevoh Chalobah,
Reece James, Wesley Fofana, Mateo Kovacic, N'Golo Kanté, Kai Havertz (77' Mason Mount),
Conor Gallagher (67' João Félix), Enzo Fernández (67' Raheem Sterling).
Coach: Frank Lampard.
Real Madrid CF: Thibaut Courtois, David Alaba (46' Antonio Rüdiger), Dani Carvajal (81'
Nacho), Éder Militão, Luka Modric, Toni Kroos (76' Dani Ceballos), Federico Valverde,
Eduardo Camavinga, Karim Benzema (71' Aurélien Tchouaméni), Vinícius Júnior, Rodrygo
(81' Marco Asensio). Coach: Carlo Ancelotti.
Goals: 58', 80' Rodrygo 0-1, 0-2.
Referee: Daniele Orsato (ITA)   Attendance: 39,453.

18.04.23   Stadio Diego Arando Maradona, Napoli: SSC Napoli – AC Milan 1-1 (0-1)
SSC Napoli: Alex Meret, Juan Jesus, Mário Rui (34' Mathías Olivera), Giovanni Di Lorenzo,
Amir Rrahmani (74' Leo Østigård), Piotr Zielinski (74' Giacomo Raspadori), Stanislav
Lobotka, Tanguy Ndombèlé (63' Eljif Elmas), Matteo Politano (34' Hirving Lozano), Victor
Osimhen, Khvicha Kvaratskhelia. Coach: Luciano Spalletti.
AC Milan: Mike Maignan, Simon Kjær, Davide Calabria, Fikayo Tomori, Theo Hernández,
Rade Krunic, Ismaël Bennacer, Brahim Díaz (59' Junior Messias), Sandro Tonali, Olivier
Giroud (68' Divock Origi), Rafael Leão (84' Alexis Saelemaekers). Coach: Stefano Pioli.
Goals: 43' Olivier Giroud 0-1, 90+3' Victor Osimhen 1-1.
Referee: Szymon Marciniak (POL)   Attendance: 52,728.

Olivier Giroud missed a penalty kick (22').
Khvicha Kvaratskhelia missed a penalty kick (82').

19.04.23   Stadio Giuseppe Meazza, Milano: Internazionale Milano – SL Benfica 3-3 (1-1)
Internazionale Milano: André Onana, Matteo Darmian, Francesco Acerbi, Federico Dimarco
(80' Robin Gosens), Denzel Dumfries, Alessandro Bastoni (80' Danilo D'Ambrosio), Henrikh
Mkhitaryan, Marcelo Brozovic, Nicolò Barella (76' Hakan Çalhanoglu), Edin Dzeko (76'
Romelu Lukaku), Lautaro Martínez (76' Joaquín Correa). Coach: Simone Inzaghi.
SL Benfica: Odisseas Vlachodimos, Nicolás Otamendi, Gilberto (46' David Neres), Álex
Grimaldo, António Silva, João Mário (89' Andreas Schjelderup), Fredrik Aursnes, Rafa Silva
(80' João Neves), Chiquinho (80' Petar Musa), Florentino, Gonçalo Ramos (74' Gonçalo
Guedes). Coach: Roger Schmidt.
Goals: 14' Nicolò Barella 1-0, 38' Fredrik Aursnes 1-1, 65' Lautaro Martínez 2-1,
78' Joaquín Correa 3-1, 86' António Silva 3-2, 90+5' Petar Musa 3-3.
Referee: Carlos del Cerro Grande (ESP)   Attendance: 75,380.

19.04.23   Allianz Arena, München: Bayern München – Manchester City 1-1 (0-0)
Bayern München: Yann Sommer, João Cancelo (63' Alphonso Davies), Benjamin Pavard (77'
Josip Stanisic), Dayot Upamecano, Matthijs de Ligt, Leon Goretzka, Joshua Kimmich, Eric
Maxim Choupo-Moting (71' Mathys Tel), Kingsley Coman, Leroy Sané (64' Sadio Mané),
Jamal Musiala (72' Thomas Müller). Coach: Thomas Tuchel.
Manchester City: Ederson, Nathan Aké (66' Aymeric Laporte), John Stones, Rúben Dias,
Manuel Akanji, Ilkay Gündogan, Kevin De Bruyne (88' Kyle Walker), Jack Grealish,
Bernardo Silva, Rodri, Erling Haaland (84' Julián Álvarez). Coach: Pep Guardiola.
Goals: 57' Erling Haaland 0-1, 83' Joshua Kimmich 1-1 (p).
Referee: Clément Turpin (FRA)   Attendance: 75,000.

Erling Haaland missed a penalty kick (37').

SEMI-FINALS

09.05.23   Estadio Santiago Bernabéu, Madrid: Real Madrid CF – Manchester City 1-1 (1-0)
Real Madrid CF: Thibaut Courtois, David Alaba, Dani Carvajal, Antonio Rüdiger, Luka
Modric (87' Nacho), Toni Kroos (84' Aurélien Tchouaméni), Federico Valverde, Eduardo
Camavinga, Karim Benzema, Vinícius Júnior, Rodrygo (81' Marco Asensio).
Coach: Carlo Ancelotti.
Manchester City: Ederson, Kyle Walker, John Stones, Rúben Dias, Manuel Akanji, Ilkay
Gündogan, Kevin De Bruyne, Jack Grealish, Bernardo Silva, Rodri, Erling Haaland.
Coach: Pep Guardiola.
Goals: 36' Vinícius Júnior 1-0, 67' Kevin De Bruyne 1-1.
Referee: Artur Soares Dias (POR)   Attendance: 63,485.

10.05.23   Stadio Giuseppe Meazza, Milano: AC Milan – Internazionale Milano 0-2 (0-2)
AC Milan: Mike Maignan, Simon Kjær (59' Malick Thiaw), Davide Calabria (82' Pierre
Kalulu), Fikayo Tomori, Theo Hernández, Rade Krunic, Ismaël Bennacer (17' Junior Messias),
Brahim Díaz (82' Tommaso Pobega), Alexis Saelemaekers (59' Divock Origi), Sandro Tonali,
Olivier Giroud. Coach: Stefano Pioli.
Internazionale Milano: André Onana, Matteo Darmian, Francesco Acerbi, Federico Dimarco
(70' Stefan de Vrij), Denzel Dumfries, Alessandro Bastoni, Henrikh Mkhitaryan (62' Marcelo
Brozovic), Hakan Çalhanoglu (78' Roberto Gagliardini), Nicolò Barella, Edin Dzeko (70'
Romelu Lukaku), Lautaro Martínez (78' Joaquín Correa). Coach: Simone Inzaghi.
Goals: 8' Edin Dzeko 0-1, 11' Henrikh Mkhitaryan 0-2.
Referee: Jesús Gil Manzano (ESP)   Attendance: 75,532.

16.05.23   Stadio Giuseppe Meazza, Milano: Internazionale Milano – AC Milan 1-0 (0-0)
Internazionale Milano: André Onana, Matteo Darmian, Francesco Acerbi, Federico Dimarco
(66' Robin Gosens), Denzel Dumfries, Alessandro Bastoni, Henrikh Mkhitaryan (44' Marcelo
Brozovic), Hakan Çalhanoglu, Nicolò Barella (84' Roberto Gagliardini), Edin Dzeko (66'
Romelu Lukaku), Lautaro Martínez (84' Joaquín Correa). Coach: Simone Inzaghi.
AC Milan: Mike Maignan, Davide Calabria, Fikayo Tomori, Theo Hernández, Malick Thiaw
(64' Pierre Kalulu), Rade Krunic, Brahim Díaz (76' Divock Origi), Sandro Tonali, Olivier
Giroud, Rafael Leão, Junior Messias (76' Alexis Saelemaekers). Coach: Stefano Pioli.
Goal: 74' Lautaro Martínez 1-0.
Referee: Clément Turpin (FRA)   Attendance: 75,567.

17.05.23   Etihad Stadium, Manchester: Manchester City – Real Madrid CF 4-0 (2-0)
Manchester City: Ederson, Kyle Walker, John Stones, Rúben Dias, Manuel Akanji, Ilkay
Gündogan (79' Riyad Mahrez), Kevin De Bruyne (84' Phil Foden), Jack Grealish, Bernardo
Silva, Rodri, Erling Haaland (89' Julián Álvarez). Coach: Pep Guardiola.
Real Madrid CF: Thibaut Courtois, David Alaba, Dani Carvajal (80' Lucas Vázquez), Éder
Militão, Luka Modric (63' Antonio Rüdiger), Toni Kroos (70' Marco Asensio), Federico
Valverde, Eduardo Camavinga (79' Aurélien Tchouaméni), Karim Benzema, Vinícius Júnior,
Rodrygo (79' Dani Ceballos). Coach: Carlo Ancelotti.
Goals: 23', 37' Bernardo Silva 1-0, 2-0, 76' Manuel Akanji 3-0, 90+1' Julián Álvarez 4-0.
Referee: Szymon Marciniak (POL)   Attendance: 52,313.

FINAL

10.06.23   <u>Atatürk Olimpiyat Stadi, Istanbul:</u>
Manchester City – Internazionale Milano 1-0 (0-0)
<u>Manchester City:</u> Ederson, Nathan Aké, John Stones (82' Kyle Walker), Rúben Dias, Manuel Akanji, Ilkay Gündogan, Kevin De Bruyne (36' Phil Foden), Jack Grealish, Bernardo Silva, Rodri, Erling Haaland. Coach: Pep Guardiola.
<u>Internazionale Milano:</u> André Onana, Matteo Darmian (84' Danilo D'Ambrosio), Francesco Acerbi, Federico Dimarco, Denzel Dumfries (76' Raoul Bellanova), Alessandro Bastoni (76' Robin Gosens), Marcelo Brozovic, Hakan Çalhanoglu (84' Henrikh Mkhitaryan), Nicolò Barella, Edin Dzeko (57' Romelu Lukaku), Lautaro Martínez. Coach: Simone Inzaghi.
<u>Goals:</u> 68' Rodri 1-0.
<u>Referee:</u> Szymon Marciniak (POL)   Attendance: 71,412.

UEFA CHAMPIONS LEAGUE
2023-2024

PRELIMINARY ROUND

Semi-Final Round

27.06.23   Kópavogsvöllur, Kópavogur:
        Atlètic Club d'Escaldes – FK Buducnost Podgorica 0-3 (0-2)
Atlètic Club d'Escaldes: Saúl Gracia, Jilmar Torres (82' David Rodríguez), Víctor Maffeo, Javi Morales, Álex Sánchez, Víctor Pérez, Martí Riverola, Hamza Ryahi (66' Víctor Alonso), Víctor Casadesús, Mathias Coureur (73' Guillaume López), Rodrigo Piloto. Coach: Federico Bessone.
FK Buducnost Podgorica: Djordije Pavlicic, Ivan Novovic, Zvonko Ceklic, Stephano Almeida (81' Milos Brnovic), Uros Ignjatovic, Petar Grbic (71' Ognjen Gasevic), Marko Pavlovski (71' Luka Mirkovic), Miomir Djurickovic (86' Jovan Dasic), Vasilije Adzic (82' Vladimir Perisic), Balsa Sekulic, Damjan Dakic. Coach: Miodrag Dzudovic.
Goals: 13' Balsa Sekulic 0-1 (p), 21' Miomir Djurickovic 0-2, 60' Balsa Sekulic 0-3.
Referee: Marcel Bîrsan (ROM)   Attendance: 103.

27.06.23   Kópavogsvöllur, Kópavogur: SP Tre Penne – Breidablik 1-7 (1-3)
SP Tre Penne: Mattia Migani, Roberto Rosini, Giacomo Nigretti, Nicola Bellucci (46' Riccardo Pieri), Antonio Barretta (76' Davide Cesarini), Piero Tamagnini, Andrea De Falco (90+1' Michele Stellato), Marcello Scarponi, Assane Fall, Luca Ceccaroli (61' Lorenzo Dormi), Imre Badalassi (77' Fabio Giovagnoli). Coach: Stefano Ceci.
Breidablik: Anton Ari Einarsson, Damir Muminovic, Höskuldur Gunnlaugsson, Davíd Ingvarsson, Oliver Stefánsson (64' Viktor Örn Margeirsson), Oliver Sigurjónsson (46' Anton Lúdvíksson), Gísli Eyjólfsson (64' Kristinn Steindórsson), Alexander Sigurdarson (75' Jason Dadi Svanthórsson), Viktor Einarsson, Ágúst Hlynsson, Klæmint Olsen (64' Stefán Ingi Sigurdarson). Coach: Óskar Hrafn Thorvaldsson.
Goals: 6' Höskuldur Gunnlaugsson 0-1, 25' Ágúst Hlynsson 0-2, 31' Antonio Barretta 1-2, 45+3' Klæmint Olsen 1-3, 67' Stefán Ingi Sigurdarson 1-4, 74' Viktor Einarsson 1-5, 89' Höskuldur Gunnlaugsson 1-6, 90+3' Ágúst Hlynsson 1-7.
Referee: Mads-Kristoffer Kristoffersen (DEN)   Attendance: 621.

Final Round

30.06.23   Kópavogsvöllur, Kópavogur: FK Buducnost Podgorica – Breidablik 0-5 (0-4)
FK Buducnost Podgorica: Djordije Pavlicic, Ivan Novovic (46' Ognjen Gasevic), Zvonko
Ceklic, Stephano Almeida, Uros Ignjatovic, Petar Grbic (77' Vladimir Perisic), Marko
Pavlovski (46' Luka Mirkovic), Miomir Djurickovic, Vasilije Adzic (46' Milos Brnovic),
Balsa Sekulic (71' Marko Mrvaljevic), Damjan Dakic. Coach: Miodrag Dzudovic.
Breidablik: Anton Ari Einarsson, Arnór Adalsteinsson (71' Davíd Ingvarsson), Damir
Muminovic, Höskuldur Gunnlaugsson, Viktor Örn Margeirsson, Andri Yeoman (71' Ágúst
Hlynsson), Oliver Sigurjónsson (81' Anton Lúdvíksson), Gísli Eyjólfsson, Viktor Einarsson,
Kristinn Steindórsson (71' Jason Dadi Svanthórsson), Stefán Ingi Sigurdarson (75' Klæmint
Olsen). Coach: Óskar Hrafn Thorvaldsson.
Goals: 5' Viktor Einarsson 0-1, 22' Stefán Ingi Sigurdarson 0-2, 28' Gísli Eyjólfsson 0-3,
33' Höskuldur Gunnlaugsson 0-4, 73' Jason Dadi Svanthórsson 0-5.
Referee: Krzysztof Jakubik (POL)   Attendance: 845.
Sent off: 90+2' Miomir Djurickovic.

FIRST QUALIFYING ROUND

11.07.23   Urartu Stadium, Yerevan: FC Urartu – Zrinjski Mostar 0-1 (0-0)
FC Urartu: Aleksandr Melikhov, Zhirayr Margaryan, Evgeniy Tsymbalyuk, Erik Piloyan, Nana
Antwi (89' Perisa Pesukic), Marcos Júnior, Narek Grigoryan, Dramane Salou (86' Pavel
Mogilevets), Ugochukwu Iwu, Leon Sabua (46' Yaya Sanogo, 86' Aras Özbiliz), Artem
Maksimenko (46' Oleg Polyakov). Coach: Dmitriy Gunko.
Zrinjski Mostar: Marko Maric, Mario Ticinovic (80' Franko Sabljic), Hrvoje Barisic, Josip
Corluka, Matej Senic, Luka Marin (90+6' Kerim Memija), Dario Canadjija, Mato Stanic (68'
Damir Zlomislic), Antonio Ivancic (80' Zvonimir Kozulj), Nemanja Bilbija, Matija
Malekinusic (46' Mario Cuze). Coach: Krunoslav Rendulic.
Goal: 89' Matej Senic 0-1.
Referee: Philip Farrugia (MLT)   Attendance: 3,900.

11.07.23   Victoria Stadium, Gibraltar: Lincoln Red Imps – Qarabag FK 1-2 (1-0)
Lincoln Red Imps: Dayle Coleing, Nano, Ibrahim Ayew, Bernando Lopes, Jack Sergeant,
Ethan Britto (64' Lee Casciaro), Mandi (55' Samson Bolaji Ajayi), Juampe (73' Juanfri), Liam
Walker (64' Santi Luque), Mustapha Yahaya, Kike Gómez. Coach: Javi Muñoz.
Qarabag FK: Sahrudin Mahammadaliyev, Marko Vesovic, Bahlul Mustafazade, Kevin Medina,
Marko Jankovic (87' Qara Qarayev), Abdellah Zoubir, Elvin Cafarquliyev, Leandro Andrade
(87' Adama Diakhaby), Júlio Romão, Nariman Axundzade (61' Hamidou Keyta), Redon
Xhixha (61' Yassine Benzia). Coach: Qurban Qurbanov.
Goals: 25' Kike Gómez 1-0, 58' Redon Xhixha 1-1, 90+4' Yassine Benzia 1-2.
Referee: Vitālijs Spasjonnikovs (LAT)   Attendance: 683.

11.07.23 Vilniaus LFF stadionas, Vilnius: FK Zalgiris – FC Struga 0-0
FK Zalgiris: Edvinas Gertmonas, Stipe Vucur, Mario Pavelic, Joël Bopesu, Nassim Hnid, Nicolás Gorobsov, Yuriy Kendysh (79' Liviu Antal), Donatas Kazlauskas (46' Árni Vilhjálmsson), Ovidijus Verbickas (62' Paulius Golubickas), Yukiyoshi Karashima (79' Marko Milickovic), Mathias Oyewusi. Coach: Vladimir Cheburin.
FC Struga: Vedran Kjosevski, Medzit Neziri, Vangjel Zguro, Edis Malikji (89' Ard Kasami), Besart Krivanjeva, Sava Radic, Bunjamin Shabani, Besmir Bojku, Mentor Mazrekaj (89' Flamur Tairi), Besart Ibraimi (78' Valentin Kochoski), Marjan Radeski (90+2' Senad Jarovic). Coach: Shpëtim Duro.
Referee: Elchin Masiyev (AZE)   Attendance: 4,647.

11.07.23 Stadion Stozice, Ljubljana: Olimpija Ljubljana – Valmiera FC 2-1 (1-0)
Olimpija Ljubljana: Matevz Vidovsek, David Sualehe, Jorge Silva (90+4' Justas Lasickas), Ivan Posavec (76' Saar Fadida), Ahmet Muhamedbegovic, Timi Elsnik, Agustin Doffo, Svit Seslar (64' Admir Bristric), Marcel Ratnik, Mustafa Nukic (64' Raul Florucz), Rui Pedro (76' Nemanja Motika). Coach: João Henriques.
Valmiera FC: Carlos Olses, Daniels Balodis, Niks Sliede, Alvis Jaunzems (67' Pape Yaré Fall), Ivan Zhelizko (77' Gustavo), Victor Diagne (65' Rifet Kapic), Adel Ghanem, Maksims Tonisevs, Camilo Mena, Alioune Ndoye (65' Leonardo "Léo" Gaúcho), Ruan Ribeiro (77' Meissa Diop). Coach: Jurgis Kalns.
Goals: 42' Mustafa Nukic 1-0, 74' Rui Pedro 2-0, 87' Meissa Diop 2-1.
Referee: Andrei Chivulete (ROM)   Attendance: 4,355.

11.07.23 Miejski Stadion Pilkarski "Raków", Czestochowa:
          Raków Czestochowa – FC Flora Tallinn 1-0 (0-0)
Raków Czestochowa: Vladan Kovacevic, Milan Rundic, Zoran Arsenic, Stratos Svarnas, Marcin Cebula (64' Mateusz Wdowiak), Bartosz Nowak (46' John Yeboah), Jean Carlos (46' Deian Sorescu), Vladyslav Kochergin, Fran Tudor, Ben Lederman (82' Gustav Berggren), Fabian Piasecki (78' Lukasz Zwolinski). Coach: Dawid Szwarga.
FC Flora Tallinn: Evert Grünvald, Märtin Kuusk, Michael Lilander, Markkus Seppik, Kristo Hussar, Konstantin Vassiljev, Martin Miller, Vladislavs Kreida (12' Rauno Alliku), Nikita Mihhailov (67' Danil Kuraksin), Henrik Ojamaa, Sten Reinkort (76' Mikhel Järviste). Coach: Jürgen Henn.
Goal: 54' Vladyslav Kochergin 1-0).
Referee: Arda Kardesler (TUR)   Attendance: 5,242.

11.07.23 MFA Centenary Stadium, Ta'Qali: Hamrun Spartans – Maccabi Haifa 0-4 (0-2)
Hamrun Spartans: Federico Marchetti, Steve Borg, Emerson Marcelina, Ryan Camenzuli, Nemanja Krstic (62' Eder), Juan Corbalan (70' Joseph Mbong), Uros Djuranovic, Roko Prsa, Ognjen Bjelicic, Jonny (70' Luke Montebello), Elionay (62' Yulian Nenov). Coach: Luciano Zauri.
Maccabi Haifa: Itamar Nizan, Daniel Sundgren, Shon Goldberg, Pierre Cornud, Abdoulaye Seck, Tjaronn Chery (80' Hamza Shibli), Dia Sabi'A (68' Anan Khalaili), Ali Muhammad (68' Mahmoud Jaber), Goni Naor, Dean David (56' Lior Refaelov), Frantzdy Pierrot (68' Erik Shuranov). Coach: Messay Dego.
Goals: 41' Frantzdy Pierrot 0-1, 45+3' Dean David 0-2, 58' Frantzdy Pierrot 0-3, 80' Anan Khalaili 0-4.
Referee: Donald Robertson (SCO)   Attendance: 1,627.

Hamrun Spartans played their home match at the MFA Centenary Stadium in Ta'Qali, instead of their regular stadium, the Victor Tedesco Stadium, in Hamrun, which did not meet UEFA requirements.

11.07.23 Stadiumi Fadil Vokrri, Pristina: KF Ballkani – PFC Ludogorets Razgrad 2-0 (1-0)
KF Ballkani: Enea Koliçi, Lorenc Trashi (76' Arbër Potoku), Bajram Jashanica, Armend
Thaqi, Lumbardh Dellova, Edvin Kuc (76' Veton Tusha), Meriton Korenica (89' Almir
Kryeziu), Qendrim Zyba, Lindon Emërllahu, Nazmi Gripshi (90+3' Albin Kapra), Albion
Rrahmani (76' Albin Berisha). Coach: Ilir Daja.
PFC Ludogorets Razgrad: Sergio Padt, Igor Plastun, Marcel Heister, Aslak Witry (30' Pipa),
Franco Russo, Claude Gonçalves, Nonato (46' Dominik Yankov), Show (46' Pedro Naressi),
Kiril Despodov, Matías Tissera (69' Spas Delev), Caio Vidal (69' Raí Nascimento).
Coach: Ivaylo Petev.
Goals: 45+1' Meriton Korenica 1-0, 55' Qendrim Zyba 2-0.
Referee: Gal Leibovitz (ISR)   Attendance: 7,656.

*KF Ballkani played their home match at the Stadiumi Fadil Vokrri in Pristina, instead of their
regular stadium, the Suva Reka City Stadium, in Suva Reka, which did not meet UEFA
requirements.*

11.07.23 Vid Djúpumýrar, Klaksvík: KÍ Klaksvík – Ferencvárosi TC 0-0
KÍ Klaksvík: Jonatan Johansson, Vegard Forren, Heini Vatnsdal, Patrick Da Silva, Børge
Petersen, C Kronberg (78' Mads Mikkelsen), Árni Frederiksberg, René Joensen, Luc Kassi
(88' Sivert Gussiås), Deni Pavlovic (55' Jóannes Danielsen), Jákup Andreasen.
Coach: Magne Hoseth.
Ferencvárosi TC: Dénes Dibusz, Endre Botka, Eldar Civic, Ibrahim Cissé, Samy Mmaee,
Anderson Esiti (73' Dávid Sigér), Kristoffer Zachariassen (90+2' Cebrails Makreckis), Péter
Baráth, Adama Traoré (I) (67' Krisztián Lisztes), Barnabás Varga, Marquinhos (66' Owusu
Kwabena). Coach: Stanislav Cherchesov.
Referee: Juri Frischer (EST)   Attendance: 1,010.

11.07.23 Air Albania Stadium, Tirana: FK Partizani Tirana – BATE Borisov 1-1 (0-0)
FK Partizani Tirana: Panajot Qirko, David Atanaskoski, Elion Sota, Andi Hadroj, Saliou
Sembene, Valentino Murataj, Arinaldo Rrapaj (86' Maguette Gueye), Adnard Mehmeti (86'
Bruno Telushi), Victor da Silva (71' Eros Grezda), Tedi Cara, Christian Mba (71' Alfred
Mensah). Coach: Zoran Zekic.
BATE Borisov: Andrey Kudravets, Ruslan Khadarkevich, Vladislav Malkevich (79' Dmitri
Podstrelov), Danila Nechaev, Sherif Jimoh, Sidi Bane, Valeriy Gromyko, Denis Grechikho
(71' Sead Islamovic), Artem Kontsevoy, Valeriy Bocherov, Dmitri Antilevski (79' Aleksandr
Shestyuk). Coach: Kirill Alshevskiy.
Goals: 58' Dmitri Antilevski 0-1, 66' Tedi Cara 1-1.
Referee: Nathan Verboomen (BEL)   Attendance: 5,000.

*FK Partizani Tirana played their home match at the Air Albania Stadium in Tirana, instead of
their regular stadium, the Partizani Complex, in Tirana, which did not meet UEFA
requirements.*

11.07.23   Tallaght Stadium, Tallaght: Shamrock Rovers – Breidablik 0-1 (0-1)
Shamrock Rovers: Leon Pöhls, Sean Kavanagh, Roberto Lopes "Pico", Sean Hoare, Dan Cleary, Ronan Finn (72' Richie Towell), Jack Byrne, Gary O'Neill, Dylan Watts (60' Graham Burke), Markus Poom, Rory Gaffney (87' Johnny Kenny). Coach: Stephen Bradley.
Breidablik: Anton Ari Einarsson, Damir Muminovic (73' Arnór Adalsteinsson), Höskuldur Gunnlaugsson, Viktor Örn Margeirsson, Andri Yeoman, Oliver Sigurjónsson (73' Alexander Sigurdarson), Gísli Eyjólfsson, Viktor Einarsson, Jason Dadi Svanthórsson (66' Ágúst Hlynsson), Kristinn Steindórsson (87' Davíd Ingvarsson), Klæmint Olsen.
Coach: Óskar Hrafn Thorvaldsson.
Goal: 39' Damir Muminovic 0-1.
Referee: Chrysovalantis Theouli (CYP)   Attendance: 7,216.

12.07.23   Astana Arena, Astana: FK Astana – Dinamo Tbilisi 1-1 (1-0)
FK Astana: Josip Condric, Abzal Beysebekov, Varazdat Haroyan, Mikhail Gabyshev (16' Kamo Hovhannisyan), Yan Vorogovskiy (88' Elkhan Astanov), Aleksa Amanovic, Marin Tomasov, Fabien Ourega (73' Timur Dosmagambetov), Dusan Jovanvic, Maks Ebong (88' Aslan Darabaev), Abat Aymbetov (73' Dembo Darboe). Coach: Grigoriy Babayan.
Dynamo Tbilisi: Giorgi Loria, Gagi Margvelashvili, Jemal Tabidze, Davit Kobouri (46' Aleksandre Kalandadze), Nikoloz Mali (72' Giorgi Maisuradze), Imran Oulad Omar (82' Moussa Sangare), Gabriel Sigua, Davit Skhirtladze, Giorgi Kharaishvili (72' Saba Khvadagiani), Barnes Osei (72' Levan Osikmashvili), Ousmane Camara.
Coach: Giorgi Chiabrishvili.
Goals: 11' Abat Aymbetov 1-0, 57 Gabriel Sigua 1-1.
Referee: Christian-Petru Ciochirca (AUT)   Attendance: 27,328.

12.07.23   Bolt Arena, Helsinki: HJK Helsinki – Larne FC 1-0 (1-0)
HJK Helsinki: Jesse Öst, Jukka Raitala, Pyry Soiri, Miro Tenho, Matti Peltola, Atomu Tanaka (64' Kevin Kouassivi-Benissan), Përparim Hetemaj, Lucas Lingman, Santeri Hostikka (81' Anthony Olusanya), Bojan Radulovic, Topi Keskinen. Coach: Toni Koskela.
Larne FC: Rohan Ferguson, Cian Bolger, Shaun Want, Aaron Donnelly, Michael Glynn, Tomas Cosgrove, Leroy Millar, Shea Gordon, Dylan Sloan (83' Daniel Kearns), Andy Ryan (86' Isaac Westendorf), Lee Bonis. Coach: Tiernan Lynch.
Goal: 3' Bojan Radulovic 1-0 (p).
Referee: Goga Kikacheishvili (GEO)   Attendance: 10,121.

12.07.23   Bravida Arena, Göteborg: BK Häcken – The New Saints 3-1 (3-1)
BK Häcken: Peter Abrahamsson, Even Hovland, Simon Sandberg (62' Franklin Tebo Uchenna), Valgeir Lunddal Fridriksson (62' Tomas Totland), Kristoffer Lund, Tobias Sana (46' Momodou Sonko), Mikkel Rygaard, Samuel Gustafson, Simon Gustafson, Ibrahim Sadiq (83' Ola Kamara), Filip Trpcevski (71' Amor Layouni). Coach: Per-Mathias Høgmo.
The New Saints: Connor Roberts, Chris Marriott, Daniel Davies, Ryan Astles, Josh Pask, Daniel Redmond, Leo Smith, Daniel Williams, Declan McManus (82' Ryan Brobbel), Joshua Daniels, Jordan Williams (76' Rory Holden). Coach: Craig Harrison.
Goals: 7' Ibrahim Sadiq 1-0, 13' Mikkel Rygaard 2-0, 32' Declan McManus 2-1, 36' Even Hovland 3-1.
Referee: Henrik Nalbandyan (ARM)   Attendance: 4,516.

12.07.23   Stadionul Viitorul, Ovidiu: FCV Farul Constanta – FC Sheriff Tiraspol 1-0 (0-0)
FCV Farul Constanta: Mihai Aioani, Kévin Boli, David Kiki, Mihai Popescu, Andrei Borza
(70' Enes Sali), Andrei Artean, Dragos Nedelcu, Tudor Baluta (58' Diogo Queirós), Denis
Alibec (84' Gustavo Maríns), Rivaldinho (58' Marco Borgnino), Adrian Mazilu (70' Dan
Sîrbu). Coach: Gheorghe Hagi.
FC Sheriff Tiraspol: Maksim Koval, Cristian Tovar, Didier Bueno, Armel Zohouri, Munashe
Garananga, Kostas Apostolakis (89' Adamou Ibrahim Djibo), Amine Talal (65' Cédric
Badolo), João Paulo, Jerome Ngom Mbekeli (72' Vinícius Paiva), Moussa Kyabou (64' Peter
Ademo), Luvannor. Coach: Roberto Bordin.
Goal: 56' David Kiki 1-0.
Referee: Sander van der Eijk (HOL)   Attendance: 4,028.

12.07.23   Stadión Tehelné pole, Bratislava: Slovan Bratislava – Swift Hesperange 1-1 (1-1)
Slovan Bratislava: Milan Borjan, Guram Kashia, Lukás Pauschek, Kenan Bajric, Lucas Lovat,
Juraj Kucka, Jaba Kankava, Vladimír Weiss (83' Zuberu Sharani), Tigran Barseghyan (46'
Kyriakos Savvidis), Jaromír Zmrhal (46' Aleksandar Cavric), Malik Abubakari (77' Marko
Tolic). Coach: Vladimir Weiss.
Swift Hesperange: Geordan Dupire, Jerry Prempeh (76' Yann Matias Marques), Toufik
Zeghdane, Négo Ekofo, Simão Martins, Dominik Stolz (76' Cédric Sacras), Bryan Nouvier
(63' Paul Ayongo), Aldin Skenderovic, Charles Morren, Gustavo (70' Olivier Marques),
Blankson Anoff (63' Lado Akhalaia). Coach: Carlos Fangueiro.
Goals: 22' Dominik Stolz 0-1 (p), 25' Vladimír Weiss 1-1.
Referee: Viktor Kopiyevskyy (UKR)   Attendance: 14,470.
Sent off: 45+6' Juraj Kucka.

18.07.23   SRC Biljanini Izvori, Ohrid: FC Struga – FK Zalgiris 1-2 (0-0)
FC Struga: Vedran Kjosevski, Medzit Neziri, Vangjel Zguro, Edis Malikji (85' Ard Kasami),
Besart Krivanjeva (81' Valentin Kochoski), Sava Radic, Bunjamin Shabani, Besmir Bojku,
Mentor Mazrekaj, Besart Ibraimi (85' Senad Jarovic), Marjan Radeski. Coach: Shpëtim Duro.
FK Zalgiris: Edvinas Gertmonas, Stipe Vucur, Mario Pavelic, Joël Bopesu, Nassim Hnid,
Nicolás Gorobsov, Yuriy Kendysh (90+3' Gustas Jarusevicius), Paulius Golubickas (87'
Ovidijus Verbickas), Yukiyoshi Karashima (46' Oliver Buff), Liviu Antal (60' Adama Fofana),
Mathias Oyewusi. Coach: Vladimir Cheburin.
Goal: 75' Besart Ibraimi 1-0 (p), 78' Yuriy Kendysh 1-1, 83' Sava Radic 1-2 (og).
Referee: Darren England (ENG)   Attendance: 1,400.

FC Struga played their home match at the SRC Biljanini Izvori in Ohrid, instead of their
regular stadium, the Gradska Plaza Stadium, in Struga, which did not meet UEFA
requirements.

18.07.23   A. Le Coq Arena, Tallinn: FC Flora Tallinn – Raków Czestochowa 0-3 (0-0)
FC Flora Tallinn: Evert Grünvald, Märtin Kuusk, Michael Lilander, Markkus Seppik (83'
Aleksandr Sapovalov), Kristo Hussar, Konstantin Vassiljev, Martin Miller, Danil Kuraksin
(68' Marko Lipp), Rauno Alliku, Henrik Ojamaa, Sten Reinkort (62 Nikita Mihhailov).
Coach: Jürgen Henn.
Raków Czestochowa: Vladan Kovacevic, Milan Rundic, Zoran Arsenic, Stratos Svarnas,
Marcin Cebula (68' Vladyslav Kochergin), Bartosz Nowak (68' John Yeboah), Jean Carlos
(79' Deian Sorescu), Fran Tudor (79' Mateusz Wdowiak), Giannis Papanikolaou, Ben
Lederman, Lukasz Zwolinski (68' Fabian Piasecki). Coach: Dawid Szwarga.
Goals: 47', 59' Lukasz Zwolinski 0-1, 0-2, 85' Giannis Papanikolaou 0-3.
Referee: Marian Alexandru Barbu (ROM)   Attendance: 3,204.

135

18.07.23   Bolshaya Sportivnaya Arena, Tiraspol:
FC Sheriff Tiraspol – FCV Farul Constanta 3-0 (1-0,1-0) (AET)
FC Sheriff Tiraspol: Maksim Koval, Didier Bueno, Armel Zohouri, Munashe Garananga,
Kostas Apostolakis (102' Cristian Tovar), Amine Talal (120' Ricardinho), João Paulo, Cédric
Badolo (69' Peter Ademo), Jerome Ngom Mbekeli (113' Adamou Ibrahim Djibo), Moussa
Kyabou (113' Cedric Ngah), Luvannor (102' Vinícius Paiva). Coach: Roberto Bordin.
FCV Farul Constanta: Mihai Aioani, Kévin Boli (58' Ionut Larie), David Kiki (87' Dan Sîrbu),
Mihai Popescu, Andrei Borza, Andrei Artean, Dragos Nedelcu (79' Marco Borgnino),
Constantin Grameni, Denis Alibec (114' Ionu Vîna), Rivaldinho (58' Tudor Baluta), Adrian
Mazilu (87' Nicolae Cârnat). Coach: Gheorghte Hagi.
Goals: 45+1' Amine Talal 1-0, 99' Jerome Ngom Mbekeli 2-0, 105+1' Peter Ademo 3-0.
Referee: Miguel Bertolo Nogueira (POR)   Attendance: 5,792.

FC Sheriff Tiraspol won after extra time.

18.07.23   Sammy Ofer Stadium, Haifa: Maccabi Haifa – Hamrun Spartans 2-1 (0-1)
Maccabi Haifa: Itamar Nizan, Pierre Cornud, Abdoulaye Seck, Maor Kandil (60' Dolev
Haziza), Ori Dahan, Lior Refaelov (61' Tjaronn Chery), Dia Sabi'A, Mahmoud Jaber, Goni
Naor (46' Ali Muhammad), Ilay Hajaj (46' Daniel Sundgren), Erik Shuranov (74' Frantzdy
Pierrot). Coach: Messay Dego.
Hamrun Spartans: Federico Marchetti, Steve Borg (89' Karlo Bilic), Emerson Marcelina, Ryan
Camenzuli, Yulian Nenov (46' Eder), Uros Djuranovic, Joseph Mbong (79' Juan Corbalan),
Roko Prsa, Ognjen Bjelicic, Jonny (78' Nemanja Krstic), Elionay (64' Seth Paintsil).
Coach: Luciano Zauri.
Goals: 31' Joseph Mbong 0-1, 69' Erik Shuranov 1-1, 84' Frantzdy Pierrot 2-1.
Referee: Igor Pajac (CRO)   Attendance: 29,000.

18.07.23   Park Hall Stadium, Oswestry: The New Saints – BK Häcken 0-2 (0-1)
The New Saints: Connor Roberts, Chris Marriott, Daniel Davies, Ryan Astles, Josh Pask (73'
Ashley Baker), Jonathan Routledge (37' Daniel Williams), Ryan Brobbel, Leo Smith, Ben
Clark (65' Rory Holden), Joshua Daniels, Jordan Williams (73' Adrian Cieslewicz).
Coach: Craig Harrison.
BK Häcken: Peter Abrahamsson, Even Hovland, Valgeir Lunddal Fridriksson, Kristoffer Lund,
Franklin Tebo Uchenna, Tobias Sana (61' Momodou Sonko), Mikkel Rygaard, Samuel
Gustafson, Simon Gustafson (44' Pontus Dahbo), Ibrahim Sadiq (80' Ola Kamara), Filip
Trpcevski (61' Tomas Totland). Coach: Per-Mathias Høgmo.
Goals: 19' Ibrahim Sadiq 0-1, 90+1' Momodou Sonko 0-2.
Referee: Dario Bel (CRO)   Attendance: 1,003.

18.07.23 Stadion Bijeli Brijeg, Mostar: Zrinjski Mostar – FC Urartu 2-3 (1-0,1-2) (AET)
Zrinjski Mostar: Marko Maric, Mario Ticinovic (80' Aldin Hrvanovic), Hrvoje Barisic, Josip
Corluka, Matej Senic, Luka Marin (80' Kerim Memija), Dario Canadjija (75' Zvonimir
Kozulj), Mato Stanic (61' Damir Zlomislic), Antonio Ivancic, Mario Cuze (61' Franko
Sabljic), Nemanja Bilbija (91' Tomislav Kis). Coach: Krunoslav Rendulic.
FC Urartu: Aleksandr Melikhov, Ivan Zotko (108' Arman Ghazaryan), Zhirayr Margaryan,
Evgeniy Tsymbalyuk, Erik Piloyan (68' Artem Maksimenko), Nana Antwi (80' Karen
Melkonyan), Pavel Mogilevets (60' Eduardo), Marcos Júnior, Narek Grigoryan, Dramane
Salou (68' Aras Özbiliz), Leon Sabua (46' Temur Dzhikiya). Coach: Dmitriy Gunko.
Goals: 27' Nemanja Bilbija 1-0, 74', 90+1' Narek Grigoryan 1-1, 1-2 (p),
94' Tomislav Kis 2-2 (p), 105+3' Artem Maksimenko 2-3.
Referee: Peter Kjærsgaard-Andersen (DEN) Attendance: 5,000.

Zrinjski Mostar won after extra time on penalties (4:3).

*Penalties: Maksimenko 1-0, Kis 1-1, Özbiliz 2-1, Kozulj 2-2, Grigoryan 3-2, Zlomislic missed,
Eduardo Teixeira missed, Senic 3-3, Ghazaryan missed, Barisic 3-4.*

18.07.23   Mezőkövesdi Városi Stadion, Mezőkövesd (HUN):
           BATE Borisov – FK Partizani Tirana 2-0 (0-0)
BATE Borisov: Andrey Kudravets, Ruslan Khadarkevich, Vladislav Malkevich (90+2'
Aleksandr Shestyuk), Danila Nechaev, Sherif Jimoh, Sidi Bane, Valeriy Gromyko, Denis
Grechikho (85' Sead Islamovic), Artem Kontsevoy (90+2' Ilya Vasilevich), Valeriy Bocherov,
Dmitri Antilevski (83' Dmitri Podstrelov). Coach: Kirill Alshevskiy.
FK Partizani Tirana: Panajot Qirko, David Atanaskoski, Elion Sota, Andi Hadroj, Saliou
Sembene, Valentino Murataj, Arinaldo Rrapaj (85' Albers Keko), Adnard Mehmeti (76' Sabit
Bilali), Victor da Silva (76' Maguette Gueye), Tedi Cara (76' Eros Grezda), Christian Mba
(85' Alfred Mensah). Coach: Zoran Zekic.
Goals: 71' Vladislav Malkevich 1-0, 90+12' Aleksandr Shestyuk 2-0.
Referee: Kevin Clancy (SCO) Attendance: 0

*Due to the involvement of Belarus in the Russian invasion of Ukraine, Belarusian teams were
ordered to play their home matches at neutral venues and behind closed doors until further
notice.*

18.07.23   Kópavogsvöllur, Kópavogur: Breidablik – Shamrock Rovers 2-1 (1-0)
Breidablik: Anton Ari Einarsson, Damir Muminovic, Höskuldur Gunnlaugsson, Viktor Örn
Margeirsson, Andri Yeoman (89' Arnór Adalsteinsson), Oliver Sigurjónsson, Gísli Eyjólfsson,
Alexander Sigurdarson (81' Davíd Ingvarsson), Viktor Einarsson, Jason Dadi Svanthórsson
(81' Ágúst Hlynsson), Kristinn Steindórsson (89' Klæmint Olsen).
Coach: Óskar Hrafn Thorvaldsson.
Shamrock Rovers: Leon Pöhls, Sean Kavanagh, Roberto Lopes "Pico", Sean Hoare, Dan
Cleary, Ronan Finn (87' Lee Grace), Richie Towell (70' Aaron Greene), Gary O'Neill, Markus
Poom (70' Dylan Watts), Rory Gaffney, Graham Burke (78' Johnny Kenny).
Coach: Stephen Bradley.
Goals: 16' Jason Dadi Svanthórsson 1-0, 57' Höskuldur Gunnlaugsson 2-0,
65' Graham Burke 2-1 (p).
Referee: Adam Ladebäck (SWE) Attendance: 1,320.

137

19.07.23   Jānis Dalina stadions, Valmiera: Valmiera FC – Olimpija Ljubljana 1-2 (0-1)
Valmiera FC: Carlos Olses, Daniels Balodis, Niks Sliede, Pape Yaré Fall, Rifet Kapic (81'
Gustavo), Alvis Jaunzems, Ivan Zhelizko (90+1' Kristers Cudars), Meissa Diop (46' Ruan
Ribeiro), Maksims Tonisevs (71' Alioune Ndoye), Camilo Mena, Leonardo "Léo" Gaúcho.
Coach: Jurgis Kalns.
Olimpija Ljubljana: Matevz Vidovsek, David Sualehe, Jorge Silva (84' Justas Lasickas), Ivan
Posavec (63' Nemanja Gavric), Ahmet Muhamedbegovic, Timi Elsnik, Agustin Doffo, Svit
Seslar (84' Nemanja Motika), Marcel Ratnik, Mustafa Nukic (67' Raul Florucz), Rui Pedro
(67' Admir Bristric). Coach: João Henriques.
Goals: 33' Rui Pedro 0-1, 64' Ahmet Muhamedbegovic 0-2, 82' Camilo Mena 1-2.
Referee: César Soto Grado (ESP)   Attendance: 1,250.

19.07.23   Groupama Aréna, Budapest: Ferencvárosi TC – KÍ Klaksvík 0-3 (0-3)
Ferencvárosi TC: Dénes Dibusz, Endre Botka, Eldar Civic (75' Marquinhos), Samy Mmaee,
Mats Knoester, Amer Gojak (46' Cebrails Makreckis), Kristoffer Zachariassen (57' Krisztián
Lisztes), Mohammad Abu Fani, Péter Baráth (46' Mohamed Ali Ben Romdhane), Adama
Traoré (I) (57' Owusu Kwabena), Barnabás Varga.
Coaches: Csaba Máté & Stanislav Cherchesov.
KÍ Klaksvík: Jonatan Johansson, Odmar Færø, Vegard Forren, Jóannes Danielsen, Børge
Petersen, Claes Kronberg (90+3' Latif Isaak Ahmed), Árni Frederiksberg (56' Mads
Mikkelsen), René Joensen (73' Patrick Da Silva), Luc Kassi (73' Sivert Gussiâs), Deni
Pavlovic (46' Hallur Hánsson), Jákup Andreasen. Coach: Magne Hoseth.
Goals: 8', 32' Árni Frederiksberg 0-1 (p), 0-2, 45+1' Luc Kassi 0-3.
Referee: David Smajc (SVN)   Attendance: 18,187.

19.07.23   Baki Olimpiya Stadionu, Baku: Qarabag FK – Lincoln Red Imps 4-0 (2-0)
Qarabag FK: Sahrudin Mahammadaliyev, Marko Vesovic (71' Toral Bayramov), Badavi
Hüseynov, Bahlul Mustafazade, Yassine Benzia (63' Hamidou Keyta), Marko Jankovic (82'
Richard Almeyda), Abdellah Zoubir (71' Adama Diakhaby), Elvin Cafarquliyev, Leandro
Andrade, Júlio Romão, Redon Xhixha (72' Nariman Axundzade). Coach: Qurban Qurbanov.
Lincoln Red Imps: Dayle Coleing, Nano, Ibrahim Ayew, Bernando Lopes, Jack Sergeant (77'
Samson Bolaji Ajayi), Ethan Britto, Mandi (83' Kyle Clinton), Liam Walker (54' Juampe),
Mustapha Yahaya (77' Djumaney Burnet), Lee Casciaro (54' Juanfri), Kike Gómez.
Coach: Javi Muñoz.
Goals: 7' Abdellah Zoubir 1-0, 45+1' Bahlul Mustafazade 2-0, 49' Redon Xhixha 3-0,
62' Marko Jankovic 4-0.
Referee: Eldorjan Hamiti (ALB)   Attendance: 19,453.

19.07.23   Boris Paichadze Dinamo Arena, Tbilisi: Dinamo Tbilisi – FK Astana 1-2 (1-0)
Dynamo Tbilisi: Giorgi Loria, Gagi Margvelashvili (57' Giorgi Maisuradze), Jemal Tabidze,
Nikoloz Mali (57' Saba Khvadagiani), Aleksandre Kalandadze, Anzor Mekvabishvili, Imran
Oulad Omar, Davit Skhirtladze (77' Zoran Marusic), Giorgi Kharaishvili (73' Giorgi
Moistsrapishvili), Barnes Osei (57' Gabriel Sigua), Ousmane Camara.
Coach: Giorgi Chiabrishvili.
FK Astana: Josip Condric, Zarko Tomasevic, Abzal Beysebekov (65' Stjepan Loncar), Yan
Vorogovskiy (86' Elkhan Astanov), Aleksa Amanovic, Aleksandr Marochkin, Marin Tomasov,
Fabien Ourega (76' Timur Dosmagambetov), Dusan Jovanvic (46' Kamo Hovhannisyan),
Maks Ebong, Dembo Darboe (86' Abat Aymbetov). Coach: Grigoriy Babayan.
Goals: 22' Ousmane Camara 1-0, 50' Abzal Beysebekov 1-1, 51' Dembo Darboe 1-2.
Referee: Stuart Attwell (ENG)   Attendance: 10,736.

138

19.07.23 Huvepharma Arena, Razgrad: PFC Ludogorets Razgrad – KF Ballkani 4-0 (2-0)
PFC Ludogorets Razgrad: Sergio Padt, Igor Plastun, Marcel Heister, Aslak Witry, Franco Russo, Claude Gonçalves, Jakub Piotrowski (83' Ivan Yordanov), Dominik Yankov (70' Pedro Naressi), Kiril Despodov (76' Olivier Verdon), Bernard Tekpetey (70' Caio Vidal), Matías Tissera (76' Spas Delev). Coach: Ivaylo Petev.
KF Ballkani: Enea Koliçi, Lorenc Trashi, Bajram Jashanica, Armend Thaqi (56' Almir Kryeziu), Lumbardh Dellova, Edvin Kuc (75' Albin Berisha), Meriton Korenica, Qendrim Zyba (75' Arbër Potoku), Lindon Emërllahu, Nazmi Gripshi (75' Bleart Tolaj), Albion Rrahmani (89' Yoan Marc-Olivier). Coach: Ilir Daja.
Goals: 4', 45+1' Bernard Tekpetey 1-0, 2-0, 49' Matías Tissera 3-0, 78' Caio Vidal 4-0.
Referee: Luca Pairetto (ITA)   Attendance: 5,353.

19.07.23   Stade de Luxembourg, Luxembourg:
             Swift Hesperange – Slovan Bratislava 0-2 (0-0)
Swift Hesperange: Geordan Dupire, Jerry Prempeh (66' Bryan Nouvier), Cédric Sacras (65' Blankson Anoff), Négo Ekofo, Simão Martins, Dominik Stolz (80' Dylan Cardoso), Clément Couturier (80' Lado Akhalaia), Aldin Skenderovic, Charles Morren, Dejvid Sinani (87' Gustavo), Paul Ayongo. Coach: Carlos Fangueiro.
Slovan Bratislava: Milan Borjan, Guram Kashia, Kevin Wimmer, Kenan Bajric, Lucas Lovat, Jaba Kankava, Vladimír Weiss (82' Jaromír Zmrhal), Tigran Barseghyan (82' Malik Abubakari), Kyriakos Savvidis (90+5' Nino Marcelli), Marko Tolic (73' Filip Lichý), Aleksandar Cavric (82' Zuberu Sharani). Coach: Vladimír Weiss.
Goals: 55', 62' Vladimír Weiss 0-1 (p), 0-2 (p).
Referee: Abdulkadir Bitigen (TUR)   Attendance: 3,054.

Dominik Stolz missed a penalty kick (10').

Swift Hesperange played their home match at the Stade de Luxembourg in Luxembourg, instead of their regular stadium, Stade Alphonse Theis, in Hesperange, which did not meet UEFA requirements.

19.07.23   Solitude, Belfast: Larne FC – HJK Helsinki 2-2 (0-1,2-1) (AET)
Larne FC: Rohan Ferguson, Cian Bolger (34' Craig Farquhar), Shaun Want, Aaron Donnelly, Michael Glynn (76' Isaac Westendorf), Tomas Cosgrove, Leroy Millar, Shea Gordon (98' Thomas Maguire), Dylan Sloan (76' Joe Thomson), Andy Ryan (89' Paul O'Neill), Lee Bonis. Coach: Tiernan Lynch.
HJK Helsinki: Dejan Iliev (46' Jesse Öst), Jukka Raitala, Joona Toivio, Pyry Soiri (119' Kevin Kouassivi-Benissan), Miro Tenho, Tuomas Ollila, Lucas Lingman, Georgios Kanellopoulos (90' Liam Möller), Anthony Olusanya (56' Atomu Tanaka), Bojan Radulovic, Topi Keskinen (71' Roope Riski). Coach: Toni Korkeakunnas.
Goals: 26' Tuomas Ollila 0-1, 65' Lee Bonis 1-1 (p), 87' Joe Thomson 2-1,
96' Shaun Want 2-2 (og).
Referee: Aristotelis Diamantopoulos (GRE)   Attendance: 1,993.

HJK Helsinki won after extra time.

Larne FC played their home match at the Solitude in Belfast, instead of their regular stadium, the Inver Park, in Larne, which did not meet UEFA requirements.

SECOND QUALIFYING ROUND

(Champions Path)

25.07.23 Vilniaus LFF stadionas, Vilnius: FK Zalgiris – Galatasaray 2-2 (0-0)
FK Zalgiris: Edvinas Gertmonas, Stipe Vucur, Mario Pavelic, Joël Bopesu, Nassim Hnid, Adama Fofana (60' Yukiyoshi Karashima), Nicolás Gorobsov, Yuriy Kendysh, Oliver Buff (80' Donatas Kazlauskas), Paulius Golubickas (60' Ovidijus Verbickas), Mathias Oyewusi (64' Liviu Antal). Coach: Vladimir Cheburin.
Galatasaray: Fernando Muslera, Abdülkerim Bardakçi, Angeliño (84' Léo Dubois), Victor Nelsson, Sacha Boey, Sérgio Oliveira, Nicolò Zaniolo (73' Halil Dervisoglu), Berkan Kutlu (62' Fredrik Midtsjø), Yunus Akgün (73' Olimpiu Morutan), Kerem Aktürkoglu, Baris Yilmaz (61' Dries Mertens). Coach: Okan Buruk.
Goals: 47' Mathias Oyewusi 1-0, 75' Abdülkerim Bardakçi 1-1, 78' Halil Dervisoglu 1-2, 90+1' Donatas Kazlauskas 2-2.
Referee: Luís Godinho (POR) Attendance: 4,864.
Sent off: 90+2' Donatas Kazlauskas.

25.07.23 Bolt Arena, Helsinki: HJK Helsinki – Molde FK 1-0 (1-0)
HJK Helsinki: Jesse Öst, Jukka Raitala, Joona Toivio, Pyry Soiri, Miro Tenho, Kevin Kouassivi-Benissan, Atomu Tanaka (78' Aapo Halme), Lucas Lingman, Georgios Kanellopoulos (70' Përparim Hetemaj), Bojan Radulovic, Topi Keskinen (78' Anthony Olusanya). Coach: Toni Korkeakunnas.
Molde FK: Jacob Karlstrøm, Martin Linnes, Kristoffer Haugen, Martin Bjørnbak, Benjamin Hansen, Anders Hagelskjær, Kristian Eriksen (67' Markus Kaasa), Eric Bugale Kitolano (67' Magnus Eikrem), Ola Brynhildsen (67' Veton Berisha), Emil Breivik, Sivert Heggheim Mannsverk. Coach: Erling Moe.
Goal: 25' Topi Keskinen 1-0.
Referee: Sven Jablonski (GER) Attendance: 8,154.

25.07.23 Stadion Maksimir, Zagreb: Dinamo Zagreb – FK Astana 4-0 (3-0)
Dinamo Zagreb: Dominik Livakovic, Stefan Ristovski, Sadegh Moharrami, Josip Sutalo, Josip Misic, Luka Ivanusec (90+5' Petar Sucic), Marko Bulat (71' Bogdan Mykhaylychenko), Robert Ljubicic, Martin Baturina (81' Antonio Marin), Bruno Petkovic (80' Mahir Emreli), Dario Spikic (71' Luka Menalo). Coach: Igor Biscan.
FK Astana: Josip Condric, Zarko Tomasevic, Abzal Beysebekov (60' Dusan Jovanvic), Yan Vorogovskiy (83' Abat Aymbetov), Aleksa Amanovic, Aleksandr Marochkin, Marin Tomasov, Kamo Hovhannisyan, Fabien Ourega (68' Elkhan Astanov), Maks Ebong, Dembo Darboe (83' Timur Dosmagambetov). Coach: Grigoriy Babayan.
Goals: 35' Dario Spikic 1-0, 41', 43' 56' Luka Ivanusec 2-0, 3-0, 4-0.
Referee: Guillermo Cuadra Fernández (ESP) Attendance: 7,123.

25.07.23 Stadion Bijeli Brijeg, Mostar: Zrinjski Mostar – Slovan Bratislava 0-1 (0-0)
Zrinjski Mostar: Marko Maric, Mario Ticinovic (64' Ivan Jukic), Hrvoje Barisic, Josip
Corluka, Kerim Memija, Matej Senic (46' Slobodan Jakovljevic), Dario Canadjija, Mato Stanic
(64' Zvonimir Kozulj), Antonio Ivancic (64' Nemanja Bilbija), Mario Cuze (83' Matija
Malekinusic), Tomislav Kis. Coach: Krunoslav Rendulic.
Slovan Bratislava: Milan Borjan, Guram Kashia, Lukás Pauschek, Kenan Bajric, Lucas Lovat,
Jaba Kankava, Tigran Barseghyan (67' Filip Lichý), Kyriakos Savvidis, Marko Tolic (67'
Malik Abubakari, Aleksandar Cavric (77' Jaromír Zmrhal), Zuberu Sharani (83' Kevin
Wimmer). Coach: Vladimir Weiss.
Goal: 53' Zuberu Sharani 0-1.
Referee: Bram Van Driessche (BEL)   Attendance: 4,900.

25.07.23 Kópavogsvöllur, Kópavogur: Breidablik – FC København 0-2 (0-2)
Breidablik: Anton Ari Einarsson, Damir Muminovic, Höskuldur Gunnlaugsson, Viktor Örn
Margeirsson, Andri Yeoman (80' Davíd Ingvarsson), Oliver Sigurjónsson (83' Anton
Lúdvíksson), Gísli Eyjólfsson, Alexander Sigurdarson (74' Ágúst Hlynsson), Viktor Einarsson,
Jason Dadi Svanthórsson, Kristinn Steindórsson (80' Klæmint Olsen).
Coach: Óskar Hrafn Thorvaldsson.
FC København: Kamil Grabara, Denis Vavro, Kevin Diks, Valdemar Lund Jensen, Elias Jelert,
Rasmus Falk, Lukas Lerager, Diogo Gonçalves (71' Orri Óskarsson), Roony Bardghji (58'
Ísak Bergmann Jóhannesson), William Clem, Jordan Larsson (72' Elias Achouri).
Coach: Jacob Neestrup.
Goals: 1' Jordan Larsson 0-1, 32' Rasmus Falk 0-2.
Referee: Gergö Bogár (HUN)   Attendance: 1,485.

26.07.23 Bolshaya Sportivnaya Arena, Tiraspol:
          FC Sheriff Tiraspol – Maccabi Haifa 1-0 (1-0)
FC Sheriff Tiraspol: Maksim Koval, Cristian Tovar, Armel Zohouri, Munashe Garananga,
Kostas Apostolakis, Amine Talal (90+2' Cedric Ngah), João Paulo, Jerome Ngom Mbekeli
(69' Vinícius Paiva), Moussa Kyabou, Peter Ademo, Luvannor (90+2' David Ankeye).
Coach: Roberto Bordin.
Maccabi Haifa: Itamar Nizan, Daniel Sundgren, Shon Goldberg, Pierre Cornud (81' Ilay
Hajaj), Abdoulaye Seck, Tjaronn Chery (81' Dean David), Dia Sabi'A (62' Lior Refaelov), Ali
Muhammad, Dolev Haziza (88' Maor Kandil), Goni Naor (46' Mahmoud Jaber), Frantzdy
Pierrot. Coach: Messay Dego.
Goal: 28' Amine Talal 1-0.
Referee: Sebastian Gishamer (AUT)   Attendance: 7,933.

26.07.23 Alphamega Stadium, Limassol: Aris Limassol – BATE Borisov 6-2 (3-0)
Aris Limassol: Vaná, Steeve Yago, Caju, Franz Brorsson, Alex Moucketou-Moussounda,
Veljko Nikolic (46' Július Szöke), Leo Bengtsson (46' Mariusz Stepinski), Karol Struski,
Shavy Warren Babicka (80' Jaden Montnor), Mihlali Mayambela (87' Mamadou Sané),
Yannick Gomis (80' Matija Spoljaric). Coach: Aleksey Shpilevski.
BATE Borisov: Andrey Kudravets, Ruslan Khadarkevich (70' Aleksandr Martynov), Vladislav
Malkevich (62' Denis Laptev), Danila Nechaev, Sherif Jimoh, Sidi Bane (85' Sergey Volkov),
Valeriy Gromyko, Denis Grechikho (85' Sead Islamovic), Artem Kontsevoy, Valeriy
Bocherov, Dmitri Antilevski (71' Dmitri Podstrelov). Coach: Kirill Alshevskiy.
Goals: 17' Yannick Gomis 1-0 (p), 32' Leo Bengtsson 2-0, 39' Sidi Bane 3-0 (og),
48' Artem Kontsevoy 3-1, 60' Yannick Gomis 4-1, 65' Ruslan Khadarkevich 4-2,
83' Jaden Montnor 5-2, 90+1' Mariusz Stepinski 6-2 (p).
Referee: Yigal Frid (ISR)   Attendance: 3,338.

26.07.23   Miejski Stadion Pilkarski "Raków", Czestochowa:
Raków Czestochowa – Qarabag FK   3-2 (0-0)
Raków Czestochowa: Vladan Kovacevic, Zoran Arsenic, Stratos Svarnas, Bogdan Racovitan, Marcin Cebula (65' John Yeboah), Jean Carlos (84' Deian Sorescu), Vladyslav Kochergin (81' Sonny Kittel), Fran Tudor, Giannis Papanikolaou, Ben Lederman (66' Gustav Berggren), Lukasz Zwolinski (65' Fabian Piasecki). Coach: Dawid Szwarga.
Qarabag FK: Sahrudin Mahammadaliyev, Bahlul Mustafazade, Kevin Medina, Yassine Benzia (70' Hamidou Keyta), Marko Jankovic (70' Patrick Andrade), Abdellah Zoubir, Toral Bayramov, Elvin Cafarquliyev (71' Maksim Medvedev), Leandro Andrade (83' Richard Almeyda), Júlio Romão, Redon Xhixha (83' Nariman Axundzade). Coach: Qurban Qurbanov.
Goals: 55' Elvin Cafarquliyev 1-0 (og), 71' Fabian Piasecki 2-0, 73', 75' Redon Xhixha 2-1, 2-2, 90+1' Sonny Kittel 3-2.
Referee: Lukas Fähndrich (SUI)   Attendance: 5,451.

26.07.23   Huvepharma Arena, Razgrad:
PFC Ludogorets Razgrad – Olimpija Ljubljana 1-1 (1-1)
PFC Ludogorets Razgrad: Sergio Padt, Igor Plastun, Marcel Heister, Aslak Witry, Franco Russo, Claude Gonçalves, Jakub Piotrowski (54' Pedro Naressi), Dominik Yankov (73' Spas Delev), Kiril Despodov (73' Rick), Kwadwo Duah (7' Matías Tissera), Bernard Tekpetey (54' Caio Vidal). Coach: Ivaylo Petev.
Olimpija Ljubljana: Matevz Vidovsek, David Sualehe, Jorge Silva, Ivan Posavec (76' Raul Florucz), Ahmet Muhamedbegovic, Timi Elsnik, Agustin Doffo, Svit Seslar (86' Nemanja Motika), Marcel Ratnik, Mustafa Nukic (66' Pedro Lucas), Rui Pedro (76' Nemanja Gavric). Coach: João Henriques.
Goals: 14' Timi Elsnik 0-1, 44' Dominik Yankov 1-1.
Referee: Rohit Saggi (NOR)   Attendance: 5,532.

26.07.23   Vid Djúpumýrar, Klaksvík: KÍ Klaksvík – BK Häcken 0-0
KÍ Klaksvík: Jonatan Johansson, Odmar Færø, Vegard Forren, Jóannes Danielsen, Børge Petersen, Claes Kronberg (81' Patrick Da Silva), Hallur Hánsson (68' Deni Pavlovic), Árni Frederiksberg, René Joensen, Luc Kassi (81' Sivert Gussiås), Jákup Andreasen.
Coach: Magne Hoseth.
BK Häcken: Peter Abrahamsson, Even Hovland, Simon Sandberg, Valgeir Lunddal Fridriksson, Kristoffer Lund, Tobias Sana (46' Momodou Sonko), Mikkel Rygaard, Samuel Gustafson, Pontus Dahbo, Ibrahim Sadiq, Filip Trpcevski (75' Amor Layouni).
Coach: Per-Mathias Høgmo.
Referee: Michal Ocenás (SVK)   Attendance: 1,224.

01.08.23   Stadion Stozice, Ljubljana:
Olimpija Ljubljana – PFC Ludogorets Razgrad 2-1 (1-1)
Olimpija Ljubljana: Matevz Vidovsek, David Sualehe, Jorge Silva, Ivan Posavec (81' Nemanja Motika), Ahmet Muhamedbegovic, Timi Elsnik, Agustin Doffo, Svit Seslar (90+5' Nemanja Gavric), Marcel Ratnik, Mustafa Nukic (60' Pedro Lucas), Rui Pedro (90+5' Aljaz Krefl). Coach: João Henriques.
PFC Ludogorets Razgrad: Sergio Padt, Marcel Heister, Son, Olivier Verdon, Franco Russo, Claude Gonçalves (69' Caio Vidal), Pedro Naressi (83' Ivan Yordanov), Dominik Yankov (83' Aslak Witry), Kiril Despodov, Bernard Tekpetey (55' Jakub Piotrowski), Matías Tissera (55' Spas Delev). Coach: Ivaylo Petev.
Goals: 15' Kiril Despodov 0-1, 18', 90+2' Timi Elsnik 1-1, 2-1.
Referee: Christian Dingert (GER)   Attendance: 9,265.
Sent off: 82' Son.

Kiril Despodov missed a penalty kick (90+12')

01.08.23   Mezőkövesdi Városi Stadion, Mezőkövesd (HUN):
BATE Borisov – Aris Limassol 3-5 (1-3)
BATE Borisov: Andrey Kudravets, Ruslan Khadarkevich, Danila Nechaev, Sherif Jimoh (69' Vladislav Malkevich), Sidi Bane (42' Aleksandr Martynov), Valeriy Gromyko (84' Sergey Volkov), Dmitri Podstrelov (69' Dmitri Antilevski), Denis Grechikho (68' Sead Islamovic), Artem Kontsevoy, Valeriy Bocherov, Denis Laptev. Coach: Kirill Alshevskiy.
Aris Limassol: Vaná, Steeve Yago, Caju (57' Slobodan Urosevic), Franz Brorsson (46' Mamadou Sané), Alex Moucketou-Moussounda, Július Szöke, Leo Bengtsson, Karol Struski (57' Veljko Nikolic), Shavy Warren Babicka (46' Mariusz Stepinski), Mihlali Mayambela, Yannick Gomis (74' Jaden Montnor). Coach: Aleksey Shpilevski.
Goals: 8' Shavy Warren Babicka 0-1, 25' Valeriy Gromyko 1-1 (p),
26' Yannick Gomis 1-2, 35' Caju 1-3, 48' Aleksandr Martynov 2-3, 56' Leo Bengtsson 2-4,
74' Mariusz Stepinski 2-5, 90+3' Denis Laptev 3-5 (p).
Referee: Morten Krogh (DEN)   Attendance: behind closed doors.

Due to the involvement of Belarus in the Russian invasion of Ukraine, Belarusian teams were required to play their home matches at neutral venues and behind closed doors until further notice.

01.08.23   Stadión Tehelné pole, Bratislava: Slovan Bratislava – Zrinjski Mostar 2-2 (1-0)
Slovan Bratislava: Milan Borjan, Guram Kashia, Lukás Pauschek, Kenan Bajric, Lucas Lovat, Juraj Kucka, Jaba Kankava, Vladimír Weiss (78' Tigran Barseghyan), Kyriakos Savvidis, Aleksandar Cavric (88' Malik Abubakari), Zuberu Sharani (77' Nino Marcelli). Coach: Vladimir Weiss.
Zrinjski Mostar: Marko Maric, Mario Ticinovic (65' Ivan Jukic), Slobodan Jakovljevic, Hrvoje Barisic, Josip Corluka, Kerim Memija, Dario Canadjija, Zvonimir Kozulj (46' Tomislav Kis), Mato Stanic (46' Antonio Ivancic), Mario Cuze (65' Matija Malekinusic), Nemanja Bilbija (73' Damir Zlomislic). Coach: Krunoslav Rendulic.
Goals: 5' Aleksandar Cavric 1-0, 66' Zuberu Sharani 2-0, 75' Hrvoje Barisic 2-1,
90+3' Antonio Ivancic 2-2.
Referee: Jérémie Pignard (FRA)   Attendance: 20,498.

02.08.23   Astana Arena, Astana: FK Astana – Dinamo Zagreb 0-2 (0-1)
FK Astana: Josip Condric, Zarko Tomasevic, Yan Vorogovskiy, Aleksa Amanovic (41' Timur Dosmagambetov), Aleksandr Marochkin, Marin Tomasov (46' Dusan Jovanvic), Kamo Hovhannisyan, Stjepan Loncar, Maks Ebong, Abat Aymbetov (69' Elkhan Astanov), Vladislav Prokopenko (46' Dembo Darboe). Coach: Grigoriy Babayan.
Dinamo Zagreb: Dominik Livakovic, Stefan Ristovski, Sadegh Moharrami, Bogdan Mykhaylychenko, Josip Sutalo (67' Maxime Bernauer), Josip Misic (79' Luka Lukanic), Robert Ljubicic (78' Martin Baturina), Mahir Emreli (79' Josip Drmic), Bruno Petkovic (68' Antonio Marin), Dario Spikic, Petar Sucic. Coach: Igor Biscan.
Goals: 24' Aleksandr Marochkin 0-1 (og), 89' Antonio Marin 0-2.
Referee: Dennis Higler (HOL)   Attendance: 26,978.

02.08.23   Baku Olimpiya Stadionu, Baku: Qarabag FK – Raków Czestochowa 1-1 (0-0)
Qarabag FK: Sahrudin Mahammadaliyev, Bahlul Mustafazade, Kevin Medina, Yassine Benzia (70' Juninho), Marko Jankovic, Abdellah Zoubir, Toral Bayramov, Elvin Cafarquliyev (79' Adama Diakhaby), Leandro Andrade (86' Nariman Axundzade), Júlio Romão, Redon Xhixha (70' Hamidou Keyta). Coach: Qurban Qurbanov.
Raków Czestochowa: Vladan Kovacevic, Zoran Arsenic, Stratos Svarnas, Bogdan Racovitan, Marcin Cebula (61' Sonny Kittel), Gustav Berggren, Jean Carlos, Fran Tudor (82' Deian Sorescu), Giannis Papanikolaou, Lukasz Zwolinski (46' Fabian Piasecki), John Yeboah (31' Bartosz Nowak, 61' Vladyslav Kochergin). Coach: Dawid Szwarga.
Goals: 51' Fran Tudor 0-1, 60' Redon Xhixha 1-1.
Referee: Sven Jablonski (GER)   Attendance: 31,257.

02.08.23   Bravida Arena, Göteborg: BK Häcken – KÍ Klaksvík 3-3 (1-1,2-2) (AET)
BK Häcken: Peter Abrahamsson, Even Hovland, Johan Hammar (96' Franklin Tebo Uchenna), Valgeir Lunddal Fridriksson (70' Simon Sandberg), Kristoffer Lund, Tobias Sana (79' Romeo Amané), Mikkel Rygaard, Samuel Gustafson, Amor Layouni, Ibrahim Sadiq (110' Ali Youssef), Filip Trpcevski (70' Momodou Sonko). Coach: Per-Mathias Høgmo.
KÍ Klaksvík: Jonatan Johansson, Odmar Færø (106' Jonn Johannessen), Vegard Forren, Jóannes Danielsen, Børge Petersen (64' Heini Vatnsdal), Claes Kronberg (73' Patrick Da Silva), Árni Frederiksberg, René Joensen (91' Sivert Gussiås), Luc Kassi (119' Latif Isaak Ahmed), Deni Pavlovic (73' Hallur Hánsson), Jákup Andreasen. Coach: Magne Hoseth.
Goals: 17' Árni Frederiksberg 0-1, 24' Tobias Sana 1-1, 48' Amor Layouni 2-1,
52' Árni Frederiksberg 2-2, 105+1' Ibrahim Sadiq 3-2, 109' Peter Abrahamsson 3-3 (og).
Referee: Andrew Madley (ENG)   Attendance: 4,396.

KÍ Klaksvïk won after extra time on penalties (4:3).

Penalties: Hovland 1-0, Frederiksberg 1-1, Layouni 2-1, J.Andreasen 2-2,
*   Samuel Gustafson 3-2, Da Silva 3-3, Rygaard missed, Gussiås missed,*
*   Sandberg missed, Forren 3-4.*

144

02.08.23   Aker Stadion, Molde: Molde FK – HJK Helsinki 2-0 (0-0)
Molde FK: Jacob Karlstrøm, Martin Linnes, Kristoffer Haugen, Martin Bjørnbak, Eirik
Haugan, Anders Hagelskjær (71' Veton Berisha), Magnus Eikrem (59' Eric Bugale Kitolano),
Markus Kaasa (59' Kristian Eriksen), Ola Brynhildsen (90+4' Benjamin Hansen), Emil Breivik
(90+4' Martin Ellingsen), Sivert Heggheim Mannsverk. Coach: Erling Moe.
HJK Helsinki: Jesse Öst, Jukka Raitala (90+1' Roope Riski), Joona Toivio, Pyry Soiri, Miro
Tenho, Kevin Kouassivi-Benissan (82' Tuomas Ollila), Atomu Tanaka (63' Filip Rogic),
Lucas Lingman, Georgios Kanellopoulos (82' Përparim Hetemaj), Bojan Radulovic, Topi
Keskinen (63' Anthony Olusanya). Coach: Toni Korkeakunnas.
Goals: 74' Kristian Eriksen 1-0, 89' Ola Brynhildsen 2-0.
Referee: Igor Pajac (CRO)   Attendance: 5,205.

02.08.23   Sammy Ofer Stadium, Haifa:
           Maccabi Haifa – FC Sheriff Tiraspol 4-1 (1-1,2-1) (AET)
Maccabi Haifa: Itamar Nizan, Daniel Sundgren (82' Erik Shuranov), Shon Goldberg,
Abdoulaye Seck, Tjaronn Chery, Lior Refaelov (74' Mahmoud Jaber), Dia Sabi'A (60' Dean
David), Ali Muhammad (106' Maor Kandil), Dolev Haziza (74' Suf Podgoreanu), Frantzdy
Pierrot, Anan Khalaili (60' Hamza Shibli). Coach: Messay Dego.
FC Sheriff Tiraspol: Maksim Koval, Cristian Tovar, Armel Zohouri, Munashe Garananga,
Kostas Apostolakis (107' Ricardinho), Amine Talal (84 Cedric Ngah), João Paulo, Jerome
Ngom Mbekeli (56' Vinícius Paiva), Moussa Kyabou (45+14' Cédric Badolo), Peter Ademo,
Luvannor (57' David Ankeye). Coach: Roberto Bordin.
Goals: 20' Amine Talal 0-1 (p), 33' Tjaronn Chery 1-1, 85' Mahmoud Jaber 2-1,
105+2' Dean David 3-1, 107' Erik Shuranov 4-1.
Referee: Damian Sylwestrzak (POL)   Attendance: 29,000.
Sent off: 86' Luvannor, 90+4' Amine Talal.

Maccabi Haifa won after extra time.

02.08.23   Stadion Parken, København: FC København – Breidablik 6-3 (4-1)
FC København: Kamil Grabara, Denis Vavro, Kevin Diks (46' Christian Sørensen), Valdemar
Lund Jensen, Elias Jelert (46' Peter Ankersen), Rasmus Falk, Lukas Lerager, Diogo Gonçalves
(57' Roony Bardghji), William Clem (29' Elias Achouri, 46' Oscar Højlund), Jordan Larsson,
Orri Óskarsson. Coach: Jacob Neestrup.
Breidablik: Anton Ari Einarsson, Damir Muminovic, Höskuldur Gunnlaugsson, Viktor Örn
Margeirsson, Andri Yeoman (65' Davíd Ingvarsson), Oliver Sigurjónsson (65' Alexander
Sigurdarson), Gísli Eyjólfsson, Viktor Einarsson, Jason Dadi Svanthórsson (80' Ágúst
Thorsteinsson), Anton Lúdvíksson (65' Ágúst Hlynsson), Kristinn Steindórsson (65' Klæmint
Olsen). Coach: Óskar Hrafn Thorvaldsson.
Goals: 9' Jason Dadi Svanthórsson 0-1, 33' Diogo Gonçalves 1-1, 35' Elias Achouri 2-1,
37' Jordan Larsson 3-1, 45+1', 47' Orri Óskarsson 4-1, 5-1, 51' Kristinn Steindórsson 5-2,
56' Orri Óskarsson 6-2, 74' Höskuldur Gunnlaugsson 6-3.
Referee: Fabio Maresca (ITA)   Attendance: 20,886.

02.08.23 Rams Global Stadium, Istanbul: Galatasaray – FK Zalgiris 1-0 (1-0)
Galatasaray: Fernando Muslera, Abdülkerim Bardakçi, Angeliño, Victor Nelsson, Sacha Boey,
Sérgio Oliveira (69' Fredrik Midtsjø), Berkan Kutlu, Dries Mertens (78' Olimpiu Morutan),
Kerem Aktürkoglu (89' Kaan Ayhan), Halil Dervisoglu (46' Yunus Akgün), Baris Yilmaz (79'
Cédric Bakambu). Coach: Okan Buruk.
FK Zalgiris: Edvinas Gertmonas, Stipe Vucur, Mario Pavelic, Petar Mamic (59' Árni
Vilhjálmsson), Joël Bopesu, Nassim Hnid, Nicolás Gorobsov, Yuriy Kendysh (89' Ovidijus
Verbickas), Oliver Buff (74' Yukiyoshi Karashima), Paulius Golubickas, Mathias Oyewusi.
Coach: Vladimir Cheburin.
Goal: 31' Dries Mertens 1-0.
Referee: Willy Delajod (FRA)   Attendance: 41,505.

(League Path)

25.07.23 Kosická futbalová aréna, Kosice (SVK): SK Dnipro-1 – Panathinaikos 1-3 (0-1)
SK Dnipro-1: Yakiv Kinareykin, Denys Miroshnichenko, Oleksandr Svatok (61' Igor Kogut),
Vasyl Kravets (73' Oleksandr Kaplienko), Ruslan Babenko (83' Volodymyr Tanchyk),
Maksym Tretyakov (61' Volodymyr Adamyuk), Domingo Blanco (83' Oleg Gorin), Oleksiy
Gutsulyak, Valentyn Rubchynskyi, Eduard Sarapii, Artem Dovbyk. Coach: Oleksandr Kucher.
Panathinaikos: Alberto Brignoli, Hördur Magnússon, Bart Schenkeveld (23' Tin Jedvaj),
Juankar, Giannis Kotsiras, Rubén Pérez, Filip Djuricic (78' Daniel Mancini), Tonny Vilhena
(70' Enis Çokaj), Bernard (70' Benjamin Verbic), Andraz Sporar (78' Fotis Ioannidis),
Sebastián Palacios. Coach: Ivan Jovanovic.
Goals: 10' Andraz Sporar 0-1, 73' Filip Djuricic 0-2, 84' Fotis Ioannidis 0-3 (p),
90' Volodymyr Tanchyk 1-3.
Referee: Daniele Chiffi (ITA)   Attendance: 5,248.

Due to the Russian invasion of Ukraine, Ukrainian teams were required to play their home
matches at neutral venues until further notice.

25.07.23 Stade de Genève, Lancy: Servette FC – KRC Genk 1-1 (0-1)
Servette FC: Jérémy Frick, Steve Rouiller, Yoan Severin, Bradley Mazikou, Keigo Tsunemoto,
David Douline (80' Gaël Ondoua), Dereck Kutesa (72' Boubacar Fofana), Timothé Cognat,
Alexis Antunes (72' Jérémy Guillemenot), Enzo Crivelli, Chris Bedia (80' Ronny Rodelin).
Coach: René Weiler.
KRC Genk: Maarten Vandevoordt, Joris Kayembe, Carlos Cuesta, Mark McKenzie, Daniel
Muñoz, Patrik Hrosovský (86' Matías Galarza), Bryan Heynen (68' Aziz Ouattara), Bilal El
Khannouss (60' Anouar Ait El Hadj), Joseph Paintsil, Toluwalase Arokodare (86' Yira Sor),
Alieu Fadera (46' Mike Trésor). Coach: Wouter Vrancken.
Goals: 21' Toluwalase Arokodare 0-1, 77' Steve Rouiller 1-1.
Referee: István Vad (II) (HUN)   Attendance: 18,026.

01.08.23   Stadio Apostolos Nikolaidis, Athens: Panathinaikos – SK Dnipro-1 2-2 (1-1)
Panathinaikos: Alberto Brignoli, Hördur Magnússon, Juankar, Tin Jedvaj, Giannis Kotsiras, Rubén Pérez, Filip Djuricic (79' László Kleinheisler), Tonny Vilhena (66' Enis Çokaj), Bernard (90+1' Benjamin Verbic), Andraz Sporar (79' Fotis Ioannidis), Sebastián Palacios (46' Daniel Mancini). Coach: Ivan Jovanovic.
SK Dnipro-1: Yevgen Volynets (36' Yakiv Kinareykin), Oleksandr Kaplienko (69' Igor Kogut), Denys Miroshnichenko, Volodymyr Adamyuk, Ruslan Babenko, Domingo Blanco, Oleksandr Pikhalyonok (69' Oleksiy Gutsulyak), Yevgeniy Pasich, Valentyn Rubchynskyi (69' Volodymyr Tanchyk), Eduard Sarapii (57' Oleksandr Svatok), Artem Dovbyk.
Coach: Oleksandr Kucher.
Goals: 15' Andraz Sporar 1-0, 23' Artem Dovbyk 1-1, 54' Eduard Sarapii 1-2, 69' Andraz Sporar 2-2.
Referee: Bastian Dankert (GER)   Attendance: 14,098.
Sent off: 75' Volodymyr Tanchyk.

02.08.23   Cegeka Arena, Genk: KRC Genk – Servette FC 2-2 (1-1,2-2) (AET)
KRC Genk: Maarten Vandevoordt, Joris Kayembe (46' Gerardo Arteaga), Carlos Cuesta, Mark McKenzie, Daniel Muñoz, Patrik Hrosovský, Bryan Heynen (8' Matías Galarza, 106' Aziz Ouattara), Mike Trésor (69' Alieu Fadera), Bilal El Khannouss (69' Anouar Ait El Hadj), Joseph Paintsil (106' Christopher Bonsu Baah), Toluwalase Arokodare.
Coach: Wouter Vrancken.
Servette FC: Jérémy Frick (59' Joël Mall), Steve Rouiller, Yoan Severin, Bradley Mazikou, Nicolas Vouilloz (119' Ronny Rodelin), David Douline, Dereck Kutesa (75' Boubacar Fofana), Timothé Cognat (106' Gaël Ondoua), Alexis Antunes (74' Jérémy Guillemenot), Enzo Crivelli, Chris Bedia (86' Hussayn Touati). Coach: René Weiler.
Goals: 28' Mike Trésor 1-0 (p), 36' Timothé Cognat 1-1, 51' Toluwalase Arokodare 2-1, 63' Chris Bedia 2-2.
Referee: Novak Simovic (SRB)   Attendance: 16,280
Sent off: 5' Enzo Crivelli.

Servette FC won after extra time on penalties (4:1).

Penalties: Touati 1-0, Hrosovský missed, Guillemenot 2-0, Cuesta 2-1, Severin 3-1,
       Arokodare missed, Rodelin 4-1.

THIRD QUALIFYING ROUND

(Champions Path)

08.08.23   Miejski Stadion Pilkarski "Raków", Czestochowa:
Raków Czestochowa – Aris Limassol 2-1 (1-0)
Raków Czestochowa: Vladan Kovacevic, Zoran Arsenic, Stratos Svarnas, Bogdan Racovitan, Marcin Cebula (86' Sonny Kittel), Gustav Berggren (86' Ben Lederman), Jean Carlos, Vladyslav Kochergin (73' Deian Sorescu), Fran Tudor, Giannis Papanikolaou, Fabian Piasecki (73' Lukasz Zwolinski). Coach: Dawid Szwarga.
Aris Limassol: Vaná, Steeve Yago, Caju, Franz Brorsson (71' Alex Moucketou-Moussounda), Eric Boakye, Július Szöke (46' Veljko Nikolic), Leo Bengtsson (76' Jaden Montnor), Karol Struski, Shavy Warren Babicka (64' Mariusz Stepinski), Mihlali Mayambela, Yannick Gomis. Coach: Aleksey Shpilevski.
Goals: 7' Vladyslav Kochergin 1-0, 63' Fabian Piasecki 2-0 (p), 88' Mihlali Mayambela 2-1.
Referee: Duje Strukan (CRO)   Attendance: 5,500.

08.08.23   Stadion Parken, København: FC København – AC Sparta Praha 0-0
FC København: Kamil Grabara, Christian Sørensen, Denis Vavro, Kevin Diks, Elias Jelert, Rasmus Falk, Mohamed Elyounoussi (72' Victor Claesson), Lukas Lerager, Diogo Gonçalves, Roony Bardghji (57' Elias Achouri), Jordan Larsson (72' Orri Óskarsson).
Coach: Jacob Neestrup.
AC Sparta Praha: Peter Vindahl Jensen, Jaroslav Zelený, Asger Sørensen (60' Martin Vitík), Filip Panák, Jan Mejdr, Lukás Sadílek (76' Qazim Laçi), Lukás Haraslín (76' Jakub Pesek), Kaan Kairinen, Veljko Birmancevic (60' Martin Minchev), Ladislav Krejcí (II), Jan Kuchta. Coach: Brian Priske.
Referee: Benoît Bastien (FRA)   Attendance: 27,170.

08.08.23   Tórsvøllur, Tórshavn: KÍ Klaksvík – Molde FK 2-1 (0-0)
KÍ Klaksvík: Jonatan Johansson, Odmar Færø, Vegard Forren, Heini Vatnsdal, Jóannes Danielsen (72' Patrick Da Silva), Claes Kronberg, Árni Frederiksberg, René Joensen, Luc Kassi (81' Sivert Gussiâs), Deni Pavlovic (71' Hallur Hánsson), Jákup Andreasen.
Coach: Magne Hoseth.
Molde FK: Jacob Karlstrøm, Martin Linnes, Kristoffer Haugen, Martin Bjørnbak, Eirik Haugan, Anders Hagelskjær, Magnus Eikrem (66' Veton Berisha), Kristian Eriksen, Ola Brynhildsen (66' Eric Bugale Kitolano), Emil Breivik (88' Markus Kaasa), Sivert Heggheim Mannsverk (72' Martin Ellingsen). Coach: Erling Moe.
Goals: 48' Magnus Eikrem 0-1, 64', 86' Árni Frederiksberg 1-1, 2-1.
Referee: Aliyar Aghayev (AZE)   Attendance: 4,584.

KÍ Klaksvík played their home match at Tórsvøllur in Tórshavn, instead of their regular stadium the Vid Djúpumýrar in Klaksvík, which did not meet UEFA requirements.

08.08.23   Stadion Stozice, Ljubljana: Olimpija Ljubljana – Galatasaray 0-3 (0-1)
Olimpija Ljubljana: Matevz Vidovsek, David Sualehe, Jorge Silva, Ivan Posavec (77' Nemanja Gavric), Ahmet Muhamedbegovic, Timi Elsnik, Saar Fadida (46' Nemanja Motika), Svit Seslar (86' Mustafa Nukic), Marcel Ratnik, Rui Pedro (86' Aldin Jakupovic), Admir Bristric (65' Pedro Lucas). Coach: João Henriques.
Galatasaray: Fernando Muslera, Abdülkerim Bardakçi, Victor Nelsson, Sacha Boey, Kazimcan Karatas (63' Léo Dubois), Sérgio Oliveira (87' Kaan Ayhan), Berkan Kutlu, Dries Mertens (75' Yunus Akgün), Cédric Bakambu (75' Mauro Icardi), Kerem Aktürkoglu, Baris Yilmaz (86' Halil Dervisoglu). Coach: Okan Buruk.
Goals: 9' Kerem Aktürkoglu 0-1, 48' Dries Mertens 0-2, 90+1' Halil Dervisoglu 0-3.
Referee: Andreas Ekberg (SWE)   Attendance: 13,712.

09.08.23   Stadión Tehelné pole, Bratislava: Slovan Bratislava – Maccabi Haifa 1-2 (1-2)
Slovan Bratislava: Milan Borjan, Guram Kashia, Lukás Pauschek (87' Jaromír Zmrhal), Kenan Bajric, Lucas Lovat, Juraj Kucka, Jaba Kankava, Kyriakos Savvidis (75' Marko Tolic), Aleksandar Cavric, Zuberu Sharani (63' Tigran Barseghyan), Malik Abubakari (74' Dávid Strelec). Coach: Vladimir Weiss.
Maccabi Haifa: Itamar Nizan, Daniel Sundgren, Shon Goldberg, Pierre Cornud, Abdoulaye Seck, Dia Sabi'A (79' Lior Refaelov), Ali Muhammad, Dolev Haziza (63' Dean David), Mahmoud Jaber, Frantzdy Pierrot, Anan Khalaili (63' Suf Podgoreanu). Coach: Messay Dego.
Goals: 5' Frantzdy Pierrot 0-1, 12' Abdoulaye Seck 1-1 (og), 15' Dia Sabi'A 1-2.
Referee: Andris Treimanis (LVA)   Attendance: 21,375.

15.08.23   Alphamega Stadium, Kolossi: Aris Limassol – Raków Czestochowa 0-1 (0-0)
Aris Limassol: Vaná, Steeve Yago, Caju, Eric Boakye (64' Matija Spoljaric), Alex Moucketou-Moussounda, Morgan Brown (46' Veljko Nikolic), Leo Bengtsson (76' Jaden Montnor), Karol Struski, Mariusz Stepinski (46' Shavy Warren Babicka), Mihlali Mayambela, Yannick Gomis (64' Slobodan Urosevic). Coach: Aleksey Shpilevski.
Raków Czestochowa: Vladan Kovacevic, Zoran Arsenic, Stratos Svarnas (53' Deian Sorescu), Bogdan Racovitan, Marcin Cebula (64' Bartosz Nowak), Gustav Berggren, Jean Carlos, Vladyslav Kochergin (86' Szymon Czyz), Fran Tudor, Giannis Papanikolaou, Fabian Piasecki (63' Lukasz Zwolinski). Coach: Dawid Szwarga.
Goal: 49' Fran Tudor 0-1.
Referee: Matej Jug (SVN)   Attendance: 3,959.

15.08.23   Sammy Ofer Stadium, Haifa: Maccabi Haifa – Slovan Bratislava 3-1 (2-0)
Maccabi Haifa: Itamar Nizan, Daniel Sundgren (77' Anan Khalaili), Shon Goldberg, Pierre Cornud, Abdoulaye Seck, Tjaronn Chery, Dia Sabi'A (71' Dean David), Ali Muhammad (77' Goni Naor), Dolev Haziza (64' Lior Refaelov), Mahmoud Jaber (65' Maor Kandil), Frantzdy Pierrot. Coach: Messay Dego.
Slovan Bratislava: Milan Borjan, Guram Kashia, Lukás Pauschek, Kenan Bajric, Lucas Lovat, Juraj Kucka (68' Nino Marcelli), Jaba Kankava, Tigran Barseghyan (46' Malik Abubakari), Aleksandar Cavric (46' Filip Lichý), Dávid Strelec (80' César Blackman), Zuberu Sharani (67' Marko Tolic). Coach: Vladimir Weiss.
Goals: 29' Frantzdy Pierrot 1-0, 45+2' Dia Sabi'A 2-0, 85' Marko Tolic 2-1,
90+3' Dean David 3-1.
Referee: Craig Pawson (ENG)   Attendance: 29,000.

149

15.08.23   epet ARENA, Praha: AC Sparta Praha – FC København 3-3 (0-1,1-1) (AET)
AC Sparta Praha: Peter Vindahl Jensen, Jaroslav Zelený, Asger Sørensen, Filip Panák (46'
Martin Vitík), Tomás Wiesner (77' Jan Mejdr), Lukás Sadílek (89' Qazim Laçi), Lukás
Haraslín (72' Victor Olatunji), Kaan Kairinen, Veljko Birmancevic (94' Jakub Pesek), Ladislav
Krejcí (II), Jan Kuchta (94' Martin Minchev). Coach: Brian Priske.
FC København: Kamil Grabara, Christian Sørensen, Denis Vavro (55' Nicolai Boilesen),
Kevin Diks, Elias Jelert, Rasmus Falk (108' Orri Óskarsson), Mohamed Elyounoussi (108'
Roony Bardghji), Lukas Lerager, Diogo Gonçalves (84' William Clem), Jordan Larsson (74'
Victor Claesson), Elias Achouri. Coach: Jacob Neestrup.
Goals: 1' Jordan Larsson 0-1, 80' Veljko Birmancevic 1-1, 105' Qazim Laçi 2-1,
105+3' Victor Claesson 2-2, 107' Victor Olatunji 3-2, 112' Victor Claesson 3-3.
Referee: Serdar Gözübüyük (HOL)   Attendance: 18,109.

FC København won after extra time on penalties (4:2).

Penalties: Krejci missed, Diks 0-1, Laçi 1-1, Claesson 1-2, Kairinen 2-2, Boilesen 2-3,
Sørensen missed, Bardghji 2-4.

15.08.23   Aker Stadion, Molde: Molde FK – KÍ Klaksvík 2-0 (1-0,1-0) (AET)
Molde FK: Jacob Karlstrøm, Martin Linnes, Kristoffer Haugen, Martin Bjørnbak (90' Anders
Hagelskjær), Eirik Haugan, Magnus Eikrem (69' Veton Berisha), Martin Ellingsen (90'
Magnus Grødem), Kristian Eriksen (120' Benjamin Hansen), Ola Brynhildsen (100' Erling
Knudtzon), Emil Breivik (81' Markus Kaasa), Sivert Heggheim Mannsverk.
Coach: Erling Moe.
KÍ Klaksvík: Jonatan Johansson, Odmar Færø (81' Børge Petersen), Vegard Forren, Heini
Vatnsdal (113' Jonn Johannessen), Jóannes Danielsen, Claes Kronberg (46' Patrick Da Silva),
Árni Frederiksberg, René Joensen, Luc Kassi (100' Sivert Gussiâs), Deni Pavlovic (79' Mads
Mikkelsen), Jákup Andreasen. Coach: Magne Hoseth.
Goals: 17' Kristian Eriksen 1-0, 112' Martin Linnes 2-0.
Referee: Nikola Dabanovic (MNE)   Attendance: 10,346.

Molde FK won after extra time.

15.08.23   Stadion Maksimir, Zagreb: Dinamo Zagreb – AEK Athens 1-2 (1-0)
Dinamo Zagreb: Dominik Livakovic, Stefan Ristovski, Sadegh Moharrami, Bogdan
Mykhaylychenko, Josip Sutalo, Josip Misic (84' Takuro Kaneko), Luka Ivanusec (72' Martin
Baturina), Marko Bulat (72' Petar Sucic), Robert Ljubicic, Bruno Petkovic, Dario Spikic (46'
Mahir Emreli). Coach: Igor Biscan.
AEK Athens: Cican Stankovic, Domagoj Vida, Djibril Sidibé, Harold Moukoudi, Ehsan
Hajisafi, Steven Zuber (84' Sergio Araújo), Jens Jønsson (67' Konstantinos Galanopoulos),
Niclas Eliasson (55' Nordin Amrabat), Orbelín Pineda (84' Rodolfo Pizarro), Damian
Szymanski (84' Petros Mantalos), Levi García. Coach: Matías Almeyda.
Goals: 39' Marko Bulat 1-0, 59' Steven Zuber 1-1, 90' Konstantinos Galanopoulos 1-2.
Referee: João Pedro Pinheiro (POR)   Attendance: 13,311.

150

15.08.23   Rams Global Stadium, Istanbul: Galatasaray – Olimpija Ljubljana 1-0 (1-0)
Galatasaray: Fernando Muslera, Kaan Ayhan, Angeliño, Sacha Boey, Emin Bayram (78'
Sérgio Oliveira), Lucas Torreira, Berkan Kutlu, Dries Mertens (46' Cédric Bakambu), Mauro
Icardi (71' Abdülkerim Bardakçi), Kerem Aktürkoglu (46' Wilfried Zaha), Baris Yilmaz (60'
Halil Dervisoglu). Coach: Okan Buruk.
Olimpija Ljubljana: Matevz Vidovsek, David Sualehe (70' Aljaz Krefl), Jorge Silva, Ivan
Posavec (78' Admir Bristric), Ahmet Muhamedbegovic, Mateo Karamatic, Agustin Doffo (78'
Saar Fadida), Svit Seslar, Marcel Ratnik, Mustafa Nukic (56' Pedro Lucas), Rui Pedro.
Coach: João Henriques.
Goal: 24' Mauro Icardi 1-0.
Referee: Marco Guida (ITA)   Attendance: 38,383.
Sent off: 64' Lucas Torreira.

19.08.23   OPAP Arena, Athens: AEK Athens – Dinamo Zagreb 2-2 (0-1)
AEK Athens: Cican Stankovic, Domagoj Vida, Harold Moukoudi, Lazaros Rota, Nordin
Amrabat (67' Niclas Eliasson), Ehsan Hajisafi, Steven Zuber (67' Sergio Araújo), Jens Jønsson
(76' Petros Mantalos), Orbelín Pineda (76' Konstantinos Galanopoulos), Damian Szymanski
(67' Mijat Gacinovic), Levi García. Coach: Matías Almeyda.
Dinamo Zagreb: Dominik Livakovic, Stefan Ristovski, Sadegh Moharrami, Bogdan
Mykhaylychenko, Josip Sutalo, Josip Misic, Luka Ivanusec, Marko Bulat, Robert Ljubicic,
Bruno Petkovic, Dario Spikic (86' Antonio Marin). Coach: Igor Biscan.
Goals: 45+1' Josip Sutalo 0-1, 65' Robert Ljubicic 0-2, 90+2' Sergio Araújo 1-2,
90+11' Domagoj Vida 2-2.
Referee: Espen Eskås (NOR)   Attendance: 30,100.

Levi García missed a penalty kick (90+10').

*The first leg was originally scheduled to be played on 8th August 2023, but was postponed
following supporter riots in which one person died. The match was rescheduled for 19th
August 2023 and was designated as the second leg of the tie.*

(League Path)

08.08.23   Philips Stadion, Eindhoven: PSV Eindhoven – Sturm Graz 4-1 (3-1)
PSV Eindhoven: Walter Benítez, Patrick van Aanholt, André Ramalho, Olivier Boscagli,
Jordan Teze, Ibrahim Sangaré, Joey Veerman, Luuk de Jong (84' Ricardo Pepi), Noa Lang,
Johan Bakayoko (84' Yorbe Vertessen), Isaac Babadi (65' Ismael Saibari). Coach: Peter Bosz.
Sturm Graz: Kjell Scherpen, Gregory Wüthrich, Jusuf Gazibegovic, David Affengruber, David
Schnegg (46' Amadou Danté), Stefan Hierländer (70' Javier Serrano), Jon Gorenc Stankovic,
Otar Kiteishvili (70' Tomi Horvat), Alexander Prass, William Bøving (78' Mohammed
Fuseini), Szymon Wlodarczyk (61' Bryan Teixeira). Coach: Christian Ilzer.
Goals: 4' Isaac Babadi 1-0, 22', 32' Luuk de Jong 2-0, 3-0, 40' Jon Gorenc Stankovic 3-1,
73' Ibrahim Sangaré 4-1.
Referee: Radu Petrescu (ROM)   Attendance: 31,500.

08.08.23   Estádio Municipal de Braga, Braga: Sporting Braga – TSC Backa Topola 3-0 (2-0)
Sporting Braga: Matheus Magalhães, José Fonte, Cristián Borja, Víctor Gómez (90' Joe
Mendes), Sikou Niakaté, Pizzi (68' Álvaro Djaló), Ali Al Musrati, Vitor Carvalho (77'
Rodrigo Zalazar), Bruma, Ricardo Horta (90' Simon Banza), Abe Ruiz (77' André Horta).
Coach: Artur Jorge.
TSC Backa Topola: Veljko Ilic, Nemanja Petrovic, Milos Cvetkovic, Josip Calusic, Nemanja
Stojic, Mateja Djordjevic, Nikola Kuveljic (79' Petar Stanic), Milos Pantovic (59' Aleksandar
Cirkovic), Ifet Djakovac (87' Goran Antonic), Sasa Jovanovic, Marko Rakonjac (46' Milán
Rádin). Coach: Zarko Lazetic.
Goals: 17' Bruma 1-0, 19' Pizzi 2-0, 87' Álvaro Djaló 3-0.
Referee: Harald Lechner (AUT)   Attendance: 22,186.

09.08.23   Leoforos Alexandras Stadium, Athens:
          Panathinaikos – Olympique Marseille 1-0 (0-0)
Panathinaikos: Alberto Brignoli, Hördur Magnússon, Juankar (79' Filip Mladenovic), Tin
Jedvaj, Georgios Vagiannidis, Rubén Pérez, Filip Djuricic (72' Bernard), Tonny Vilhena (78'
Adam Gnezda Cerin), Benjamin Verbic (58' László Kleinheisler), Daniel Mancini, Andraz
Sporar (72' Fotis Ioannidis). Coach: Ivan Jovanovic.
Olympique Marseille: Pau López, Jonathan Clauss, Samuel Gigot, Renan Lodi, Leonardo
Balerdi, Geoffrey Kondogbia, Jordan Veretout (85' Mattéo Guendouzi), Azzedine Ounahi (67'
Valentin Rongier), Pierre-Emerick Aubameyang (86' Chancel Mbemba), Ismaïla Sarr (75'
Amine Harit), Iliman Ndiaye (75' François Mughe). Coach: Marcelino.
Goal: 83' Bernard 1-0.
Referee: István Kovács (ROM)   Attendance: 11,270.
Sent off: 65' Geoffrey Kondogbia.

09.09.23   Ibrox Stadium, Glasgow: Glasgow Rangers FC – Servette FC 2-1 (2-1)
Glasgow Rangers FC: Jack Butland, James Tavernier, Connor Goldson, John Souttar, Borna
Barisic, Ryan Jack (77' José Cifuentes), Todd Cantwell, Nicolas Raskin (89' Scott Wright),
Cyriel Dessers (89' Ianis Hagi), Sam Lammers (78' Kieran Dowell), Danilo (66' Abdallah
Sima). Coach: Michael Beale.
Servette FC: Joël Mall, Steve Rouiller (90+4' Anthony Baron), Yoan Severin, Bradley
Mazikou, Nicolas Vouilloz, David Douline, Dereck Kutesa, Timothé Cognat, Chris Bedia (79'
Ronny Rodelin), Jérémy Guillemenot, Boubacar Fofana (64' Samba Diba).
Coach: René Weiler.
Goals: 6' James Tavernier 1-0 (p), 15' Cyriel Dessers 2-0, 44' Chris Bedia 2-1 (p).
Referee: Donatas Rumsas (LTU)   Attendance: 48,956.
Sent off: 59' David Douline.

15.08.23   TSC Arena, Backa Topola: TSC Backa Topola – Sporting Braga 1-4 (1-4)
TSC Backa Topola: Nikola Simic, Dusan Cvetinovic, Nemanja Petrovic, Josip Calusic, Mateja
Djordjevic (46' Goran Antonic), Milán Rádin, Nikola Kuveljic (46' Ivan Milosavjlevic), Milos
Pantovic (60' Bence Sós), Petar Stanic, Sasa Jovanovic (46' Jovan Vlalukin), Marko Rakonjac
(69' Uros Milovanovic). Coach: Zarko Lazetic.
Sporting Braga: Matheus Magalhães, José Fonte, Adrián Marín, Víctor Gómez (60' Joe
Mendes), Sikou Niakaté, Pizzi (79' El Hadji Soumaré), Ali Al Musrati (46' Rodrigo Zalazar),
Vitor Carvalho, Bruma (46' Rony Lopes), Ricardo Horta (46' Roger Fernandes), Álvaro Djaló.
Coach: Artur Jorge.
Goals: 8' Pizzi 0-1, 12' Bruma 0-2, 16' Álvaro Djaló 0-3, 20' Ali Al-Musrati 0-4,
40' Marko Rakonjac 1-4.
Referee: Jakob Kehlet (DEN)   Attendance: 4,200.

15.08.23   Stade De Genève, Lancy: Servette FC – Glasgow Rangers FC 1-1 (1-0)
Servette FC: Joël Mall, Steve Rouiller, Yoan Severin, Bradley Mazikou (77' Anthony Baron),
Nicolas Vouilloz, Dereck Kutesa (71' Miroslav Stevanovic), Gaël Ondoua (71' Samba Diba),
Timothé Cognat, Enzo Crivelli, Chris Bedia (85' Ronny Rodelin), Jérémy Guillemenot (77'
Boubacar Fofana). Coach: René Weiler.
Glasgow Rangers FC: Jack Butland, James Tavernier, Connor Goldson, John Souttar, Borna
Barisic, Ryan Jack, José Cifuentes (84' Dujon Sterling), Todd Cantwell (90+6' Kieran
Dowell), Nicolas Raskin, Danilo (61' Cyriel Dessers), Abdallah Sima (61' Sam Lammers).
Coach: Michael Beale.
Goals: 22' Dereck Kutesa 1-0, 50' James Tavernier 1-1.
Referee: Maurizio Mariani (ITA)   Attendance: 26,000.

15.08.23   Merkur Arena, Graz: Sturm Graz – PSV Eindhoven 1-3 (1-2)
Sturm Graz: Kjell Scherpen, Gregory Wüthrich, Jusuf Gazibegovic (71' Max Johnston), David
Affengruber, Amadou Danté, Stefan Hierländer, Jon Gorenc Stankovic (71' Javier Serrano),
Otar Kiteishvili (71' Tomi Horvat), Alexander Prass (80' Jakob Jantscher), William Bøving,
Bryan Teixeira (59' Szymon Wlodarczyk). Coach: Christian Ilzer.
PSV Eindhoven: Walter Benítez, Patrick van Aanholt, André Ramalho, Olivier Boscagli,
Jordan Teze (86' Shurandy Sambo), Ibrahim Sangaré, Joey Veerman, Luuk de Jong (46'
Ricardo Pepi), Yorbe Vertessen (86' Isaac Babadi), Ismael Saibari, Johan Bakayoko (60' Guus
Til). Coach: Peter Bosz.
Goals: 26' William Bøving 1-0, 32' Joey Veerman 1-1, 39' Luuk de Jong 1-2,
85' Ricardo Pepi 1-3 (p).
Referee: Srdjan Jovanovic (SRB)   Attendance: 12,571.

15.08.23   Stade Orange Vélodrome, Marseille:
           Olympique Marseille – Panathinaikos 2-1 (2-0,2-1) (AET)
Olympique Marseille: Pau López (120+4' Rubén Blanco), Jonathan Clauss, Chancel Mbemba,
Samuel Gigot, Renan Lodi, Jordan Veretout, Valentin Rongier, Azzedine Ounahi (59' Amine
Harit), Pierre-Emerick Aubameyang (80' Vítinha), Ismaïla Sarr, Iliman Ndiaye (68' Mattéo
Guendouzi). Coach: Marcelino.
Panathinaikos: Alberto Brignoli, Hördur Magnússon, Juankar (70' Filip Mladenovic), Tin
Jedvaj, Georgios Vagiannidis, Rubén Pérez, Filip Djuricic (63' Bernard), Tonny Vilhena (70'
Adam Gnezda Cerin), Benjamin Verbic (46' Sebastián Palacios), Daniel Mancini (106' László
Kleinheisler), Andraz Sporar (63' Fotis Ioannidis). Coach: Ivan Jovanovic.
Goals: 2', 45+1' Pierre-Emerick Aubameyang 1-0, 2-0, 90+9' Fotis Ioannidis 2-1 (p).
Referee: Michael Oliver (ENG)   Attendance: 63,050.

Panathinaikos won after extra time on penalties (5:3).
Penalties: Ioannidis 1-0, Guendouzi missed, Bernard 2-0, Veretout 2-1, Kleinheisler 3-1,
*   Sarr 3-2, Palacios 4-2, Vitinha 4-3, Mladenovic 5-3.*

PLAY-OFF ROUND

The winners of the ties advanced to the Group Stage.

The losers were transferred to the UEFA Europa League Group Stage.

(Champions Path)

22.08.23   Bosuilstadion, Deurne: Royal Antwerp FC – AEK Athens 1-0 (1-0)
Royal Antwerp FC: Jean Butez, Ritchie De Laet, Toby Alderweireld, Jelle Bataille, Soumaïla
Coulibaly, Mandela Keita, Jurgen Ekkelenkamp (56' Zeno Van Den Bosch), Jacob Ondrejka
(56' Sam Vines), Arthur Vermeeren, Vincent Janssen (70' Arbnor Muja), Michel Balikwisha.
Coach: Mark van Bommel.
AEK Athens: Georgios Athanasiadis, Ehsan Hajsafi, Domagoj Vida, Djibril Sidibé (68' Sergio
Araújo), Harold Moukoudi, Mijat Gacinovic (67' Niclas Eliasson), Orbelín Pineda, Damian
Szymanski (46' Jens Jønsson), Nordin Amrabat, Steven Zuber (67' Petros Mantalos), Levi
García (36' Ezequiel Ponce). Coach: Matías Almeyda.
Goal: 16' Vincent Janssen 1-0.
Referee: François Letexier (FRA)   Attendance: 13,376.
Sent off: 50' Jelle Bataille.

22.08.23   ArcelorMittal Park, Sosnowiec:
                Raków Czestochowa – FC København 0-1 (0-1)
Raków Czestochowa: Vladan Kovacevic, Milan Rundic (80' Srdjan Plavsic), Adnan
Kovacevic, Bogdan Racovitan, Marcin Cebula (60' Sonny Kittel), Gustav Berggren, Jean
Carlos (23' Deian Sorescu), Vladyslav Kochergin (80' Ben Lederman), Fran Tudor, Giannis
Papanikolaou, Fabian Piasecki (80' Lukasz Zwolinski). Coach: Dawid Szwarga.
FC København: Kamil Grabara, Denis Vavro, Birger Meling, Kevin Diks, Elias Jelert, Rasmus
Falk (86' Oscar Højlund), Victor Claesson (65' Lukas Lerager), Mohamed Elyounoussi (81'
Nicolai Boilesen), Diogo Gonçalves (81' Christian Sørensen), Roony Bardghji (64' Orri
Óskarsson), Jordan Larsson. Coach: Jacob Neestrup.
Goal: 9' Bogdan Racovitan 0-1 (og).
Referee: Irfan Peljto (BIH)   Attendance: 11,600.

*Raków Czestochowa played their home match at the Zaglebiowski Park Sportowy in
Sosnowiec, instead of their regular stadium the Miejski Stadion Pilkarski "Raków" in
Czestochowa, which did not meet UEFA requirements.*

23.08.23   Sammy Ofer Stadium, Haifa: Maccabi Haifa – BSC Young Boys 0-0
Maccabi Haifa: Itamar Nizan, Daniel Sundgren, Shon Goldberg, Pierre Cornud, Abdoulaye
Seck, Tjaronn Chery (88' Lior Refaelov), Dia Sabi'A (73' Anan Khalaili), Ali Muhammad,
Dolev Haziza (79' Dean David), Mahmoud Jaber, Frantzdy Pierrot. Coach: Messay Dego.
BSC Young Boys: Anthony Racioppi, Loris Benito, Saïdy Janko, Mohamed Camara, Noah
Persson, Sandro Lauper (70' Miguel Chaiwa), Filip Ugrinic, Kastriot Imeri (61' Joël
Monteiro), Fabian Rieder, Cedric Itten (70' Jean-Pierre Nsame), Meschack Elia (88' Silvère
Ganvoula). Coach: Raphaël Wicky.
Referee: Davide Massa (ITA)   Attendance: 29,864.

23.08.23   Aker Stadion, Molde: Molde FK – Galatasaray 2-3 (1-2)
Molde FK: Jacob Karlstrøm, Kristoffer Haugen, Martin Bjørnbak, Eirik Haugan, Erling
Knudtzon, Magnus Eikrem (78' Eric Bugale Kitolano), Martin Ellingsen, Kristian Eriksen (69'
Markus Kaasa), Emil Breivik, Sivert Heggheim Mannsverk, Ola Brynhildsen.
Coach: Erling Moe.
Galatasaray: Fernando Muslera, Abdülkerim Bardakçi, Angeliño, Victor Nelsson, Sacha Boey,
Sérgio Oliveira (70' Kaan Ayhan), Berkan Kutlu (82' Fredrik Midtsjø), Dries Mertens (59'
Kerem Demirbay), Mauro Icardi, Yunus Akgün (82' Tetê), Kerem Aktürkoglu (70' Baris
Yilmaz). Coach: Okan Buruk.
Goals: 8' Martin Ellingsen 1-0, 25' Sérgio Oliveira 1-1, 29' Mauro Icardi 1-2,
56' Kristoffer Haugen 2-2, 90+3' Fredrik Midtsjø 2-3.
Referee: Anthony Taylor (ENG)   Attendance: 9,553.

29.08.23   Stadion Wankdorf, Bern: BSC Young Boys – Maccabi Haifa 3-0 (2-0)
BSC Young Boys: Anthony Racioppi, Loris Benito, Saïdy Janko (83' Lewin Blum), Mohamed
Camara, Noah Persson, Sandro Lauper, Filip Ugrinic (83' Darian Males), Kastriot Imeri (70'
Joël Monteiro), Fabian Rieder (74' Lukasz Lakomy), Cedric Itten (69' Silvère Ganvoula),
Meschack Elia. Coach: Raphaël Wicky.
Maccabi Haifa: Itamar Nizan, Daniel Sundgren, Shon Goldberg, Abdoulaye Seck, Tjaronn
Chery (69' Lior Refaelov), Ali Muhammad, Dolev Haziza, Mahmoud Jaber (69' Lorenco
Simic), Dean David (76' Eric Shuranov), Frantzdy Pierrot (55' Suf Podgoreanu), Anan
Khalaili (55' Dia Sabi'A). Coach: Messay Dego.
Goals: 23' Cedric Itten 1-0, 28' Abdoulaye Seck 2-0 (og), 46' Filip Ugrinic 3-0.
Referee: Slavko Vincic (SVN)   Attendance: 31,500.

29.08.23   Rams Global Stadium, Istanbul: Galatasaray – Molde FK 2-1 (1-0)
Galatasaray: Fernando Muslera, Abdülkerim Bardakçi, Angeliño, Victor Nelsson, Sacha Boey,
Kerem Demirbay (90' Berkan Kutlu), Lucas Torreira, Dries Mertens (72' Kaan Ayhan), Mauro
Icardi, Kerem Aktürkoglu (71' Baris Yilmaz), Tetê (80' Cédric Bakambu).
Coach: Okan Buruk.
Molde FK: Jacob Karlstrøm, Kristoffer Haugen, Martin Bjørnbak, Eirik Haugan, Erling
Knudtzon (22' Mathias Løvik, 85' Magnus Grødem), Magnus Eikrem (76' Veton Berisha),
Martin Ellingsen, Markus Kaasa (21' Eirik Hestad), Emil Breivik (76' Kristian Eriksen), Sivert
Heggheim Mannsverk, Ola Brynhildsen. Coach: Erling Moe.
Goals: 7' Mauro Icardi 1-0 (p), 66' Eirik Hestad 1-1, 90+3' Angeliño 2-1.
Referee: Szymon Marciniak (POL)   Attendance: 47,845.

30.08.23   OPAP Arena, Athens: AEK Athens – Royal Antwerp FC 1-2 (0-0)
AEK Athens: Cican Stankovic, Ehsan Hajsafi, Domagoj Vida, Harold Moukoudi, Lazaros Rota
(80' Jens Jønsson), Mijat Gacinovic (80' Petros Mantalos), Orbelín Pineda, Damian Szymanski
(80' Rodolfo Pizarro), Nordin Amrabat (69' Niclas Eliasson), Steven Zuber (70' Sergio
Araújo), Ezequiel Ponce. Coach: Matías Almeyda.
Royal Antwerp FC: Jean Butez, Ritchie De Laet, Toby Alderweireld (65' Zeno Van Den
Bosch), Sam Vines, Soumaïla Coulibaly, Mandela Keita, Jurgen Ekkelenkamp (66' Gyrano
Kerk), Arthur Vermeeren, Vincent Janssen (83' Alhassan Yusuf), Arbnor Muja, Michel
Balikwisha (90+8' Jacob Ondrejka). Coach: Mark van Bommel.
Goals: 73' Gyrano Kerk 0-1, 90' Sergio Araújo 1-1, 90+5' Michel Balikwisha 1-2.
Referee: Jesús Gil Manzano (ESP)   Attendance: 29,300.

30.08.23   Parken, København: FC København – Raków Czestochowa 1-1 (1-0)
FC København: Kamil Grabara, Denis Vavro, Birger Meling, Kevin Diks, Elias Jelert, Rasmus Falk, Victor Claesson, Mohamed Elyounoussi (60' Elias Achouri), Lukas Lerager, Diogo Gonçalves (88' Valdemar Lund Jensen), Jordan Larsson (61' Andreas Cornelius). Coach: Jacob Neestrup.
Raków Czestochowa: Vladan Kovacevic, Milan Rundic, Adnan Kovacevic, Zoran Arsenic (76' Bogdan Racovitan), Marcin Cebula (59' Sonny Kittel), Gustav Berggren (59' Ben Lederman), Vladyslav Kochergin (76' John Yeboah), Fran Tudor, Deian Sorescu, Giannis Papanikolaou, Fabian Piasecki (84' Lukasz Zwolinski). Coach: Dawid Szwarga.
Goals: 35' Denis Vavro 1-0, 87' Lukasz Zwolinski 1-1.
Referee: István Kovács (ROM)   Attendance: 34,737.

(League Path)

22.08.23   Ibrox Stadium, Glasgow: Glasgow Rangers FC – PSV Eindhoven 2-2 (1-0)
Glasgow Rangers FC: Jack Butland, James Tavernier, Connor Goldson, John Souttar, Borna Barisic, Ryan Jack (67' John Lundstram), José Cifuentes (81' Kieran Dowell), Todd Cantwell (86' Sam Lammers), Nicolas Raskin, Cyriel Dessers (81' Danilo), Abdallah Sima (67' Rabbi Matondo). Coach: Michael Beale.
PSV Eindhoven: Walter Benítez, André Ramalho (90' Jerdy Schouten), Olivier Boscagli (90' Isaac Babadi), Jordan Teze, Sergiño Dest (82' Shurandy Sambo), Ibrahim Sangaré, Joey Veerman, Luuk de Jong, Noa Lang (81' Yorbe Vertessen), Ismael Saibari (69' Guus Til), Johan Bakayoko. Coach: Peter Bosz.
Goals: 45' Abdallah Sima 1-0, 61' Ibrahim Sangaré 1-1, 76' Rabbi Matondo 2-1, 80' Luuk de Jong 2-2.
Referee: Clément Turpin (FRA)   Attendance: 47,537.

23.08.23   Estádio Municipal de Braga, Braga: Sporting Braga – Panathinaikos 2-1 (0-0)
Sporting Braga: Matheus Magalhães, José Fonte, Adrián Marín, Víctor Gómez, Sikou Niakaté, Pizzi (66' Álvaro Djaló), Ali Al Musrati (36' André Horta), Vitor Carvalho, Bruma (86' Andre Castro), Ricardo Horta (86' Rony Lopes), Abel Ruiz (86' Simon Banza). Coach: Artur Jorge.
Panathinaikos: Alberto Brignoli, Hördur Magnússon, Juankar, Tin Jedvaj, Georgios Vagiannidis, Rubén Pérez (82' Willian Arão), Filip Djuricic (65' Bernard), Tonny Vilhena (76' Adam Gnezda Cerin), Daniel Mancini, Andraz Sporar (65' Fotis Ioannidis), Sebastián Palacios (76' Aitor Cantalapiedra). Coach: Ivan Jovanovic.
Goals: 51' Abel Ruiz 1-0, 73' Álvaro Djaló 2-0, 90+5' Daniel Mancini 2-1.
Referee: Felix Zwayer (GER)   Attendance: 23,401.

29.08.23   Olympiako Stadio Spyros Louis, Athens: Panathinaikos – Sporting Braga 0-1 (0-0)
Panathinaikos: Alberto Brignoli, Hördur Magnússon, Juankar, Tin Jedvaj (43' Bart
Schenkeveld), Georgios Vagiannidis, Rubén Pérez (78' Adam Gnezda Cerin), Tonny Vilhena,
Bernard (77' Filip Djuricic), Daniel Mancini, Sebastián Palacios (62' Aitor Cantalapiedra),
Fotis Ioannidis (62' Andraz Sporar). Coach: Ivan Jovanovic.
Sporting Braga: Matheus Magalhães, José Fonte, Adrián Marín, Víctor Gómez, Sikou Niakaté
(49' Serdar Saatçi), André Horta (65' Pizzi), Vitor Carvalho, Bruma (88' Paulo Oliveira),
Ricardo Horta, Abel Ruiz (88' Simon Banza), Álvaro Djaló (65' Rodrigo Zalazar).
Coach: Artur Jorge.
Goal: 83' Bruma 0-1.
Referee: Daniele Orsato (ITA)   Attendance: 61,390.
Sent off: 90+1' Juankar.

*Panathinaikos played their home match at the Olympic Stadium in Athens, instead of their
regular stadium the Leoforos Alexandras Stadium in Athens.*

30.08.23   Philips Stadion, Eindhoven: PSV Eindhoven – Glasgow Rangers FC 5-1 (1-0)
PSV Eindhoven: Walter Benítez, Olivier Boscagli (83' Guus Til), Jordan Teze (83' Shurandy
Sambo), Sergiño Dest, Ibrahim Sangaré, Jerdy Schouten, Joey Veerman, Luuk de Jong, Noa
Lang (69' André Ramalho), Ismael Saibari (87' Yorbe Vertessen), Johan Bakayoko (87' Malik
Tillman). Coach: Peter Bosz.
Glasgow Rangers FC: Jack Butland, James Tavernier, Connor Goldson, John Souttar, Borna
Barisic (51' Dujon Sterling), John Lundstram, José Cifuentes, Todd Cantwell, Nicolas Raskin
(61' Sam Lammers), Cyriel Dessers (61' Danilo), Rabbi Matondo (85' Ryan Jack).
Coach: Michael Beale.
Goals: 35', 53' Ismael Saibari 1-0, 2-0, 64' James Tavernier 2-1, 66' Luuk de Jong 3-1,
78' Joey Veerman 4-1, 81' Connor Goldson 5-1 (og).
Referee: José María Sánchez Martínez (ESP)   Attendance: 34,560.

GROUP STAGE

The top two teams of each group advanced to the Round of 16.

The third-placed teams were transferred to the UEFA Europa League Knockout Round Play-
offs.

GROUP A

Bayern München	6	5	1	0	12	-	6	16
FC København	6	2	2	2	8	-	8	8
Galatasaray	6	1	2	3	10	-	13	5
Manchester United	6	1	1	4	12	-	15	4

GROUP B

Arsenal FC	6	4	1	1	16 - 4	13
PSV Eindhoven	6	2	3	1	8 - 10	9
Racing Club Lens	6	2	2	2	6 - 11	8
Sevilla FC	6	0	2	4	7 - 12	2

GROUP C

Real Madrid CF	6	6	0	0	16 - 7	18
SSC Napoli	6	3	1	2	10 - 9	10
Sporting Braga	6	1	1	4	6 - 12	4
1.FC Union Berlin	6	0	2	4	6 - 10	2

GROUP D

Real Sociedad	6	3	3	0	7 - 2	12
Internazionale Milano	6	3	3	0	8 - 5	12
SL Benfica	6	1	1	4	7 - 11	4
Red Bull Salzburg	6	1	1	4	4 - 8	4

GROUP E

Atlético Madrid	6	4	2	0	17 - 6	14
Lazio Roma	6	3	1	2	7 - 7	10
Feyenoord Rotterdam	6	2	0	4	9 - 10	6
Celtic FC	6	1	1	4	5 - 15	4

GROUP F

Borussia Dortmund	6	3	2	1	7 - 4	11
Paris Saint-Germain	6	2	2	2	9 - 8	8
AC Milan	6	2	2	2	5 - 8	8
Newcastle United	6	1	2	3	6 - 7	5

GROUP G

Manchester City	6	6	0	0	18 - 7	18
RB Leipzig	6	4	0	2	13 - 10	12
BSC Young Boys	6	1	1	4	7 - 13	4
Crvena Zvezda Beograd	6	0	1	5	7 - 15	1

GROUP H

FC Barcelona	6	4	0	2	12 - 6	12
FC Porto	6	4	0	2	15 - 8	12
Shakhtar Donetsk	6	3	0	3	10 - 12	9
Royal Antwerp FC	6	1	0	5	6 - 17	3

GROUP A

20.09.23   Rams Park, Istanbul: Galatasaray – FC København 2-2 (0-1)
Galatasaray: Fernando Muslera, Abdülkerim Bardakçi, Angeliño, Victor Nelsson (76' Tanguy Ndombèlè), Sacha Boey, Kerem Demirbay (59' Sérgio Oliveira), Hakim Ziyech (66' Baris Yilmaz), Lucas Torreira, Dries Mertens (59' Tetê), Mauro Icardi, Kerem Aktürkoglu (66' Wilfried Zaha). Coach: Okan Buruk.
FC København: Kamil Grabara, Denis Vavro, Birger Meling, Kevin Diks, Elias Jelert, Rasmus Falk, Mohamed Elyounoussi (90+3' Oscar Højlund), Lukas Lerager, Diogo Gonçalves (70' Victor Claesson), Jordan Larsson (70' Orri Óskarsson, 75' Peter Ankersen), Elias Achouri (76' Valdemar Lund Jensen). Coach: Jacob Neestrup.
Goals: 35' Mohamed Elyounoussi 0-1, 58' Diogo Gonçalves 0-2, 86' Sacha Boey 1-2, 88' Tetê 2-2.
Referee: Georgi Kabakov (BUL)   Attendance: 46,911.
Sent off: 73' Elias Jelert.

20.09.23   Allianz Arena, München: Bayern München – Manchester United 4-3 (2-0)
Bayern München: Sven Ulreich, Dayot Upamecano, Alphonse Davies, Kim Min-Jae, Leon Goretzka, Joshua Kimmich, Konrad Laimer, Harry Kane (87' Thomas Müller), Serge Gnabry (63' Kingsley Coman), Leroy Sané (87' Mathys Tel), Jamal Musiala (75' Eric Maxim Choupo-Moting). Coach: Thomas Tuchel.
Manchester United: André Onana, Victor Lindelöf, Sergio Reguilón, Diogo Dalot, Lisandro Martínez, Christian Eriksen (69' Scott McTominay), Casemiro, Bruno Fernandes, Facundo Pellistri (81' Alejandro Garnacho), Marcus Rashford, Rasmus Højlund (81' Anthony Martial). Coach: Erik ten Hag.
Goals: 28' Leroy Sané 1-0, 32' Serge Gnabry 2-0, 49' Rasmus Højlund 2-1, 53' Harry Kane 3-1 (p), 88' Casemiro 3-2, 90+2' Mathys Tel 4-2, 90+5' Casemiro 4-3.
Referee: Glenn Nyberg (SWE)   Attendance: 75,000.

03.10.23   Old Trafford, Manchester: Manchester United – Galatasaray 2-3 (1-1)
Manchester United: André Onana, Victor Lindelöf, Raphaël Varane, Diogo Dalot, Casemiro, Bruno Fernandes, Sofyan Amrabat (89' Anthony Martial), Mason Mount (85' Antony), Hannibal Mejbri (46' Christian Eriksen), Marcus Rashford (68' Alejandro Garnacho), Rasmus Højlund. Coach: Erik ten Hag.
Galatasaray: Fernando Muslera, Kaan Ayhan (84' Victor Nelsson), Abdülkerim Bardakçi, Davinson Sánchez, Angeliño (84' Tanguy Ndombèlè), Sacha Boey, Lucas Torreira (61' Sérgio Oliveira), Wilfried Zaha (72' Dries Mertens), Mauro Icardi, Kerem Aktürkoglu, Tetê (61' Baris Yilmaz). Coach: Okan Buruk.
Goals: 17' Rasmus Højlund 1-0, 23' Wilfried Zaha 1-1, 67' Rasmus Højlund 2-1, 71' Kerem Aktürkoglu 2-2, 81' Mauro Icardi 2-3.
Referee: Ivan Kruzliak (SVK)   Attendance: 73,204.
Sent off: 77' Casemiro.

Mauro Icardi missed a penalty kick (78').

03.10.23   Parken, København: FC København – Bayern München 1-2 (0-0)
FC København: Kamil Grabara, Peter Ankersen, Denis Vavro, Birger Meling, Kevin Diks (78'
Valdemar Lund Jensen), Rasmus Falk, Victor Claesson, Mohamed Elyounoussi (85' Jordan
Larsson), Lukas Lerager, Diogo Gonçalves (85' Orri Óskarsson), Elias Achouri (65' Roony
Bardghji). Coach: Jacob Neestrup.
Bayern München: Sven Ulreich, Noussair Mazraoui, Dayot Upamecano, Alphonse Davies,
Kim Min-Jae, Joshua Kimmich, Konrad Laimer (77' Thomas Müller), Harry Kane, Kingsley
Coman (87' Eric Maxim Choupo-Moting), Leroy Sané (77' Mathys Tel), Jamal Musiala (77'
Leon Goretzka). Coach: Thomas Tuchel.
Goals: 56' Lukas Lerager 1-0, 67' Jamal Musiala 1-1, 83' Mathys Tel 1-2.
Referee: Orel Grinfeld (ISR)   Attendance: 35,690.

24.10.23   Rams Park, Istanbul: Galatasaray – Bayern München 1-3 (1-1)
Galatasaray: Fernando Muslera, Kaan Ayhan (80' Tanguy Ndombèlé), Abdülkerim Bardakçi,
Davinson Sánchez, Sacha Boey, Kazimcan Karatas (74' Angeliño), Lucas Torreira, Wilfried
Zaha (75' Hakim Ziyech), Mauro Icardi, Kerem Aktürkoglu (74' Baris Yilmaz), Tetê (56'
Dries Mertens). Coach: Okan Buruk.
Bayern München: Sven Ulreich, Noussair Mazraoui (78' Bouna Sarr), Matthijs de Ligt,
Alphonse Davies, Kim Min-Jae, Joshua Kimmich, Konrad Laimer, Harry Kane (83' Eric
Maxim Choupo-Moting), Kingsley Coman (83' Mathys Tel), Leroy Sané, Jamal Musiala.
Coach: Thomas Tuchel.
Goals: 8' Kingsley Coman 0-1, 30' Mauro Icardi 1-1 (p), 73' Harry Kane 1-2,
79' Jamal Musiala 1-3.
Referee: Davide Massa (ITA)   Attendance: 51,776.

24.10.23   Old Trafford, Manchester: Manchester United – FC København 1-0 (0-0)
Manchester United: André Onana, Raphaël Varane, Harry Maguire, Sergio Reguilón (63'
Victor Lindelöf), Diogo Dalot, Bruno Fernandes, Sofyan Amrabat (46' Christian Eriksen),
Scott McTominay, Marcus Rashford, Antony (63' Alejandro Garnacho), Rasmus Højlund (86'
Anthony Martial). Coach: Erik ten Hag.
FC København: Kamil Grabara, Peter Ankersen, Denis Vavro, Kevin Diks, Elias Jelert (77'
Christian Sørensen), Rasmus Falk, Victor Claesson (76' Orri Óskarsson), Mohamed
Elyounoussi, Lukas Lerager, Diogo Gonçalves (85' Jordan Larsson), Elias Achouri (90+1'
Oscar Højlund). Coach: Jacob Neestrup.
Goal: Manchester United: 72' Harry Maguire 1-0.
Referee: Marco Guida (ITA)   Attendance: 73,249.

Jordan Larsson missed a penalty kick (90+7').

08.11.23   Allianz Arena, München: Bayern München – Galatasaray 2-1 (0-0)
Bayern München: Manuel Neuer, Noussair Mazraoui, Dayot Upamecano (72' Konrad Laimer),
Alphonse Davies, Kim Min-Jae, Leon Goretzka, Joshua Kimmich, Harry Kane, Kingsley
Coman (87' Serge Gnabry), Leroy Sané (72' Mathys Tel), Jamal Musiala (40' Thomas
Müller). Coach: Thomas Tuchel.
Galatasaray: Fernando Muslera, Kaan Ayhan (69' Sérgio Oliveira), Abdülkerim Bardakçi,
Davinson Sánchez, Angeliño (78' Victor Nelsson), Sacha Boey, Hakim Ziyech (58' Baris
Yilmaz), Lucas Torreira, Wilfried Zaha (78' Cédric Bakambu), Mauro Icardi (69' Tetê),
Kerem Aktürkoglu. Coach: Okan Buruk.
Goals: Bayern München: 80' Harry Kane 1-0, 86' Harry Kane 2-0.
Galatasaray: 90+3' Cédric Bakambu 2-1.
Referee: António Nobre (POR)   Attendance: 75,000.

160

08.11.23   Parken, København: FC København – Manchester United 4-3 (2-2)
FC København: Kamil Grabara, Peter Ankersen (70' Christian Sørensen), Denis Vavro (78'
Nicolai Boilesen), Kevin Diks, Elias Jelert, Rasmus Falk, Victor Claesson, Mohamed
Elyounoussi (63' Roony Bardghji), Lukas Lerager, Diogo Gonçalves (70' Orri Óskarsson),
Elias Achouri (78' Jordan Larsson). Coach: Jacob Neestrup.
Manchester United: André Onana, Jonny Evans (15' Raphaël Varane), Harry Maguire, Diogo
Dalot, Aaron Wan-Bissaka, Christian Eriksen (46' Sofyan Amrabat), Bruno Fernandes, Scott
McTominay, Marcus Rashford, Alejandro Garnacho, Rasmus Højlund (84' Mason Mount).
Coach: Erik ten Hag.
Goals: FC København: 45' Mohamed Elyounoussi 1-2, 45+9' Diogo Gonçalves 2-2 (p),
83' Lukas Lerager 3-3, 87' Roony Bardghji 4-3.
Manchester United: 3' Rasmus Højlund 0-1, 28' Rasmus Højlund 0-2,
69' Bruno Fernandes 2-3 (p).
Referee: Donatas Rumsas (LTU)   Attendance: 36,099.
Sent off: 42' Marcus Rashford.

29.11.23   Rams Park, Istanbul: Galatasaray – Manchester United 3-3 (1-2)
Galatasaray: Fernando Muslera, Kaan Ayhan, Abdülkerim Bardakçi, Angeliño (83' Victor
Nelsson), Sacha Boey, Hakim Ziyech (83' Baris Yilmaz), Tanguy Ndombèlé (60' Sérgio
Oliveira), Lucas Torreira, Dries Mertens (60' Kerem Aktürkoglu), Wilfried Zaha (88' Kerem
Demirbay), Mauro Icardi. Coach: Okan Buruk.
Manchester United: André Onana, Victor Lindelöf, Harry Maguire, Luke Shaw, Aaron Wan-
Bissaka (78' Diogo Dalot), Bruno Fernandes, Sofyan Amrabat (58' Kobbie Mainoo), Scott
McTominay, Antony, Alejandro Garnacho (78' Facundo Pellistri), Rasmus Højlund (58'
Anthony Martial). Coach: Erik ten Hag.
Goals: Galatasaray: 29' Hakim Ziyech 1-2, 62' Hakim Ziyech 2-3, 71' Kerem Aktürkoglu 3-3.
Manchester United: 11' Alejandro Garnacho 0-1, 18' Bruno Fernandes 0-2,
55' Scott McTominay 1-3.
Referee: José María Sánchez Martínez (ESP)   Attendance: 51,733.

29.11.23   Allianz Arena, München: Bayern München – FC København 0-0
Bayern München: Manuel Neuer, Raphaël Guerreiro (64' Aleksandar Pavlovic), Dayot
Upamecano, Alphonse Davies (86' Frans Krätzig), Leon Goretzka, Joshua Kimmich, Konrad
Laimer, Thomas Müller, Harry Kane, Kingsley Coman (64' Leroy Sané), Mathys Tel (64'
Serge Gnabry). Coach: Thomas Tuchel.
FC København: Kamil Grabara, Nicolai Boilesen (71' Peter Ankersen), Denis Vavro, Kevin
Diks, Elias Jelert, Rasmus Falk, Victor Claesson (60' Orri Óskarsson), Mohamed Elyounoussi,
Lukas Lerager, Diogo Gonçalves (90+5' Oscar Højlund), Roony Bardghji (60' Elias Achouri).
Coach: Jacob Neestrup.
Referee: Stéphanie Frappart (FRA)   Attendance: 75,000.

12.12.23   Old Trafford, Manchester: Manchester United – Bayern München 0-1 (0-0)
Manchester United: André Onana, Raphaël Varane (80' Kobbie Mainoo), Harry Maguire (40'
Jonny Evans), Luke Shaw (46' Aaron Wan-Bissaka), Diogo Dalot, Bruno Fernandes, Sofyan
Amrabat, Scott McTominay, Antony (75' Facundo Pellistri), Alejandro Garnacho (74'
Hannibal Mejbri), Rasmus Højlund. Coach: Erik ten Hag.
Bayern München: Manuel Neuer, Noussair Mazraoui (46' Konrad Laimer), Dayot Upamecano,
Alphonse Davies, Kim Min-Jae, Leon Goretzka, Joshua Kimmich, Harry Kane, Kingsley
Coman (77' Mathys Tel), Leroy Sané (90' Raphaël Guerreiro), Jamal Musiala (67' Thomas
Müller). Coach: Thomas Tuchel.
Goal: 71' Kingsley Coman 0-1.
Referee: Espen Eskås (NOR)   Attendance: 73,073.

12.12.23   Parken, København: FC København – Galatasaray 1-0 (0-0)
FC København: Kamil Grabara, Peter Ankersen, Denis Vavro, Kevin Diks, Elias Jelert, Rasmus Falk, Victor Claesson, Mohamed Elyounoussi (90+3' Oscar Højlund), Lukas Lerager, Diogo Gonçalves (67' Andreas Cornelius), Elias Achouri (81' Nicolai Boilesen). Coach: Jacob Neestrup.
Galatasaray: Fernando Muslera, Kaan Ayhan (61' Dries Mertens), Abdülkerim Bardakçi, Davinson Sánchez, Angeliño (77' Baris Yilmaz), Sacha Boey, Lucas Torreira (77' Sérgio Oliveira), Wilfried Zaha (65' Cédric Bakambu), Mauro Icardi, Kerem Aktürkoglu, Tetê (61' Hakim Ziyech). Coach: Okan Buruk.
Goal: FC København: 58' Lukas Lerager 1-0.
Referee: Daniele Orsato (ITA)   Attendance: 34,726.
Sent off: 90' Lukas Lerager.

GROUP B

20.09.23   Estadio Ramón Sánchez Pizjuán, Sevilla: Sevilla FC – Racing Club Lens 1-1 (1-1)
Sevilla FC: Marko Dmitrovic, Sergio Ramos, Adrià Pedrosa, Ivan Rakitic (74' Suso), Fernando, Érik Lamela (63' Dodi Lukébakio), Nemanja Gudelj, Lucas Ocampos, Djibril Sow (63' Boubakary Soumaré), Juanlu Sánchez (80' Jesús Navas), Youssef En-Nesyri (80' Mariano Díaz). Coach: José Luis Mendilíbar.
Racing Club Lens: Brice Samba, Jonathan Gradit, Deiver Machado (85' Massadio Haïdara), Kevin Danso, Facundo Medina, Nampalys Mendy (71' Andy Diouf), Przemyslaw Frankowski, Angelo Fulgini (76' Adrien Thomasson), Salis Abdul Samed, Florian Sotoca, Elye Wahi (71' Morgan Guilavogui). Coach: Franck Haise.
Goals: 9' Lucas Ocampos 1-0, 24' Angelo Fulgini 1-1.
Referee: Tobias Stieler (GER)   Attendance: 33,544.

20.09.23   Emirates Stadium, London: Arsenal FC – PSV Eindhoven 4-0 (3-0)
Arsenal FC: David Raya, Oleksandr Zinchenko (58' Takehiro Tomiyasu), Gabriel Magalhães, Ben White, William Saliba, Martin Ødegaard, Declan Rice (76' Jorginho), Kai Havertz, Leandro Trossard (58' Reiss Nelson), Gabriel Jesus (69' Emile Smith Rowe), Bukayo Saka (69' Fábio Vieira). Coach: Mikel Arteta.
PSV Eindhoven: Walter Benítez, Olivier Boscagli, Jordan Teze, Sergiño Dest, Armel Bella-Kotchap (76' André Ramalho), Jerdy Schouten, Joey Veerman, Luuk de Jong (90' Ricardo Pepi), Noa Lang (76' Yorbe Vertessen), Ismael Saibari (66' Malik Tillman), Johan Bakayoko (66' Hirving Lozano). Coach: Peter Bosz.
Goals: 8' Bukayo Saka 1-0, 20' Leandro Trossard 2-0, 38' Gabriel Jesus 3-0, 70' Martin Ødegaard 4-0.
Referee: Felix Zwayer (GER)   Attendance: 58,860.

03.10.23   Stade Bollaert-Delelis, Lens: Racing Club Lens – Arsenal FC 2-1 (1-1)
Racing Club Lens: Brice Samba, Jonathan Gradit, Deiver Machado (81' Ruben Aguilar), Kevin Danso, Facundo Medina, Nampalys Mendy (73' Andy Diouf), Adrien Thomasson (73' Angelo Fulgini), Przemyslaw Frankowski, Salis Abdul Samed, Florian Sotoca, Elye Wahi (74' Wesley Saïd). Coach: Franck Haise.
Arsenal FC: David Raya, Oleksandr Zinchenko (70' Ben White), Takehiro Tomiyasu, Gabriel Magalhães, William Saliba, Martin Ødegaard (80' Eddie Nketiah), Declan Rice, Kai Havertz (71' Emile Smith Rowe), Leandro Trossard (71' Reiss Nelson), Gabriel Jesus, Bukayo Saka (34' Fábio Vieira). Coach: Mikel Arteta.
Goals: 14' Gabriel Jesus 0-1, 25' Adrien Thomasson 1-1, 69' Elye Wahi 2-1.
Referee: Marco Guida (ITA)   Attendance: 37,040.

162

03.10.23   Philips Stadion, Eindhoven: PSV Eindhoven – Sevilla FC 2-2 (0-0)
PSV Eindhoven: Walter Benítez, André Ramalho (82' Armel Bella-Kotchap), Olivier Boscagli (82' Ricardo Pepi), Jordan Teze, Sergiño Dest, Jerdy Schouten, Joey Veerman (71' Ismael Saibari), Malik Tillman, Luuk de Jong, Noa Lang, Johan Bakayoko (71' Hirving Lozano). Coach: Peter Bosz.
Sevilla FC: Ørjan Nyland, Sergio Ramos, Jesús Navas (73' Juanlu Sánchez), Adrià Pedrosa (72' Marcos Acuña), Ivan Rakitic, Fernando (66' Djibril Sow), Nemanja Gudelj, Lucas Ocampos (87' Loïc Badé), Suso (66' Óliver Torres), Dodi Lukébakio, Youssef En-Nesyri. Coach: José Luis Mendilíbar.
Goals: 68' Nemanja Gudelj 0-1, 86' Luuk de Jong 1-1 (p), 87' Youssef En-Nesyri 1-2, 90+5' Jordan Teze 2-2.
Referee: Daniele Orsato (ITA)   Attendance: 34,206.

24.10.23   Estadio Ramón Sánchez Pizjuán, Sevilla: Sevilla FC – Arsenal FC 1-2 (0-1)
Sevilla FC: Ørjan Nyland, Sergio Ramos, Jesús Navas (78' Juanlu Sánchez), Marcos Acuña, Ivan Rakitic, Nemanja Gudelj, Lucas Ocampos, Djibril Sow (57' Mariano Díaz), Boubakary Soumaré, Dodi Lukébakio (57' Érik Lamela), Youssef En-Nesyri. Coach: Diego Alonso.
Arsenal FC: David Raya, Takehiro Tomiyasu, Gabriel Magalhães, Ben White, William Saliba, Jorginho, Martin Ødegaard (73' Kai Havertz), Declan Rice, Gabriel Jesus (81' Eddie Nketiah), Bukayo Saka (81' Leandro Trossard), Gabriel Martinelli (90+1' Jakub Kiwior). Coach: Mikel Arteta.
Goals: 45+4' Gabriel Martinelli 0-1, 53' Gabriel Jesus 0-2, 58' Nemanja Gudelj 1-2.
Referee: Glenn Nyberg (SWE)   Attendance: 39,595.

24.10.23   Stade Bollaert-Delelis, Lens: Racing Club Lens – PSV Einhoven 1-1 (0-0)
Racing Club Lens: Brice Samba, Jonathan Gradit, Deiver Machado (82' Massadio Haïdara), Kevin Danso, Facundo Medina, Nampalys Mendy (63' David Pereira da Costa), Przemyslaw Frankowski, Angelo Fulgini (63' Adrien Thomasson), Salis Abdul Samed, Florian Sotoca (63' Wesley Saïd), Elye Wahi (72' Morgan Guilavogui). Coach: Franck Haise.
PSV Eindhoven: Walter Benítez, André Ramalho, Olivier Boscagli, Jordan Teze, Sergiño Dest, Jerdy Schouten, Joey Veerman, Malik Tillman (71' Ismael Saibari), Luuk de Jong (90+1' Ricardo Pepi), Hirving Lozano (82' Yorbe Vertessen), Johan Bakayoko (82' Guus Til). Coach: Peter Bosz.
Goals: 54' Johan Bakayoko 0-1, 65' Elye Wahi 1-1.
Referee: Radu Petrescu (ROM)   Attendance: 38,133.

08.11.23   Emirates Stadium, London: Arsenal FC – Sevilla FC 2-0 (1-0)
Arsenal FC: David Raya, Takehiro Tomiyasu (46' Oleksandr Zinchenko), Gabriel Magalhães, Ben White, William Saliba, Jorginho (90' Mohamed Elneny), Declan Rice, Kai Havertz, Leandro Trossard (81' Fábio Vieira), Bukayo Saka (85' Jakub Kiwior), Gabriel Martinelli (81' Reiss Nelson). Coach: Mikel Arteta.
Sevilla FC: Marko Dmitrovic, Adrià Pedrosa (76' Tanguy Nianzou), Loïc Badé, Kike Salas (76' Lucas Ocampos), Fernando, Érik Lamela, Nemanja Gudelj, Joan Jordán (65' Boubakary Soumaré, 73' Mariano Díaz), Djibril Sow (65' Ivan Rakitic), Juanlu Sánchez, Youssef En-Nesyri. Coach: Diego Alonso.
Goals: 29' Leandro Trossard 1-0, 64' Bukayo Saka 2-0.
Referee: István Kovács (ROM)   Attendance: 60,024.

163

08.11.23   Philips Stadion, Eindhoven: PSV Eindhoven – Racing Club Lens 1-0 (1-0)
PSV Eindhoven: Walter Benítez, André Ramalho, Olivier Boscagli, Jordan Teze, Sergiño Dest,
Jerdy Schouten, Guus Til (66' Malik Tillman), Joey Veerman (66' Ismael Saibari), Luuk de
Jong (90+3' Ricardo Pepi), Hirving Lozano (90+3' Yorbe Vertessen), Johan Bakayoko.
Coach: Peter Bosz.
Racing Club Lens: Brice Samba, Jonathan Gradit, Deiver Machado (78' Massadio Haïdara),
Kevin Danso, Facundo Medina, Nampalys Mendy (66' Neil El Aynaoui), Adrien Thomasson
(65' Angelo Fulgini), Przemyslaw Frankowski (78' Morgan Guilavogui), Salis Abdul Samed,
Florian Sotoca, Elye Wahi (82' Wesley Saïd). Coach: Franck Haise.
Goal: 12' Luuk de Jong 1-0.
Referee: Daniel Siebert (GER)   Attendance: 34,200.
Sent off: 90+2' Morgan Guilavogui.

29.11.23   Estadio Ramón Sánchez Pizjuán, Sevilla: Sevilla FC – PSV Eindhoven 2-3 (1-0)
Sevilla FC: Marko Dmitrovic, Sergio Ramos, Jesús Navas (58' Juanlu Sánchez), Marcos
Acuña, Ivan Rakitic, Fernando (84' Óliver Torres), Nemanja Gudelj, Lucas Ocampos, Djibril
Sow (74' Joan Jordán), Dodi Lukébakio (73' Tanguy Nianzou), Youssef En-Nesyri (74' Rafa
Mir). Coach: Diego Alonso.
PSV Eindhoven: Walter Benítez, André Ramalho (58' Ismael Saibari), Olivier Boscagli (82'
Patrick van Aanholt), Jordan Teze, Sergiño Dest, Jerdy Schouten (82' Ricardo Pepi), Guus Til
(58' Malik Tillman), Joey Veerman, Luuk de Jong, Hirving Lozano (44' Yorbe Vertessen),
Johan Bakayoko. Coach: Peter Bosz.
Goals: 24' Sergio Ramos 1-0, 47' Youssef En-Nesyri 2-0, 68' Ismael Saibari 2-1,
81' Nemanja Gudelj 2-2 (og), 90+2' Ricardo Pepi 2-3.
Referee: Davide Massa (ITA)   Attendance: 29,403.
Sent off: 66' Lucas Ocampos, 90+8' Fernando.

29.11.23   Emirates Stadium, London: Arsenal FC – Racing Club Lens 6-0 (5-0)
Arsenal FC: David Raya, Oleksandr Zinchenko (46' Jakub Kiwior), Takehiro Tomiyasu (46'
Ben White), Gabriel Magalhães, William Saliba, Martin Ødegaard, Declan Rice (75' Jorginho),
Kai Havertz, Gabriel Jesus (82' Eddie Nketiah), Bukayo Saka (66' Reiss Nelson), Gabriel
Martinelli. Coach: Mikel Arteta.
Racing Club Lens: Brice Samba, Massadio Haïdara, Jonathan Gradit (62' Abduqodir
Khusanov), Kevin Danso, Facundo Medina (46' Deiver Machado), Nampalys Mendy (76'
David Pereira da Costa), Przemyslaw Frankowski, Angelo Fulgini, Salis Abdul Samed (46'
Neil El Aynaoui), Florian Sotoca (46' Adrien Thomasson), Elye Wahi. Coach: Franck Haise.
Goals: 13' Kai Havertz 1-0, 21' Gabriel Jesus 2-0, 23' Bukayo Saka 3-0,
27' Gabriel Martinelli 4-0, 45+1' Martin Ødegaard 5-0, 86' Jorginho 6-0 (p).
Referee: Artur Soares Dias (POR)   Attendance: 59,987.

12.12.23   Stade Bollaert-Delelis, Lens: Racing Club Lens – Sevilla FC 2-1 (0-0)
Racing Club Lens: Brice Samba, Ruben Aguilar, Jonathan Gradit (90+8' Abduqodir
Khusanov), Kevin Danso, Facundo Medina, Nampalys Mendy (23' Neil El Aynaoui),
Przemyslaw Frankowski, Salis Abdul Samed, David Pereira da Costa (72' Angelo Fulgini),
Florian Sotoca, Elye Wahi (72' Morgan Guilavogui). Coach: Franck Haise.
Sevilla FC: Marko Dmitrovic, Sergio Ramos, Adrià Pedrosa, Kike Salas, Ivan Rakitic,
Nemanja Gudelj, Óliver Torres (70' Rafa Mir), Djibril Sow, Boubakary Soumaré, Juanlu
Sánchez, Youssef En-Nesyri. Coach: Diego Alonso.
Goals: 63' Przemyslaw Frankowski 1-0 (p), 79' Sergio Ramos 1-1 (p),
90+6' Angelo Fulgini 2-1.
Referee: Felix Zwayer (GER)   Attendance: 37,456.

12.12.23   Philips Stadion, Eindhoven: PSV Eindhoven – Arsenal FC 1-1 (0-1)
PSV Eindhoven: Walter Benítez, Patrick van Aanholt, André Ramalho, Mauro Júnior, Armando Obispo, Jordan Teze, Malik Tillman (82' Guus Til), Yorbe Vertessen (90' Fredrik Oppegård), Ricardo Pepi, Ismael Saibari (74' Sergiño Dest), Johan Bakayoko (74' Isaac Babadi). Coach: Peter Bosz.
Arsenal FC: Aaron Ramsdale, Cédric Soares (62' Declan Rice), Gabriel Magalhães, Jakub Kiwior, William Saliba (62' Ben White), Mohamed Elneny (62' Martin Ødegaard), Jorginho, Kai Havertz (89' Emile Smith Rowe), Leandro Trossard, Eddie Nketiah, Reiss Nelson (89' Gabriel Jesus). Coach: Mikel Arteta.
Goals: 42' Eddie Nketiah 0-1, 50' Yorbe Vertessen 1-1.
Referee: Tobias Stieler (GER)   Attendance: 35,000.

GROUP C

20.09.23   Estadio Santiago Bernabéu, Madrid: Real Madrid CF – 1.FC Union Berlin 1-0 (0-0)
Real Madrid CF: Kepa, David Alaba, Nacho (73' Fran García), Antonio Rüdiger, Luka Modric (80' Brahim Díaz), Lucas Vázquez, Aurélien Tchouaméni (66' Federico Valverde), Eduardo Camavinga (66' Toni Kroos), Jude Bellingham, Joselu, Rodrygo. Coach: Carlo Ancelotti.
1.FC Union Berlin: Frederik Rønnow, Leonardo Bonucci (80' Paul Jaeckel), Robin Gosens, Josip Juranovic, Diogo Leite, Danilho Doekhi, Aïssa Laïdouni (66' Brenden Aaronson), Lucas Tousart (83' Aljoscha Kemlein), Alex Král, Kevin Behrens (66' Kevin Volland), Sheraldo Becker (80' David Fofana). Coach: Urs Fischer.
Goal: 90+4' Jude Bellingham 1-0.
Referee: Espen Eskås (NOR)   Attendance: 65,207.

20.09.23   Estádio Municipal de Braga, Braga: Sporting Braga – SSC Napoli 1-2 (0-1)
Sporting Braga: Matheus Magalhães, José Fonte, Cristián Borjá (85' Adrián Marín), Víctor Gómez, Sikou Niakaté, Ali Al Musrati, Vitor Carvalho (67' Rodrigo Zalazar), Bruma, Ricardo Horta, Abel Ruiz (85' Pizzi), Álvaro Djaló (77' Simon Banza). Coach: Artur Jorge.
SSC Napoli: Alex Meret, Juan Jesus, Giovanni Di Lorenzo, Amir Rrahmani (13' Leo Østigård), Mathías Olivera, Piotr Zielinski (90' Natan), Stanislav Lobotka, Frank Anguissa, Matteo Politano (67' Giacomo Raspadori), Victor Osimhen (90' Giovanni Simeone), Khvicha Kvaratskhelia (66' Eljif Elmas). Coach: Rudi García.
Goals: 45+1' Giovanni Di Lorenzo 0-1, 84' Bruma 1-1, 88' Sikou Niakaté 1-2 (og).
Referee: Serdar Gözübüyük (HOL)   Attendance: 18,422.

03.10.23   Olympiastadion, Berlin: 1.FC Union Berlin – Sporting Braga 2-3 (2-1)
1.FC Union Berlin: Frederik Rønnow, Leonardo Bonucci, Robin Gosens (86' Jérôme Roussillon), Josip Juranovic, Diogo Leite, Danilho Doekhi, Janik Haberer (81' Brenden Aaronson), Lucas Tousart (63' Aïssa Laïdouni), Alex Král, Kevin Behrens (63' Kevin Volland), Sheraldo Becker. Coach: Urs Fischer.
Sporting Braga: Matheus Magalhães, Cristián Borjá (74' Adrián Marín), Sikou Niakaté, Serdar Saatçi, Joe Mendes (86' Andre Castro), Ali Al Musrati, Rodrigo Zalazar (73' João Moutinho), Bruma, Ricardo Horta (83' Vitor Carvalho), Simon Banza, Álvaro Djaló (84' Abel Ruiz). Coach: Artur Jorge.
Goals: 30' Sheraldo Becker 1-0, 37' Sheraldo Becker 2-0, 41' Sikou Niakaté 2-1, 51' Bruma 2-2, 90+4' Andre Castro 2-3.
Referee: Srdjan Jovanovic (SRB)   Attendance: 73,345.

1.FC Union Berlin played their home matches at the Olympiastadion, in Berlin, instead of their regular stadium, Stadion An der Alten Försterei, in Berlin.

03.10.23 Stadio Diego Armando Maradona, Napoli: SSC Napoli – Real Madrid CF 2-3 (1-2)
SSC Napoli: Alex Meret, Giovanni Di Lorenzo, Mathías Olivera (88' Mário Rui), Leo
Østigård, Natan, Piotr Zielinski (75' Giacomo Raspadori), Stanislav Lobotka (88' Jens-Lys
Cajuste), Frank Anguissa (88' Giovanni Simeone), Matteo Politano (70' Eljif Elmas), Victor
Osimhen, Khvicha Kvaratskhelia. Coach: Rudi García.
Real Madrid CF: Kepa, Nacho, Dani Carvajal, Antonio Rüdiger, Toni Kroos (65' Luka
Modric), Federico Valverde, Aurélien Tchouaméni, Eduardo Camavinga (64' Ferland Mendy),
Jude Bellingham, Vinícius Júnior (84' Dani Ceballos), Rodrygo (75' Joselu).
Coach: Carlo Ancelotti.
Goals: 19' Leo Østigård 1-0, 27' Vinícius Júnior 1-1, 34' Jude Bellingham 1-2,
54' Piotr Zielinski 2-2 (p), 78' Alex Meret 2-3 (og).
Referee: Clément Turpin (FRA)   Attendance: 51,649.

24.10.23 Estádio Municipal de Braga, Braga: Sporting Braga – Real Madrid CF 1-2 (0-1)
Sporting Braga: Matheus Magalhães, Cristián Borjá, Sikou Niakaté, Serdar Saatçi, Joe Mendes
(73' Diogo Fonseca), Ali Al Musrati (78' João Moutinho), Vitor Carvalho (66' Bruma),
Rodrigo Zalazar, Ricardo Horta, Simon Banza (67' Abel Ruiz), Álvaro Djaló.
Coach: Artur Jorge.
Real Madrid CF: Kepa, Nacho, Dani Carvajal, Antonio Rüdiger, Fran García (75' Ferland
Mendy), Luka Modric, Federico Valverde, Eduardo Camavinga, Jude Bellingham (89' Lucas
Vázquez), Vinícius Júnior, Rodrygo (71' Aurélien Tchouaméni). Coach: Carlo Ancelotti.
Goals: 16' Rodrygo 0-1, 61' Jude Bellingham 0-2, 63' Álvaro Djaló 1-2.
Referee: Michael Oliver (ENG)   Attendance: 29,820.

24.10.23 Olympiastadion, Berlin: 1.FC Union Berlin – SSC Napoli 0-1 (0-0)
1.FC Union Berlin: Frederik Rønnow, Christopher Trimmel, Robin Knoche, Robin Gosens,
Diogo Leite, Danilho Doekhi (80' Lucas Tousart), Rani Khedira (70' Alex Král), Janik
Haberer (80' Kevin Volland), Brenden Aaronson (70' Aïssa Laïdouni), Sheraldo Becker,
David Fofana (70' Kevin Behrens). Coach: Urs Fischer.
SSC Napoli: Alex Meret, Mário Rui (71' Mathías Olivera), Giovanni Di Lorenzo, Amir
Rrahmani, Natan, Piotr Zielinski, Stanislav Lobotka, Jens-Lys Cajuste (46' Eljif Elmas),
Matteo Politano (81' Jesper Lindstrøm), Khvicha Kvaratskhelia (89' Leo Østigård), Giacomo
Raspadori (71' Giovanni Simeone). Coach: Rudi García.
Goal: 65' Giacomo Raspadori 0-1.
Referee: Irfan Peljto (BIH)   Attendance: 72,062.

08.11.23 Stadio Diego Armando Maradona, Napoli:
            SSC Napoli – 1.FC Union Berlin 1-1 (1-0)
SSC Napoli: Alex Meret, Mário Rui (77' Mathías Olivera), Giovanni Di Lorenzo, Amir
Rrahmani, Natan, Piotr Zielinski (90+1' Jens-Lys Cajuste), Stanislav Lobotka (77' Giovanni
Simeone), Frank Anguissa, Matteo Politano (87' Jesper Lindstrøm), Khvicha Kvaratskhelia,
Giacomo Raspadori. Coach: Rudi García.
1.FC Union Berlin: Frederik Rønnow, Leonardo Bonucci, Jérôme Roussillon (80' Robin
Gosens), Josip Juranovic (64' Christopher Trimmel), Paul Jaeckel, Diogo Leite, Rani Khedira
(70' Lucas Tousart), Janik Haberer (79' Brenden Aaronson), Aïssa Laïdouni (70' Alex Král),
Sheraldo Becker, David Fofana. Coach: Urs Fischer.
Goals: 39' Matteo Politano 1-0, 52' David Fofana 1-1.
Referee: Danny Makkelie (HOL)   Attendance: 42,449.

08.11.23   Estadio Santiago Bernabéu, Madrid: Real Madrid CF – Sporting Braga 3-0 (1-0)
Real Madrid CF: Andriy Lunin, Nacho, Antonio Rüdiger, Ferland Mendy (84' Fran García),
Toni Kroos, Lucas Vázquez (74' Dani Carvajal), Federico Valverde (77' Nico Paz), Brahim
Díaz (74' Luka Modric), Eduardo Camavinga, Vinícius Júnior, Rodrygo (77' Joselu).
Coach: Carlo Ancelotti.
Sporting Braga: Matheus Magalhães, José Fonte, Cristián Borjá, Víctor Gómez (62' Joe
Mendes), Sikou Niakaté, João Moutinho, Vitor Carvalho, Rodrigo Zalazar (62' Ali Al
Musrati), Bruma (77' André Horta), Ricardo Horta (62' Abel Ruiz), Álvaro Djaló (77' Simon
Banza). Coach: Artur Jorge.
Goals: 27' Brahim Díaz 1-0, 58' Vinícius Júnior 2-0, 61' Rodrygo 3-0.
Referee: Halil Umut Meler (TUR)   Attendance: 68,509.

Álvaro Djaló missed a penalty kick (6').

29.11.23   Estadio Santiago Bernabéu, Madrid: Real Madrid CF – SSC Napoli 4-2 (2-1)
Real Madrid CF: Andriy Lunin, David Alaba, Dani Carvajal, Antonio Rüdiger, Ferland Mendy
(87' Nacho), Toni Kroos, Dani Ceballos (57' Joselu), Federico Valverde, Brahim Díaz (65'
Nico Paz), Jude Bellingham, Rodrygo (87' Lucas Vázquez). Coach: Carlo Ancelotti.
SSC Napoli: Alex Meret, Juan Jesus (87' Alessandro Zanoli), Giovanni Di Lorenzo, Amir
Rrahmani, Natan, Piotr Zielinski (65' Eljif Elmas), Stanislav Lobotka (87' Giacomo
Raspadori), Frank Anguissa, Matteo Politano (78' Jens-Lys Cajuste), Giovanni Simeone (46'
Victor Osimhen), Khvicha Kvaratskhelia. Coach: Walter Mazzarri.
Goals: 9' Giovanni Simeone 0-1, 11' Rodrygo 1-1, 22' Jude Bellingham 2-1,
47' Frank Anguissa 2-2, 84' Nico Paz 3-2, 90+4' Joselu 4-2.
Referee: François Letexier (FRA)   Attendance: 73,562.

29.11.23   Estádio Municipal de Braga, Braga: Sporting Braga – 1.FC Union Berlin 1-1 (0-1)
Sporting Braga: Matheus Magalhães, José Fonte, Cristián Borjá, Víctor Gómez (82' Joe
Mendes), Sikou Niakaté, João Moutinho, Vitor Carvalho (36' Serdar Saatçi), Rodrigo Zalazar
(81' André Horta), Ricardo Horta, Simon Banza (68' Abel Ruiz), Álvaro Djaló (82' Roger
Fernandes). Coach: Artur Jorge.
1.FC Union Berlin: Frederik Rønnow, Robin Knoche, Jérôme Roussillon, Robin Gosens, Josip
Juranovic, Diogo Leite, Rani Khedira (78' Brenden Aaronson), Aïssa Laïdouni (78' Alex
Král), Lucas Tousart (62' Janik Haberer), Kevin Volland, Kevin Behrens (62' David Fofana).
Coach: Nenad Bjelica.
Goals: 42' Robin Gosens 0-1, 51' Álvaro Djaló 1-1.
Referee: Clément Turpin (FRA)   Attendance: 15,855.
Sent off: 31' Sikou Niakaté.

12.12.23   Stadio Diego Armando Maradona, Napoli: SSC Napoli – Sporting Braga 2-0 (2-0)
SSC Napoli: Alex Meret, Juan Jesus (73' Leo Østigård), Giovanni Di Lorenzo, Amir
Rrahmani, Natan, Piotr Zielinski (61' Jens-Lys Cajuste), Stanislav Lobotka (69' Gianluca
Gaetano), Frank Anguissa, Matteo Politano (60' Eljif Elmas), Victor Osimhen (69' Giacomo
Raspadori), Khvicha Kvaratskhelia. Coach: Walter Mazzarri.
Sporting Braga: Matheus Magalhães, José Fonte, Cristián Borjá, Víctor Gómez (81' Joe
Mendes), Serdar Saatçi, João Moutinho (81' André Horta), Pizzi (46' Abel Ruiz), Rodrigo
Zalazar (68' Ali Al Musrati), Bruma, Ricardo Horta (88' Rony Lopes), Simon Banza.
Coach: Artur Jorge.
Goals: 9' Serdar Saatçi 1-0 (og), 33' Victor Osimhen (33').
Referee: Slavko Vincic (SVN)   Attendance: 37,841.

167

12.12.23   Olympiastadion, Berlin: 1.FC Union Berlin – Real Madrid CF 2-3 (1-0)
1.FC Union Berlin: Frederik Rønnow, Robin Knoche, Jérôme Roussillon, Robin Gosens (75'
Aïssa Laïdouni), Josip Juranovic (82' Christopher Trimmel), Paul Jaeckel (75' Sheraldo
Becker), Diogo Leite, Rani Khedira (75' Alex Král), Janik Haberer, Kevin Volland (82'
Brenden Aaronson), Kevin Behrens. Coach: Nenad Bjelica.
Real Madrid CF: Kepa, David Alaba (71' Antonio Rüdiger), Nacho, Fran García, Luka
Modric, Lucas Vázquez, Dani Ceballos (90' Nico Paz), Federico Valverde (46' Toni Kroos),
Jude Bellingham, Joselu, Rodrygo (80' Brahim Díaz). Coach: Carlo Ancelotti.
Goals: 45+1' Kevin Volland 1-0, 61' Joselu 1-1, 72' Joselu 1-2, 85' Alex Král 2-2,
89' Dani Ceballos 2-3.
Referee: Rade Obrenovic (SVN)   Attendance: 73,420.

Luka Modric missed a penalty kick (45').

GROUP D

20.09.23   Reale Arena, San Sebastián: Real Sociedad – Internazionale Milan 1-1 (1-0)
Real Sociedad: Álex Remiro, Hamari Traoré, Robin Le Normand, Kieran Tierney (62' Aihen
Muñoz), Brais Méndez (85' Jon Pacheco), Mikel Merino, Zubeldía, Martín Zubimendi,
Takefusa Kubo (72' Álvaro Odriozola), Mikel Oyarzabal (72' Umar Sadiq), Ander
Barrenetxea (61' Mohamed Cho). Coach: Imanol Alguacil.
Internazionale Milano: Yann Sommer, Stefan de Vrij (76' Francesco Acerbi), Denzel
Dumfries, Benjamin Pavard, Alessandro Bastoni (55' Federico Dimarco), Carlos Augusto,
Henrikh Mkhitaryan (70' Alexis Sánchez), Nicolò Barella, Kristjan Asllani (55' Davide
Frattesi), Marko Arnautovic (55' Marcus Thuram), Lautaro Martínez. Coach: Simone Inzaghi.
Goals: 4' Brais Méndez 1-0, 87' Lautaro Martínez 1-1.
Referee: Michael Oliver (ENG)   Attendance: 36,591.

20.09.23   Estádio do Sport Lisboa e Benfica, Lisboa:
SL Benfica – Red Bull Salzburg 0-2 (0-1)
SL Benfica: Anatoliy Trubin, Nicolás Otamendi, Alexander Bah, António Silva, Ángel Di
María (72' David Neres), João Mário (16' Morato), Fredrik Aursnes, Rafa Silva (83' Tiago
Gouveia), Orkun Kökçü (72' Chiquinho), João Neves, Petar Musa (83' Casper Tengstedt).
Coach: Roger Schmidt.
Red Bull Salzburg: Alexander Schlager, Aleksa Terzic, Strahinja Pavlovic (89' Kamil
Piatkowski), Amar Dedic, Samson Baidoo (72' Oumar Solet), Mads Bidstrup, Maurits
Kjærgaard, Lucas Gourna-Douath, Oscar Gloukh (71' Luka Sucic), Roko Simic (71' Petar
Ratkov), Karim Konaté (59' Sékou Koïta). Coach: Gerhard Struber.
Goals: 15' Roko Simic 0-1 (p), 51' Oscar Gloukh 0-2.
Referee: Halil Umut Meler (TUR)   Attendance: 60,917.
Sent off: 13' António Silva.

Karim Konaté missed a penalty kick (3').

03.10.23   Red Bull Arena, Wals-Siezenheim: Red Bull Salzburg – Real Sociedad 0-2 (0-2)
Red Bull Salzburg: Alexander Schlager, Aleksa Terzic, Oumar Solet (46' Samson Baidoo),
Strahinja Pavlovic, Amar Dedic, Mads Bidstrup (65' Nicolás Capaldo), Maurits Kjærgaard
(46' Amankwah Forson), Lucas Gourna-Douath, Oscar Gloukh (78' Luka Sucic), Roko Simic,
Karim Konaté (46' Petar Ratkov). Coach: Gerhard Struber.
Real Sociedad: Álex Remiro, Hamari Traoré (84' Aritz Elustondo), Robin Le Normand (46'
Jon Pacheco), Aihen Muñoz, Brais Méndez (82' Beñat Turrientes), Mikel Merino, Zubeldía,
Martín Zubimendi, Takefusa Kubo (63' Mohamed Cho), Mikel Oyarzabal, Ander Barrenetxea
(64' Carlos Fernández). Coach: Imanol Alguacil.
Goals: 7' Mikel Oyarzabal 0-1, 27' Brais Méndez 0-2.
Referee: Bartosz Frankowski (POL)   Attendance: 28,227.

03.10.23   Stadio Giuseppe Meazza, Milano: Internazionale Milano – SL Benfica 1-0 (0-0)
Internazionale Milano: Yann Sommer, Francesco Acerbi, Federico Dimarco (84' Carlos
Augusto), Denzel Dumfries (73' Matteo Darmian), Benjamin Pavard, Alessandro Bastoni,
Henrikh Mkhitaryan, Hakan Çalhanoglu (84' Kristjan Asllani), Nicolò Barella (90+2' Davy
Klaassen), Marcus Thuram (73' Alexis Sánchez), Lautaro Martínez. Coach: Simone Inzaghi.
SL Benfica: Anatoliy Trubin, Nicolás Otamendi, Juan Bernat (80' Arthur Cabral), Alexander
Bah (22' Tomás Araújo), Morato, Ángel Di María (80' David Jurásek), Fredrik Aursnes, Rafa
Silva (69' Chiquinho), Orkun Kökçü (69' Petar Musa), João Neves, David Neres.
Coach: Roger Schmidt.
Goal: 62' Marcus Thuram 1-0.
Referee: Danny Makkelie (HOL)   Attendance: 66,573.

24.10.23   Stadio Giuseppe Meazza, Milano:
          Internazionale Milano – Red Bull Salzburg 2-1 (1-0)
Internazionale Milano: Yann Sommer, Stefan de Vrij, Denzel Dumfries (65' Matteo Darmian),
Benjamin Pavard, Alessandro Bastoni, Carlos Augusto, Henrikh Mkhitaryan (46' Nicolò
Barella), Hakan Çalhanoglu (76' Kristjan Asllani), Davide Frattesi, Alexis Sánchez (65'
Marcus Thuram), Lautaro Martínez (85' Davy Klaassen). Coach: Simone Inzaghi.
Red Bull Salzburg: Alexander Schlager, Andreas Ulmer, Oumar Solet, Strahinja Pavlovic,
Amar Dedic, Mads Bidstrup (72' Karim Konaté), Luka Sucic, Maurits Kjærgaard (71'
Dorgeles Nene), Lucas Gourna-Douath (85' Nicolás Capaldo), Oscar Gloukh (85' Amankwah
Forson), Roko Simic (71' Petar Ratkov). Coach: Gerhard Struber.
Goals: 19' Alexis Sánchez 1-0, 57' Oscar Gloukh 1-1, 64' Hakan Çalhanoglu 2-1 (p).
Referee: François Letexier (FRA)   Attendance: 71,825.

24.10.23   Estádio do Sport Lisboa e Benfica, Lisboa: SL Benfica – Real Sociedad 0-1 (0-0)
SL Benfica: Anatoliy Trubin, Nicolás Otamendi, Alexander Bah (81' Chiquinho), David
Jurásek (59' Juan Bernat), António Silva, João Mário (46' Orkun Kökçü), Fredrik Aursnes,
Rafa Silva, João Neves, Petar Musa (46' Arthur Cabral), David Neres (69' Tiago Gouveia).
Coach: Roger Schmidt.
Real Sociedad: Álex Remiro, Hamari Traoré (70' Aritz Elustondo), Robin Le Normand, Aihen
Muñoz, Brais Méndez, Mikel Merino, Zubeldía, Martín Zubimendi, Takefusa Kubo (76'
Carlos Fernández), Mikel Oyarzabal (90+2' Mohamed Cho), Ander Barrenetxea (76' Arsen
Zakharyan). Coach: Imanol Alguacil.
Goal: 63' Brais Méndez 0-1.
Referee: Clément Turpin (FRA)   Attendance: 56,002.

08.11.23   Reale Arena, San Sebastián: Real Sociedad – SL Benfica 3-1 (3-0)
Real Sociedad: Álex Remiro, Aritz Elustondo (86' Álvaro Odriozola), Robin Le Normand,
Aihen Muñoz, Brais Méndez (70' Beñat Turrientes), Mikel Merino, Zubeldía, Martín
Zubimendi, Takefusa Kubo (70' Carlos Fernández), Mikel Oyarzabal, Ander Barrenetxea (78'
Arsen Zakharyan). Coach: Imanol Alguacil.
SL Benfica: Anatoliy Trubin, Nicolás Otamendi, Morato, António Silva, Ángel Di María (85'
Casper Tengstedt), João Mário (85' Chiquinho), Fredrik Aursnes, Rafa Silva (85' Gonçalo
Guedes), Florentino (31' David Jurásek), João Neves, Arthur Cabral (64' Petar Musa).
Coach: Roger Schmidt.
Goals: 6' Mikel Merino 1-0, 11' Mikel Oyarzabal 2-0, 21' Ander Barrenetxea 3-0,
49' Rafa Silva 3-1.
Referee: Anthony Taylor (ENG)   Attendance: 36,815.

Brais Méndez missed a penalty kick (29').

08.11.23   Red Bull Arena, Wals-Siezenheim:
            Red Bull Salzburg – Internazionale Milano 0-1 (0-0)
Red Bull Salzburg: Alexander Schlager, Andreas Ulmer (46' Lucas Gourna-Douath), Strahinja
Pavlovic, Amar Dedic, Samson Baidoo, Mads Bidstrup, Luka Sucic, Nicolás Capaldo, Oscar
Gloukh (87' Amankwah Forson), Roko Simic (79' Petar Ratkov), Karim Konaté (87' Dorgeles
Nene). Coach: Gerhard Struber.
Internazionale Milano: Yann Sommer, Matteo Darmian, Francesco Acerbi, Alessandro
Bastoni, Yann Bisseck (46' Stefan de Vrij), Carlos Augusto (86' Federico Dimarco), Henrikh
Mkhitaryan (69' Nicolò Barella), Hakan Çalhanoglu (61' Kristjan Asllani), Davide Frattesi,
Alexis Sánchez (68' Lautaro Martínez), Marcus Thuram. Coach: Simone Inzaghi.
Goal: 85' Lautaro Martínez 0-1 (p).
Referee: Serdar Gözübüyük (HOL)   Attendance: 30,071.

29.11.23   Estádio do Sport Lisboa e Benfica, Lisboa:
            SL Benfica – Internazionale Milano 3-3 (3-0)
SL Benfica: Anatoliy Trubin, Nicolás Otamendi, Morato, António Silva, Ángel Di María (89'
Tomás Araújo), João Mário (90+9' Chiquinho), Fredrik Aursnes, Rafa Silva (90+9' Tiago
Gouveia), Florentino (79' Orkun Kökçü), João Neves, Casper Tengstedt (79' Petar Musa).
Coach: Roger Schmidt.
Internazionale Milano: Emil Audero, Matteo Darmian (67' Juan Cuadrado), Stefan de Vrij (77'
Federico Dimarco), Francesco Acerbi, Yann Bisseck, Carlos Augusto, Davy Klaassen (68'
Nicolò Barella), Davide Frattesi, Kristjan Asllani, Alexis Sánchez (79' Lautaro Martínez),
Marko Arnautovic (68' Marcus Thuram). Coach: Simone Inzaghi.
Goals: 5' João Mário 1-0, 13' João Mário 2-0, 34' João Mário 3-0, 53' Marko Arnautovic 3-1,
58' Davide Frattesi 3-2, 72' Alexis Sánchez 3-3 (p).
Referee: Andris Treimanis (LVA)   Attendance: 52,944.
Sent off: 84' António Silva.

29.11.23 Reale Arena, San Sebastián: Real Sociedad – Red Bull Salzburg 0-0
Real Sociedad: Álex Remiro, Álvaro Odriozola (74' Hamari Traoré), Aritz Elustondo (46' Jon Pacheco), Aihen Muñoz, Brais Méndez (65' Ander Barrenetxea), Zubeldía, Martín Zubimendi, Beñat Turrientes, Arsen Zakharyan, Mikel Oyarzabal (80' Umar Sadiq), Mohamed Cho (74' Takefusa Kubo). Coach: Imanol Alguacil.
Red Bull Salzburg: Alexander Schlager, Andreas Ulmer (84' Samson Baidoo), Strahinja Pavlovic (46' Leandro Morgalla), Amar Dedic, Kamil Piatkowski, Mads Bidstrup, Luka Sucic, Nicolás Capaldo, Oscar Gloukh (78' Amankwah Forson), Dorgeles Nene (62' Karim Konaté), Petar Ratkov (62' Roko Simic). Coach: Gerhard Struber.
Referee: Mykola Balakin (UKR) Attendance: 34,419.

12.12.23 Stadio Giuseppe Meazza, Milano: Internazionale Milano – Real Sociedad 0-0
Internazionale Milano: Yann Sommer, Matteo Darmian, Francesco Acerbi, Federico Dimarco (77' Alessandro Bastoni), Carlos Augusto, Henrikh Mkhitaryan (65' Nicolò Barella), Juan Cuadrado, Hakan Çalhanoglu (82' Kristjan Asllani), Davide Frattesi, Alexis Sánchez (65' Lautaro Martínez), Marcus Thuram (65' Marko Arnautovic). Coach: Simone Inzaghi.
Real Sociedad: Álex Remiro, Hamari Traoré, Robin Le Normand, Aihen Muñoz (86' Kieran Tierney), Mikel Merino, Zubeldía (77' Aritz Elustondo), Martín Zubimendi, Takefusa Kubo (86' Carlos Fernández), Arsen Zakharyan (77' Jon Magunazelaia), Umar Sadiq (61' Beñat Turrientes), Mikel Oyarzabal. Coach: Imanol Alguacil.
Referee: Sandro Schärer (SUI) Attendance: 69,010.

12.12.23 Red Bull Arena, Wals-Siezenheim: Red Bull Salzburg – SL Benfica 1-3 (0-2)
Red Bull Salzburg: Alexander Schlager, Strahinja Pavlovic, Amar Dedic, Kamil Piatkowski, Samson Baidoo, Mads Bidstrup (90+5' Roko Simic), Luka Sucic, Lucas Gourna-Douath, Oscar Gloukh (82' Dijon Kameri), Dorgeles Nene (55' Sékou Koïta), Petar Ratkov (55' Fernando). Coach: Gerhard Struber.
SL Benfica: Anatoliy Trubin, Nicolás Otamendi, Tomás Araújo, Morato, Ángel Di María, João Mário (90+1' Arthur Cabral), Fredrik Aursnes, Rafa Silva (90+4' Florentino), Orkun Kökçü (68' Gonçalo Guedes), João Neves, Casper Tengstedt (46' Petar Musa).
Coach: Roger Schmidt.
Goals: 32' Ángel Di María 0-1, 45+1' Rafa Silva 0-2, 57' Luka Sucic 1-2, 90+2' Arthur Cabral 1-3.
Referee: Daniel Siebert (GER) Attendance: 27,134.

GROUP E

19.09.23 De Kuip, Rotterdam: Feyenoord Rotterdam – Celtic FC 2-0 (1-0)
Feyenoord Rotterdam: Timon Wellenreuther, Gernot Trauner, Dávid Hancko, Lutsharel Geertruida, Quilindschy Hartman, Luka Ivanusec (89' Leo Sauer), Calvin Stengs, Quinten Timber (73' Ramiz Zerrouki), Mats Wieffer, Igor Paixão (67' Alireza Jahanbakhsh), Yankuba Minteh (67' Ondrej Lingr). Coach: Arne Slot.
Celtic FC: Joe Hart, Greg Taylor, Liam Scales, Gustaf Lagerbielke, Alistair Johnston, Callum McGregor, Matt O'Riley (82' Paulo Bernardo), Reo Hatate (58' Odin Holm), Daizen Maeda (82' Oh Hyeon-Gyu), Kyogo Furuhashi (67' Tomoki Iwata), Luis Palma (58' Yang Hyun-Jun). Coach: Brendan Rodgers.
Goals: 45+2' Calvin Stengs 1-0, 76' Alireza Jahanbakhsh 2-0.
Referee: Irfan Peljto (BIH) Attendance: 44,008.
Sent off: 64' Gustaf Lagerbielke, 68' Odin Holm.

Igor Paixão missed a penalty kick (66').

171

19.09.23   Stadio Olimpico, Roma: Lazio Roma – Atlético Madrid 1-1 (0-1)
Lazio Roma: Ivan Provedel, Patric, Alessio Romagnoli, Adam Marusic, Luca Pellegrini (38'
Manuel Lazzari), Matías Vecino (76' Danilo Cataldi), Luis Alberto, Felipe Anderson (62'
Gustav Isaksen), Mattia Zaccagni (76' Pedro), Daichi Kamada (62' Mattéo Guendouzi), Ciro
Immobile. Coach: Maurizio Sarri.
Atlético Madrid: Jan Oblak, Stefan Savic, Mario Hermoso, Nahuel Molina, Axel Witsel (75'
Ángel Correa), Saúl, Marcos Llorente, Pablo Barrios (46' José Giménez), Antoine Griezmann,
Álvaro Morata, Samuel Lino (79' Rodrigo Riquelme). Coach: Diego Simeone.
Goals: 29' Pablo Barrios 0-1, 90+5' Ivan Provedel 1-1.
Referee: Slavko Vincic (SVN)   Attendance: 46,168.

04.10.23   Estádio Cívitas Metropolitano, Madrid:
           Atlético Madrid – Feyenoord Rotterdam 3-2 (2-2)
Atlético Madrid: Jan Oblak, César Azpilicueta, Mario Hermoso, Nahuel Molina (79' Rodrigo
Riquelme), Axel Witsel, Saúl, Koke, Rodrigo De Paul (46' Marcos Llorente), Antoine
Griezmann (79' Ángel Correa), Álvaro Morata (90+4' Ilias Kostis), Samuel Lino (62' Javi
Galán). Coach: Diego Simeone.
Feyenoord Rotterdam: Timon Wellenreuther, Gernot Trauner (73' Bart Nieuwkoop), Dávid
Hancko, Lutsharel Geertruida, Quilindschy Hartman, Calvin Stengs, Quinten Timber, Mats
Wieffer (74' Ondrej Lingr), Ramiz Zerrouki (78' Alireza Jahanbakhsh), Ayase Ueda (60'
Yankuba Minteh), Igor Paixão. Coach: Arne Slot.
Goals: 7' Mario Hermoso 0-1 (og), 12' Álvaro Morata 1-1, 34' Dávid Hancko 1-2,
45+4' Antoine Griezmann 2-2, 47' Álvaro Morata 3-2.
Referee: François Letexier (FRA)   Attendance: 61,742.

04.10.23   Celtic Park, Glasgow: Celtic FC – Lazio Roma 1-2 (1-1)
Celtic FC: Joe Hart, Greg Taylor, Liam Scales, Nathaniel Phillips (62' Cameron Carter-
Vickers), Alistair Johnston, Callum McGregor, Matt O'Riley, Reo Hatate (72' Paulo
Bernardo), Daizen Maeda, Kyogo Furuhashi (86' Oh Hyeon-Gyu), Yang Hyun-Jun (62' Luis
Palma). Coach: Brendan Rodgers.
Lazio Roma: Ivan Provedel, Elseid Hysaj, Patric, Alessio Romagnoli, Matías Vecino, Luis
Alberto (68' Mattéo Guendouzi), Felipe Anderson (68' Gustav Isaksen), Manuel Lazzari (84'
Adam Marusic), Mattia Zaccagni (84' Pedro), Daichi Kamada, Ciro Immobile (72' Taty
Castellanos). Coach: Maurizio Sarri.
Goals: 12' Kyogo Furuhashi 1-0, 29' Matías Vecino 1-1, 90+5' Pedro 1-2.
Referee: Donatas Rumsas (LTU)   Attendance: 56,063.

25.10.23   De Kuip, Rotterdam: Feyenoord Rotterdam – Lazio Roma 3-1 (2-0)
Feyenoord Rotterdam: Justin Bijlow, Bart Nieuwkoop (46' Marcos López), Dávid Hancko,
Lutsharel Geertruida, Quilindschy Hartman, Calvin Stengs (78' Luka Ivanusec), Quinten
Timber, Mats Wieffer, Ramiz Zerrouki (89' Ondrej Lingr), Santiago Giménez (79' Ayase
Ueda), Igor Paixão (71' Alireza Jahanbakhsh). Coach: Arne Slot.
Lazio Roma: Ivan Provedel, Elseid Hysaj (46' Manuel Lazzari), Alessio Romagnoli, Adam
Marusic, Nicolò Casale, Matías Vecino (78' Danilo Cataldi), Luis Alberto, Felipe Anderson
(68' Pedro), Mattia Zaccagni, Nicolò Rovella (46' Mattéo Guendouzi), Ciro Immobile (55'
Taty Castellanos). Coach: Maurizio Sarri.
Goals: 31' Santiago Giménez 1-0, 45+2' Ramiz Zerrouki 2-0, 74' Santiago Giménez 3-0,
83' Pedro 3-1 (p).
Referee: Tobias Stieler (GER)   Attendance: 44,031.

172

25.10.23   Celtic Park, Glasgow: Celtic FC – Atlético Madrid 2-2 (2-1)
Celtic FC: Joe Hart, Cameron Carter-Vickers, Greg Taylor, Liam Scales, Alistair Johnston, Callum McGregor, Matt O'Riley, Reo Hatate (7' Paulo Bernardo), Daizen Maeda, Kyogo Furuhashi (80' James Forrest), Luis Palma (62' Nathaniel Phillips). Coach: Brendan Rodgers.
Atlético Madrid: Jan Oblak, Stefan Savic, Mario Hermoso, Javi Galán (46' Marcos Llorente), Nahuel Molina, Axel Witsel, Saúl (46' Rodrigo Riquelme), Koke, Rodrigo De Paul, Antoine Griezmann, Álvaro Morata (73' Ángel Correa). Coach: Diego Simeone.
Goals: 4' Kyogo Furuhashi 1-0, 25' Antoine Griezmann 1-1, 28' Luis Palma 2-1, 53' Álvaro Morata 2-2.
Referee: Felix Zwayer (GER)   Attendance: 55,844.
Sent off: 82' Rodrigo De Paul.

Antoine Griezmann missed a penalty kick (25').

07.11.23   Estádio Cívitas Metropolitano, Madrid: Atlético Madrid – Celtic FC 6-0 (2-0)

Atlético Madrid: Jan Oblak, José Giménez (77' Çaglar Söyüncü), Mario Hermoso, Nahuel Molina (71' César Azpilicueta), Axel Witsel, Koke, Rodrigo Riquelme (65' Samuel Lino), Pablo Barrios (46' Marcos Llorente), Antoine Griezmann (65' Saúl), Álvaro Morata, Ángel Correa. Coach: Diego Simeone.
Celtic FC: Joe Hart, Cameron Carter-Vickers, Greg Taylor, Liam Scales, Alistair Johnston, Callum McGregor (71' Tomoki Iwata), Matt O'Riley (46' Odin Holm), Paulo Bernardo (61' David Turnbull), Daizen Maeda, Kyogo Furuhashi (61' Yang Hyun-Jun), Luis Palma (46' Oh Hyeon-Gyu). Coach: Brendan Rodgers.
Goals: 6' Antoine Griezmann 1-0, 45+2' Álvaro Morata 2-0, 60' Antoine Griezmann 3-0, 66' Samuel Lino 4-0, 76' Álvaro Morata 5-0, 84' Saúl 6-0.
Referee: Ivan Kruzliak (SVK)   Attendance: 60,863.
Sent off: 23' Daizen Maeda.

07.11.23   Stadio Olimpico, Roma: Lazio Roma – Feyenoord Rotterdam 1-0 (1-0)
Lazio Roma: Ivan Provedel, Elseid Hysaj (78' Luca Pellegrini), Patric, Alessio Romagnoli, Matías Vecino (78' Nicolò Rovella), Luis Alberto, Felipe Anderson, Manuel Lazzari, Mattia Zaccagni (63' Pedro), Daichi Kamada (53' Mattéo Guendouzi), Ciro Immobile (63' Taty Castellanos). Coach: Maurizio Sarri.
Feyenoord Rotterdam: Justin Bijlow, Bart Nieuwkoop (20' Gernot Trauner, 74' Alireza Jahanbakhsh), Dávid Hancko, Lutsharel Geertruida, Quilindschy Hartman, Calvin Stengs, Quinten Timber (81' Antoni Milambo), Mats Wieffer, Ramiz Zerrouki (81' Ayase Ueda), Santiago Giménez, Igor Paixão (74' Luka Ivanusec). Coach: Arne Slot.
Goal: 45+1' Ciro Immobile 1-0.
Referee: Szymon Marciniak (POL)   Attendance: 36,612.

28.11.23   Stadio Olimpico, Roma: Lazio Roma – Celtic FC 2-0 (0-0)
Lazio Roma: Ivan Provedel, Patric, Adam Marusic, Mario Gila, Luis Alberto (84' Daichi Kamada), Felipe Anderson (61' Pedro), Manuel Lazzari, Mattéo Guendouzi, Nicolò Rovella (79' Danilo Cataldi), Gustav Isaksen, Taty Castellanos (61' Ciro Immobile). Coach: Maurizio Sarri.
Celtic FC: Joe Hart, Cameron Carter-Vickers, Greg Taylor, Liam Scales, Alistair Johnston, James Forrest (61' Mikey Johnston), Callum McGregor, Matt O'Riley, Paulo Bernardo (69' Oh Hyeon-Gyu), Kyogo Furuhashi, Yang Hyun-Jun (86' David Turnbull). Coach: Brendan Rodgers.
Goals: 82' Ciro Immobile 1-0, 85' Ciro Immobile 2-0.
Referee: Halil Umut Meler (TUR)   Attendance: 50,555.

28.11.23   De Kuip, Rotterdam: Feyenoord Rotterdam – Atlético Madrid 1-3 (0-1)
Feyenoord Rotterdam: Justin Bijlow, Gernot Trauner (64' Antoni Milambo), Dávid Hancko,
Lutsharel Geertruida, Quilindschy Hartman, Calvin Stengs (70' Luka Ivanusec), Quinten
Timber (78' Leo Sauer), Mats Wieffer, Santiago Giménez, Igor Paixão (46' Ayase Ueda),
Yankuba Minteh (63' Ondrej Lingr). Coach: Arne Slot.
Atlético Madrid: Jan Oblak, José Giménez, Mario Hermoso, Nahuel Molina, Axel Witsel,
Koke (84' Ángel Correa), Rodrigo De Paul (74' Saúl), Marcos Llorente (56' Pablo Barrios),
Rodrigo Riquelme, Antoine Griezmann, Álvaro Morata (74' Memphis Depay).
Coach: Diego Simeone.
Goals: 14' Lutsharel Geertruida 0-1 (og), 57' Mario Hermoso 0-2, 77' Mats Wieffer 1-2,
81' Santiago Giménez 1-3 (og).
Referee: Anthony Taylor (ENG)   Attendance: 43,992.

13.12.23   Estádio Cívitas Metropolitano, Madrid: Atlético Madrid – Lazio Roma 2-0 (1-0)
Atlético Madrid: Jan Oblak, Stefan Savic (68' César Azpilicueta), José Giménez (46' Çaglar
Söyüncü), Mario Hermoso, Nahuel Molina, Axel Witsel (63' Koke), Saúl, Rodrigo De Paul,
Antoine Griezmann (46' Memphis Depay), Ángel Correa (63' Álvaro Morata), Samuel Lino.
Coach: Diego Simeone.
Lazio Roma: Ivan Provedel, Elseid Hysaj (70' Luca Pellegrini), Adam Marusic (58' Manuel
Lazzari), Nicolò Casale, Mario Gila, Matías Vecino, Luis Alberto (63' Daichi Kamada), Mattia
Zaccagni, Mattéo Guendouzi, Pedro (58' Felipe Anderson), Ciro Immobile (63' Taty
Castellanos). Coach: Maurizio Sarri.
Goals: 6' Antoine Griezmann 1-0, 51' Samuel Lino 2-0.
Referee: Serdar Gözübüyük (HOL)   Attendance: 63,574.

13.12.23   Celtic Park, Glasgow: Celtic FC – Feyenoord Rotterdam 2-1 (1-0)
Celtic FC: Joe Hart, Greg Taylor, Liam Scales, Stephen Welsh (75' Gustaf Lagerbielke),
Alistair Johnston, Callum McGregor, Tomoki Iwata (19' Paulo Bernardo), Matt O'Riley,
Mikey Johnston (68' James Forrest), Kyogo Furuhashi (68' Oh Hyeon-Gyu), Luis Palma (75'
Mitchel Frame). Coach: Brendan Rodgers.
Feyenoord Rotterdam: Justin Bijlow, Dávid Hancko, Lutsharel Geertruida, Quilindschy
Hartman, Thomas Beelen (79' Javairô Dilrosun), Luka Ivanusec (67' Ayase Ueda), Calvin
Stengs (54' Mats Wieffer), Quinten Timber (54' Thomas van den Belt), Ramiz Zerrouki,
Santiago Giménez, Igor Paixão (54' Yankuba Minteh). Coach: Arne Slot.
Goals: 33' Luis Palma 1-0 (p), 82' Yankuba Minteh 1-1, 90+1' Gustaf Lagerbielke 2-1.
Referee: Benoît Bastien (FRA)   Attendance: 56,391.

GROUP F

19.09.23   Stadio Giuseppe Meazza, Milano: AC Milan – Newcastle United 0-0
AC Milan: Mike Maignan (81' Marco Sportiello), Davide Calabria (46' Alessandro Florenzi),
Fikayo Tomori, Theo Hernández, Malick Thiaw, Ruben Loftus-Cheek (72' Yunus Musah),
Rade Krunic, Tommaso Pobega (61' Tijjani Reijnders), Olivier Giroud, Rafael Leão, Samuel
Chukwueze (61' Christian Pulisic). Coach: Stefano Pioli.
Newcastle United: Nick Pope, Kieran Trippier, Fabian Schär, Dan Burn, Sven Botman, Jacob
Murphy (63' Callum Wilson), Bruno Guimarães, Sean Longstaff, Sandro Tonali (72' Elliot
Anderson), Alexander Isak (90+1' Harvey Barnes), Anthony Gordon (63' Miguel Almirón).
Coach: Eddie Howe.
Referee: José María Sánchez Martínez (ESP)   Attendance: 65,695.

19.09.23   Parc des Princes, Paris: Paris Saint-Germain – Borussia Dortmund 2-0 (0-0)
Paris Saint-Germain: Gianluigi Donnarumma, Marquinhos, Milan Skriniar, Lucas Hernández
(88' Danilo Pereira), Achraf Hakimi, Manuel Ugarte, Vitinha (80' Lee Kang-In), Warren
Zaïre-Emery, Ousmane Dembélé, Kylian Mbappé, Randal Kolo Muani (80' Gonçalo Ramos).
Coach: Luis Enrique.
Borussia Dortmund: Gregor Kobel, Mats Hummels, Niklas Süle, Julian Ryerson, Nico
Schlotterbeck, Marcel Sabitzer (14' Felix Nmecha), Emre Can (76' Jamie Bynoe-Gittens),
Julian Brandt (62' Marco Reus), Marius Wolf (78' Ramy Bensebaïni), Donyell Malen (62'
Niclas Füllkrug), Karim Adeyemi. Coach: Edin Terzic.
Goals: 49' Kylian Mbappé 1-0 (p), 58' Achraf Hakimi 2-0.
Referee: Jesús Gil Manzano (ESP)   Attendance: 47,379.

04.10.23   SIGNAL IDUNA PARK, Dortmund: Borussia Dortmund – AC Milan 0-0
Borussia Dortmund: Gregor Kobel, Mats Hummels, Ramy Bensebaïni, Julian Ryerson, Nico
Schlotterbeck, Marco Reus (72' Felix Nmecha), Emre Can, Julian Brandt (64' Karim
Adeyemi), Salih Özcan, Niclas Füllkrug (85' Youssoufa Moukoko), Donyell Malen (72' Jamie
Bynoe-Gittens). Coach: Edin Terzic.
AC Milan: Mike Maignan, Davide Calabria (69' Alessandro Florenzi), Fikayo Tomori, Theo
Hernández, Malick Thiaw, Christian Pulisic (69' Samuel Chukwueze), Tommaso Pobega (58'
Yacine Adli), Tijjani Reijnders, Yunus Musah, Olivier Giroud (69' Noah Okafor), Rafael
Leão. Coach: Stefano Pioli.
Referee: Szymon Marciniak (POL)   Attendance: 81,365.

04.10.23   St. James' Park, Newcastle upon Tyne:
          Newcastle United – Paris Saint-Germain 4-1 (2-0)
Newcastle United: Nick Pope, Kieran Trippier, Fabian Schär, Dan Burn, Jamaal Lascelles,
Miguel Almirón (71' Jacob Murphy), Bruno Guimarães, Sean Longstaff, Sandro Tonali (65'
Elliot Anderson), Alexander Isak, Anthony Gordon (90+3' Matt Targett). Coach: Eddie Howe.
Paris Saint-Germain: Gianluigi Donnarumma, Marquinhos, Milan Skriniar, Lucas Hernández,
Achraf Hakimi, Manuel Ugarte (64' Vitinha), Warren Zaïre-Emery, Ousmane Dembélé, Kylian
Mbappé, Randal Kolo Muani (57' Bradley Barcola), Gonçalo Ramos. Coach: Luis Enrique.
Goals: 17' Miguel Almirón 1-0, 39' Dan Burn 2-0, 50' Sean Longstaff 3-0,
56' Lucas Hernández 3-1, 90+1' Fabian Schär 4-1.
Referee: István Kovács (ROM)   Attendance: 52,009.

25.10.23   Parc des Princes, Paris: Paris Saint-Germain – AC Milan 3-0 (1-0)
Paris Saint-Germain: Gianluigi Donnarumma, Marquinhos, Milan Skriniar, Lucas Hernández,
Achraf Hakimi (90+3' Nordi Mukiele), Manuel Ugarte (71' Fabián Ruiz), Vitinha, Warren
Zaïre-Emery, Ousmane Dembélé (71' Lee Kang-In), Kylian Mbappé, Randal Kolo Muani (82'
Gonçalo Ramos). Coach: Luis Enrique.
AC Milan: Mike Maignan, Fikayo Tomori (90' Simon Kjær), Theo Hernández, Pierre Kalulu,
Malick Thiaw (46' Davide Calabria), Rade Krunic (77' Yacine Adli), Christian Pulisic, Tijjani
Reijnders, Yunus Musah (77' Tommaso Pobega), Olivier Giroud, Rafael Leão.
Coach: Stefano Pioli.
Goals: 32' Kylian Mbappé 1-0, 53' Randal Kolo Muani 2-0, 89' Lee Kang-In 3-0.
Referee: Slavko Vincic (SVN)   Attendance: 47,356.

25.10.23   St. James' Park, Newcastle upon Tyne:
Newcastle United – Borussia Dortmund 0-1 (0-1)
Newcastle United: Nick Pope, Kieran Trippier, Fabian Schär, Dan Burn (70' Matt Targett),
Jamaal Lascelles, Miguel Almirón, Bruno Guimarães, Sean Longstaff (65' Sandro Tonali),
Joelinton (65' Jacob Murphy, 70' Joe Willock), Alexander Isak (15' Callum Wilson), Anthony
Gordon. Coach: Eddie Howe.
Borussia Dortmund: Gregor Kobel, Mats Hummels, Ramy Bensebaïni, Nico Schlotterbeck,
Marco Reus (63' Karim Adeyemi), Marcel Sabitzer, Emre Can (43' Salih Özcan), Marius
Wolf, Felix Nmecha (79' Gio Reyna), Niclas Füllkrug (79' Sébastien Haller), Donyell Malen
(79' Niklas Süle). Coach: Edin Terzic.
Goal: 45' Felix Nmecha 0-1.
Referee: Artur Soares Dias (POR)   Attendance: 52,024.

07.11.23   SIGNAL IDUNA PARK, Dortmund:
Borussia Dortmund – Newcastle United 2-0 (1-0)
Borussia Dortmund: Gregor Kobel, Mats Hummels, Niklas Süle, Julian Ryerson, Nico
Schlotterbeck, Marcel Sabitzer, Julian Brandt, Salih Özcan, Felix Nmecha, Niclas Füllkrug
(87' Youssoufa Moukoko), Karim Adeyemi (80' Marco Reus). Coach: Edin Terzic.
Newcastle United: Nick Pope, Kieran Trippier, Fabian Schär, Jamaal Lascelles, Tino
Livramento, Lewis Hall (46' Miguel Almirón), Joe Willock (80' Lewis Miley), Bruno
Guimarães, Sean Longstaff, Callum Wilson (46' Anthony Gordon), Joelinton.
Coach: Eddie Howe.
Goals: 26' Niclas Füllkrug 1-0, 79' Julian Brandt 2-0.
Referee: Alejandro Hernández Hernández (ESP)   Attendance: 81,365.

07.11.23   Stadio Giuseppe Meazza, Milano: AC Milan – Paris Saint-Germain 2-1 (1-1)
AC Milan: Mike Maignan, Davide Calabria, Fikayo Tomori, Theo Hernández, Malick Thiaw,
Ruben Loftus-Cheek, Christian Pulisic (90+2' Alessandro Florenzi), Tijjani Reijnders, Yunus
Musah (84' Rade Krunic), Olivier Giroud, Rafael Leão (85' Noah Okafor).
Coach: Stefano Pioli.
Paris Saint-Germain: Gianluigi Donnarumma, Marquinhos, Milan Skriniar (89' Bradley
Barcola), Lucas Hernández (64' Nordi Mukiele), Achraf Hakimi, Manuel Ugarte (60' Fabián
Ruiz), Vitinha (60' Lee Kang-In), Warren Zaïre-Emery, Ousmane Dembélé, Kylian Mbappé,
Randal Kolo Muani (60' Gonçalo Ramos). Coach: Luis Enrique.
Goals: 9' Milan Skriniar 0-1, 12' Rafael Leão 1-1, 50' Olivier Giroud 2-1.
Referee: Jesús Gil Manzano (ESP)   Attendance: 75,649.

28.11.23   Parc des Princes, Paris: Paris Saint-Germain – Newcastle United 1-1 (0-1)
Paris Saint-Germain: Gianluigi Donnarumma, Milan Skriniar, Lucas Hernández, Achraf
Hakimi, Danilo Pereira (85' Gonçalo Ramos), Fabián Ruiz, Manuel Ugarte (62' Vitinha), Lee
Kang-In (82' Marco Asencio), Ousmane Dembélé, Kylian Mbappé, Randal Kolo Muani (62'
Bradley Barcola). Coach: Luis Enrique.
Newcastle United: Nick Pope, Kieran Trippier, Fabian Schär, Jamaal Lascelles, Tino
Livramento, Miguel Almirón, Bruno Guimarães, Lewis Miley, Joelinton, Alexander Isak,
Anthony Gordon. Coach: Eddie Howe.
Goals: 24' Alexander Isak 0-1, 90+8' Kylian Mbappé 1-1 (p).
Referee: Szymon Marciniak (POL)   Attendance: 46,435.

176

28.11.23   Stadio Giuseppe Meazza, Milano: AC Milan – Borussia Dortmund 1-3 (1-1)
AC Milan: Mike Maignan, Davide Calabria, Fikayo Tomori, Theo Hernández, Malick Thiaw
(53' Rade Krunic), Ruben Loftus-Cheek, Christian Pulisic, Yacine Adli (77' Luka Jovic),
Tijjani Reijnders, Olivier Giroud, Samuel Chukwueze (77' Chaka Traoré).
Coach: Stefano Pioli.
Borussia Dortmund: Gregor Kobel, Mats Hummels, Ramy Bensebaïni, Julian Ryerson, Nico
Schlotterbeck (55' Salih Özcan), Marco Reus (79' Julian Brandt), Marcel Sabitzer, Emre Can,
Niclas Füllkrug, Donyell Malen (55' Karim Adeyemi), Jamie Bynoe-Gittens (66' Marius
Wolf). Coach: Edin Terzic.
Goals: 10' Marco Reus 0-1 (p), 37' Samuel Chukwueze 1-1, 59' Jamie Bynoe-Gittens 1-2,
69' Karim Adeyemi 1-3.
Referee: István Kovács (ROM)   Attendance: 75,292.

Olivier Giroud missed a penalty kick (6').

13.12.23   SIGNAL IDUNA PARK, Dortmund:
            Borussia Dortmund – Paris Saint-Germain 1-1 (0-0)
Borussia Dortmund: Gregor Kobel, Mats Hummels, Niklas Süle, Ramy Bensebaïni, Marco
Reus, Julian Brandt, Marius Wolf (69' Nico Schlotterbeck), Salih Özcan (69' Marcel Sabitzer),
Niclas Füllkrug (81' Sébastien Haller), Karim Adeyemi (81' Gio Reyna), Jamie Bynoe-Gittens
(60' Donyell Malen). Coach: Edin Terzic.
Paris Saint-Germain: Gianluigi Donnarumma, Marquinhos, Milan Skriniar, Lucas Hernández,
Achraf Hakimi, Vitinha, Lee Kang-In (68' Manuel Ugarte), Warren Zaïre-Emery, Kylian
Mbappé, Randal Kolo Muani (90+6' Carlos Soler), Bradley Barcola (82' Marco Asensio).
Coach: Luis Enrique.
Goals: 51' Karim Adeyemi 1-0, 56' Warren Zaïre-Emery 1-1.
Referee: Glenn Nyberg (SWE)   Attendance: 81,365.

13.12.23   St. James' Park, Newcastle upon Tyne: Newcastle United – AC Milan 1-2 (1-0)
Newcastle United: Martin Dúbravka, Kieran Trippier (63' Dan Burn), Fabian Schär, Jamaal
Lascelles, Tino Livramento, Miguel Almirón, Bruno Guimarães, Lewis Miley (71' Sean
Longstaff), Callum Wilson, Joelinton, Anthony Gordon (62' Alexander Isak).
Coach: Eddie Howe.
AC Milan: Mike Maignan, Alessandro Florenzi, Davide Calabria, Fikayo Tomori, Theo
Hernández, Ruben Loftus-Cheek (73' Tommaso Pobega), Christian Pulisic (73' Luka Jovic),
Tijjani Reijnders, Yunus Musah (83' Samuel Chukwueze), Olivier Giroud (83' Noah Okafor),
Rafael Leão (88' Davide Bartesaghi). Coach: Stefano Pioli.
Goals: 33' Joelinton 1-0, 59' Christian Pulisic 1-1, 84' Samuel Chukwueze 1-2.
Referee: Danny Makkelie (HOL)   Attendance: 52,037.

GROUP G

19.09.23   Stadion Wankdorf, Bern: BSC Young Boys – RB Leipzig 1-3 (1-1)
BSC Young Boys: Anthony Racioppi, Loris Benito, Saïdy Janko (69' Lewin Blum), Ulisses
Garcia (77' Noah Persson), Mohamed Camara, Aurèle Amenda, Sandro Lauper (77' Darian
Males), Filip Ugrinic, Cheikh Niasse (85' Jean-Pierre Nsame), Cedric Itten (69' Silvère
Ganvoula), Meschack Elia. Coach: Raphaël Wicky.
RB Leipzig: Janis Blaswich, Benjamin Henrichs, David Raum, Mohamed Simakan, Castello
Lukeba, Emil Forsberg (79' Christoph Baumgartner), Kevin Kampl, Xaver Schlager, Xavi
Simons (88' Timo Werner), Yussuf Poulsen (64' Benjamin Sesko), Loïs Openda (88'
Christopher Lenz). Coach: Marco Rose.
Goals: 3' Mohamed Simakan 0-1, 33' Meschack Elia 1-1, 73' Xaver Schlager 1-2,
90+2' Benjamin Sesko 1-3.
Referee: Enea Jorgji (ALB)   Attendance: 31,500.

19.09.23   Etihad Stadium, Manchester: Manchester City – Crvena Zvezda Beograd 3-1 (0-1)
Manchester City: Ederson, Kyle Walker, Nathan Aké, Rúben Dias (84' Rico Lewis), Bernardo
Silva (44' Jérémy Doku), Rodri (83' Kalvin Phillips), Phil Foden (83' Oscar Bobb), Sergio
Gómez (58' Manuel Akanji), Matheus Nunes, Erling Haaland, Julián Álvarez.
Coach: Pep Guardiola.
Crvena Zvezda Beograd: Omri Glazer, Aleksandar Dragovic, Milan Rodic, Nasser Djiga,
Srdjan Mijailovic, Mirko Ivanic (68' Peter Olayinka), Hwang In-Beom (82' Kings Kangwa),
Osman Bukari (83' Milos Degenek), Marko Stamenic, Stefan Mitrovic (77' Vladimir Lucic),
Cherif Ndiaye (68' Jean-Philippe Krasso). Coach: Barak Bakhar.
Goals: 45' Osman Bukari 0-1, 47' Julián Álvarez 1-1, 60' Julián Álvarez 2-1, 73' Rodri 3-1.
Referee: João Pedro Pinheiro (POR)   Attendance: 50,204.

04.10.23   Red Bull Arena, Leipzig: RB Leipzig – Manchester City 1-3 (0-1)
RB Leipzig: Janis Blaswich, Lukas Klostermann, David Raum, Mohamed Simakan, Castello
Lukeba, Emil Forsberg (70' Benjamin Sesko), Xaver Schlager, Nicolas Seiwald (85' Amadou
Haïdara), Xavi Simons, Yussuf Poulsen (75' Christoph Baumgartner), Loïs Openda (70' Timo
Werner). Coach: Marco Rose.
Manchester City: Ederson, Kyle Walker, Rúben Dias, Manuel Akanji (72' Jérémy Doku),
Josko Gvardiol, Rico Lewis, Jack Grealish (72' Nathan Aké), Bernardo Silva (87' Matheus
Nunes), Rodri, Phil Foden (79' Julián Álvarez), Erling Haaland. Coach: Pep Guardiola.
Goals: 25' Phil Foden 0-1, 48' Loïs Openda 1-1, 84' Julián Álvarez 1-2,
90+2' Jérémy Doku 1-3.
Referee: Artur Soares Dias (POR)   Attendance: 45,228.

04.10.23   Stadion Rajko Mitic, Beograd:
          Crvena Zvezda Beograd – BSC Young Boys 2-2 (1-0)
Crvena Zvezda Beograd: Omri Glazer, Aleksandar Dragovic, Milan Rodic (62' Peter
Olayinka), Nasser Djiga, Srdjan Mijailovic, Mirko Ivanic, Hwang In-Beom, Osman Bukari,
Marko Stamenic (69' Vladimir Lucic), Stefan Mitrovic (70' Aleksandar Katai), Cherif Ndiaye
(80' Jean-Philippe Krasso). Coach: Barak Bakhar.
BSC Young Boys: Anthony Racioppi, Loris Benito (47' Aurèle Amenda), Saïdy Janko, Ulisses
Garcia, Mohamed Camara, Filip Ugrinic, Cheikh Niasse, Darian Males (74' Miguel Chaiwa),
Cedric Itten (75' Silvère Ganvoula), Meschack Elia, Joël Monteiro. Coach: Raphaël Wicky.
Goals: 35' Cherif Ndiaye 1-0, 48' Filip Ugrinic 1-1, 61' Cedric Itten 1-2 (p),
88' Osman Bukari 2-2.
Referee: William Collum (SCO)   Attendance: 47,201.

25.10.23   Red Bull Arena, Leipzig: RB Leipzig – Crvena Zvezda Beograd 3-1 (1-0)
RB Leipzig: Janis Blaswich, Benjamin Henrichs (58' Lukas Klostermann), David Raum, Mohamed Simakan, Castello Lukeba, Emil Forsberg (58' Christoph Baumgartner), Kevin Kampl, Xaver Schlager, Xavi Simons (75' Dani Olmo), Yussuf Poulsen (82' Timo Werner), Loïs Openda (82' Benjamin Sesko). Coach: Marco Rose.
Crvena Zvezda Beograd: Omri Glazer, Aleksandar Dragovic, Milan Rodic (65' Kosta Nedeljkovic), Nasser Djiga, Srdjan Mijailovic, Mirko Ivanic, Peter Olayinka (46' Osman Bukari), Hwang In-Beom, Marko Stamenic (81' Aleksandar Katai), Stefan Mitrovic (65' Vladimir Lucic), Cherif Ndiaye (65' Jovan Mijatovic). Coach: Barak Bakhar.
Goals: 12' David Raum 1-0, 59' Xavi Simons 2-0, 70' Marko Stamenic 2-1, 84' Dani Olmo 3-1.
Referee: José María Sánchez Martínez (ESP)   Attendance: 42,209.

25.10.23   Stadion Wankdorf, Bern: BSC Young Boys – Manchester City 1-3 (0-0)
BSC Young Boys: Anthony Racioppi, Loris Benito, Ulisses Garcia (80' Noah Persson), Mohamed Camara, Lewin Blum (80' Saïdy Janko), Sandro Lauper (80' Darian Males), Filip Ugrinic, Cheikh Niasse, Cedric Itten (73' Jean-Pierre Nsame), Meschack Elia, Joël Monteiro (72' Silvère Ganvoula). Coach: Raphaël Wicky.
Manchester City: Ederson, Nathan Aké, Rúben Dias, Manuel Akanji, Rico Lewis, Mateo Kovacic, Jack Grealish, Rodri (90' Kalvin Phillips), Matheus Nunes (72' Julián Álvarez), Erling Haaland (90' Sergio Gómez), Jérémy Doku (72' Bernardo Silva).
Coach: Pep Guardiola.
Goals: 48' Manuel Akanji 0-1, 52' Meschack Elia 1-1, 67' Erling Haaland 1-2 (p), 86' Erling Haaland 1-3.
Referee: Morten Krogh Hansen (DEN)   Attendance: 31,500.

07.11.23   Etihad Stadium, Manchester: Manchester City – BSC Young Boys 3-0 (2-0)
Manchester City: Ederson, Kyle Walker (61' Kalvin Phillips), John Stones (46' Nathan Aké), Rúben Dias, Josko Gvardiol, Rico Lewis, Mateo Kovacic (80' Jérémy Doku), Jack Grealish, Phil Foden, Matheus Nunes, Erling Haaland (61' Oscar Bobb). Coach: Pep Guardiola.
BSC Young Boys: Anthony Racioppi, Loris Benito, Saïdy Janko (65' Lewin Blum), Ulisses Garcia (78' Noah Persson), Mohamed Camara, Aurèle Amenda, Sandro Lauper, Filip Ugrinic (88' Darian Males), Cheikh Niasse, Cedric Itten (65' Miguel Chaiwa), Meschack Elia (78' Silvère Ganvoula). Coach: Raphaël Wicky.
Goals: 23' Erling Haaland 1-0 (p), 45+1' Phil Foden 2-0, 51' Erling Haaland 3-0.
Referee: Erik Lambrechts (BEL)   Attendance: 51,049.
Sent off: 53' Sandro Lauper.

07.11.23   Stadion Rajko Mitic, Beograd: Crvena Zvezda Beograd – RB Leipzig 1-2 (0-1)
Crvena Zvezda Beograd: Omri Glazer, Aleksandar Dragovic, Milan Rodic (85' Aleksandar Katai), Nasser Djiga, Srdjan Mijailovic (46' Kosta Nedeljkovic), Guélor Kanga, Mirko Ivanic (70' Peter Olayinka), Hwang In-Beom, Osman Bukari, Jean-Philippe Krasso (46' Cherif Ndiaye), Vladimir Lucic (78' Jovan Mijatovic). Coach: Barak Bakhar.
RB Leipzig: Janis Blaswich, Benjamin Henrichs, David Raum, Mohamed Simakan, Castello Lukeba, Emil Forsberg (70' Christoph Baumgartner), Xaver Schlager (84' Kevin Kampl), Amadou Haïdara (83' Nicolas Seiwald), Xavi Simons (75' Fábio Carvalho), Loïs Openda, Benjamin Sesko (70' Lukas Klostermann). Coach: Marco Rose.
Goals: 8' Xavi Simons 0-1, 77' Loïs Openda 0-2, 81' Benjamin Henrichs 1-2 (og).
Referee: Daniele Orsato (ITA)   Attendance: 41,961.

179

28.11.23   Etihad Stadium, Manchester: Manchester City – RB Leipzig 3-2 (0-2)
Manchester City: Stefan Ortega, Kyle Walker (54' Julián Álvarez), Rúben Dias (46' Nathan
Aké), Manuel Akanji, Josko Gvardiol (90+3' Sergio Gómez), Rico Lewis, Jack Grealish (54'
Jérémy Doku), Bernardo Silva, Rodri, Phil Foden, Erling Haaland. Coach: Pep Guardiola.
RB Leipzig: Janis Blaswich, Lukas Klostermann, David Raum, Mohamed Simakan, Castello
Lukeba, Emil Forsberg (60' Christoph Baumgartner), Xaver Schlager (88' Kevin Kampl),
Amadou Haïdara (74' Fábio Carvalho), Nicolas Seiwald, Xavi Simons (75' Yussuf Poulsen),
Loïs Openda (60' Benjamin Sesko). Coach: Marco Rose.
Goals: 13' Loïs Openda 0-1, 33' Loïs Openda 0-2, 54' Erling Haaland 1-2, 70' Phil Foden 2-2,
87' Julián Álvarez 3-2.
Referee: Glenn Nyberg (SWE)   Attendance: 51,402.

28.11.23   Stadion Wankdorf, Bern: BSC Young Boys – Crvena Zvezda Beograd 2-0 (2-0)
BSC Young Boys: Anthony Racioppi, Loris Benito, Ulisses Garcia, Mohamed Camara, Lewin
Blum, Filip Ugrinic, Cheikh Niasse, Darian Males (46' Ebrima Colley), Jean-Pierre Nsame
(74' Silvère Ganvoula), Meschack Elia, Joël Monteiro (74' Miguel Chaiwa).
Coach: Raphaël Wicky.
Crvena Zvezda Beograd: Omri Glazer, Aleksandar Dragovic, Milan Rodic, Nasser Djiga,
Kosta Nedeljkovic, Srdjan Mijailovic (83' Aleksandar Katai), Mirko Ivanic (59' Jean-Philippe
Krasso), Hwang In-Beom (90' Guélor Kanga), Osman Bukari, Marko Stamenic (59' Vladimir
Lucic), Cherif Ndiaye (46' Jovan Mijatovic). Coach: Barak Bakhar.
Goals: 8' Kosta Nedeljkovic 1-0 (og), 29' Lewin Blum 2-0.
Referee: Danny Makkelie (HOL)   Attendance: 31,500.

13.12.23   Red Bull Arena, Leipzig: RB Leipzig – BSC Young Boys 2-1 (0-0)
RB Leipzig: Péter Gulácsi, Christopher Lenz, Benjamin Henrichs, Mohamed Simakan (59'
Lukas Klostermann), Castello Lukeba (80' Xaver Schlager), Emil Forsberg (74' Xavi Simons),
Kevin Kampl, Nicolas Seiwald, Fábio Carvalho, Yussuf Poulsen (74' Loïs Openda), Benjamin
Sesko (74' Timo Werner). Coach: Marco Rose.
BSC Young Boys: David von Ballmoos, Fabian Lustenberger, Saïdy Janko, Ulisses Garcia,
Aurèle Amenda, Sandro Lauper (70' Lukasz Lakomy), Filip Ugrinic (70' Darian Males),
Cheikh Niasse, Jean-Pierre Nsame (62' Silvère Ganvoula), Meschack Elia (62' Joël Monteiro),
Ebrima Colley (82' Donat Rrudhani). Coach: Raphaël Wicky.
Goals: 51' Benjamin Sesko 1-0, 53' Ebrima Colley 1-1, 56' Emil Forsberg 2-1.
Referee: Manfredas Lukjancukas (LTU)   Attendance: 43,331.

13.12.23   Stadion Rajko Mitic, Beograd: Crvena Zvezda Beograd – Manchester City 2-3 (0-1)
Crvena Zvezda Beograd: Omri Glazer, Aleksandar Dragovic, Uros Spajic (65' Milan Rodic),
Nasser Djiga, Kosta Nedeljkovic (78' Uros Kabic), Srdjan Mijailovic, Guélor Kanga (57'
Aleksandar Katai), Peter Olayinka (57' Vladimir Lucic), Hwang In-Beom, Osman Bukari,
Cherif Ndiaye (57' Jovan Mijatovic). Coach: Barak Bakhar.
Manchester City: Stefan Ortega, John Stones (86' Nathan Aké), Manuel Akanji, Rico Lewis,
Mateo Kovacic (76' Mahamadou Susoho), Jack Grealish (46' Phil Foden), Kalvin Phillips,
Sergio Gómez, Matheus Nunes (82' Bernardo Silva), Micah Hamilton, Oscar Bobb.
Coach: Pep Guardiola.
Goals: 19' Micah Hamilton 0-1, 62' Oscar Bobb 0-2, 76' Hwang In-Beom 1-2,
85' Kalvin Phillips 1-3 (p), 90+1' Aleksandar Katai 2-3.
Referee: Aliyar Aghayev (AZE)   Attendance: 49,443.

GROUP H

19.09.23   Estadi Olímpic Lluís Companys, Barcelona:
FC Barcelona – Royal Antwerp FC 5-0 (3-0)
FC Barcelona: Marc-André ter Stegen, João Cancelo (76' Sergi Roberto), Andreas Christensen, Jules Koundé, Alejandro Balde, Ilkay Gündogan, Frenkie de Jong (58' Oriol Romeu), Gavi (58' Fermín López), Robert Lewandowski, Raphinha (68' Ferran Torres), João Félix (68' Lamine Yamal). Coach: Xavi.
Royal Antwerp FC: Jean Butez, Toby Alderweireld, Owen Wijndal, Jelle Bataille (73' Gyrano Kerk), Soumaïla Coulibaly, Jurgen Ekkelenkamp (61' Alhassan Yusuf), Mandela Keita, Arthur Vermeeren, Vincent Janssen (60' George Ilenikhena), Arbnor Muja (83' Anthony Valencia), Michel Balikwisha (61' Ritchie De Laet). Coach: Mark van Bommel.
Goals: 11' João Félix 1-0, 19' Robert Lewandowski 1-0, 22' Jelle Bataille 3-0 (og), 54' Gavi 4-0, 66' João Félix 5-0.
Referee: Radu Petrescu (ROM)   Attendance: 40,989.

FC Barcelona played their home matches at the Estadi Olímpic Lluís Companys, in Barcelona, instead of their regular stadium, Camp Nou, in Barcelona, which was being renovated.

19.09.23   Volksparkstadion, Hamburg (GER): Shakhtar Donetsk – FC Porto 1-3 (1-3)
Shakhtar Donetsk: Dmytro Riznyk, Yaroslav Rakitskyi, Yukhym Konoplya (76' Giorgi Gocholeishvili), Stav Lemkin (65' Irakli Azarovi), Taras Stepanenko (65' Oleksiy Kashchuk), Oleksandr Zubkov, Yegor Nazaryna, Georgiy Sudakov, Novatus Miroshi, Danylo Sikan (81' Eguinaldo), Kevin Kelsy (65' Artem Bondarenko), Coach: Patrick van Leeuwen.
FC Porto: Diogo Costa, Pepe, Zaidu Sanusi (46' Wendell), João Mário (73' Jorge Sánchez), David Carmo, Stephen Eustáquio, André Franco (82' Gonçalo Borges), Iván Jaime (73' Nico González), Alan Varela, Mehdi Taremi, Galeno (90+1' Francisco Conceição). Coach: Sérgio Conceição.
Goals: 8 Galeno 0-1, 13' Kevin Kelsy 1-1, 15' Galeno 1-2, 29' Mehdi Taremi 1-3.
Referee: Davide Massa (ITA)   Attendance: 46,729.

Due to the Russian invasion of Ukraine, Ukrainian teams were required to play their home matches at neutral venues until further notice.

04.10.23   Bosuilstadion, Deurne: Royal Antwerp FC – Shakhtar Donetsk 2-3 (2-0)
Royal Antwerp FC: Jean Butez, Toby Alderweireld, Owen Wijndal (83' George Ilenikhena), Jelle Bataille, Soumaïla Coulibaly, Jurgen Ekkelenkamp (74' Anthony Valencia), Mandela Keita (83' Alhassan Yusuf), Arthur Vermeeren, Vincent Janssen, Arbnor Muja (87' Zeno Van den Bosch), Michel Balikwisha. Coach: Mark van Bommel.
Shakhtar Donetsk: Dmytro Riznyk, Yaroslav Rakitskyi, Mykola Matvienko, Yukhym Konoplya, Irakli Azarovi, Taras Stepanenko, Oleksandr Zubkov, Yegor Nazaryna, Dmytro Kryskiv, Georgiy Sudakov, Danylo Sikan (87' Marian Shved). Coach: Patrick van Leeuwen.
Goals: 3' Arbnor Muja 1-0, 33' Michel Balikwisha 2-0, 48' Danylo Sikan 2-1, 71' Yaroslav Rakitskyi 2-2, 76' Danylo Sikan 2-3.
Referee: Rade Obrenovic (SVN)   Attendance: 13,509.

Toby Alderweireld missed a penalty kick (90+7).

04.10.23   Estádio Do Dragão, Porto: FC Porto – FC Barcelona 0-1 (0-1)
FC Porto: Diogo Costa, Wendell, Fábio Cardoso, João Mário (85' Nico González), David
Carmo, Stephen Eustáquio, Romário Baró (64' Evanilson), Alan Varela (85' Francisco
Conceição), Mehdi Taremi (85' Danny Namaso), Galeno (85' Iván Jaime), Pepê Aquino.
Coach: Sérgio Conceição.
FC Barcelona: Marc-André ter Stegen, João Cancelo, Jules Koundé, Ronald Araujo, Alejandro
Balde, Ilkay Gündogan, Oriol Romeu (69' Sergi Roberto), Gavi, Robert Lewandowski (34'
Ferran Torres), João Félix (69' Fermín López), Lamine Yamal (80' Marcos Alonso).
Coach: Xavi.
Goal: 45+1' Ferran Torres 0-1.
Referee: Anthony Taylor (ENG)   Attendance: 49,722.
Sent off: 90+3' Gavi.

25.10.23   Estadi Olímpic Lluís Companys, Barcelona:
           FC Barcelona – Shakhtar Donetsk 2-1 (2-0)
FC Barcelona: Marc-André ter Stegen, Marcos Alonso (71' Alejandro Balde), Iñigo Martínez
(82' Andreas Christensen), João Cancelo, Ronald Araújo, Ilkay Gündogan, Oriol Romeu,
Fermín López (82' Marc Casadó), Ferran Torres, João Félix (75' Marc Guiu), Lamine Yamal.
Coach: Xavi.
Shakhtar Donetsk: Dmytro Riznyk, Mykola Matvienko, Valeriy Bondar, Yukhym Konoplya,
Irakli Azarovi, Taras Stepanenko (90+2' Eguinaldo), Oleksandr Zubkov, Dmytro Kryskiv (63'
Newerton), Artem Bondarenko, Georgiy Sudakov, Danylo Sikan (70' Kevin Kelsy).
Coach: Marino Pusic.
Goals: 28' Ferran Torres 1-0 36' Fermín López 2-0, 62' Georgiy Sudakov 2-1.
Referee: Ivan Kruzliak (SVK)   Attendance: 41,409.

25.10.23   Bosuilstadion, Deurne: Royal Antwerp FC – FC Porto 1-4 (1-0)
Royal Antwerp FC: Jean Butez, Ritchie De Laet (60' Owen Wijndal), Toby Alderweireld, Jelle
Bataille, Soumaïla Coulibaly, Jurgen Ekkelenkamp, Alhassan Yusuf, Arthur Vermeeren,
Vincent Janssen (77' George Ilenikhena), Arbnor Muja (77' Chidera Ejuke), Michel
Balikwisha (77' Anthony Valencia, 90' Gyrano Kerk). Coach: Mark van Bommel.
FC Porto: Diogo Costa, Pepe, Wendell (44' Evanilson), João Mário, David Carmo, Stephen
Eustáquio (82' Marko Grujic), André Franco (65' Jorge Sánchez), Alan Varela (83' Nico
González), Mehdi Taremi, Galeno, Pepê Aquino (83' Francisco Conceição).
Coach: Sérgio Conceição.
Goals: 37' Alhassan Yusuf 1-0, 46' Evanilson 1-1, 54' Stephen Eustáquio 1-2,
69' Evanilson 1-3, 84' Evanilson 1-4.
Referee: Benoît Bastien (FRA)   Attendance: 13,651.

07.11.23   Volksparkstadion, Hamburg (GER): Shakhtar Donetsk – FC Barcelona 1-0 (1-0)
Shakhtar Donetsk: Dmytro Riznyk, Yaroslav Rakitskyi, Mykola Matvienko, Valeriy Bondar,
Giorgi Gocholeishvili, Taras Stepanenko (72' Yegor Nazaryna), Oleksandr Zubkov, Dmytro
Kryskiv, Georgiy Sudakov, Danylo Sikan (62' Kevin Kelsy), Newerton (90+8' Marian Shved).
Coach: Marino Pusic.
FC Barcelona: Marc-André ter Stegen, Marcos Alonso (60' Alejandro Balde), João Cancelo,
Andreas Christensen, Ronald Araújo, Ilkay Gündogan, Oriol Romeu (59' Pedri), Gavi (81'
Fermín López), Robert Lewandowski, Ferran Torres (59' João Félix), Raphinha (59' Lamine
Yamal). Coach: Xavi.
Goal: 40' Danylo Sikan 1-0.
Referee: Irfan Peljto (BIH)   Attendance: 49,147.

182

07.11.23   Estádio Do Dragão, Porto: FC Porto – Royal Antwerp FC 2-0 (1-0)
FC Porto: Diogo Costa, Pepe, Zaidu Sanusi (83' Jorge Sánchez), João Mário, David Carmo, Stephen Eustáquio, André Franco (82' Danny Namaso), Alan Varela, Mehdi Taremi (69' Francisco Conceição), Pepê Aquino, Evanilson (83' Fran Navarro). Coach: Sérgio Conceição.
Royal Antwerp FC: Senne Lammens, Ritchie De Laet (46' Jelle Bataille), Owen Wijndal (69' Kobe Corbanie), Soumaïla Coulibaly, Zeno Van den Bosch, Jurgen Ekkelenkamp, Alhassan Yusuf, Arthur Vermeeren, Gyrano Kerk (75' Chidera Ejuke), Michel Balikwisha (69' Arbnor Muja), George Ilenikhena (75' Vincent Janssen). Coach: Mark van Bommel.
Goals: 32' Evanilson 1-0 (p), 90+1' Pepe 2-0.
Referee: Maurizio Mariani (ITA)   Attendance: 44,830.
Sent off: 52' Jurgen Ekkelenkamp.

28.11.23   Volksparkstadion, Hamburg (GER):
            Shakhtar Donetsk – Royal Antwerp FC 1-0 (1-0)
Shakhtar Donetsk: Dmytro Riznyk, Mykola Matvienko, Valeriy Bondar, Giorgi Gocholeishvili, Irakli Azarovi, Taras Stepanenko, Oleksandr Zubkov, Dmytro Kryskiv (89' Kevin Kelsy), Georgiy Sudakov, Danylo Sikan (90+6' Yaroslav Rakitskyi), Newerton (70' Artem Bondarenko). Coach: Marino Pusic.
Royal Antwerp FC: Jean Butez, Toby Alderweireld, Owen Wijndal, Jelle Bataille, Soumaïla Coulibaly, Alhassan Yusuf (73' George Ilenikhena), Arthur Vermeeren, Vincent Janssen, Gyrano Kerk (46' Chidera Ejuke), Arbnor Muja, Michel Balikwisha.
Coach: Mark van Bommel.
Goal: 12' Mykola Matvienko 1-0.
Referee: Bartosz Frankowski (POL)   Attendance: 47,209.
Sent off: 90+7' Arbnor Muja.

28.11.23   Estadi Olímpic Lluís Companys, Barcelona: FC Barcelona – FC Porto 2-1 (1-1)
FC Barcelona: Iñaki Peña, Iñigo Martínez, João Cancelo (82' Alejandro Balde), Jules Koundé, Ronald Araújo, Ilkay Gündogan, Frenkie de Jong, Pedri, Robert Lewandowski, Raphinha (90' Lamine Yamal), João Félix (75' Ferran Torres). Coach: Xavi.
FC Porto: Diogo Costa, Pepe, Fábio Cardoso (90' Danny Namaso), Zaidu Sanusi, João Mário (67' Jorge Sánchez), Stephen Eustáquio (81' Nico González), Alan Varela, Mehdi Taremi, Galeno (90' Toni Martínez), Pepê Aquino, Evanilson (81' Francisco Conceição).
Coach: Sérgio Conceição.
Goals: 30' Pepê Aquino 0-1, 32' João Cancelo 1-1, 57' João Félix 2-1.
Referee: Daniele Orsato (ITA)   Attendance: 43,533.

13.12.23   Estádio Do Dragão, Porto: FC Porto – Shakhtar Donetsk 5-3 (2-1)
FC Porto: Diogo Costa, Pepe, Fábio Cardoso, Jorge Sánchez (77' João Mário), Zaidu Sanusi, Stephen Eustáquio (82' Marko Grujic), Alan Varela, Mehdi Taremi, Galeno (88' Iván Jaime), Pepê Aquino (81' Francisco Conceição), Evanilson (82' André Franco).
Coach: Sérgio Conceição.
Shakhtar Donetsk: Dmytro Riznyk, Yaroslav Rakitskyi (73' Kevin Kelsy), Mykola Matvienko, Valeriy Bondar, Giorgi Gocholeishvili, Taras Stepanenko, Oleksandr Zubkov (86' Eguinaldo), Dmytro Kryskiv (59' Newerton), Artem Bondarenko (85' Yegor Nazaryna), Georgiy Sudakov, Danylo Sikan. Coach: Marino Pusic.
Goals: 9' Galeno 1-0, 29' Danylo Sikan 1-1, 43' Galeno 2-1, 62' Mehdi Taremi 3-1, 72' Stephen Eustáquio 3-2 (og), 75' Pepe 4-2, 82' Francisco Conceição 5-2, 88' Eguinaldo 5-3.
Referee: István Kovács (ROM)   Attendance: 48,113.

13.12.23   Bosuilstadion, Deurne: Royal Antwerp FC – FC Barcelona 3-2 (1-1)
Royal Antwerp FC: Jean Butez, Ritchie De Laet (90+4' Zeno Van den Bosch), Toby
Alderweireld, Owen Wijndal, Soumaïla Coulibaly, Alhassan Yusuf, Mandela Keita, Arthur
Vermeeren, Vincent Janssen (79' George Ilenikhena), Gyrano Kerk (69' Jelle Bataille),
Chidera Ejuke (80' Kobe Corbanie). Coach: Mark van Bommel.
FC Barcelona: Iñaki Peña, Sergi Roberto (76' Marc Casadó), Andreas Christensen, Jules
Koundé, Alejandro Balde, Héctor Fort (60' João Cancelo), Oriol Romeu (60' Ilkay Gündogan),
Fermín López (60' Pedri), Robert Lewandowski (72' Marc Guiu), Ferran Torres, Lamine
Yamal. Coach: Xavi.
Goals: 2' Arthur Vermeeren 1-0, 35' Ferran Torres 1-1, 56' Vincent Janssen 2-1,
90+1' Marc Guiu 2-2, 90+2' George Ilenikhena 3-2.
Referee: Marco Guida (ITA)   Attendance: 13,550.

KNOCKOUT PHASE

ROUND OF 16

13.02.24   Parken, København: FC København – Manchester City 1-3 (1-2)
FC København: Kamil Grabara, Denis Vavro, Scott McKenna, Kevin Diks, Elias Jelert,
Rasmus Falk, Victor Claesson (55' Andreas Cornelius), Mohamed Elyounoussi, Diogo
Gonçalves (70' Oscar Højlund), Magnus Mattsson (81' Jordan Larsson), Elias Achouri (81'
Christian Sørensen). Coach: Jacob Neestrup.
Manchester City: Ederson, Kyle Walker, Nathan Aké, John Stones, Rúben Dias, Kevin De
Bruyne, Jack Grealish (21' Jérémy Doku), Bernardo Silva (78' Matheus Nunes), Rodri, Phil
Foden, Erling Haaland. Coach: Pep Guardiola.
Goals: 10' Kevin De Bruyne 0-1, 34' Magnus Mattsson 1-1, 45+1' Bernardo Silva 1-2,
90+2' Phil Foden 1-3.
Referee: José María Sánchez Martínez (ESP)   Attendance: 35,853.

13.02.24   Red Bull Arena, Leipzig: RB Leipzig – Real Madrid CF 0-1 (0-0)
RB Leipzig: Péter Gulácsi, Willi Orbán, Lukas Klostermann, Benjamin Henrichs (75' Amadou
Haïdara), David Raum, Mohamed Simakan, Xaver Schlager (90' Kevin Kampl), Dani Olmo
(76' Eljif Elmas), Xavi Simons, Loïs Openda (75' Yussuf Poulsen), Benjamin Sesko.
Coach: Marco Rose.
Real Madrid CF: Andriy Lunin, Nacho, Dani Carvajal, Ferland Mendy, Toni Kroos, Federico
Valverde, Brahim Díaz (84' Lucas Vázquez), Aurélien Tchouaméni, Eduardo Camavinga,
Vinícius Júnior, Rodrygo (84' Joselu). Coach: Carlo Ancelotti.
Goal: 48' Brahim Díaz 0-1.
Referee: Irfan Peljto (BIH)   Attendance: 45,028.

14.02.24   Parc des Princes, Paris: Paris Saint-Germain – Real Sociedad 2-0 (0-0)
Paris Saint-Germain: Gianluigi Donnarumma, Marquinhos, Achraf Hakimi, Lucas Beraldo,
Danilo Pereira (72' Lucas Hernández), Fabián Ruiz, Vitinha, Warren Zaïre-Emery, Ousmane
Dembélé (83' Randal Kolo Muani), Kylian Mbappé, Bradley Barcola (72' Marco Asencio).
Coach: Luis Enrique.
Real Sociedad: Álex Remiro, Hamari Traoré, Robin Le Normand (78' Jon Pacheco), Javi
Galán (88' Jon Aramburu), Brais Méndez (79' Beñat Turrientes), Mikel Merino, Zubeldía,
Martín Zubimendi, Takefusa Kubo, André Silva (79' Umar Sadiq), Ander Barrenetxea (66'
Arsen Zakharyan). Coach: Imanol Alguacil.
Goals: 58' Kylian Mbappé 1-0, 70' Bradley Barcola 2-0.
Referee: Marco Guida (ITA)   Attendance: 46,435.

14.02.24   Stadio Olimpico, Roma: Lazio Roma – Bayern München 1-0 (0-0)
Lazio Roma: Ivan Provedel, Elseid Hysaj (60' Manuel Lazzari), Alessio Romagnoli, Adam
Marusic, Mario Gila (81' Patric), Luis Alberto (81' Daichi Kamada), Felipe Anderson, Danilo
Cataldi, Mattéo Guendouzi, Ciro Immobile (74' Taty Castellanos), Gustav Isaksen (74' Pedro).
Coach: Maurizio Sarri.
Bayern München: Manuel Neuer, Raphaël Guerreiro, Noussair Mazraoui, Dayot Upamecano,
Kim Min-Jae, Leon Goretzka (73' Matthijs de Ligt), Joshua Kimmich, Thomas Müller (81'
Eric Maxim Choupo-Moting), Harry Kane, Leroy Sané (81' Mathys Tel), Jamal Musiala.
Coach: Thomas Tuchel.
Goal: 69' Ciro Immobile 1-0 (p).
Referee: François Letexier (FRA)   Attendance: 57,470.
Sent off: 67' Dayot Upamecano.

20.02.24   Stadio Giuseppe Meazza, Milano:
            Internazionale Milano – Atlético Madrid 1-0 (0-0)
Internazionale Milano: Yann Sommer, Matteo Darmian (69' Denzel Dumfries), Stefan de Vrij,
Federico Dimarco (69' Carlos Augusto), Benjamin Pavard, Alessandro Bastoni, Henrikh
Mkhitaryan (72' Davide Frattesi), Hakan Çalhanoglu, Nicolò Barella, Marcus Thuram (46'
Marko Arnautovic), Lautaro Martínez (88' Alexis Sánchez). Coach: Simone Inzaghi.
Atlético Madrid: Jan Oblak, José Giménez (46' Stefan Savic), Mario Hermoso (68' Reinildo),
Nahuel Molina (68' Pablo Barrios), Axel Witsel, Saúl (54' Álvaro Morata), Koke, Rodrigo De
Paul, Marcos Llorente, Antoine Griezmann (78' Ángel Correa), Samuel Lino.
Coach: Diego Simeone.
Goal: 79' Marko Arnautovic 1-0.
Referee: István Kovács (ROM)   Attendance: 73,709.

20.02.24   Philips Stadion, Eindhoven: PSV Eindhoven – Borussia Dortmund 1-1 (0-1)
PSV Eindhoven: Walter Benítez, Olivier Boscagli (90' Armando Obispo), Jordan Teze,
Sergiño Dest, Jerdy Schouten, Joey Veerman, Malik Tillman, Ismael Saibari (83' Mauro
Júnior), Luuk de Jong, Hirving Lozano (75' Ricardo Pepi), Johan Bakayoko.
Coach: Peter Bosz.
Borussia Dortmund: Alexander Meyer, Mats Hummels, Julian Ryerson, Nico Schlotterbeck,
Ian Maatsen, Marco Reus (62' Julian Brandt), Marcel Sabitzer, Emre Can, Niclas Füllkrug (82'
Youssoufa Moukoko), Donyell Malen (82' Salih Özcan), Jadon Sancho (68' Marius Wolf).
Coach: Edin Terzic.
Goals: 24' Donyell Malen 0-1, 56' Luuk de Jong 1-1 (p).
Referee: Srdjan Jovanovic (SRB)   Attendance: 34,950.

21.02.24   Estádio Do Dragão, Porto: FC Porto – Arsenal FC 1-0 (0-0)
FC Porto: Diogo Costa, Pepe, Wendell (90' Stephen Eustáquio), João Mário, Otávio, Nico
González (81' Iván Jaime), Alan Varela, Galeno, Pepê Aquino, Evanilson (85' Toni Martínez),
Francisco Conceição (86' Gonçalo Borges). Coach: Sérgio Conceição.
Arsenal FC: David Raya, Gabriel Magalhães, Ben White, Jakub Kiwior, William Saliba,
Martin Ødegaard, Declan Rice, Kai Havertz, Leandro Trossard (74' Jorginho), Bukayo Saka,
Gabriel Martinelli. Coach: Mikel Arteta.
Goal: 90+4' Galeno 1-0.
Referee: Serdar Gözübüyük (HOL)   Attendance: 49,111.

185

21.02.24   Stadio Diego Armando Maradona, Napoli: SSC Napoli – FC Barcelona 1-1 (0-0)
SSC Napoli: Alex Meret, Juan Jesus, Giovanni Di Lorenzo, Amir Rrahmani, Mathías Olivera, Stanislav Lobotka, Frank Anguissa, Jens-Lys Cajuste (68' Hamed Traoré), Matteo Politano (77' Giacomo Raspadori), Victor Osimhen (77' Giovanni Simeone), Khvicha Kvaratskhelia (68' Jesper Lindstrøm). Coach: Francesco Calzona.
FC Barcelona: Marc-André ter Stegen, Iñigo Martínez, João Cancelo, Andreas Christensen (86' Oriol Romeu), Jules Koundé, Ronald Araújo, Ilkay Gündogan, Frenkie de Jong, Pedri (86' João Félix), Robert Lewandowski, Lamine Yamal (80' Raphinha). Coach: Xavi.
Goals: 60' Robert Lewandowski 0-1, 75' Victor Osimhen 1-1.
Referee: Felix Zwayer (GER)   Attendance: 49,529.

05.03.24   Reale Arena, San Sebastián: Real Sociedad – Paris Saint-Germain 1-2 (0-1)
Real Sociedad: Álex Remiro, Hamari Traoré, Robin Le Normand, Javi Galán, Brais Méndez (61' Beñat Turrientes), Mikel Merino, Zubeldía (76' Jon Pacheco), Martín Zubimendi (83' Jon Ander Olasagasti), Takefusa Kubo, Sheraldo Becker (61' Ander Barrenetxea), Mikel Oyarzabal (77' André Silva). Coach: Imanol Alguacil.
Paris Saint-Germain: Gianluigi Donnarumma, Lucas Hernández, Achraf Hakimi (83' Carlos Soler), Nuno Mendes (62' Nordi Mukiele), Lucas Beraldo, Fabián Ruiz (77' Manuel Ugarte), Vitinha, Warren Zaïre-Emery, Ousmane Dembélé (82' Randal Kolo Muani), Kylian Mbappé, Bradley Barcola (46' Lee Kang-In). Coach: Luis Enrique.
Goals: 15' Kylian Mbappé 0-1, 56' Kylian Mbappé 0-2, 89' Mikel Merino 1-2.
Referee: Michael Oliver (ENG)   Attendance: 39,336.

05.03.24   Allianz Arena, München: Bayern München – Lazio Roma 3-0 (2-0)
Bayern München: Manuel Neuer, Raphaël Guerreiro (78' Alphonso Davies), Eric Dier, Matthijs de Ligt, Leon Goretzka, Joshua Kimmich, Aleksandar Pavlovic, Thomas Müller (78' Mathys Tel), Harry Kane, Leroy Sané (89' Konrad Laimer), Jamal Musiala (90+1' Serge Gnabry). Coach: Thomas Tuchel.
Lazio Roma: Ivan Provedel, Alessio Romagnoli, Adam Marusic, Luca Pellegrini, Mario Gila, Matías Vecino (61' Danilo Cataldi), Luis Alberto (80' Daichi Kamada), Felipe Anderson (75' Pedro), Mattia Zaccagni (61' Gustav Isaksen), Mattéo Guendouzi, Ciro Immobile (61' Taty Castellanos). Coach: Maurizio Sarri.
Goals: 38' Harry Kane 1-0, 45+2' Thomas Müller 2-0, 66' Harry Kane 3-0.
Referee: Slavko Vincic (SVN)   Attendance: 75,000.

06.03.24   Etihad Stadium, Manchester: Manchester City – FC København 3-1 (3-1)
Manchester City: Ederson, Rúben Dias (68' John Stones), Manuel Akanji, Josko Gvardiol, Rico Lewis, Mateo Kovacic, Rodri (46' Sergio Gómez), Matheus Nunes (74' Micah Hamilton), Oscar Bobb, Erling Haaland (88' Jacob Wright), Julián Álvarez.
Coach: Pep Guardiola.
FC København: Kamil Grabara, Peter Andersen, Denis Vavro, Scott McKenna, Kevin Diks, Elias Jelert (78' Birger Meling), Mohamed Elyounoussi, Elias Achouri (58' Roony Bardghji), William Clem (68' Oscar Højlund), Victor Froholdt (58' Magnus Mattsson), Orri Óskarsson (69' Andreas Cornelius). Coach: Jacob Neestrup.
Goals: 5' Manuel Akanji 1-0, 9' Julián Álvarez 2-0, 29' Mohamed Elyounoussi 2-1, 45+3' Erling Haaland 3-1.
Referee: Espen Eskås (NOR)   Attendance: 51,531.

06.03.24   Estadio Santiago Bernabéu, Madrid: Real Madrid CF – RB Leipzig 1-1 (0-0)
Real Madrid CF: Andriy Lunin, Nacho, Dani Carvajal, Antonio Rüdiger, Ferland Mendy, Toni
Kroos (78' Luka Modric), Federico Valverde, Aurélien Tchouaméni, Eduardo Camavinga (46'
Rodrygo), Jude Bellingham (85' Joselu), Vinícius Júnior. Coach: Carlo Ancelotti.
RB Leipzig: Péter Gulácsi, Willi Orbán, Benjamin Henrichs, David Raum, Castello Lukeba,
Xaver Schlager (85' Eljif Elmas), Dani Olmo, Amadou Haïdara (90' Kevin Kampl), Xavi
Simons, Loïs Openda (77' Yussuf Poulsen), Benjamin Sesko (85' Christoph Baumgartner).
Coach: Marco Rose.
Goals: 65' Vinícius Júnior 1-0, 68' Willi Orbán 1-1.
Referee: Davide Massa (ITA)   Attendance: 76,126.

12.03.24   Emirates Stadium, London: Arsenal FC – FC Porto 1-0 (1-0,1-0) (AET)
Arsenal FC: David Raya, Gabriel Magalhães, Ben White, Jakub Kiwior (106' Oleksandr
Zinchenko), William Saliba, Jorginho (83 Gabriel Jesus), Martin Ødegaard, Declan Rice, Kai
Havertz, Leandro Trossard (106' Eddie Nketiah), Bukayo Saka. Coach: Mikel Arteta.
FC Porto: Diogo Costa, Pepe, Wendell, João Mário (86' Jorge Sánchez), Otávio, Nico
González (101' Stephen Eustáquio), Alan Varela (90+7' Marko Grujic), Galeno, Pepê Aquino,
Evanilson (88' Mehdi Taremi), Francisco Conceição (101' Gonçalo Borges).
Coach: Sérgio Conceição.
Goal: 41' Leandro Trossard 1-0.
Referee: Clément Turpin (FRA)   Attendance: 60,257.

Arsenal FC won on penalties (4:2).

Penalties: Ødegaard 1-0, Pepê Aquino 1-1, Havertz 2-1, Wendell (missed), Saka 3-1,
Grujic 3-2, Rice 4-2, Galeno (missed).

12.03.24   Estadi Olímpic Lluís Companys, Barcelona: FC Barcelona – SSC Napoli 3-1 (2-1)
FC Barcelona: Marc-André ter Stegen, João Cancelo, Andreas Christensen (61' Oriol Romeu),
Jules Koundé, Ronald Araújo, Pau Cubarsí, Ilkay Gündogan, Fermín López (60' Sergi
Roberto), Robert Lewandowski, Raphinha (81' João Félix), Lamine Yamal. Coach: Xavi.
SSC Napoli: Alex Meret, Juan Jesus, Mário Rui (64' Mathías Olivera), Giovanni Di Lorenzo,
Amir Rrahmani, Stanislav Lobotka, Frank Anguissa, Hamed Traoré (78' Giacomo Raspadori),
Matteo Politano (64' Jesper Lindstrøm), Victor Osimhen, Khvicha Kvaratskhelia (90+2' Cyril
Ngonge). Coach: Francesco Calzona.
Goals: 15' Fermín López 1-0, 17 João Cancelo 2-0, 30' Amir Rrahmani 2-1,
83' Robert Lewandowski 3-1.
Referee: Danny Makkelie (HOL)   Attendance: 50,301.

FC Barcelona played their home matches at the Estadi Olímpic Lluís Companys, in Barcelona,
instead of their regular stadium, Camp Nou, in Barcelona, which is being renovated.

13.03.24   Estádio Cívitas Metropolitano, Madrid:
Atlético Madrid – Internazionale Milano 2-1 (1-1,2-1) (AET)
Atlético Madrid: Jan Oblak, Stefan Savic, Mario Hermoso, Nahuel Molina (79' Pablo Barrios),
Axel Witsel, Koke, Rodrigo De Paul (71' Ángel Correa), Marcos Llorente (98' César
Azpilicueta), Antoine Griezmann (105' Saúl), Álvaro Morata (79' Memphis Depay), Samuel
Lino (71' Rodrigo Riquelme). Coach: Diego Simeone.
Internazionale Milano: Yann Sommer, Stefan de Vrij, Federico Dimarco (84' Yann Bisseck),
Denzel Dumfries (73' Matteo Darmian), Benjamin Pavard, Alessandro Bastoni (73' Francesco
Acerbi), Henrikh Mkhitaryan (111' Davy Klaassen), Hakan Çalhanoglu, Nicolò Barella (84'
Davide Frattesi), Marcus Thuram (102' Alexis Sánchez), Lautaro Martínez.
Coach: Simone Inzaghi.
Goals: 33' Federico Dimarco 0-1, 35' Antoine Griezmann 1-1, 87' Memphis Depay 2-1.
Referee: Szymon Marciniak (POL)   Attendance: 69,196.

Atlético Madrid won on penalties (3:2).

Penalties: Çalhanoglu 1-0, Depay 1-1, Sánchez (missed), Saúl (missed), Klaassen (missed),
   Rodrigo Riquelme 2-1, Acerbi 2-2, Correa 3-2, Martínez (missed).

13.03.24   Signal Iduna Park, Dortmund: Borussia Dortmund – PSV Eindhoven 2-0 (1-0)
Borussia Dortmund: Gregor Kobel, Mats Hummels, Niklas Süle, Ian Maatsen, Marcel Sabitzer,
Emre Can, Julian Brandt (58' Felix Nmecha), Salih Özcan, Niclas Füllkrug, Donyell Malen
(70' Karim Adeyemi), Jadon Sancho (75' Marco Reus). Coach: Edin Terzic.
PSV Eindhoven: Walter Benítez, Olivier Boscagli, Mauro Júnior (86' Isaac Babadi), Jordan
Teze, Sergiño Dest, Jerdy Schouten, Guus Til (46' Hirving Lozano), Joey Veerman (82'
Ricardo Pepi), Malik Tillman, Luuk de Jong, Johan Bakayoko. Coach: Peter Bosz.
Goals: 3' Jadon Sancho 1-0, 90+5' Marco Reus 2-0.
Referee: Daniele Orsato (ITA)   Attendance: 81,365.

QUARTER-FINALS

09.04.24   Emirates Stadium, London: Arsenal FC – Bayern München 2-2 (1-2)
Arsenal FC: David Raya, Gabriel Magalhães, Ben White, Jakub Kiwior (46' Oleksandr
Zinchenko), William Saliba, Jorginho (67' Gabriel Jesus), Martin Ødegaard, Declan Rice, Kai
Havertz (86' Thomas Partey), Bukayo Saka, Gabriel Martinelli (66' Leandro Trossard).
Coach: Mikel Arteta.
Bayern München: Manuel Neuer, Eric Dier, Matthijs de Ligt, Alphonso Davies, Leon
Goretzka, Joshua Kimmich, Konrad Laimer, Harry Kane, Serge Gnabry (70' Raphaël
Guerreiro), Leroy Sané (66' Kingsley Coman), Jamal Musiala. Coach: Thomas Tuchel.
Goals: 12' Bukayo Saka 1-0, 18' Serge Gnabry 1-1, 32' Harry Kane 1-2 (p),
76' Leandro Trossard 2-2.
Referee: Glenn Nyberg (SWE)   Attendance: 60,221.

09.04.24　Estadio Santiago Bernabéu, Madrid: Real Madrid CF – Manchester City 3-3 (2-1)
Real Madrid CF: Andriy Lunin, Dani Carvajal, Antonio Rüdiger, Ferland Mendy, Toni Kroos (72' Luka Modric), Federico Valverde, Aurélien Tchouaméni, Eduardo Camavinga, Jude Bellingham, Vinícius Júnior (86' Joselu), Rodrygo (72' Brahim Díaz). Coach: Carlo Ancelotti.
Manchester City: Stefan Ortega, John Stones, Rúben Dias, Manuel Akanji, Josko Gvardiol, Mateo Kovacic, Jack Grealish, Bernardo Silva, Rodri, Phil Foden (87' Julián Álvarez), Erling Haaland. Coach: Pep Guardiola.
Goals: 2' Bernardo Silva 0-1, 12' Rúben Dias 1-1 (og), 14' Rodrygo 2-1, 66' Phil Foden 2-2, 71' Josko Gvardiol 2-3, 79' Federico Valverde 3-3.
Referee: François Letexier (FRA)　Attendance: 76,680.

10.04.24　Estádio Cívitas Metropolitano, Madrid:
Atlético Madrid – Borussia Dortmund 2-1 (2-0)
Atlético Madrid: Jan Oblak, César Azpilicueta, José Giménez, Nahuel Molina (90' Saúl), Axel Witsel (90+1' Stefan Savic), Koke, Rodrigo De Paul (80' Ángel Correa), Marcos Llorente, Antoine Griezmann, Álvaro Morata (64' Pablo Barrios), Samuel Lino (90+1' Rodrigo Riquelme). Coach: Diego Simeone.
Borussia Dortmund: Gregor Kobel, Mats Hummels, Julian Ryerson, Nico Schlotterbeck, Ian Maatsen, Marcel Sabitzer (84' Marco Reus), Emre Can (84' Salih Özcan), Felix Nmecha (46' Julian Brandt), Niclas Füllkrug (60' Sébastien Haller), Jadon Sancho, Karim Adeyemi (73' Jamie Bynoe-Gittens). Coach: Edin Terzic.
Goals: 4' Rodrigo De Paul 1-0, 32' Samuel Lino 2-0, 81' Sébastien Haller 2-1.
Referee: Marco Guida (ITA)　Attendance: 68,641.

10.04.24　Parc des Princes, Paris: Paris Saint-Germain – FC Barcelona 2-3 (0-1)
Paris Saint-Germain: Gianluigi Donnarumma, Marquinhos, Lucas Hernández, Nuno Mendes, Lucas Beraldo, Fabián Ruiz (85' Gonçalo Ramos), Vitinha, Lee Kang-In (61' Warren Zaïre-Emery), Ousmane Dembélé, Marco Asensio (46' Bradley Barcola), Kylian Mbappé.
Coach: Luis Enrique.
FC Barcelona: Marc-André ter Stegen, Sergi Roberto (61' Pedri), João Cancelo, Jules Koundé, Ronald Araújo, Pau Cubarsí, Ilkay Gündogan (86' Fermín López), Frenkie de Jong (75' Andreas Christensen), Robert Lewandowski, Raphinha (76' Ferran Torres), Lamine Yamal (61' João Félix). Coach: Xavi.
Goals: 37' Raphinha 0-1, 48' Ousmane Dembélé 1-1, 51' Vitinha 2-1, 62' Raphinha 2-2, 77' Andreas Christensen 2-3.
Referee: Anthony Taylor (ENG)　Attendance: 47,470.

16.04.24　Signal Iduna Park, Dortmund: Borussia Dortmund – Atlético Madrid 4-2 (2-0)
Borussia Dortmund: Gregor Kobel, Mats Hummels, Julian Ryerson, Nico Schlotterbeck, Ian Maatsen, Marcel Sabitzer, Emre Can, Julian Brandt (90' Marco Reus), Niclas Füllkrug, Jadon Sancho (86' Salih Özcan), Karim Adeyemi (66' Jamie Bynoe-Gittens). Coach: Edin Terzic.
Atlético Madrid: Jan Oblak, César Azpilicueta (46' Rodrigo Riquelme), José Giménez, Mario Hermoso, Nahuel Molina (46' Pablo Barrios), Axel Witsel, Koke, Rodrigo De Paul (84' Saúl), Marcos Llorente, Antoine Griezmann, Álvaro Morata (46' Ángel Correa).
Coach: Diego Simeone.
Goals: 34' Julian Brandt 1-0, 39' Ian Maatsen 2-0, 49' Mats Hummels 2-1 (og), 64' Ángel Correa 2-2, 71' Niclas Füllkrug 3-2, 74' Marcel Sabitzer 4-2.
Referee: Slavko Vincic (SVN)　Attendance: 81,365.

16.04.24   Estadi Olímpic Lluís Companys, Barcelona:
FC Barcelona – Paris Saint-Germain 1-4 (1-1)
FC Barcelona: Marc-André ter Stegen, João Cancelo (82' João Félix), Jules Koundé, Ronald Araújo, Pau Cubarsí, Ilkay Gündogan, Frenkie de Jong (82' Fermín López), Pedri (61' Ferran Torres), Robert Lewandowski, Raphinha, Lamine Yamal (34' Iñigo Martínez). Coach: Xavi.
Paris Saint-Germain: Gianluigi Donnarumma, Marquinhos, Lucas Hernández, Achraf Hakimi, Nuno Mendes, Fabián Ruiz (77' Marco Asensio), Vitinha, Warren Zaïre-Emery (80' Manuel Ugarte), Ousmane Dembélé (88' Randal Kolo Muani), Kylian Mbappé, Bradley Barcola (77' Lee Kang-In). Coach: Luis Enrique.
Goals: 12' Raphinha 1-0, 40' Ousmane Dembélé 1-1, 54' Vitinha 1-2, 61', 89' Kylian Mbappé 1-3 (p), 1-4.
Referee: István Kovács (ROM)   Attendance: 50,309.
Sent off: 29' Ronald Araújo, 56' Xavi (coach).

FC Barcelona played their home matches at the Estadi Olímpic Lluís Companys, in Barcelona, instead of their regular stadium, Camp Nou, in Barcelona, which is being renovated.

17.04.24   Allianz Arena, München: Bayern München – Arsenal FC 1-0 (0-0)
Bayern München: Manuel Neuer, Raphaël Guerreiro, Eric Dier, Noussair Mazraoui (76' Kim Min-Jae), Matthijs de Ligt, Leon Goretzka, Joshua Kimmich, Konrad Laimer, Harry Kane, Leroy Sané (89' Dayot Upamecano), Jamal Musiala. Coach: Thomas Tuchel.
Arsenal FC: David Raya, Takehiro Tomiyasu (86' Eddie Nketiah), Gabriel Magalhães, Ben White, William Saliba, Jorginho (67' Gabriel Jesus), Martin Ødegaard, Declan Rice, Kai Havertz, Bukayo Saka, Gabriel Martinelli (68' Leandro Trossard). Coach: Mikel Arteta.
Goal: 63' Joshua Kimmich 1-0.
Referee: Danny Makkelie (HOL)   Attendance: 75,000.

17.04.24   Etihad Stadium, Manchester:
Manchester City – Real Madrid CF 1-1 (0-1,1-1) (AET)
Manchester City: Ederson, Kyle Walker, Rúben Dias, Manuel Akanji (112' John Stones), Josko Gvardiol, Kevin De Bruyne (112' Mateo Kovacic), Jack Grealish (72' Jérémy Doku), Bernardo Silva, Rodri, Phil Foden, Erling Haaland (91' Julián Álvarez). Coach: Pep Guardiola.
Real Madrid CF: Andriy Lunin, Nacho, Dani Carvajal (110' Éder Militão), Antonio Rüdiger, Ferland Mendy, Toni Kroos (79' Luka Modric), Federico Valverde, Eduardo Camavinga, Jude Bellingham, Vinícius Júnior (102' Lucas Vázquez), Rodrygo (84' Brahim Díaz). Coach: Carlo Ancelotti.
Goals: 12' Rodrygo 0-1, 76' Kevin De Bruyne 1-1.
Referee: Daniele Orsato (ITA)   Attendance: 52,306.

Real Madrid CF won on penalties (4:3).

Penalties: Álvarez 1-0, Modic (missed), Bernardo Silva (missed), Bellingham 1-1, Kovacic (missed), Lucas Vázquez 1-2, Foden 2-2, Nacho 2-3, Ederson 3-3, Rüdiger 3-4.

SEMI-FINALS

30.04.24 Allianz Arena, München: Bayern München – Real Madrid CF 2-2 (0-1)
Bayern München: Manuel Neuer, Eric Dier, Noussair Mazraoui, Kim Min-Jae, Leon Goretzka (46' Raphaël Guerreiro), Joshua Kimmich, Konrad Laimer, Thomas Müller (80 Serge Gnabry), Harry Kane, Leroy Sané (87' Alphonso Davies), Jamal Musiala. Coach: Thomas Tuchel.
Real Madrid CF: Andriy Lunin, Nacho (65 Eduardo Camavinga), Antonio Rüdiger, Ferland Mendy, Toni Kroos (76' Brahim Díaz), Lucas Vázquez, Federico Valverde, Aurélien Tchouaméni, Jude Bellingham (75' Luka Modric), Vinícius Júnior, Rodrygo (87' Joselu). Coach: Carlo Ancelotti.
Goals: 24' Vinícius Júnior 0-1, 53' Leroy Sané 1-1, 57' Harry Kane 2-1 (p), 83' Vinícius Júnior 2-2 (p).
Referee: Clément Turpin (FRA) Attendance: 75,000.

01.05.24 Signal Iduna Park, Dortmund: Borussia Dortmund – Paris Saint-Germain 1-0 (1-0)
Borussia Dortmund: Gregor Kobel, Mats Hummels, Julian Ryerson (87' Marius Wolf), Nico Schlotterbeck, Ian Maatsen, Marcel Sabitzer, Emre Can, Julian Brandt (87' Felix Nmecha), Niclas Füllkrug (90+1' Youssoufa Moukoko), Jadon Sancho, Karim Adeyemi (83' Marco Reus). Coach: Edin Terzic.
Paris Saint-Germain: Gianluigi Donnarumma, Marquinhos, Lucas Hernández (42' Lucas Beraldo), Achraf Hakimi, Nuno Mendes, Fabián Ruiz, Vitinha, Warren Zaïre-Emery, Ousmane Dembélé, Kylian Mbappé, Bradley Barcola (65' Randal Kolo Muani). Coach: Luis Enrique.
Goal: 36' Niclas Füllkrug 1-0.
Referee: Anthony Taylor (ENG) Attendance: 81,365.

07.05.24 Parc des Princes, Paris: Paris Saint-Germain – Borussia Dortmund 0-1 (0-0)
Paris Saint-Germain: Gianluigi Donnarumma, Marquinhos, Achraf Hakimi, Nuno Mendes, Lucas Beraldo, Fabián Ruiz (63' Marco Asensio), Vitinha, Warren Zaïre-Emery (76' Lee Kang-In), Ousmane Dembélé, Kylian Mbappé, Gonçalo Ramos (63' Bradley Barcola). Coach: Luis Enrique.
Borussia Dortmund: Gregor Kobel, Mats Hummels, Julian Ryerson, Nico Schlotterbeck, Ian Maatsen, Marcel Sabitzer, Emre Can, Julian Brandt (85' Felix Nmecha), Niclas Füllkrug, Jadon Sancho (67' Niklas Süle), Karim Adeyemi (56' Marco Reus). Coach: Edin Terzic.
Goal: 50' Mats Hummels (0-1).
Referee: Daniele Orsato (ITA) Attendance: 46,435.

08.05.24 Estsadio Santiago Bernabéu, Madrid: Real Madrid CF – Bayern München 2-1 (0-0)
Real Madrid CF: Andriy Lunin, Nacho, Dani Carvajal, Antonio Rüdiger, Ferland Mendy, Toni Kroos (69' Luka Modric), Federico Valverde (81' Joselu), Aurélien Tchouaméni (70' Eduardo Camavinga), Jude Bellingham (90+10' Éder Militão), Vinícius Júnior, Rodrygo (81' Brahim Díaz). Coach: Carlo Ancelotti.
Bayern München: Manuel Neuer, Eric Dier, Noussair Mazraoui, Matthijs de Ligt, Joshua Kimmich, Konrad Laimer, Aleksandar Pavlovic, Harry Kane (85' Eric Maxim Choupo-Moting), Serge Gnabry (27' Alphonso Davies), Leroy Sané (76' Kim Min-Jae), Jamal Musiala (84' Thomas Müller). Coach: Thomas Tuchel.
Goals: 68' Alphonso Davies 0-1, 88', 90+1' Joselu 1-1, 2-1.
Referee: Szymon Marciniak (POL) Attendance: 76,579.

FINAL

01.06.24   Wembley Stadium, London: Borussia Dortmund – Real Madrid CF 0-2 (0-0)
Borussia Dortmund: Gregor Kobel, Julian Ryerson, Mats Hummels, Nico Schlotterbeck, Ian
Maatsen, Emre Can (80' Sébastian Haller), Marcel Sabitzer, Jadon Sancho (87' Jamie Bynoe-
Gittens), Julian Brandt (80' Donyell Malen), Karim Adeyemi (72' Marco Reus), Niclas
Füllkrug. Coach: Edin Terzic.
Real Madrid CF: Thibaut Courtois, Dani Carvajal, Antonio Rüdiger, Nacho, Ferland Mendy,
Eduardo Camavinga, Federico Valverde, Toni Kroos (85' Luka Modric), Jude Bellingham (85'
Joselu), Rodrygo (90' Éder Militão), Vinícius Júnior (90+4' Lucas Vázquez).
Coach: Carlo Ancelotti.
Goals: Real Madrid CF: 0-1 Dani Carvajal (74'), 0-2 Vinícius Júnior (83').
Referee: Slavko Vincic (SVN)   Attendance: 86,212.

EUROPEAN CHAMPIONS CUP / CHAMPIONS LEAGUE WINNERS

1956	Real Madrid	Spain
1957	Real Madrid	Spain
1958	Real Madrid	Spain
1959	Real Madrid	Spain
1960	Real Madrid	Spain
1961	SL Benfica	Portugal
1962	SL Benfica	Portugal
1963	AC Milan	Italy
1964	Internazionale	Italy
1965	Internazionale	Italy
1966	Real Madrid	Spain
1967	Celtic FC	Scotland
1968	Manchester United	England
1969	AC Milan	Italy
1970	Feijenoord	Netherlands
1971	AFC Ajax	Netherlands
1972	AFC Ajax	Netherlands
1973	AFC Ajax	Netherlands
1974	Bayern München	Germany
1975	Bayern München	Germany
1976	Bayern München	Germany
1977	Liverpool FC	England
1978	Liverpool FC	England
1979	Nottingham Forest	England
1980	Nottingham Forest	England
1981	Liverpool FC	England
1982	Aston Villa	England
1983	Hamburger SV	Germany
1984	Liverpool FC	England
1985	Juventus	Italy
1986	FC Steaua Bucuresti	Romania
1987	FC Porto	Portugal
1988	PSV	Netherlands
1989	AC Milan	Italy
1990	AC Milan	Italy
1991	Crvena Zvezda Beograd	Serbia
1992	FC Barcelona	Spain
1993	Olympique Marseille	France
1994	AC Milan	Italy
1995	AFC Ajax	Netherlands
1996	Juventus	Italy
1997	Borussia Dortmund	Germany
1998	Real Madrid	Spain
1999	Manchester United	England
2000	Real Madrid	Spain
2001	Bayern München	Germany
2002	Real Madrid	Spain
2003	AC Milan	Italy

2004	FC Porto	Portugal
2005	Liverpool FC	England
2006	FC Barcelona	Spain
2007	AC Milan	Italy
2008	Manchester United	England
2009	FC Barcelona	Spain
2010	Internazionale	Italy
2011	FC Barcelona	Spain
2012	Chelsea FC	England
2013	Bayern München	Germany
2014	Real Madrid	Spain
2015	FC Barcelona	Spain
2016	Real Madrid	Spain
2017	Real Madrid	Spain
2018	Real Madrid	Spain
2019	Liverpool FC	England
2020	FC Bayern München	Germany
2021	Chelsea FC	England
2022	Real Madrid	Spain
2023	Manchester City	England
2024	Real Madrid	Spain

ALL-TIME RECORD – CLUBS

Real Madrid	15
AC Milan	7
Bayern München	6
Liverpool FC	6
FC Barcelona	5
AFC Ajax	4
Internazionale	3
Manchester United	3
SL Benfica	2
Nottingham Forest	2
Juventus	2
FC Porto	2
Chelsea FC	2
Celtic FC	1
Feijenoord	1
Aston Villa	1
Hamburger SV	1
FC Steaua Bucuresti	1
PSV	1
Crvena Zvezda Beograd	1
Olympique Marseille	1
Borussia Dortmund	1
Manchester City	1

ALL-TIME RECORD – COUNTRIES

Spain	20
England	15
Italy	12
Germany	8
Netherlands	6
Portugal	4
Scotland	1
Romania	1
Serbia	1
France	1